Date D

ALL I THOUGHT ABOUT WAS BASEBALL:
WRITINGS ON A CANADIAN PASTIME

D1536412

Did you know?

- Baseball is played throughout Canada, from Victoria to St John's and as far north as Baffin Island.
- An early version of baseball was being played in Ontario at the same time that the game was being 'invented' in the United States.
- Brother Matthias, Babe Ruth's baseball mentor, was a Canadian.
- Baseball was the game of choice for young Québécois in the late nineteenth century.
- Canadian women ballplayers helped to keep interest in baseball alive during the Second World War.
- Jackie Robinson's starring role on a Canadian team marked the end of apartheid in baseball.
- Marshall McLuhan believed that baseball is culture.
- The great Satchel Paige made one of his last barnstorming stops in Saskatchewan.
- The greatest catch made in a World Series game took place in Canada.

The stories and essays in this collection make one unmistakable point: baseball is a *Canadian* game. From the first game in Canada in 1838 to the World Series victories of the Toronto Blue Jays, baseball is celebrated in this volume through news accounts, book excerpts, short stories, personal remembrances, and historical recollections. The game's popularity in all regions of Canada is vividly expressed in this diverse collection of writings.

WILLIAM HUMBER is the chair of the Faculty of Continuing Education at Seneca College. He is the author of several books, including *Diamonds of the North: A Concise History of Baseball in Canada*.

JOHN ST JAMES is a freelance editor and lifelong baseball fan.

◆

EDITED BY WILLIAM HUMBER
AND JOHN ST JAMES

All I Thought About
Was Baseball

Writings on a Canadian Pastime

UNIVERSITY OF TORONTO PRESS
Toronto Buffalo London

© University of Toronto Press Incorporated 1996
Toronto Buffalo London
Printed in Canada

ISBN 0-8020-0444-X (cloth)
ISBN 0-8020-7237-2 (paper)

Printed on acid-free paper

Canadian Cataloguing in Publication Data

Main entry under title:

All I thought about was baseball : writings on a
Canadian pastime

Includes bibliographical references.
ISBN 0-8020-0444-X (bound) ISBN 0-8020-7237-2 (pbk.)

1. Baseball – Canada.   I. Humber, William, 1949–   .
II. St James, John.

GV863.15.A1A55 1996   796.357'0971   C95-932268-X

University of Toronto Press acknowledges the financial assistance to its
publishing program of the Canada Council and the Ontario Arts Council.

May the Game
bring as much pleasure
to our children –
Bradley, Darryl, Karen,
and Jennifer –
as it has to us
over the years

Contents

Contents   ix

Contents   xi

Introduction

CANADA'S RELATIONSHIP WITH BASEBALL MANIFESTS THE CRUEL IRONIES that confront the country as an independent nation. A sport that has meant so much to us and stirred in us sublime feelings of elation is one that equally moves a neighbour (generally acknowledged to be the greatest power in the world) that claims the game as its own.

Two magnificent World Series victories by the Toronto Blue Jays became the property of all Canadians. In Saskatoon, they celebrated by rioting on 8th Street, a moment of such force that an independent-league baseball team dubbed themselves the Saskatoon Riot in homage to the moment. In Newfoundland they cheered the next-best thing to a native son, Toronto-born Rob Butler, after whose family the community of Butlerville on Conception Bay had been named some generations before. While in Thunder Bay, the Northern League team adopted the moniker 'The Whiskey Jacks,' because astute ornithologists would know this was another name for the common blue jay.

Who could imagine all of Canada being swept up in an emotional frenzy by a team from Toronto? In truth, the Blue Jays had become more than that. Dermot Bolger, in *The Tramway End*, described his national soccer team, made up of second- and third-generation Irishmen, as 'the only country I still owned, those eleven figures in green shirts, that menagerie of accents pleading with God.' So it could be said that the Toronto Blue Jays had become a rallying point for the country, even, one suspects, in such Quebec towns as St-Hyacinthe and Trois-Rivières, places too proud to express openly what they privately experienced, an elation at the moment of a 'Canadien' triumph.

The team was of course largely American, with a few Latins, in Canadian costume. We understood this. But professional sports teams draw on something deeper in us. No matter where their homes are, these people somehow represent us. In cheering for the home team, we acknowledge our longing for a tribal community we rarely experience any more.

Canadians know it is our regionalism, our pride of place beyond the fast-food hangout, that distinguishes us as a people. We don't need to travel to foreign places to see what is already in our neighbourhood. All we want is something different, but not threatening. Baseball in Canada is such a place for both locals and visitors searching for the just-off-centre exotic.

The writings in this book are about a magical place – the experience of the game of baseball in Canada, stretching back to the time of Bob Emslie, who said of his youth in the 1870s, 'All I thought about was baseball,' and forward to Scott Feschuk's description of a primitive ball diamond among Inuit children who, in an age of satellite technology, could as easily cheer for the Yankees or the Braves, but adopt the Blue Jays – because of a feeling that can't be expressed.

This is a big story: Mark Kingwell asks if baseball can ever be anything but an American game; Alan Rauch explores the playing-out of civic insecurities in Canada's big-league cities; and Stephen Brunt surveys baseball's current sad landscape (especially in Montreal) in his look at the 1994 season. It is also a small but vivid tale, set in local places like the sandlots that Tom McKillop used to frequent as a boy and the world of small-town youth baseball chronicled by Bill Humber.

Baseball has moved our writers of the imagination to tell their stories in its metaphors, and so we relish the words of W.P. Kinsella, Ralph Connor, Scott Young, George Bowering, Paul Quarrington, Hugh Hood, and Nelles Van Loon. It also inspires moments of glory within pain, as revealed in Pat Adachi's translation of her father's memories of Vancouver baseball in the period before the 'resettlement,' when Japanese Canadians temporarily overcame the majority community's derision by becoming great baseball players. So too Brenda Zeman finds humour and pride in the family recollections of the tragic life of Jimmy Rattlesnake.

It is a game that touches important periods of our history, as evidenced by Barry Broadfoot's prairie memories from the Depression years and by Mordecai Richler's recollections of the darkest days of the Second World War, when his parents feared Hitler and his Panzers, but Richler and his friends dreaded Branch Rickey and his scouts swooping down on the talent-laden Montreal Royals in the midst of an International League pennant race.

In the end, though, baseball is also a game that doesn't have to mean a thing in any larger existential sense. Its appeal finds expression in the lifelong affection for baseball cards recounted by Dave Crichton and Randy Echlin and in fans' profane but long-standing attraction to sports gambling, detailed in Larry Humber's Las Vegas spin on the Blue Jays.

Baseball in Canada takes us right across the country. We journey from Russell Field's Newfoundland baseball beginnings in 1913 to David Folster's memory of boyhood heroes in Grand Falls, New Brunswick, to Robert Ashe's re-creation of a Maritime visit by the Boston Braves. We are enlightened by Dan Ziniuk's reflections on baseball's meaning in the 'foreign' terrain of Quebec and by Roger Lemelin's apt observations in his fictional account of a French-Canadian baseball episode in which church and state collide. We join Robert Fontaine on his escape from Ottawa to nearby Hull for a Sunday baseball fix, then read Zane Grey's story of an unusual match in Guelph, an important early baseball centre that is also featured in William Bryce's 1876 survey of the game. John Ducey, Edmonton's Mr. Baseball, recalls his long involvement with the game in western Canada. And, on the Pacific Coast, thanks to Geoff LaCasse's research, we learn about Victoria's late-nineteenth-century champions, the Amity.

Along the way, we enter the lives of some of Canada's great baseball exponents: in Milt Dunnell's story about Fergie Jenkins, Jane Gross's report on Bill Lee (an adopted Canadian of sorts) in Montreal, and Penetang Phil Marchildon's remembrance of the 1947 season. We are there for Dave Shury's meeting with the legendary Satchel Paige in North Battleford, and hear Tony Techko's story of one school's unique contribution to Canadian baseball history. Jim Shearon depicts a Souris, Manitoba, ballplayer with one big-league pinch-running appearance, and Larry Wood interviews Reggie Cleveland, the first Canadian to start a World Series game.

And what about little-known heroes? We have Bruce Meyer's tale of the man who preceded (and perhaps outshone) Joe Carter in 1887; David Pietrusza's story of Knotty Lee, a league-founding entrepreneur who succeeded without regional-development grants; Lois Browne's account of the beginnings of the All-American Girls' professional league; and Laura Robinson's report on women's softball, which fills in the details of one of that league's regional predecessors. And scoundrels? David McDonald recounts the sorry tale of Canada's early response to black baseball players.

A reader with an appetite for the whimsical can choose from Adam Gopnik's study of Italian art and the Expos, Alison Gordon's 'eh-to-zed' introduction to Canada for Americans, and John St James's outline for a Canadian baseball opera. Anyone with a penchant for Marshall McLuhan in his salad days of the fifties and sixties will be intrigued by his observation that 'baseball is culture.'

For remarkable historic revelations, we need go no further than Colin Howell's surprising story of the man who taught Babe Ruth how to play baseball (he was a *Canadian*) or Adam Ford's recollections of a baseball game played in Canada in 1838, a year before the game's supposed invention in Cooperstown, New York. A *Spalding Guide* report chronicles the season of a minor league based in the coal-mining towns of Cape Breton. And Roger Angell recounts the first World Series game played in Canada, which incidentally featured the greatest catch in Series history (sorry, Willie Mays).

In the reporting mode, we have Morley Callaghan on the 1940 Toronto Maple Leafs, Jim Davidson on Canada's baseball Olympians, and Dan Turner's unusual chronicle of the Expos and the world of 1969. Readers interested in the civic architectural angle of baseball can consult Jon Caulfield on Toronto's edifice complex and Arthur Lierman's survey of some Canadian baseball paradise gardens.

Finally, what could be more appropriate, or more ironic, than to end this collection of Canadian baseball writings on a hockey-baseball note? Eric Zweig, thanks to the alphabetical luck of the draw, has the last word here.

Recently, we asked some knowledgeable baseball fans to speculate on the outcome of a game between the 1927 New York Yankees and a Toronto team, and they concluded, quite logically, that the Bronx Bombers of Ruth and Gehrig would cream *any* Toronto team, even of World Series calibre. It is a game, they suggested, that could never be put to the challenge, however. Yet in July 1927, the Yankees, on their way to Detroit for a mid-season series, and anxious to make a few dollars, stopped off in Toronto to play an exhibition game against the city's International League team in their new Maple Leaf Stadium. Ruth and Gehrig played the whole game and were duly immortalized on the front page of the July 8, 1927, edition of the *Globe*. But the Yankees lost 11–7. Lost to Toronto – those nine men in blue pleading with God in the uniform of Toronto. Such is the unpredictable wonder of baseball that we celebrate in these pages, a game too splendid and variable to be possessed by one nation alone.

One would be remiss if one failed to note that, having beaten the acknowledged greatest team in baseball history, the Maple Leafs went out for a second game that afternoon and lost to Reading, one of their International League rivals. Magic and reality are never far apart.

WILLIAM HUMBER
JOHN ST JAMES
July 1995

ALL I THOUGHT ABOUT WAS BASEBALL

———— ◆ ————

Pat Adachi's oral-history interpretation of her father's memory of baseball within the Japanese-Canadian community of Vancouver before the Second World War describes a world that no longer exists. The displacement of that community during the war sounded the death-knell for the Asahi baseball club, which had won several titles in Vancouver's mainstream senior leagues over the previous twenty years. Vancouver's Asian community had expanded rapidly in the early years of the twentieth century, amidst a climate of growing resentment and even violence from the majority white population, who accused Chinese and Japanese immigrants of working for low wages and thus depressing the entire labour market. Generally, Chinese Canadians retreated from this hostility, but those of Japanese descent sought some means of integration. What better way was there than baseball? By 1920 the Asahis were the dominant team in the Nisei community. Their story is lovingly told in Adachi's book, Asahi: A Legend in Their Time *(1992), for which the following account provides an introduction.*

The Remarkable Asahis

PAT ADACHI AND IWAICHI KAWASHIRI

HAVING BEEN ASKED TO WRITE MY RECOLLECTION OF THE REMARKABLE Asahis, I will do my best. But I am now 94 years old and perhaps there may be errors in my memory.

It was back in 1920, at Athletic Park in Vancouver, when I saw my first Asahi baseball game. I remember Kasahara and Miyasaki. Harry Miyasaki later became the very famous Asahi Manager of all times.

In 1928 I lived on Powell Street, running a rooming house. My greatest pleasure in those difficult times was to grab 10 cents and head for the ball park to see the Asahis play. That was the beginning of my love for baseball. Powell Grounds was their stamping ground. Then they became members of the Senior City League. We followed the Asahis wherever they played. I learned baseball strategy, the true meaning of fair play and sportsmanship.

During those years the Japanese people were discriminated against at every turn. To have a Japanese language school to teach our children Japanese culture was highly suspect. We were constantly criticized for congregating in one area or working too hard in order to eke out a living. No matter what we did we were the targets of political organizations. It was a world where the Japanese Canadian people had a pathetic existence.

But the barriers came down whenever the Asahis played ball. Naturally there were the Japanese fans. But, it was the applause from the Occidental fans which would make us so proud. There was one coach on one of the opposing teams named Don Stewart. When his team was at bat, some of the Occidental fans would encourage the Asahis to execute a double play. This made Don Stewart so angry, he became livid and grabbed the wire fence and yelled at the fans to shut up. 'You root for Japs!' Stewart would holler. I felt good.

There were several brothers playing at various times, as well as many childhood friends, so that the team members were in tune with each other. They did not look for individual glory but played their best for the good of the team.

I am a strong Blue Jays fan. Yet watching them play, I feel they lack the polish and finesse of the Asahis. There is a great physical difference between the Caucasian stature and the Japanese. Caucasians have the ability to hit the 'long-ball.' So the Asahis created their own style of play – bunting to perfection and the amazing 'squeeze plays.' As soon as the ball left the pitcher's hand, the Asahi runner was already running from third to home plate. While the fielder was bewildered, the second base runner was well on his way to third and home, scoring two runs on a single bunt. And that would bring the house down, with resounding cheers from the fans. These memories appear before my eyes.

Why did these Caucasian fans look upon the Asahis so favourably? These fans appreciated the sportsmanlike attitude, the skill and fervour the Asahis displayed in their game, and thought of them not as a team of a different race, but as equal in the name of sports.

Harry Miyasaki was a great leader. He was a man who won everyone's respect, fans and players alike. It was not just to teach these youngsters to play baseball, but to provide guidance and build strong characters.

Today during the World Series we have six umpires who are paid a handsome salary. Each specializes in his own position but frequently they misjudge a call, as shown on a TV replay. I regret we were so critical of umpire White, who used to come out to Powell Grounds just for the love of the game.

Powell Grounds was a sand lot compared to the fabulous SkyDome. If the Asahis could play today at the Dome, how impressive they would be. How regrettable to see so many of the players have passed away in their prime.

———————— ◆ ————————

On October 20, 1992, the first World Series game ever played outside the United States was to be held in Toronto, Canada. The country was facing a constitutional referendum in another week, and its first-ever World Series offered merciful relief from its topsy-turvy political state. On October 18, as the national anthems were being played before Game 2 in Atlanta, however, startled Canadian television viewers had seen their country's flag unfurled upside down by an ill-informed (but perhaps politically intuitive) member of the U.S. Marines colour guard. A great fuss ensued the next day in the Canadian media, reaching a boisterous pitch on the call-in radio shows in Toronto. 'We'd better show those dumb Yanks' was the general tenor of the response, and it wasn't entirely clear how the home crowd would greet the visitors' anthem before Game 3 the next night. But, as Roger Angell notes in 'Shades of Blue,' his chronicle of the 1992 major-league season, an 'international crisis was averted by a graceful apology [gracefully accepted by the Canadian crowd, it should be added] over the loudspeakers before game time ... and a gallant second try by the Marines, who got it right this time.' What followed was a crackerjack ball game.

Catch

ROGER ANGELL

G AME THREE HAD EVERYTHING: SIZZLING PITCHING BY THE YOUNG STARTERS Steve Avery and Juan Guzman; an all-time-grade fielding play by Toronto center fielder Devon White; a hatful of little indicators about the depth and mettle of the rival clubs; a low score that flickered this way and that before the late last run came home; and a rapturously yelling audience of 51,813 Ontarians, who had come into the great white meringue of the SkyDome for a tourist event, Canada's first-ever World Series game, and were given a classic as gate prize. (The Dome, I have begun to notice, feels a bit smaller when its vast reaches are stuffed with noise, although I'm not sure that every flea-circus observer up at the back of the fifth-level SkyDeck would agree.)

White's catch came in the top of the fourth, when he ran extensively back in dead center field and, without breaking stride, sailed up onto the fence, where he gloved Dave Justice's drive just before smashing face first into the blue padding. The catch saved a run and very probably two runs, and led to a frabjous mixup on the base paths, when Terry

Pendleton, scooting around from first, passed his teammate Deion Sanders on the straightaway between second and third, and then – oops, *yow* – jammed on the brakes and headed back the other way. Sanders, standing aghast, threw both arms back and flattened himself like a trapped pedestrian as Terry zoomed by for the second time. The Blue Jay infielders, meanwhile, were throwing the ball back and forth distractedly as they tried to remember the rule book (Pendleton was out the moment he went past the prior runner), but then somehow caught Sanders in a little rundown between second and third, culminating in a tag-out by third baseman Kelly Gruber, who dived at Deion and touched him on one foot with his mitt. A triple play by all counts, and only the second one in Series history, except that umpire Bob Davidson blew the call. No one doubts this – least of all Davidson himself, who made a handsome apology the next day, after he saw a taped rerun – but of course nothing can be done; we fans must wait with equal grace for the *next* Series triple play, which, by the rules of probability, will arrive in October of 2064.

Joe Carter hit a solo home run in the bottom of the same inning (great catches often breed such an aftermath), but a Deion Sanders double in the sixth was converted into the game-tying counter. Sanders, released at last from mere celebrity, was having a terrific day at the plate. The pitchers toiled on: Avery, with his cap pulled down to his eye-brows, throwing high heat; and Guzman pausing now and then between strike-outs to pour his gold necklace back into his shirt. (He is stocky and powerfully built, with the same trapezoidal upper-body profile as a Gordie Howe or a Paul Hornung, the old Green Bay hero – what their teammates used to call 'goat shoulders.') The Atlanta hitters seemed to have a better idea of Guzman on their third and fourth at-bats: the sign of an experienced and optimistic team. The Braves went ahead after their lead-off man, Nixon, got aboard in the eighth on a Gruber error, stole second, and zipped home on a Lonnie Smith single, but Gruber made amends with his tying home run in the bottom half, which also snapped his gruesome oh-for-twenty-three string at the plate.

Every pitch and play felt freighted and scary now, and when Pat Borders, the Blue Jay catcher, at last threw out a base runner, Brian Hunter, at second in the ninth, completing a K–2–6 double play, the Dome seemed to throb and quiver with noise. A thin celebratory fog hung above the outfield – leftovers from the little fireworks show that had greeted the Gruber home run. Braves manager Bobby Cox, enraged over what he had thought was a ball on the previous pitch, sent a helmet spinning out onto the carpet in front of his dugout, and was ejected. The end arrived quickly. Robbie Alomar, on a lovely little stroke, skimmed a single up the middle to start off the Toronto ninth. Avery departed, and Robbie, on a 2–0 count, flew into second base untouched.

Alomar, at once cool and upbeat, has become the kind of player that enemy pitchers and managers have on their minds even when his next at-bat is several notches away in the game. Once on base, he looks released and joyful, rather than cautious: *Let's see, now – what next?* Several Blue Jay players said later that they had *known* he would be part of the script that brought the game home in the end. The fans, for their part, were on their feet for good now, and you could see them wildly flapping or pumping the big scarlet-and-white flags they had brought to the park that day for quite a different reason. (One of the fans down below me, a kid in a baseball cap, was wielding a flag he'd tied onto a hockey stick.) The obligatory Atlanta ripostes – intentional pass, new pitcher, *another* new pitcher – resembled the fluttery last moves of a lost chess position, and the slick winning gambit in the middle of it all was Winfield's sacrifice bunt up the right side, to move the runners into scoring position. Reardon, an ensuing Braves hurler, was greeted with happy applause by the Toronto rooters (a last sign of sophistication, if we needed one), because of his home-run ball to Sprague back in Atlanta. Now, sure enough, he delivered a third successive slider to the same outer sector of the plate, and Candy Maldonado, not trying to do too much with the pitch, rapped it into center field for the run and, at last, the great game.

It is rarely the case in games of this nature that a very early play appears to be the critical one, but that was how Bobby Cox described the Devon White catch, which had come way back in the fourth inning. The catch itself, regardless of its subsequent effects, was already beginning to come clear in memory, like a photograph emerging in the developing tray. Watching him in full flight toward the wall, we could somehow see or sense that he would get up there all in one motion, and that the ball would converge with his upthrust, back-turned glove. The wonder was that he held on to it and, what's more, kept his feet as he rebounded from that aerial collision and came down ready to get on with the rest of the play. He hit the fence just to the left of the big '400' marker out there (and the smaller '121.9' metre indicator just below), and his lean body and white uniform, smack in the wall, made it look for an instant as if he had rewritten that figure into '1400.' Other fabled Series catches now came to mind and were passed back and forth among the writers: Willie Mays against Vic Wertz, deep in the Polo Grounds in 1954; Joe Rudi hung up to dry on the left-field fence in Cincinnati in 1972; and – perhaps the closest approximation – Willie McGee's long sprint and cat-up-the-wall play to rob Gorman Thomas in Milwaukee in 1982. (One of the writers – Mike Lupica, of the *News* – told me that the catch had brought to mind a great line by the old Dodger veep Fresco Thompson: 'Willie Mays' glove is where triples go to die.')

Full-flight, non-stop catches of this order are breathtaking at the instant they happen, but there is something else about them, a deeper sort of satisfaction, that comes to us and seems to last longer. It's my guess that this has to do with the player's foreknowledge, shared by each of us in the stands, that the play will be made. White himself said later that he never had any doubt that he would catch up to the ball. Such certainty may come not just from experience but from another kind of wisdom that exceptional athletes possess and the rest of us never discover – a phenomenon that the Harvard psychologist Howard Gardner has speculated about in his work on multiple intelligences. A different prime example of these occult skills is Wayne Gretzky's admission that at any moment when he is on the ice he is aware of the exact location and speed and direction of the eleven other players in the game as well as of the puck.

In the Toronto clubhouse, we writers surrounded Devon White, telling him that his catch now belonged among the all-timers, that it would be mentioned (one man said) in his obituary one day. He was up there with Mays now. White, who is tall and lean, and speaks quietly, said that he would never compare himself to Mays, and did not smile when he was invited to think about the fame and lifelong replays his catch would assure him. Finally, he said, 'I don't worry about that stuff, as long as when I'm gone, when I'm out of the game, someone will come along and say, "Did you ever see Devon White play center field?"'

———————— ◆ ————————

From 1931 through 1939 the St. Stephen–Milltown, New Brunswick, amateur baseball team won seven Maritime titles and nine consecutive New Brunswick senior ball championships. Known variously as the Mohawks, Kiwanis, and St. Croixs, the team drew its personnel and its enthusiastic crowds from the border towns of St. Stephen and Calais, Maine, on the St. Croix River. Big games were front-page news in these towns and the team's players were community heroes. In his book Even the Babe Came to Play, *Robert Ashe tells the story of the St. Stephen team in the 'Dirty Thirties' – lean years to live through, but a glorious period for community baseball in the Maritimes.*

The Day the Braves Came to Town

ROBERT ASHE

LEN WEBBER WAS A PUNCTUAL MAN WHO SMOKED A PIPE, WORKED FOR THE federal government, and always seemed to be carrying around a stack of papers. He was not a gambler. Nevertheless, one day in the middle of the Great Depression, Len Webber tested fate.

Webber's gamble involved an amateur baseball team, the St. Stephen Kiwanis, for which he was secretary. The Kiwanis were perhaps the best amateur team in the country during the 1930s. By 1934 they had already won three New Brunswick and three Maritime amateur, or 'senior,' championships. Before the end of the decade, when the demands of war would force the team to disband, they would capture nine New Brunswick and seven Maritime titles. All this occurred during an era when such titles had regional import and playdowns were front-page news.

As the 1934 season began, the Kiwanis were $500 in debt – a considerable sum for the local service club that sponsored the team. So Webber proposed that the Kiwanis play a major-league team in an exhibition game. He had heard the Boston Braves of the National League did such barnstorming tours, and he reasoned such a contest would draw a large crowd and pull the team out of debt. If all went well ... if it didn't rain.

Rain. Therein lay the gamble. The Braves would require a $1000 guarantee – rain or shine – and so far the summer of 1934 had saturated the St. Croix Valley. Moreover, there would be other expenses such as advertising. If the game was rained out the Kiwanis would go so deeply in debt that they would be unable to finish the season. Next season too would be in jeopardy. Perhaps there would be no more seasons at all.

Webber made a telephone call to Boston.

The game was set for July 17.

Tickets for the game went briskly. Webber watched as the 500-seat grandstand sold out at $2.50 a head – ten times the usual price. Indeed, the idea of such a match set the border town afloat. Talk on the street was of little else. Would Boston field a second-rate line-up? If so, could the defending Maritime senior baseball champions upset the overconfident National Leaguers? After all, the Kiwanis had beaten several barnstorming Negro American teams reputed to be of professional calibre. The *Saint Croix Courier*, the St. Stephen weekly newspaper, sought to quash such optimism: the Kiwanis were just 'a community team ... [and] this game is not expected to be hotly contested by any means.'

Still, talk continued. And Len Webber continued to pray for sunshine.

Like other senior ball players of the era, the Kiwanis were both for and of their community. Sharing a zeal for competition and a quest for some fashion of public status, players were often neighbours or relatives, and their accomplishments generated familial pride. In the Depression Maritimes, baseball linked all strata in a rural community. Relatively affluent professionals possessing social élan played alongside men of humble means and wayward inclinations.

The Kiwanis featured players from St. Stephen and environs and from Calais, Maine. The American connection could have caused problems with the New Brunswick amateur baseball association, but Webber and other Kiwanis officials usually arranged to have American players use a Canadian address and sleep in St. Stephen a night or two during the summer months. Such meticulousness – if less than noble – was typical of the Kiwanis. 'It was a class outfit,' reflected one team member many decades later. 'They were tie and tails.'

Few said that about the Boston Braves.

In 1934, the Braves were an eclectic tribe of has-beens loosely governed by just two rules: show up for games on time and stay out of jail. Even these ordinances were selectively enforced by soft-spoken manager Bill McKechnie. Moreover, their pitching staff was old and their hitting mediocre. The Braves' pre-eminent attraction was 29-year-old Wally Berger, a good-looking, blond outfielder and one of the National League's leading sluggers. He would hit 34 homers in 1934. (All other Braves combined would hit just 49.)

The Braves were one of the original National League teams of 1876. In the 58 years since, their successes had been few. Indeed, they would forever remain a distant second in the hearts and minds of Bostonians to the affluent Red Sox of the American League. Worse, the Braves neared bankruptcy throughout the 1930s. So, to help matters, they played exhibition games for $1000 and a percentage of the gate in alien places like St. Stephen, N.B., population 3400.

St. Stephen in the 1930s was a town with resolute rural grace and an economy diverse enough to fend off the economic virus that felled many Canadian towns. Nestled in the southwestern corner of New Brunswick, on the Maine border, St. Stephen sat directly across the St. Croix River from Calais, Maine, a municipality of similar size. The juxtaposition gave the area an international pretense that continues today.

As with many Maritime centres, St. Stephen enjoyed close communion with New England, Boston in particular. That city and the Maritime region were bonded by historical and social links influencing everything from accent to architecture. For generations, Maritimers had repaired to the 'Boston states' to experience the erudite city that effortlessly blended the exotic with the familiar. Montreal and Toronto lacked similar cachet, similar comfort.

The Braves' game transformed the town. Unaccustomed to such cosmopolitan excesses as traffic jams, the locals were overwhelmed and fascinated by the torrent of cars that descended upon St. Stephen's downtown. 'The crowds on the streets and the presence of the inevitable balloon peddlers were reminiscent of the days when the traveling circus was an annual event in the life of a small town,' wrote the *Saint Croix Courier*. Local municipalities proclaimed July 17 a public holiday, and merchants gave employees the afternoon off. Stores closed, factories stopped. Press from Boston and all over the Maritimes converged. Recalled Kiwanis playing coach Orville Mitchell, 'I know a lot of people were in awe.'

All this under a glorious sun. Len Webber was a grateful man on July 17, 1934.

The press estimated that 5000 people engulfed the diamond that day, but Orville Mitchell says the guess was low. 'The guy selling tickets at the gate went to watch the game. We lost a good many hundreds of dollars right there because the people were still coming in. And others sneaked through the back woods – the fellas that couldn't pay a dollar [general admission].'

The two teams arrived in full uniform and followed the Calais marching band onto the St. Stephen exhibition grounds, although the Braves probably wished they could have kept right on marching. The facility was basic even by the day's standards.

The St. Stephen Exhibition Grounds was, foremost, a metaphor for Depression life in a Maritime town. A flag-pole stood ominously in deep centre field, and a race track encircled the entire facility. Spectators ostensibly on hand to watch a ball game would scurry to and fro to watch the horses, then restore their attention to the ball game when the race ended. The infield had a robust allure with a dirt, or 'skin,' surface that repelled ground balls at life-threatening speed. 'That diamond was lightning fast,' said Mitchell, 'and before [the Braves] started they were told, "Christ, don't kill anybody out there today." If they hit a ball at somebody they were likely to blow their head off. They worried about the pitcher. Hittin' him and hurtin' him.'

As the game time neared, the teams stood caps-over-hearts at their benches as the Calais band clattered out the 'The Star Spangled Banner.' (It is unclear whether 'O Canada' or 'God Save the King' was played.) Players on both teams were introduced to polite applause. Then came the ceremonial first pitch, followed by more polite applause.

On the sidelines, Bill McKechnie, Jr., the Boston manager's son who would play briefly in the game, smiled at this rural theatre. The Braves had played the night before in Bangor, Maine, 100 miles south, and had arrived in St. Stephen late at night, weary and uninspired. But McKechnie Jr. noticed that his team-mates' faces no longer showed the tedium. 'It's sometimes hard to get the boys enthusiastic in their regular league games, but when they come on a trip like this and realize that some of the people there in the stands have traveled a hundred miles or more just to see them play, it means something,' he told the press.

The Kiwanis sprinted onto the field.

Kenny Kallenberg, a right-hander just 16 years old, was the Kiwanis' starting pitcher and the young talent being featured for the scouts. Only the day before did he learn of this honour. It resulted in a night of broken sleep, followed by a day of broken dreams.

'I was scared out of my wits,' remembered Kallenberg more than 50 years later. 'We had no television and I had never seen a major league baseball game. I used to hear them on the radio. These guys were heroes to me ... I didn't even feel my feet touching the ground. I didn't walk out [onto the field], I floated. The hair was standing up on the back of my neck out there ... There was a helluva crowd and I was wondering myself what was going to happen. Whatever it was, I was hoping that it happened quick.'

Wish granted.

Boston lead-off hitter Tommy Thompson doubled, moved to second on an infield out, then scored on a single. Still, Kallenberg slipped out of the inning, allowing just one run. Following St. Stephen's three-up, three-down first inning, Kallenberg returned to the mound and struck out the first batter. Then the trouble started. The next batter singled, as did the three after that. After getting the second out, Kallenberg hit slugger Wally Berger, then balked in a run. A third run crossed, then another and another and another. In all, eight runs and 10 hits. The score after two innings was 9–0.

Kallenberg finished the inning and slumped alone at the end of the Kiwanis bench. The crowd was silent. 'I didn't feel like hangin' around,' he recalled. 'I mean I didn't figure I was gonna pitch a no-hitter or anything, but Christ ... I felt like I just wanted to get the hell out of there.'

Cecil 'Lefty' Brownell, a head-strong southpaw who was born right-handed, pitched the third inning. Brownell, too, had a memorable moment when, with two out and the bases empty, slugger Wally Berger arched the ball over the temporary outfield fencing. 'He teed off on me and I don't think I have ever heard anything sound so nice,' recalled Brownell. 'Oh, man. I swear that the thing landed [40 miles away]. He flattened 'er right out, I swear.' Brownell got the next batter on a ground ball, stranding the great Berger on second base.

Then the game and its tone suddenly changed. In the third inning, with the outcome assured, and with the home side no longer paralysed with wonderment, the Kiwanis relaxed and started to swing freely at 38-year-old Leo Mangum, Boston's starting pitcher. The result was intriguing.

Kiwanis second baseman Bill McIntosh began the inning with his team's first hit of the game, a single over shortstop. Lefty Brownell then reached base on a fielder's choice. Rightfielder Earl 'Squirrely' Ross doubled, advancing Brownell to third. Playing coach Orville Mitchell looped a double into centre field, scoring both Brownell and Ross. Nine–two. Mitchell subsequently scored the final run of the inning when Kiwanis shortstop Rainnie Moffatt singled to right. It was a superb display of mature, refined baseball, and the spectators greeted the effort accordingly. Nine–three.

The Braves touched Brownell for two more runs in the fourth, but he blanked them in the fifth inning, finishing his stint with four hits over three innings. Veteran right-hander Roy Boles worked the sixth and seventh, facing just seven men in the two innings and yielding only one hit. It was evident that this game was not going to be the embarrassment some townspeople had feared.

As he watched this unexpected home-town magic at work, coach Orville Mitchell felt a tap on this shoulder. An acquaintance nodded in the general direction of the ball basket, near the Kiwanis bench. Mitchell blinked. They were running out of baseballs! The humiliating spectre of Kiwanis players begging patrons to return their souvenirs floated through his mind. Mitchell turned ashen. 'We had six dozen balls for that game and that would ordinarily last us for an entire season. I didn't realize that they were going to rope off the outfield. And every time you hit a two-bagger in the crowd you lost the ball. With all the foul balls that were being hit, we were down to less than a dozen balls.'

Mitchell desperately searched the crowd. Finally he spotted a friend who worked in a sporting-goods store in Calais. On Mitchell's pleading he ran to retrieve all the balls he had in stock – only a dozen or so, but enough to complete the game ... barely.

Meanwhile, Big Mike Calder inherited the mound from Roy Boles. Calder was magnificent, holding Boston hitless over the final two innings and striking out three. In the ninth, he made a bare-handed stop and tossed the ball to first for an easy out.

The final score was 11–3.

It could have been – and likely should have been – worse. 'The "pures" put up a much better argument than the semi-pros of Bangor,' wrote Joe Cashman of the *Boston Herald*.

The game raised $2952.97, from which the Braves claimed $1140. After expenses and repayment to creditors, the Kiwanis and Len Webber held more than $1200 – a tidy sum that turned a $500 deficit into a $700 balance.

In all, 14 Braves and 15 Kiwanis played. Boston had 15 hits, the Kiwanis 10. There were four errors, all by St. Stephen. The game lasted an hour and 33 minutes, about half the time of a modern major-league game.

Yet, as these numbers pour forth, as the glory of the game is retold, one especially interesting statistic emerges. Over the last seven innings ... when the Kiwanis starting line-up was on the field ... when the regular pitchers were on the mound ... when the team relaxed ... the score was St. Stephen Kiwanis 3, Boston Braves 2.

—————— ◆ ——————

*In a 1985 article entitled 'Baseball and the Canadian Imagination,' poet and fiction writer (and part-time amateur ball player) George Bowering discusses the hold that baseball – 'the great American game' – has had on his imagination, and on that of many other Canadian writers from the late nineteenth century on. 'I have always thought that it was the great Canadian game, too.' He notes that he has just finished writing a historical novel (*Caprice*) with some baseball in it. 'The setting for the novel is the Thompson Valley in 1889 and 1890. While doing my research ... I found that a Kamloops team, fortified with some American players, won the British Columbia baseball tournament in 1889. Even though the villain of the novel is an American who shot a French-Canadian ranch hand near Kamloops, I resisted temptation. Then I found out that New Year's Day of 1890 was preternaturally warm and that the Kamloops team played the CPR team in a game that day, and that the game had to be suspended in the fifth inning because of an eclipse of the sun! What was I supposed to do? Refuse a gift from a muse who has been watching over me since my teenage days when I reported the doings of the Kamloops baseball team for newspapers in the South Okanagan?' This is Bowering's story of a game later that year, and some attendant goings-on.*

A Rifle in Deep Centre

GEORGE BOWERING

THE TEAM WAS GIDDY, AS WILL OFTEN HAPPEN AT THE BEGINNING OF A season. They were filled with confidence, and showed it by their imitation of children on the short train trip west. For some, the imports from Minneapolis, this would be their first road game as Canadian ball players, specifically as Kamloops Elks. For the others, simultaneously envious of the money the Yanks would be getting and hopeful that the addition of the pros would take them to the Provincial tournament in September, it would be their first chance to strut in another town, one of the nicest parts of the game.

Even without the Yanks they were a pretty good club. Last year's Provincial tournament had taken place on their home field, and they had lost to New Westminster in ten innings.

We can look back to what they looked forward to. These young men would indeed run away from their own league this year, and go to the championships, and come home champions of the Province.

The Indians, if they had been asked, could have told them so. They would have directed their memories to New Year's Day that year, only a few months ago. It had been a warm bright day, as if the hard white sun knew something was up and were trying to make the best of things as long as it could.

People in the Thompson Valley were acting almost as if they were responsible for the mildness of the winter. At least they felt as if they should show proper appreciation for it. On Christmas Day Santa Claus rode the length of Main Street on the cowcatcher of Engine 373, carrying his enormous sack and wearing a red union suit with no white fur. On New Year's Day, the town team and the CPR side took off their jackets and played a baseball game in front of a large crowd of picnickers. It was not an overly serious game, and there was a little mud around home plate, but the joy and effrontery of playing the summer pastime on January 1st, hangovers ebbing away as blood coursed through bodies and brains, filled the eighteen players with pride, that they could for an afternoon deny the conditions of their employment.

Then in the sixth inning there was a chill, and the light dimmed a little. The game was suspended for a half-hour as the moon slid across the face of the warmth. The ball players and their spectators cheered and toasted the eclipse of the sun, and cheered louder when it reappeared. The game continued, and the town team, whose Minnesotans had not yet arrived, eked out a narrow victory over their local rivals.

If the Indians had been asked, they could have told the townies they were going to have a good year. As long as the pitching held up, and if they could execute the hit and run.

Now, or rather a then that we call now, the train was coming to a stop, and the young men were switching crumbs off their vests, running combs through their hair, ready to step off the train and dazzle the local citizens. Baseball players have always loved to dress up fancy off the field. These young fellows were sporting candy-stripe suits, wing collars and cravats, watch chains across their vests, straw boaters on their heads, and elegant walking sticks in their hands. Their hair was shaved short and parted just off the middle. Then as now, baseball players liked to dress like pimps. If there had been motorcars then, they would have driven here in the kinds of vehicles that pimps favour. No one has ever explained this similarity of tastes.

In fact one of the Kamloops outfielders *was* a pimp. But the rest of them had regular Thompson Valley jobs, even the stars from across the line. Some of them worked on ranches, but most of them had relatively easy jobs in town. The second baseman was a teacher at the Kamloops Indian School. This was Roy Smith.

As the train squealed and steamed to a stop, Smith remained sitting while his team-mates staggered to remain upright during the last jerks of the car. He was looking out the window, forward and back along the platform. He didn't see what he was looking for.

But she was there. From her perch on the top rail of the loading pen she watched the regular passengers and the dandies step down from their car. She knew he would be the last one off, and she smiled at her knowledge. It was not a matter of pride but it was a matter of amusement to her that she could figure him out so easily while remaining a puzzle to his methodical and serious mind. It drove him crazy, for instance, that she spoke English with a barely discernible accent. Well, not crazy. With a mind like that he would never know a minute of craziness. At certain moments, when he was a little too much convinced of his role as teacher and wise moral guide, she would put on an accent and a demure feminine whimper. That would always stop his paragraph and make him just a little cool. Then she would see about warming him.

She would see. When he finally stepped down, carrying his beaten leather bag, stovepipe pantlegs wading through the steam that was still drifting across the boards of the platform, she put her gloved hands on the rail on either side of her and then she was the best athlete within a mile, as she landed on her feet and walked quickly but without haste to his side.

'Hello, teacher,' she said.

He was really happy to see her. Just about everybody was happy to see her. Utter strangers were happy to see her walking along a boardwalk or riding past on a high black horse or sipping tea at a dry camp somewhere on the Interior Plateau. But Roy Smith had to pretend that he was not happy to see her here.

'I know why you're here,' he said.

She put out her gloved hand and pushed a cowlick back into place above his forehead. That would have made just about anybody happy.

'I came to watch a ball game,' she said.

Whether with their mothers or with women who have their own ways, young men somehow have to sulk. Roy Smith was sulking now. As he and Caprice walked to the Chinese restaurant, he said nothing. Observing this, she walked beside but at a little distance. Her strides were equal in length to his. For fun she walked in step, and sulking, he tried to change his rhythm.

But when she had her tea and toast in front of her and he had his out-of-town beer, he began talking again.

'Is Frank Spencer back in the Valley?'

'I dont know. He's back in the country.'

She had her gloves off. The teacup looked wonderful as it was held by her long bony fingers. They were not soft and white. The backs of her hands had freckles on them. But her hands were not cracked and toughened like the hands of a ranch wife, either. They were strong enough to control a powerful horse and to propel a whip. But they were wonderful to look at as they busied themselves at toast and strawberry preserves with a white tablecloth as background.

'What are you doing in this town, Caprice?'

'I told you, handsome. I'm going to a ball game. I am a supporter of the Kamloops Elks.'

'Caprice, I have already heard what you did two days ago. Do you think you can cause a public scandal like that and avoid the consequences?'

'He followed me to the hostler's, Roy. He could have killed the poor little man who tried to stop him in his ugly little game.'

'Damn it, it makes me crazy to know you could get hurt or killed doing what you're doing in some town I cant get to quick. Or some place I havent even heard of.'

She knew he was right. It was not easy to find a thoroughly peaceful man in this kind of country, and there were thousands of women who had given up hope of ever finding such a man. She knew that Roy Smith wanted her to forget all this trail riding, to forget Quebec, then, to remember what she did best. He was the only person within two thousand miles to have read anything she had written. It would have been hard enough for him to ask her to combine the sensibility that had made her a poet with the dusty routine of a western schoolteacher's wife. To ask her to give up her hate was too complicated for these two minds faced with their now undeniable love. This should all have been a long drama in verse, all this death and hate and love and whatever that fourth force was. That fourth force made a person surrender to something a verse-dramatist would call fate, a destiny. Necessity. Family revenge belonged to Jacobean tragedies, all that blood and all those curses, and the off-stage horrors. No one could imagine taking such a scenario seriously into a personal modern life. It was theatre. Even the words were stupid, silly. They should be intoned by a tremulous voice or the shrieks of an old matron driven crazy by blood and sword-clash. She would never say the word fate or the word revenge out loud, especially to Roy Smith. But family revenge was something she had heard of on this continent, too, in recent times on just this sort of landscape.

'Teacher?'
It was a new tone, a quiet voice that said all fencing and parrying was over.
'Yes?'
'That man I had my run-in with? His name is Loop Groulx.'
'That's what I heard. From what I was told, he has been loafing around town all winter.'
'I heard his name mentioned in Arizona, Roy.'

It can be pretty dangerous to stay in a town after you have humiliated a person everyone perceives to be a potential bully. Strange Loop did not have a bad reputation as a gunfighter and brawler here, but he was far from refined. His language was no better than it should have been, and he spent most of his time lounging around in the bars or tracking mud into the Canadian Cafe. Strange was an outsider several months ago, and could not now (or rather the present then) be considered a citizen. That is, he didnt work. But if a newer outsider who was a man had come into town and thrashed him at the hostler's, that stranger would have to keep an eye out for retaliation in dark places. Nobody knew what the situation was likely to be if the stranger was a woman, or a girl, as most people called her.

'What kind of girl beats a man with a whip,' was the semi-rhetorical question of a young woman wearing laced boots in the bar of the Nicola.
'I'm not so sure she's a girl,' said Gert the Whore.

But Gert was of two minds, or three. She didnt much like Loop Groulx, or men like Loop, partly because they were brutish and dirty, and partly because they tried to get as much as they could for as little as they could pay, nothing if possible. On the other hand, she felt a little like the most famous desperado in town who loses a bit of glamour when Wild Bill rides in. On the third hand she liked the whiff of danger that had crept into town. She knew that danger and business went together.

'Well,' said Addie the afternoon bartender, 'it seems to me like there's two kinds of women. There's the kind you want to be your mother or the mother of your kids, and there's the other kind.'
'Listen,' said Gert, 'there's only one kind of man, and you're it, an asshole.'
'Nice language, Gert. We sure know what kind of woman you are.'
'You'll never find out,' she said.

'No, but I mean it. This one with the whip aint natural. You sure couldnt imagine marrying her, and she's too big to even imagine getting into the bedroll with.'

Everyday Luigi, his face varying in colour from yellow to purple, was having an amaro at the bar. He didnt like either side of this conversation. It was this kind of conversation that had enlivened his nights with the Kamloops Italian band a few years ago, but now it was fixed on a person he knew, and loved.

'Capriccia should take her whip to you two,' he said.

Everyday Luigi was tolerated, but there wasnt anyone in town who would admit to caring about him. A man who went to work for the Chinaman. Gert the Whore had once taunted him by offering a free sample, and was of two minds when the little man turned and left with speed.

'You find your true love, Dago?' Addie winked at the girls.

'Ah, leave him alone, Addie,' said the one in the laced boots. 'You might bruise his feelings.'

Everyday Luigi didnt even get the lame joke, but he gulped the rest of his brown drink and left anyway. He wanted to be on the street as often as he could today, between deliveries and odd jobs. He wanted to keep an eye out for Loop Groulx.

At the Canadian Cafe there were three ranch wives having tea and scones with orange marmalade. Their husbands were in town because it was Saturday and the first day of the baseball season. They were in town because they could get a ride and look at the shops. Their names were probably Ruth, Clara and Jeanette.

'Now be fair, Ruth, that Frenchman Groulx had it coming to him.'

'I agree. From a *man*. But what kind of woman comes riding into a peaceful town, comes riding *alone* into a peaceful town, and gets into a fight the first hour she's here?'

'What was she supposed to do? Just let that filthy devil have his *way* with her?'

'He wasnt trying to have his way with her, from what I have heard. She butted into a quarrel with the Italian.'

'It was hardly a quarrel, Ruth. That filthy devil was killing the old man.'

'Well, I wont have any truck with a perfect stranger who comes into my town and starts a brawl. A scandal. And a woman! Can you imagine doing such a thing, Jeanette? Of course not.'

Jeanette was imagining doing such a thing. She imagined doing it to several different men. She imagined being nearly six feet tall.

'It is just not *natural*,' proclaimed Ruth.

As one can imagine, there was at least as much talk about the whipping as there was about the ball game around town.

'What would we be doing if it was a man who did it,' asked the first constable.

'The same thing we're doing now,' said the second constable. 'No one has entered a complaint, have they?'

'I wouldn't want to be Loop Groulx,' said the first constable. 'Do you figger he's lit out?'

'I wouldnt want to be that girl,' said the second constable.

'I would,' said the first constable. 'Only I'd carry a revolver the next time I saw him.'

'You *are* carrying a revolver.'

At the baseball grounds the young athletes were beginning to throw baseballs at each other while other men in vests were laying lines of quicklime on the ground. There were already dozens of boys running around, kicking holes in the dry earth, throwing cactuses at each other, looking for snakes to bash.

The ball players on both sides were like everyone else, more likely to talk about the incident than the game.

'Tell you what I'd do, I'd take a whip to *her*,' said one of the first basemen.

'You dont even know how to use a baseball bat,' said the second first baseman, 'what do you think you could do with a whip?'

'It just aint right for a woman to ride around alone like that, beating up on fellows. I'll wager she's an invert,' opined the first first baseman.

'I dont care what she is. I'd like to get her in a hay loft,' said the second first baseman.

J.C. Tunstall, the manager of the Kamloops side, had been listening. He spit a stream of tobacco juice between the feet of his first baseman. This was always a signal that he had something to tell one or more of his players. If he hit your foot it was a sign that you would be sitting on the plank this day. His own players now became quite like boys waiting for admonition to be finished. The players from the other side listened in. They could enjoy what he had to say without having to appear contrite or compliant.

'I dont want you boys to talk like that about her. She might be anything, she might be everything you say. All I know is that she is one hell of a lookin' woman, and she could probably beat the tarnation out of any three of you. And one more thing. She's Roy Smith's woman.'

'That lucky son of a bitch,' said one ball player.

'That poor bastard,' offered another.
'Say, where the hell *is* Roy?' put in a third.

Roy was in a second-storey room at the Nicola Hotel, out of uniform, out of his regular weekend clothes, too. He was lying on his back, and on his left shoulder lay the head and loose red hair of the most famous person in town. There was a single sheet covering the two long bodies as high as their waists. The rest of the bed covers were on the floor at the foot of the brass bed.

'I wish I could see you more often,' said Roy Smith. 'It aint much fun going home at night and imagining you sleeping under the stars in Arizona or some such place.'

'Teacher, I'm surprised at you. If you say aint, what are your little Indian children going to say?'

'I wish you would forget all this unhappy travelling. I wish – '

'Shh, I know what you wish.'

Indeed she did. He used to say it every night. Now he seldom did. There was a kind of hope held out, from one of them, maybe both of them, that when this trailing was over with somehow, when they heard some news about the pursued, maybe she would say to herself and to him that she would be what he wanted. He wanted her to be Mrs Smith. When she left Quebec such a notion had never passed through her mind.

But here she was, a poet, with a schoolteacher's left leg lying under her long right leg. She turned her head and took his left nipple in her mouth and gave it a slightly more than tender bite.

'When are you supposed to be at the ballpark?' she asked.

'Right now,' he said.

'Are you supposed to do this before a match?'

'Game. A game.'

'*Ah oui, un game.*'

'No, I am not supposed to do this for twelve hours before a game.'

'Now that you have broken the rule, what do you think about doing it one more time before you go to the game?'

He knew she was kidding. He thought she was kidding. She was probably kidding. He would get up in a few seconds and go. A minute or two more. Just kiss her body a few times, and then go and play ball. Just a few kisses on the freckles above her breasts.

◆ ◆ ◆

The ballpark gave off the scent of fresh lumber. People were in the habit of attending games in their buckboards, parking them around the perimeter of the outfield except right field, whose boundary was the river. But there was a new grandstand, and that is where the unaccompanied ladies and drifters sat. Boys and girls wandered around the grounds, vaguely aware of the game but not the score, except for one ten-year-old who sat in the grandstand directly behind home plate with a pencil and his school scribbler.

In the second inning, Ed Chesley hit a ball that rattled off the spokes of a wagon in left, and Kamloops was ahead 2–0.

Caprice was reminded of a snowy day in the high country of New Mexico, a day when she and her horse had both been persuaded to abandon the sky and look for a valley farther north. All through the baseball game the wind from behind the high cottonwoods along the river bank carried a flurry of white puffballs across the playing field. The locals considered it an omen or at least a part of the home field advantage. The Kamloops Elks just laughed at the idea, they were that confident. One of the Minnesota lads continually cracked jokes about playing the great Canadian game in arctic conditions.

In the fourth inning Willy Schoonmaker slid into home plate with his spikes up, driving the catcher off his knees and onto his back. There were gutteral threats from the crowd, but the Elks were ahead 3–0.

'I cannot help wondering,' said the first Indian, 'why these people call themselves elks.'

'Well, the elk is a beautiful and noble animal,' said the second Indian. 'As a hunter and an artist I respect all the animals, of course, but the elk fills me with awe when I see him standing with his head up.'

'That elk there does not have his head up. He is all crouched over with a stick in his hand.'

The second Indian had his mouth full of ice cream. His older companion had tried some and liked it immensely, but had not taken a second bite. One had to put up with certain sacrifices to retain the kind of dignity one was expected to show in the ceremonial meetings and the photographs.

'The elk is admirable in its hauteur,' said the second Indian, licking his fingers. 'On the prairie there are Indian people who name their children after elk. I have even heard of cases in which fathers have pretended to see an elk at the birth of their children so they can call them things such as Running Elk, or Elk Who Fears No Hunter.'

'Elk, however, are stupid. I do not know how you young people do it, but we always found it easier to have the elk come to us than to go stalking him among the trees. All we had to do was put a salt lick by the side of the lake, or a snare made of vines for them to stumble into. Then we picked up our bows and picked out the one we wanted to eat. Even Coyote could get himself an elk for the winter.'

'Do you call that sport?'

'Crouching down with a stick in your hands. Do you call that sport?'

'Times are changing, old teacher. That stick is called a Louisville Slugger.'

'Do you think we should crouch down behind the willows and wait for the elk to stick his tongue on the salt lick and then bang him with a Louisville Slugger?'

'Times are changing. Maybe we would have more success doing what that man behind the brown-and-white horse is doing, crouching with a .30–30 Winchester.'

'You saw him too, did you? I was beginning to have doubts about these old eyes, but it is wonderful what a proper traditional diet will do for them.'

In the fifth inning, Joe McCrum stepped into a gopher hole while chasing down a high fly, and two unearned runs crossed the plate, tightening the score to 3–2.

Everyday Luigi was at the Canadian Cafe, getting another tub of vanilla ice cream. When he came out onto the boardwalk with the weight hanging off both ends of the pole across his shoulders, he saw two men come out of the Bank of Commerce and mount their horses. Out of habit he checked the brands. They were different from each other, but they were both unknown in the area. He would have stayed and watched which way the riders were headed, but Soo Woo had a very strong attitude toward melting.

Still, he had some data filed away. Someone might need it.

When Everyday Luigi got back to the ballpark it was the sixth inning. The cotton was falling like Christmas, and the locals had a man on second with one out. There was a ripple of excitement around the ring of buckboards and through the grandstand, where Gert the Whore could be heard excoriating the manliness of the Kamloops pitcher.

'You shoulda spent a quiet morning in church, ya dumb bunny,' she shouted, and her companions laughed heartily.

The boy with the scribbler and pencil looked at her and then at her friends with irritation and lust. Baseball was a complicated game, but it was going to be necessary in the coming years. He would find out. Baseball would be beautiful when some things were not.

'Ball two,' said the umpire.

'You coulda fooled me,' shouted Gert the Whore, and her companions guffawed.

The banker's wife hustled her kids off for another dose of ice cream.

The next pitch came off the bat twice as fast as it had come in. Smack, went the bat, and the ball hit the pitcher right on the head.

'Hooray,' shouted Gert.

But the ball landed right in the hands of Roy Smith the second baseman.

'Phooey,' said Gert.

Roy Smith moved like a cougar. With the ball in his sore hand, he ran over second base, much to the surprise of the runner who had not even thought of returning there yet. Roy Smith had two put-outs, and the pitcher, though he did not know it yet because he was still lying with his face on the ground, had an assist.

'Darn it all to heck,' said Gert the Whore.

At the end of six innings it was still 3–2.

Roy Smith dropped the ball at the pitcher's box as he trotted off the field, no expression on this face. Ball players love this moment. They always run off the field with no expressions on their faces. A smile might make it look as if they were pleased by an extraordinary stroke of mortal luck. A smile might make the victims feel a little better. If you act as if it is all in a day's work, your luck will stay good, and you will appear invincible to your opponents and fans.

Caprice sat in the grandstand and did not applaud. This was, after all, an away game. But she kept her grey eyes on Roy Smith as he joined his team-mates on the bench. Some of them were smiling; that was all right. She looked intently at him to see whether he would glance in her direction. She was really proud of him when he didnt. It would have been nice, though. Hooray, she said inside.

She would cut the piece out of the *Journal* tomorrow if it mentioned that play.

It was not going to matter now who won the game. She knew that this moment for Roy Smith was a lot like that moment for her had been when she was still a poet and not a fury.

The instant of inspiration seemed now to be reflected from all sides at once, from a multitude of sunny and snowy circumstance of what had happened or of what might have happened. The instant flashed forth like a point of light, and now from puff ball to puff ball of vague circumstance confused form was veiling softly its afterglow. In the virgin womb of the imagination the word was made flesh.

The boy with the spectacles and the scribbler watched the white stuff blowing across the outfield, and wondered whether this was what manna looked like for the people of Moses exiled in the desert.

'Ice cream here,' shouted Everyday Luigi.

On the fresh yellow wood of the plank on which Caprice was sitting a jagged rip appeared. Then there was a smack like the sound of a Louisville Slugger creating an extra-base hit. She moved like a cougar, even as the other spectators in the ballpark were gathering their wits. She was off her seat and running before anyone else had decided that what they had heard was a rifle shot.

Roy Smith ran toward her while other men ran for their horses or for cover. A man on a brown-and-white mount was already over the ridge and out of sight, even of the Indian eyes that had been alone in seeing him. There was an awful commotion in and around the ballpark, women picking up their skirts and screaming or cursing, depending on who they were, men looking for their children, children trying to save their ice cream from accidental loss.

Roy Smith had his baseball arms around the tall woman with the gleaming red hair. He held her and again had no expression on his face. Another woman in her place might have had her face buried in his chest. She was looking with her grey eyes over his shoulder, perhaps scanning the hillside.

The boy with the scribbler still sat in his seat directly behind home plate, wondering whether this was a suspension or a forfeiture of the game.

———————— ◆ ————————

Sport has always provided people with merciful relief, at little cost, in hard times. In Canada, few times have been harder than the 1930s. Barry Broadfoot's Ten Lost Years, 1929–1939: Memories of Canadians Who Survived the Depression *(1973) offers this anonymous, plain-spoken reminiscence of what baseball gave Prairie people in the Dirty Thirties.*

There Was Always the Baseball

BARRY BROADFOOT

BASEBALL! GOD, IF YOU CAME FROM THE PRAIRIES YOU HAD TO REMEMBER baseball. There was nothing else to do. You'd work your land and put in the seed and watch the Russian thistle knock out the new wheat or barley and then the blistering heat would come and you could just see everything shrivelling. Then you'd get, maybe, the grasshoppers, and that was it for the year. No crop insurance, nothing, but there was always the baseball.

If you had a car you could get to a tournament every weekend. All through Manitoba, Saskatchewan, Alberta, and teams used to come out from the Okanagan Valley too. I remember one team that came from Penticton, I think, and they rode the freights to get to a tournament at Vulcan.

Each town would have a sports day, beginning early in June and running right through to Labor Day, sports all over the country. There would be men's fastball, just ordinary baseball, and then there was softball, and a men and women's senior team and usually a girls' and boys', or junior teams. Most towns, if they were big enough, and they had the surrounding farms and villages to draw on, they had four teams, and there were some damn good teams. I've seen senior teams from towns in Saskatchewan which could go up against anybody in the country today. It was just that they were stuck out there in the wilds and nobody ever heard of them, but some of that pitching was strictly big league. Mostly fastball, you understand. There wasn't much slider or curve. The boys got up there and for seven or so innings they just threw that ball as hard as they could and nobody can tell me there weren't a couple of potential Dizzy Deans or Lefty Groves out there in The Thirties. Hell, those fellows had nothing to do except practise, and they loved baseball. I've seen men of 40 playing just as hard as a guy of 20, and some of their women, whew! Those gals could play. Softball, of course, but you get a big, hefty Ukrainian girl throwing a big softball and it just comes screaming in.

Each town would have a tournament and they'd get the prize money, hook or by crook, from entries, small admission charge if they could, although not always, because a lot of it was cow pasture ballparks, and gifts from the merchants and the banker, and perhaps a rummage sale or two. Some of those pots got up to $500 and even – for a place like Swift Current or Weyburn or Brandon or Wetaskawin or Lethbridge – even higher. As much as $1,000, and that was enough to bring real good teams from all over hell's half acre and including up from the United States if their entry was allowed. I've seen 10 teams playing, in the men's senior, on three diamonds, from 10 in the morning and when the last fly was caught just as the sun was going down, several thousand people would have watched.

They were big events. Real big. An awful lot of fun. Some teams used to bring in ringers, a Yankee, or a guy from the East, if the pot was big enough. There was nothing wrong with it, I guess, but the ringer never got the royal type of welcome he probably thought he deserved. Not even from his team mates because if he was that good, then he'd have a deal to take a third of the pot, and a third could mean a lot of dollars from the other guys' pockets.

There was one guy that Stavely brought in and he was a pitcher, a fastballer, but he had a nice curve too and a curve wasn't seen much at those tourneys, and he pitched a no-hitter the first game, a one hitter and a two hitter, and Stavely won the tournament. Naturally. If you don't believe me you can look it up. It was in Robert Ripley's *Believe It Or Not.* Three great games in one day. This big gink had played pro ball for Seattle or San Francisco and hadn't got the attention he probably thought he deserved, but he sure did on the Canadian prairies.

Sports days were fun days. Everybody came, and there was a dance and a lot of drinking, out in the cars and trucks parked around, and sometimes a fight or two. The cops usually stayed away, let the folks have their fun. Not like a Polish wedding where they stayed parked at the corner of the hall just waiting for the bomb to explode. They were good times, not prosperous times, but everybody did what they could to help the next fellow, and a lot of planning by the ladies and the committee went into them tournaments. Some of the rivalries between towns got pretty fierce, at the ball park level, for the big prize, but otherwise it was just people of Saskatchewan or Manitoba or Alberta trying to make the best of a tough situation.

Sitting in the little bleachers most towns had at the fairgrounds, you wouldn't know that if you dumped everybody's pockets, everybody in the stands and along the sidelines, you'd be lucky to come up with $50 in spending money. Nobody really cared that much. One thing I've always thought I'd like to have seen. Like to have seen some of those town kids and those big farm boys get a chance to try out for some big league team. Likely they wouldn't have made it anyway, but then again, you might have been real surprised. Some of those boys were real good.

◆

For years the exploits of the All-American Girls Professional Baseball League, which flourished in the American Midwest from 1943 to 1954, were ignored, but all that changed with the release of books like Browne's Girls of Summer *(1992), and with*

Penny Marshall's 1993 feature film, A League of Their Own. *Chicago Cubs owner Phil Wrigley started the league in response to the declining quality of major-league ball during the war years. Women from all over North America were scouted, and close to 10 per cent of all recruits were Canadian, including Regina's Mary ('Bonnie') Baker, who recalled that, when she was a child, her father 'just hated that baseball ... I got whipped more than once because I stayed in school to play ball.' Baker eventually became the league's only female manager and once appeared on the popular television show 'What's My Line.'*

The Hoydens Meet Helena Rubinstein

LOIS BROWNE

WRIGLEY HAD DISPATCHED HIS SCOUTS TO THE WORLD SOFTBALL Championships, held in Detroit in September 1942. The unknown author of the report handed to Wrigley displays considerable style in describing many of the League's first players. The New Orleans Jax had been the playoff favorites. 'In their attack,' said the scout, 'they could be compared with the heavy-hitting New York Yankees of old. The majority are long-ball clouters. Their base running and fielding keep pace with their hitting. Flashing spikes and perfect hook slides are regular practice with them. They can bunt to perfection. All in all they possess remarkable baseball sense and are considered by many fans as the greatest girls' softball team in the game's history.'

Despite this glowing recommendation, however, none of the Jax was signed by Wrigley's organization. *Time* magazine might have been referring to the Jax when it reported that, in recruiting for the League, scouts 'turned down several outstanding players because they were either too uncouth, too hard-boiled or too masculine.' *The Saturday Evening Post* described the New Orleans brigade: 'Good, substantial girls like the sinewy Savona sisters and the strapping Miss Korgan. Give 'em a cud of tobacco and these female softball players would look just like their big-league brothers.' This was not the image Wrigley had in mind. Nonetheless, Freda Savona, the captain, was supposedly offered a contract, but she refused; the Jax were about to lose their (male) coach to the draft, and she was slated to take his place. In any event, the Jax stayed intact. It didn't matter; a wealth of talent remained.

Close behind the New Orleans contingent were teams from Chicago, St. Louis, Detroit and Cleveland, as well as Canadian teams from

Saskatchewan and Toronto. All displayed a hard-driving style, and many of their players made favorable impressions. Edythe Perlick of the Chicago Rockolas, who later joined the Racine Belles, 'out-hit most of the right fielders in this district.' Her teammate, Twila 'Twi' Shively, who would be assigned to the Grand Rapids Chicks, was considered to be the championship's most outstanding defensive outfielder, covering her position with 'long, easy strides.' The pick of the 'short fielders,' a second shortstop position peculiar to softball, was the 'diminutive speed-merchant,' Shirley Jameson of the Garden City Brew Maids: 'Fast as lightning on the bases or in the field, she has a great arm and is a good hitter. Opposing pitchers say she is one of the hardest hitters to pitch to, because of her size and the power in her bat. She is smart and plays heads-up ball at all times.' Jameson went to the Kenosha Comets, and on retirement from active service became a scout for the All-American.

Charlotte Armstrong, a pitcher with the Phoenix Ramblers, was fast, with good control and a good hook: 'Her delivery is also very deceptive. Although there is plenty of back swing in her normal windup, she has a habit of releasing the ball with no windup at all. To a batter at the plate, it seems that she just flicks her shoulder a trifle, flips her right hand, and the ball comes sailing over the plate.' These skills earned Armstrong a place with the South Bend Blue Sox.

Ann 'Toots' Harnett was already well known to the scouts, thanks to her third-base duties with Chicago's Rheingold Brew Maids. Sturdy, well-built and blessed with a strong, accurate arm, Harnett was 'a free-swinging power-ball hitter who sends her drives whistling over the infielders' heads. She covers her position beautifully and has one of the best cross-diamond throws in softball.' She was the first player to be signed by the All-American and was soon after sitting at a head-office desk, phoning prospects in remote corners of the continent and urging them not to commit themselves to their teams until they heard what the new League had to offer.

Canadian teams had taken part in the championships and in occasional U.S. exhibition games since 1933. The scouting reports noted with approval that the Canadian teams 'show more of the girlish side of the picture when it comes to the style of their play. Their actions in throwing and batting do not have the tinge of masculine play like the United States girls. They do not go for boyish bobs and do not have the fire and fight of the average American team.'

Nevertheless, only two Canadians caught the scout's eye. Olive Bend

Little of the Moose Jaw Royals (later a mainstay of the Rockford Peaches) was a 'fire-baller' and 'one of the fastest pitchers in the game.' Thelma Golden played with Toronto's Sunday Morning Class, a team organized by a church parish, who were then the Canadian champions. Golden was supposedly one of the hardest pitchers to bat against. To see her in the daytime, the scout reported, she was almost skinny and didn't seem to have much on the ball. Under the lights, however, 'she seems even taller than she really is. She cups the softball in front of her and draws her arms close to her sides, leaning over at the same time. As she gets ready to release the ball, the batter has a vision of a giant spider unfolding on the mound. And out of those uncoiling long thin arms, the ball comes zooming over the plate.'

Golden's performance must have lived up to this heated prose. She was recruited early in 1943 and assigned to the Peaches. Before the end of spring training, however, she packed her bags and returned to Canada. The explanations for her departure differ markedly. Rumor had it that she demanded special privileges, including, according to Bonnie Baker, a separate hotel room. But Gladys 'Terrie' Davis, another Canadian who, with Baker and Olive Bend Little, could be counted on to project the requisite feminine grace under pressure, noted that Golden couldn't cope with power-sluggers: 'They started hitting her into the lake.'

Golden told Canadian sportswriters that she didn't like the League's grueling schedule. As a rule, Canadian teams tended to play less frequently – perhaps only two or three times a week. The League's season was, by comparison, action-packed, with games six nights a week and a double-header on either Saturday or Sunday.

Wrigley's scouts uncovered a wealth of talent at the Detroit championships, but they were confirming what they already knew or had heard about. Though softball in the United States and Canada was supposedly an amateur sport, in reality, it followed the Chicago model; it was highly commercialized, especially in large cities. Firms such as Dr. Pepper or the Bank of America in Los Angeles, Admiral Corporation in Chicago and every brewing company everywhere sponsored workplace teams. Many were all-female teams. Chrysler had sixty such clubs in the Detroit area alone. Companies offered people jobs based on their ball-playing skills – a variation on today's athletic scholarships. This was a tremendous inducement to compete, especially during the Depression, and was as much the norm in Canada as in the United States. Many firms recruited from distant parts in order to field a winning team. Players were offered higher salaries than their non-playing co-work-ers, along with time off for games, free meals, travel expenses and other perks. This practice continued even when jobs became more plentiful.

In 1939 in Toronto, a talented left-handed pitcher named Bea Hughey, then unemployed, had agreed to play for Toronto's Langley Lakesiders on the condition that they get her a job. When a team owned by Orange Crush came up with a job for her within a couple of days, she switched – to loud complaints from the Lakesiders, who refused to release her. The dispute went to arbitration, but the Lakesiders lost Hughey to Orange Crush.

Helen Nicol, of Edmonton, Alberta was western Canada's foremost pitcher of the early 1940s and would win the All-American League's pitching championship in 1943 and 1944. Both she and Bonnie Baker, who lived in Regina, Saskatchewan, worked in Army and Navy de-partment stores by day and played ball on a company-sponsored team a couple of times a week. For her efforts, Nicol received twice the normal rate of pay.

By February 1943, Wrigley's plans were well under way. Thanks to judicious use of the Cubs' scouting network, he had targeted players as far away as New York City and Memphis, Tennessee. On the Canadian prairies, the driving force was Johnny Gottselig, who had enjoyed a successful career as a defensemen with the Chicago Blackhawks hockey team during the 1920s and 1930s. He came from Regina, where he had played amateur baseball before injuring his pitching arm, and he coached women's teams in the off-season. By 1942, he was managing the Blackhawks' Kansas City farm team, but he still had useful contacts among sports figures in the prairie provinces. One of his friends, a Regina-based hockey scout named Hub Bishop, was the person respon-sible for signing Bonnie Baker, who in turn pointed out to him an extraordinary number of top-ranked western Canadian players. No one has ever figured out why half of the fifty-odd Canadians who would eventually play in the All-American came from Saskatchewan, but Baker's theory is as good as any: there was nothing else to do there 'except play ball and chase grasshoppers.'

At any rate, Wrigley went public with his plans for the League – known then as the All-American Girls Softball League – in February 1943. The press release was couched in predictably patriotic terms, with emphasis on the need to entertain war workers and bolster civic pride. It introduced the four cities and their teams, heaped praise on local backers and hinted at imminent expansion to centers both large and small. This was the first suggestion that the League might eventually include franchises in cities as large as Chicago and Detroit. Wrigley stressed that the presumably greater attendance in such locations would mean more money that could then be distributed to help carry the smaller cities. The League's non-profit charter was unveiled to general applause. No one said anything about Wrigley's actual concern – that major-league ball might be headed down the tubes.

At this point, matters began to pick up steam. Word spread among players that something was happening in the midwest, and that it would be wise to get in line. Mary Baker, whose nickname 'Bonnie' was given to her by a reporter smitten by her smile, first learned about the League in the Regina newspaper: 'I was in the coffee shop I went to every morning before work, and I opened up the sports page and there was a picture of Mrs. Wrigley with Johnny Gottselig and a model with this uniform on. I read it and said to myself, "Oh, God, it's happening. Now, am I going to be lucky enough to get in?"' That very afternoon, she got a call from Hub Bishop. 'I was ecstatic,' she says. 'I knew I was on my way to what I'd dreamed of.'

Dorothy 'Dottie' Hunter, a tall, striking brunette who worked in a Winnipeg, Manitoba, department store and played ball during the summer months, heard about the League from her friend Olive Bend Little. Little called to say that a scout had arrived at the city's Marlborough Hotel. 'It was on Good Friday, and I was entertaining some fellows who were over at Carberry [an armed forces base]. But Olive came flying out to my place in a taxi and said, "Come on, get in here, you got to go down for an interview." So I just left everybody and went down there, and before the day was over I'd signed a contract, even though I was twenty-seven years old. The scout told me he wasn't sure they'd take me at that age, that they were looking for younger girls. But they took me, so I went down to play.'

By May 1943, newspapers in Toronto and Edmonton reported that the League's recruiting was 'playing havoc with some Canadian teams.' An Edmonton columnist suggested that the softball clubs 'who make it possible for these girls to develop their latent talents' should be suitably compensated for players lured away by the All-American, much as amateur teams were reimbursed by the National Hockey League. In Chicago, two entire teams were wiped out by Wrigley's raiding. The Chicago owner-managers were incensed, and they publicly berated Wrigley for taking these players, some of whom held war-related day jobs, out of the work force.

Elsewhere, players were signed up by ones and twos. Mildred Deegan, a catcher, came from Brooklyn, New York. Irene 'Choo Choo' Hickson, the alleged twenty-eight-year-old who wound up being called 'Grandma' by the fans, came from North Carolina. Madeline 'Maddy' English, third baseman in a Boston league that played indoors on a cement field with painted bases, was from Everett, Massachusetts. Ralph Wheeler, a Boston sportswriter and sometime scout for the Cubs, came to her home to offer her a tryout, having heard of her from male athletes at her high school. She made the League, along with two other Massachusetts players, Mary Pratt and Dorothy 'Dottie' Green.

Were they eager to go when the All-American came knocking? You'd better believe they were. Younger players especially jumped at the chance to get paid for doing what they'd have done for free. Plus, they were dazzled by the sums involved. Most were making a pittance – perhaps $10 a week – in offices or factories. Store clerks made rather less. Dottie Hunter's father, a family man, was making $35 a week. The League's $55 entry-level salary was unheard of for young women. Besides, players would be on the road half the time, with those travelling and living expenses paid. They could bank money and plan on attending college to make something of themselves, or they could at least escape from the limited horizons of dead-end jobs and one-horse towns.

But there were obstacles. Many prospective players were still teenagers, and subject to the wishes of their families; even those in their twenties, holding down steady jobs, were often living at home with protective parents, people who had barely survived the Depression. To a Saskatchewan farm family, South Bend or Kenosha sounded like Sodom and Gomorrah. They were hopeful of a better life for their daughters, but this seemed a bit much.

While most parents had misgivings, however, few were adamantly against the idea. Convinced of Wrigley's bona fides, and having learned that chaperons would be thick on the ground, they usually relented. The players, of course, had their suitcases packed and were two steps out the door. Professional softball represented the opportunity of a lifetime. Amid a climate of wartime restraint, as North America battened down for rationing and sacrifice, this was a chance for adventure.

In a few cases, it wasn't parents but husbands who cried foul. Bonnie Baker's husband, Maury, was stationed overseas with the Royal Canadian Air Force when Bonnie was given her chance to play pro ball. She had good reason to believe that he would be less than thrilled at the prospect. They had been married for nearly five years. In 1942, she had had to pass up a chance to play in Montreal for a team sponsored by Ogilvie Oats because he insisted she stay home. This time, however, her mother-in-law encouraged her to go now and tell Maury later. This bold maneuver worked. When Baker became the South Bend Blue Sox catcher – and the League's most widely recognized star – Maury burst with pride. But he accepted her ball career on the understanding that Bonnie would call it quits when he came marching home.

The players reported for 1943 spring training – held for the first and only time at Wrigley Field itself – in a state of great anticipation. Only sixty players would survive, chosen to fill berths on the All-American's four founding teams. They traveled by train, with one or two delays en route. War work had priority; so did anyone in service uniform. Players scrambled for early-morning or late-night connections, clutching cardboard suitcases and other must-have gear, including, in one case, a portable gramophone. Some had never been on a train before.

To many of them, Chicago must have seemed like another planet. Lillian Jackson, recruited from Nashville, Tennessee, was thrilled to discover that she and the other hopefuls would use the same locker rooms and showers as the Cubs.

All the players had been told beforehand that there'd be myriad rules and regulations governing personal conduct. They had received the patented no-shame, no-blame pep talk, and knew that chaperons would monitor their every move. Unsuitable behavior was spelled out in their contracts, complete with the penalties – $10 for back-chatting umpires, $50 for appearing 'unkempt' in public. The League was keen on comparing its standard document to an Actors' Equity agreement. This suggestion added a touch of show-biz panache. Smoking and drinking hard liquor in public were forbidden. Every social engagement had to be cleared ahead of time with the chaperon. A curfew called for players to be tucked safely into bed two hours after the game – just time enough for a shower, change and a bite to eat. Even close friends and blood relatives were kept well away from the bench; a no-fraternization clause prohibited off-the-field contacts with rival club members. All this was understood – but the League uniform came as an unwelcome surprise. Unless the players had seen the photograph that caught Bonnie Baker's eye, they hadn't realized they'd be playing in skirts.

By the early 1940s, young women everywhere were wearing pants. Rosie the Riveter – the symbol of a woman's ability to do a man's work

– went about her business in slacks or overalls. Shorts were customary for casual wear; jeans (known as dungarees) were big with teenagers. But the All-American wanted something entirely different.

Most female softball teams wore modified men's uniforms, but there were exceptions. Clubs from the southwestern states, notably the Arizona Ramblers, wore shorts. So did the Moose Jaw Royals, from wind-swept Saskatchewan – but in deference to the prairie climate they wore them with leotards, which made the players look like trapeze artists. The ultimate fashion statement was made by Toronto's Sunday Morning Class, as described in the 1942 scouting report: 'Their entire uniform is white. On their heads they wear a small stocking cap about the size of a small plate. The fact that none of the girls have a boyish haircut makes the tiny cap appear even smaller than it really is. Instead of shirts they wear a tight-fitting long-sleeved sweater that makes them appear like a group of Hollywood sweater girls. Flowing out from the bottom of the sweater is a short full-pleated skirt that barely reaches their knees. The pleats are very small and as the players cavort about the field they give one the impression of a group of ballet dancers as their skirts flare out.'

Dazzled by this image, the League opted for skirts. The final version was apparently designed by Mrs. Wrigley, with the aid of Ann Harnett and Otis Shepherd, the artist responsible for most of Wrigley's advertising billboards. The result was a belted tunic dress with short sleeves that buttoned up the front, but on the left side, leaving the chest free for a circular team logo. The dress came in four team colors: pastel shades of green, blue, yellow and peach. Only the Blue Sox and Peaches were fortunate enough to match color and name. The skirt was flared and unhemmed. Players were expected to hem it to suit their size, but no shorter than six inches above the knee. Underneath they wore elasticized shorts, an absolute necessity given their energetic style of play. They wore a small cap with a large peak and stockings rolled to reach just below the knee. It looked like a tennis outfit or, more precisely, a British field hockey uniform. The result, according to Marie Keenan, the League secretary, nicely fulfilled Wrigley's intentions: 'We do not want our uniforms to stress sex, but they should be feminine, with emphasis on the clean American sports girl.'

The sports girls, for their part, found the design ridiculous. Dorothy Hunter, playing first base for the Racine Belles, thought some of the players looked 'like some old lady walking around with an old-fashioned dress ... I was tall enough that mine came right to my knees. Besides, I had heavy legs and I didn't want to show them off too much.' Players stuck to the hem rule at first, but gradually shortened them how they pleased. Lucille Moore, the South Bend Blue Sox chaperon, remembers that a lot of people were rather shocked because some of the players showed a lot of thigh. 'Each year,' she said, 'the hemlines went up and up.'

The skirts raised eyebrows and created problems. Joanne Winter, who was assigned to the Racine Belles, found that they cramped her pitching style. The shoulders tended to bind and the skirt flared out, impeding her release. 'It was great from the spectator viewpoint,' she said. 'From our standpoint, not many of us enjoyed it. If I'd had a brain and a seamstress, I would have changed it.'

Perhaps the most serious difficulty – aside from chilblains inevitable when playing games in the midwest in early spring – was that the skirts made sliding an exercise in masochism. Most players carried terrible abrasions known as 'strawberries' – large areas of raw, scraped skin that would scarcely heal before another slide tore them open again. At least one manager was so undone by the inevitable pain and suffering that he averted his eyes each time a player came careening into base.

Occasionally, the League would attempt to tinker with the uniform design, but the solutions were always worse. At one point, Marie Keenan wrote the manufacturer suggesting that the pitcher might be issued a skirt fitted with an elastic band that would hold it close to her legs, into which she could step like a pair of slacks. This tube-dress or stovepipe concept was never inaugurated.

Some aspects of the uniform had players in stitches. Winter and teammate Sophie Kurys remember their first glimpse of Thelma Walmsley in a catcher's uniform. Walmsley sported a high pompadour, a popular hairdo of the time. It was without question feminine, but when coupled with a catcher's mask, it was also absurd. On the pitcher's mound, Joanne Winter recalls, 'I turned my back to the plate and then turned around. And there's Walmsley behind the plate, and I cracked up.' Kurys looked at Winter and joined in. But soon she was charging the mount, yelling, 'Cut it out, will'ya! Straighten up!' 'The whole bunch of them were after me,' says an unrepentant Winter, 'but you know how it is when you get the giggles.'

During the League's earliest days, the publicity mill was working overtime. The writer of a Muskegon *Chronicle* article celebrating Arleene Johnson, another player from small-town Saskatchewan, was baffled when told that she liked curling, an activity many Americans had never heard of. The writer felt compelled to explain the game's mysteries:

'The sport where the players wear kilts and make with the brooms on an ice rink, pushing little black pots that vaguely resemble cuspidors. The game is a sort of a cross between shuffleboard, bowling, ice hockey and floor sweeping.'

Press releases centered on domesticity at every turn. Ann Harnett was presented as 'an accomplished coffee maker.' Clara Schillace 'enjoyed nothing better than to whip up a spaghetti dinner, work with her father in the Victory Garden and wash dishes with her pretty niece.'

Shirley Jameson was distinguished by 'roguish eyes that refuse to behave, a saucy, turned-up little Irish pug nose, and enough concentrated personality to lend oomph to a carload of Hollywood starlets, all wrapped up in a four-foot, eleven-inch chassis.' A League questionnaire, distributed to every player, sought to elicit human-interest data by means of questions such as 'Do you get many mash notes from the fans?'

Extracurricular interests were blown out of all proportion. If someone had taken flying lessons, she became an accomplished aviatrix. Anyone who'd posed for a department-store snapshot was described as a former model. Choo Choo Hickson, who had just once donned boxing gloves as part of a publicity stunt in Tennessee, was labelled 'Chattanooga's Only Girl Pugilist.' The pity is that Wrigley and Co. didn't highlight the players' real achievements. Lib Mahon had a university degree and taught school, as did Shirley Jameson, who has also won speed-skating awards nationwide. Oddly, even the players' wide-ranging athletic interests received relatively little attention. Schillace (in-between bouts of dish-washing) had competed in national track-and-field meets. Dorothy Ferguson was Manitoba's top-ranked speed-skater, and Betsy Jochum was the Amateur Softball Association's throwing champion. The League preferred to feature more 'womanly' activities – housework or piano playing, pasting pictures into scrapbooks and writing letters home.

Perhaps the strangest aspect of the 1943 spring training was its 'Charm School,' actually a mandatory course in good grooming and ladylike behavior. No one remembers who first came up with this bright idea, but Arthur Meyerhoff was an avid supporter. His conversion took place while visiting the summer home of Patricia Stevens, who owned a well-known Chicago modeling studio. 'We spent the day there and everyone was in swimming,' he said. 'I remember looking around and these were all girls from her school, and I said to myself, "What a bunch of homely-looking mugs." When they left for their rooms and got ready for dinner, out came the most beautiful group of girls you've ever seen.' Thus inspired, Meyerhoff arranged for none other than Helena Rubinstein, whose chain of beauty salons had made her name synonymous with the feminine ideal, to coach the players in elegant deportment.

Players were issued loose-leaf binders in which to record 'Notes of a Star To Be.' The idea of farm girls and small-town rowdies being given lessons in how to walk, sit, apply make-up, put on coats and introduce themselves at social functions was public relations gold. The Charm School session was the obligatory lead paragraph in every subsequent magazine article. Some of the players were grateful – to a degree. Because Dorothy Kamenshek's family never ate out in restaurants, she 'didn't know what all those forks were for,' and was mildly interested to learn. Even the stylish Bonnie Baker, who could have conducted the seminars herself, was appreciative: 'It was important, because everybody was watching you all the time. Much as I liked slacks and shorts, I was glad that we couldn't wear them, because people tend to get slovenly, especially with slacks, and I thought it was good discipline.'

There were dissenting opinions. Lavonne 'Pepper' Paire remarks darkly that 'some of us could have used a little polish, but it was hard to walk in high heels with a book on your head when you had a charley horse. This we were required to do in the evenings, after we'd been busting our butts for ten hours on the field.' Besides, as Choo Choo Hickson admits, a fair number of players 'didn't look any better with make-up on.' Thrown suddenly into the limelight, meeting prominent people for the first time, having to cope with the attentions of the press, they needed help.

So the cosmetics industry triumphed, to the delight of newspapers everywhere. Aside from stiff and unconvincing 'action poses,' the typical All-American photo showed players lined up in the dressing room, anxiously fluffing their hair before taking the field. Another much-repeated shot captured Ruth 'Tex' Lessing, an attractive blonde who played catcher for the Grand Rapids Chicks, with her mask tilted back to reveal a carefully coiffed head, a powder puff in one hand and mirror in the other.

Catchers did not want for coverage. Bonnie Baker was front and center in South Bend's advertisements, minus both unbecoming chest protector and the face-mask, which would have obscured her dark good looks. Some of Baker's teammates recall that she managed to garner more than her share of coverage, at the expense of the other players, which Baker acknowledges: 'Libby Mahon would go out and make four spectacular catches and maybe get three hits. In the same game, I'd run after four pop flies. But I got the headlines. Of course, if I dropped a ball and someone else hit a home run, I got the write-up for that, too, for four days in a row.' Stardom had its price.

The Charm School was discontinued after a couple of seasons, even though a beauty kit, complete with full instructions, was issued for many years. But its message lingered on, in the form of a ten-page booklet, penned by Mme. Rubinstein's staff, with the imperative title 'A Guide for All-American Girls: How To Look Better, Feel Better, Be More Popular.' Copy read thus: 'The All-American girl is a symbol of health, glamor, physical perfection, vim, vigor and a glowing personality. Being included on the All-American roster is indeed a privilege to be granted only to those who are especially chosen for looks, deportment and feminine charm, in addition to natural athletic ability. The accent, of course, is on neatness and feminine appeal. That is true of appearances on the playing field, on the street or in leisure moments. Avoid noisy, rough and raucous talk and actions and be in all respects a truly All-American Girl.'

At one point, Bonnie Baker got a chance to thank Philip Wrigley in person. In the midst of 1943 spring training, after an early-morning Charm School session and a couple of hours at the hairdresser ('They dolled me up and I had a sort of upsweep'), Baker went to the ballpark and reported to Ken Sells, the League president, who led her to Wrigley's box seats. 'The closest I had ever got was chewing his gum,' says Baker, 'so I was quite excited. But when I took my mask off, my hair was hanging down. It was one of the most embarrassing moments of my life.' Sells assured her that it didn't matter, and introduced her to Wrigley and his wife: 'And they were very nice, very ordinary kind of people. I thanked him kindly for starting the League because it had been one of my dreams to play professional ball.' This was the only time that Baker and Wrigley met – and one of the very few times he saw a player in the flesh. Years later, he confessed to a reporter that he never saw an All-American team in action. He knew, he said, that he'd have been disappointed, because he wouldn't have been able to stop comparing the players to men.

◆

In 1994 the unthinkable happened. The World Series was cancelled. Baseball fans in cities like Montreal and Cleveland (in particular) were left to wonder whether their attachment to the game – and their loyalty to their teams – counted for anything when the big-money game was being played. Major-league baseball's ugly underside – the decades-long dysfunctional marriage between the owners and the players – erupted in the longest, and most intransigent, work stoppage in the game's history. On August 12, when the players' strike began, the Montreal Expos were the best team in baseball. They could have gone to The Dance ... but now we'll never know. What is more certain is that fans everywhere will be reluctant to care again about the carefree 'summer game.'

1994: Breaking the Heart of the Game

STEPHEN BRUNT

AS THE HOURS TICKED AWAY TOWARDS THE AUGUST DEADLINE, IN MONTREAL they already knew what would happen. There would be a strike, there would have to be a strike.

The Expos were in first place with the best record in baseball, fans were finally filing into that horrid park in respectable numbers, the front office hadn't said anything threatening of late. And so, to complete the tragic cycle of professional baseball in Montreal, something held dear would be lost. By the time the season's demise was made official, most of the team's staff had been laid off, and the death-knell of the franchise was tolling once again. The best Expos baseball team ever would be denied its chance, perhaps its last chance, at a championship.

Such is the lot of the modern sports fan, to love forever unrequited, to feel passion for an illusion. There are few more perfect examples than what happened in Montreal in 1994 of why it has become so difficult to suspend disbelief.

Long ago, when it secured its anti-trust exemption in return for a pledge of moral purity, major-league baseball was declared a pastime by the United States Congress – a recreation, and not just another business. Who can pretend that's now the case? With 8 work stoppages in the last 22 years, this latest strike wasn't a novel experience. In fact, the last (and only) time the Montreal Expos won a pennant was during the bastard season of 1981, when a strike split the schedule in two, and in each division the first-half and second-half winners faced each other in a pre-playoff playoff. Montreal beat Philadelphia in that one, which is far less remembered than the horrors that would follow: Steve Rogers, Rick Monday, and the pall of broken promises that has never really lifted from the Olympic Stadium.

That moment changed everything, Expo loyalists will tell you, but it was really the moments that followed which told the story – the team's inability to get beyond that one crushing disappointment. Anyone who doubts that need look no further than 500 miles down the MacDonald-Cartier freeway, where that other Canadian franchise experienced its own heartbreak in 1985, losing in the seventh game of its first playoff, but afterwards seemed touched by the divine.

Consecutive World Series victories were only the final, happily-ever-after of the Toronto Blue Jays' fairy tale. More amazing was the way they managed to rise from expansion franchise to contender without a major setback, the way they played better than .500 baseball season after season, the way they continued to rebuild the squad without ever collapsing in a heap, the way they never gave their fans reason to despair.

Combine that with the best socio-cultural-economic fortune imaginable – the team became a contender when Toronto was rich and fast and very much in need of some new way of showing itself to the world – and you wind up with four million people in the stands every year, a new, ridiculously opulent stadium built with public money, and a re-markable force that crosses the barriers of race, age, gender, and class better than any other form of popular entertainment in the country.

But while the Blue Jays perfectly caught their wave, the Expos wiped out again and again, until they retained only a tenuous connection with their customers. Next to the sport colossus of the city, the Montréal Canadiens, and to the long history of hockey greatness to which they would always be unfavourably compared, the Expos were a cultural afterthought.

In the last few seasons, it has been the apparently dim future of the franchise as much as the burgeoning young talent that has captured the headlines. The Expos just barely managed to stay in Montreal when Charles Bronfman sold the club to an undercapitalized local consortium headed by Claude Brochu. Since then, the cavernous Big O has been renovated, so that it feels slightly more intimate, and the uniforms have been redesigned, adding a discreet little fleur-de-lys above the heart and an *accent aigu* to the word Montreal – a none-too-subtle attempt to make the Expos true *gens de pays*. During the 1994 season, on St. Jean Baptiste Day, the team went a step further in that direction, promising not to play O Canada before the game, relenting when that plan became public, and then in a true act of courage playing the anthem an hour before game time, when only a handful of fans were in the stands watching batting practice.

None of that really worked. It couldn't work, because you can't forge an organic relationship with gimmicks. You can temporarily put people in the park if you hand out toasters at the gate, but attracting fans in the long term is like building a lasting relationship – never quick or easy or particularly logical.

In Montreal, given the history, that romance could be reborn only through a particular, unlikely set of circumstances. Without the money to purchase high-priced free agents, the team would have to forge a contender from within. The organization would have to have the smarts to select the right talent, that talent would have to be nurtured in a very good farm system, and a core group of those players would have to come into their own at exactly the same time – before salary demands inevitably sent them scurrying elsewhere. There would have to be a field manager in charge who could not only bring that kind of team together, but also woo the city's francophone population; as charming as Buck Rodgers, but a winner as well.

This was kismet. The emergence of young stars Larry Walker, Marquis Grissom, and Delino DeShields. Savvy trades for Ken Hill, Pedro Martinez, John Wetteland, Moises Alou. And, after the disastrous appointment of Tom Runnells as field manager, the hiring of loyal organization man Felipe Alou – in a backhanded, by-default kind of way – to run the team. The club gelled in 1993, finishing second in the division behind the Philadelphia Phillies while posting the second-best regular-season record in franchise history. DeShields was dealt for Martinez in the off-season, which, coupled with rumours that Walker would also be traded, seemed like the beginning of a fiscally-motivated dismantling of the team.

But management held the line, maintaining the second-lowest payroll in major-league baseball while keeping the team essentially intact. The fatherly, philosophical Alou, who was married to a Québécoise and who, as a Dominican, seemed to bond especially well with what is continentally a minority culture, proved the perfect leader. The Expos sailed into the mid-summer of 1994 with the best winning percentage in the sport, comfortably ahead in their division. It was just that much sweeter that the team down the road, the one that could do no wrong, was finally struggling with mortality. By the end of July, Montreal already seemed a lock to reach the playoffs, a favourite to win, finally, the World Series.

Then came the strike.

Though it was the players who walked, it was the owners who brought it on, intent on restructuring the economics of the game – to protect small-market franchises like Montreal, they maintained. Still, it wouldn't last, wise men opined. It would be over by Labour Day. It would certainly be finished in time to save the post-season.

Instead it went on and on, becoming more bitter by the day, wiping out the World Series, the same World Series the Montreal Expos just might have won. Brochu allied himself with the hard-liners in ownership, even though the new salary-cap system the owners proposed would leave his team with four key free agents in 1995 – Walker, Wettleland, Grissom, and Hill – all of them likely to depart. Win the strike, and lose forever what was potentially the best baseball team in Montreal history. Win the war, and lose the one real chance the franchise had for lasting success, to win a world championship. As spring training in 1995 approached, Brochu appeared ready to fight for the right to use replacement players at Olympic Stadium. The fans will love them, he said.

Of course, the truth is, nobody bothered to ask them.

The same despairing cry is uttered every time there is a labour dispute that threatens to disrupt the season of one professional sport or another: What about us? The owners obviously don't care – they're the ones who raise ticket prices, who charge exorbitant rates at the concessions, who extort sweetheart deals from local politicians to keep their teams in town, making pro sport part of the tax burden. And the players may well pledge their fidelity long enough for a 30-second television clip, but clearly they lead a mercenary existence, their loyalty can be bought. Just beneath the surface (or, in the case of Vince Coleman of the New York Mets, who tossed a firecracker at fans who were invading his 'personal space,' well above the surface) lurks a contempt for the paying customers, relayed through sports reporters, for whom the athletes' contempt is even more obvious.

To be a fan means pretending that's not the case. The essential fantasy that goes with any team spectator sport is that the contest is in some way a shared experience between players and supporters. Common ground comes in the motivation, in wanting to win for the place, for the city, the community, for home. At the heart of real, passionate support for sports teams is self-affirmation. It's a way of saying to the world, I come from this place, these are my representatives, the representatives of my friends, my family, my neighbours. And we are as good as or better than those people down the road. It's not just the allure of the product. In a consumer society, those things desired most passionately – hula hoops, pet rocks, Mighty Morphin Power Rangers – don't tend to have a whole lot of staying power. At best, it is not just a buyer-seller relationship between baseball teams and their fans, but one of a united passion, of a consensus. In a post-religious, fragmented world, how many of those bonds remain?

A strike or a lock-out destroys that fantasy even more than contract hold-outs, a free-agent departure, or a points-shaving scandal. When the twin forces of greed, the players' and the owners', clash, it becomes all too clear that the fans – as consumers of baseball entertainment – mean no more to the process than do car buyers when it's Ford or Chrysler that's about to be shut down by a strike. In fact, they matter a good deal less, since by virtue of its anti-trust exemption, baseball enjoys a legal monopoly. Consumers can't simply switch from one brand to another. If they want the best baseball being played, there is only one place they can get it, and history has shown that no matter how ugly the circumstances, the fans always come back in droves.

This strike, if the owners' rhetoric was to be believed, carried with it greater implications. Without a salary cap, the bosses said, small-market franchises wouldn't be able to survive – small-market franchises like Montreal, that is, though the Expos were also a prime example of why the owners' argument about competitive balance didn't hold water. Still, an extended strike might well kill the club just as surely as market forces might if there wasn't one, and as far as the players were concerned, that was no real problem. As long as there were people in other places desperate for a team – in Phoenix and St. Petersburg and Buffalo, to name just three – those jobs would continue to exist. The notion of loyalty to a place had no bearing whatsoever. There used to be a team in Brooklyn. Not any more. As the marketplace and the money shifted, the Dodgers went west.

And there's the rub, in the economics that force the business of sport to the forefront, in the portability of franchises, in owners saying 'Give me a better lease or I'm gone,' in free agency, in catching a plane minutes after the final pitch of the season and flying elsewhere. It cuts away at what makes sports different than other forms of entertainment, the illusory two-way commitment. No one believes that Sylvester Stallone acts for them, but a considerable number of people believe that Moises Alou plays for me.

Breed cynicism and break the bond.

In Montreal, there was the chance that 1994 might have been like those early days in Jarry Park, with Le Grand Orange and Jonesville, when the home of Expo 67, newly international, newly self-aware, found expression through sport. It would have been good for the city. It might have preserved the franchise in the long term. It would, like a religious revival, have sent the fans to the exits with a sense of a welcoming, orderly universe of which they were an essential part.

Instead, they were left thinking: it's just a game, it's just a diversion, it's just a way to kill an afternoon ... or it will be if it ever comes back. And if that's all there is, it might just as well be gone.

The strike ended in April, or at least it paused, a truce forced by the courts that resolved nothing, that left both parties to regroup and plot strategy for the battle that still lay ahead. But the players did come back, reporting to spring training just hours before the scabs were scheduled to take the field for Opening Day.

In West Palm Beach, though, spring training home of the Expos, any joy at the return of the real major leaguers was tempered by the team's continued hard-line stance. The injunction that ended the strike meant that the business of baseball would continue under the same collective-bargaining agreement that was in place during 1994. The Expos, then, would retain Wetteland, Hill, and Grissom. Only Larry Walker would be a free agent, and he was gone anyway, off to the Colorado Rockies.

No matter. The big three were eligible for arbitration, all three would surely be entitled to huge raises, and so all three were history as far as the Expos were concerned. Kevin Malone, Montreal's new general manager, has the honesty of a country boy, and all spring long he served as the poster boy for the 'small market' problem. 'Come and get it,' Malone said to the rest of baseball. 'We're going to have the lowest payroll in the game this year – maybe even as low as $10 million, down from $18 million in 1994 – and so we're open for business.'

Wetteland went first, to the New York Yankees, dealt for a couple of middling minor-league prospects. Hill went next, to St. Louis, for much the same kind of package. And then it was Grissom's turn. At least Atlanta threw in a couple of guys who could play – outfielders Tony Tarasco and Roberto Kelly – but the reason the Expos made the deal was because the Braves also threw in the cash equivalent of Kelly's salary.

Through it all, the Expos' upper management acted as though they almost relished the opportunity to dismantle the best team in baseball. Claude Brochu promised the fans that the club would be competitive – not that they'd win a championship, not that they'd make the post-season, but that they'd be 'competitive' – which for the remaining hard-core support in Montreal was hardly an encouraging word. Season's ticket sales stalled at about 9000, up from the already pitiable total of 8000 the year before, only because a pharmacy chain bought 2000 at the last minute to sell to its customers.

Perhaps Brochu didn't sound completely depressed because of reports that circulated during the spring suggesting that interests in Northern Virginia, spurned in their attempt to secure an expansion franchise, were willing to offer serious money to move the Expos there in 1996. If that were to take place, Brochu and the rest of the owners – once they'd paid back the City of Montreal and the Province of Quebec for their investment in the consortium – stood to make a very handsome profit. Shed a tear for the Expos, shed a tear for baseball in Montreal, but be consoled by watching that bank balance grow.

Come the home opener at the Olympic Stadium, the uncertainty about the future of the franchise remained. Before the game, Felipe Alou said that he was optimistic about what the team could achieve on the field, but he wasn't making any promises. 'Give me the team we had last year,' he said, 'and then I'll make promises.'

Then something peculiar happened. All over baseball, attendance was down dramatically after the strike. The Toronto Blue Jays, who had never had the slightest trouble selling tickets, didn't sell the last one for their home opener until more than an hour after the game had started. They followed that up a day later with the smallest baseball crowd in the history of the SkyDome.

But at the Big O, they packed the place to see the Expos play the New York Mets. They cheered and sang while baseball fans in other places were booing and throwing things at the players. They reacted to having the best team in baseball snatched away from them with an outpouring of unconditional love. And though the attendance returned to its previous dreary levels in the games that immediately followed, the sense remained that maybe the spirit wasn't quite dead yet, maybe the cynical conspiracy to destroy baseball in Montreal hadn't been entirely successful. Something of Jarry Park and 1969 and the teams that might have been remained. Perhaps it was just the franchise death throes, just the loyal and the dim grasping at straws. But for one night, it was there, and it was grand.

At a meeting in Toronto's Walker House Hotel in early April, 1876, plans for the first Canadian baseball association were confirmed, with teams from London, Guelph, Toronto, Hamilton, and Kingston. In spirit at least it was a Canadian response to the National League, also formed that year in the United States. Bryce's Canadian Base Ball Guide *of 1876 was the first such publishing effort in Canada, but its ambition to return as an annual, like that of the new Canadian baseball league, went unfulfilled. One reason was the ambivalent attitude of local papers like the* Toronto Globe, *which despaired at the hiring of professionals by London and Guelph. 'As baseball loses the character of amateur amusement for players who love it for its own sake, and partakes of speculation in the engagement of mercenaries, as a game for gamblers, its sordid side is sure to extinguish its favour in the eyes of the Canadian public.'*

Base Ball in Canada, 1876

WILLIAM BRYCE

WITHIN THE PAST SIX YEARS BASE BALL HAS MADE RAPID STRIDES IN public favor in Canada, and in the western and northern portions of Ontario, especially, it has to a great extent displaced Cricket and Lacrosse as a favorite summer out-door recreation. In its earlier years, we are informed, the game first found a foothold in Hamilton. Woodstock next became the centre of its operations, and for many seasons base ball was confined to that town, Ingersoll, Dundas and Hamilton, the game being almost entirely unknown outside of these places. Gradually it spread to London, Guelph, Stratford, St. Mary's, St. Thomas and other towns in the West. With the single exception of a defeat by Ingersoll, Woodstock held the Silver Ball, emblematic of the Canadian championship, until it twice became the property of the Young Canadians of that town. In 1869, the 'Young Canadians' presented to the Tecumsehs, of London, for competition at a tournament held under the auspices of that club, a new silver ball, which, with the title of Champions of Canada, was to become the property of the club winning the majority of games. The Maple Leafs, of Guelph came off victors, and the silver ball has ever since been held by that club, and is now their property. The Young Canadians survived the loss of the title of 'champions' only a brief time. Pascoe, Clyde, Douglass, Hill and others who formed the backbone of the old champion nine, retired from the field through various causes; the rising generation failed to furnish successors equal to the task of upholding the high reputation of the once famous 'Young Canadians' and as a consequence the club name lives only in the memories of old admirers of the game. Similar causes led to the falling away of the 'Victorias' of Ingersoll. Gibson, Hearn, Jackson and other crack players abandoned the field to younger and less skillful men and the 'Victorias' were soon lost to sight. Dundas had long been a strong competitor for the championship. In the days of slow and medium paced pitching, Williams, of the Dundas 'Independents,' was a terror to Canadian batsmen, owing to the speed with which he could deliver the ball, and many a victory he won for his club. The Maple Leafs alone narrowly escaped defeat on several occasions. But frequent failures to achieve the object of their ambition – the possession of the silver ball – had a damaging effect upon the players, and at last Dundas went the way of Woodstock and Ingersoll. Hamilton, too, about the same time, ceased to be regarded as a base ball town, continuous defeats at the hands of all its neighbors having the effect of causing the long established Maple Leafs of that city to quit the arena in despair. The Guelph champions had meantime strengthened their nine by the importation of several excellent players from the United States, who took the place of Nicholls, Sunley, Goldie, Steele, McLean and other well known local experts. About the same time, W. Smith mastered the knack of underhand throwing and developed into a formidable pitcher; Maddocks, their old third baseman, possessing the requisite nerve, skill and endurance to face the new style pitching, the club contained in itself the nucleus of a strong team. The old infielders were wiped out and a new infield of experienced players substituted. These changes made the Maple Leafs, so far as Canadian amateurs were concerned, invincible. They did not even rest content with Canadian conquests, but carrying the Maple Leaf across the border gained decisive victories over the best of the American so-called amateurs. Professionals, too, have had in one or two instances to lower their banner to the Canadian champions.

A new era in base ball was inaugurated in Canada. The Tecumsehs, of London, the only Canadian club that for several years had ventured with any prospect of success to encounter the Maple Leafs, pluckily maintained its organization, invited professional nines to visit them, and profiting by the experience gained in its contests with the latter and the champions, developed strong playing powers. A namesake of the Guelph pitcher, though a mere lad in years, discovered the art of underhand throwing, and catchers soon sprung up who were able to handle his swift delivery. Some fine contests were the result, the most notable being that of the season of 1874, when the champions won a game in London by the close score of 5 to 3. This was undoubtedly the finest game played in Canada up to that date. The Tecumsehs were composed entirely of local amateurs, while the Guelphs had the advantage of the services of Myers, of Ilion, 1st base; Keerl, of Chicago, 2nd; Jones, of Ilion, short stop, and Spence, of Detroit, 3rd base, all of whom had been induced by the lovers of base ball in Guelph to settle in that town, and attach themselves to the Maple Leafs. Kingston the same year called in the aid of foreign players, and made a bold dash for the championship, but they were unequal to the task. Toronto also began to loom up as a likely contestant. The season of 1875 opened with a strong amateur nine in London, McLean, their present pitcher, taking the place of Smith. Guelph added a catcher to their nine in the person of Foley, a young Chicagoan, and Lapham, of the Westerns, of Keokuk, took the place of Myers, at first base, the latter returning to his home in Ilion, N.Y. Kingston secured almost an entire nine from over the border. Toronto, by amalgamating its best clubs, and adding a foreign pitcher, also presented a strong nine, and there were prospects of a lively struggle, but the end of the year saw the contesting clubs in about the same relative positions they held at the commencement of the season. The Maple Leafs defeated all comers on their own grounds, suffering only one defeat in Canada – at the hands of the Kingston club, in one of the most remarkable contests ever played either in Canada or the United States. Twelve innings were necessary to decide the game, the result being in favor of Kingston, by the astonishingly low score of 3 to 2.

Base ball has now reached such a stage of perfection in Canada that its leading clubs are able to cope successfully with the best of the same class in the United States. The victories by the Maple Leafs in New York State were repeated by the Tecumsehs in Michigan, where they defeated the State champions, the Mutuals, of Jackson, on their own grounds, and also won signal victories over the Detroit Etnas in the City of the Straits. Following the example set by Guelph, Kingston and Toronto, the London Tecumsehs, during the season of 1875, strengthened themselves by securing the services of a second baseman, from the United States, and as the season was closing, they induced Mr. Latham, the captain of the New Haven professionals, to settle permanently in their city. The impetus given to base ball by the greatly improved style of play resulting from the introduction of foreign talent, is manifesting itself in the increased patronage bestowed upon the game by the public in all parts of Ontario. The formation of a Base Ball Association and the re-entry of Hamilton, Dundas and Woodstock, into the base ball arena, are tangible tokens of the hold the game has obtained in the country and the renewed interest awakened in its progress and prosperity. The season of 1876 will, undoubtedly, be the most exciting in Canadian base ball circles yet experienced. The championship is to be contested for under new rules which place competing clubs on a greater equality than heretofore, when every championship game had to be played on the grounds of the holders of the silver ball. Guelph appears determined to maintain its supremacy, although the rivalry is far greater than it has ever yet been called upon to contend against; London seems determined to be no longer content with second position; Kingston threatens to carry out last year's design of flying the champion pennant in the Limestone City; Hamilton, Toronto, Woodstock, Dundas and Dunnville are actively preparing for the struggle on the diamond field, and all are reasonably hopeful of success. May the best nine win, and the contests be characterized by good play and an honest, manly rivalry between the clubs and players to excel on their merits alone.

◆

If he hadn't become a writer, Morley Callaghan would have been quite happy being a ball player. He loved the game. In his youth he was a pitcher for the Broadview YMCA team, the Toronto juvenile city champions in 1919. Morley followed baseball all his life, and it appears often in his writings. Baseball, skilfully played, was to him a metaphor for art – a hard-worked-at craft that at its best should appear gracefully easy. This journalistic piece, on the 1940 Toronto Maple Leafs, examines how, for ball players, staying 'loose as a goose' can be their greatest asset.

Fast and Loose

MORLEY CALLAGHAN

THE OTHER DAY OUT AT THE BALL PARK WE HEARD THAT DICK PORTER, the Syracuse manager, had said of some hitter he was high on, that 'he was loose as a goose and he swung from the hips.' And as we sat there in the sunlight behind the third base brooding over the stylistic perfection of this description, we began to see that this reflection on the goose which was turned into a tribute to a ball player applied not just to hitting but to everything that was done perfectly out there on the ball field.

It got us thinking of an infielder we used to play with in the sandlot leagues some years ago. He was really one of the best and most dependable players we had. If you were pitching and the ball was smacked down his way you knew that chances were he'd come up with it, and yet each time you felt like going over and congratulating him, or extending him another vote of confidence. It was the same when he was hitting. He stood up at the plate quivering with a lust for battle, all tightened up, and giving you the notion that whatever happened he would die fiercely. What was there that was wrong with him? Why did you know so surely in your soul that no pro scout would ever pick him up no matter how good he looked in our league? Well, just that fact that he was tight as a drum, there was no flow in his movements; in short, he was often sensational but he had no style.

While the blessed memory of this infielder of our youth was with us out there on the diamond, the ball was suddenly hit hard a little to the left of second base, and Chapman, the new Leaf shortstop, went after it; it was a hard chance, but he didn't seem to be tearing after it, he seemed to flow toward it, and he came up with it in a scoop of his glove and he had to pivot and throw balanced on one foot, and throw underhand and you saw how loose his shoulder and body muscles were, and what control he had of them when he was fielding and how much this helped him in making the hard chances look easy. Chapman may be a bit erratic, but you will always feel surprise and regret when he misses one because his fielding approach looks so right and smooth. Unfortunately, he doesn't look quite this way at the plate. It's hard to say what it is in his swing, but somewhere around the wrists there seems to be a lack of flexibility.

However, still haunted by Mr. Porter's goose, we looked around for Dink Carroll, the publicity man, and we asked, 'Look, Dink, have you seen many of those guys with their clothes off?'

'Just a minute,' he said, 'what's this leading to?'

'Well, what do they look like? In the showers.'

'It all depends on whether we win or lose.'

'All we want to know about is the style of muscular development. Is it any different than that of a football player or a fighter?'

'It's a funny thing,' he said. 'Some of them look a little fat like babies and they never seem to be muscle-bound, especially around the shoulders.'

Well, there you are. If you want to raise your children to grow up to be ball players, don't have them go in for wrestling or weight lifting; they will develop the wrong muscles. Someone can always bob up and say, 'What about Eric Tipton? Or what about Ace Parker? Both great football players and in football the brawny men ride high.' But you only need to take one look at Tipton to see the answer. He is not the biggest man in the world but he must weigh about one hundred and ninety pounds, and he has heavy, powerful legs that undoubtedly gave him great drive on an end sweep, but he doesn't seem at all heavy and unduly muscular around the shoulders. In fact, there isn't a more relaxed hitter on the Toronto team than Tipton. He looks to us like an easy, natural hitter, but he makes it look so easy that people don't notice him. A while back there he was in a slump, and an irate mining man sitting behind us kept crying, 'Why do they leave that bum in there? He never looked like a hitter to me.' And we were so high on Tipton that we turned and asked, 'Have you noticed that the guy nearly always hits the ball?'

'Hits it where?' he asked.

'Hits it hard and sometimes to left, and sometimes to right and sometimes to centre,' we said. But we didn't think the mining man had noticed Tipton at all because Tipton looked as if he was taking it easy with a nice relaxed looseness at the plate when the mining man was probably praying for some guy to come along and stand up there and look as if he was going to murder the ball.

But it will always be in the pitchers that you get the best chance to see how much this muscular looseness and repose means to ball players. It's a good idea to watch the pitchers doing the thing they're good at, which is pitching, in the main, and then watch them doing the thing for which God, for some reason this writer has never been able to fathom, has denied them talent, which is hitting. If you want to see a lot of pitchers all hitting at the same time come around to the park about one o'clock in the afternoon: there you see them at batting practice and they are what Tim Daly calls the 1.10 hitters: we were never sure whether it referred to the hour or the batting average, but it aptly covers both as far as most of them are concerned. But in case some of them read this and plan to come rushing to the *New World* office with bricks in their hands, we hasten to add that many of them are inordinately proud of their batting prowess. Take Carl Fischer, for example. One season he hit about .213 and he wanted to have somebody do something about it, and now he is conscious of himself as a hitter, so he has two approaches to life: the approach of the hitter and the approach of the pitcher: if he is hitting and drives the ball at an infielder and the infielder muffs it, and the scorer calls it an error and doesn't give Fischer a hit, Fischer says, 'Why, the bum, that ball was far too hot to handle, it should have been scored as a hit.' And then if he is pitching, and the same kind of a ball is hit to an infielder and the infielder muffs it, then he cries to the gods to witness that it was an easy chance and should never be scored as a hit. It just depends on whether he is thinking of himself as a pitcher or a hitter.

Anyway, if you watch the pitchers at the batting practice you'll see how few of them swing from the hips and how that nice looseness is missing. Marchildon, who has a better style than most of them, always looks like a four hundred hitter among them. But when that same group of ball players starts doing their specialty, which is pitching, you see how much depends on that looseness and ease they have to have when they are working right. The Toronto club this year has as nice a looking lot of pitchers as you'd want to see. Reninger, Walkup, Pezzullo and Fischer are all nice to watch, and if there is a better pitcher in the league than Fischer we don't know his name at the moment. It is our unalterable opinion that any team which has a swell pitching staff, if the rest of the team belongs in the league at all, must finish at least as high as fifth. This is aside from the point that any one of these pitchers is apt to give a clear demonstration at any time of how much looseness means to a pitcher. Someone with a trained eye could stand on the grandstand roof as a look-out, watching for signs of a pitcher tightening up on himself and therefore losing control – it would be something like watching the sea for the great white whale – a cry would echo down over the grandstand, 'Thar she blows,' and the customers would look at the pitcher and see that for some inexplicable reason he had thrown four balls in a row, not deliberately at all, his control just suddenly went on him: if he starts to tighten up on himself to get the ball over, the chances are they will knock it out of the lot.

You can notice this easily in Marchildon; he throws much more smoothly this year, he seems to be looser in every way, and his change of pace is smoother, too, but you still feel that at the end of the seventh or around there, he will tighten up on himself. This, they say, is because of his shoulder muscles, which have been too well developed by hard work up north: that loose flow of muscles just isn't in Marchildon's shoulders the way it should be; but, of course, he may get it in the course of time.

A funny thing is that Krakauskas, the Washington pitcher that Griffith is so high on, and a Canadian like Marchildon, is supposed to have the same kind of muscular development around the shoulders as Marchildon, and it seems to stand in his way. They say that Griffith has spent a lot of money submitting the Krakauskas shoulder muscles to the steam treatment. The chances are that Griffith still stops and wonders what a pitcher Krakauskas might be if he were only 'loose as a goose,' around the shoulders.

———————— ◆ ————————

It's unlikely many long-standing Toronto Blue Jays fans have nostalgic feelings about the damp, bone-chillingly cold April evenings they used to spend at Exhibition Stadium, the Jays' first 'ballpark.' No one – no ball fans, at least – doubted that Toronto's major-league team needed a decent park, one that matched the quality of the team being fielded in the mid-1980s. A covered facility, for frigid April evenings and other inclemencies, seemed inevitable from early on in the new-stadium campaign. Then the daring concept of a retractable roof, to bring the game back outside to the sweet breezes and golden sun it thrives in, was espoused. For a time there was even the hope of having real grass on the new park's indoor/outdoor field. Somewhere along the line, however, as Jon Caulfield points out, imagination was swallowed up by commercial interest. It's doubtful that SkyDome will ever evoke the kind of feelings, or create the sort of attachments, that real ballparks (old and new) do with real baseball fans.

All We Really Wanted Was a Ballpark

JON CAULFIELD

O N THE NORTH WALL OF THE BROBDINGNAGIAN CONCRETE BUNKER named SkyDome in which Toronto's Blue Jays play baseball, twenty metres above a pedestrian concourse, are fifteen sculptures of oversized human figures. The sculptures are arranged in two groups, eight on the east façade and seven on the west. Named *The Audience* and designed by artist Michael Snow, they are made of plastic foam moulded over steel skeletons and covered with metallic paint to simulate bronze. They appear to be upper-deck fans at a baseball game looking out at the field, and their animated manner suggests that something important has just happened in the game.

Some of the figures do have their attention directed elsewhere. A smiling woman points toward the northeast distance, oblivious to whatever is occurring below, and three other figures face directly down at passers-by on the walkway beneath them instead of out toward where the action appears to be: a woman waving one hand over her head, shielding the sun from her eyes with the other; a man looking through the viewfinder of a camera; and another man, wearing what appears to be a ten-gallon hat, with a thumb pressed to his nose and waggling his fingers.

But most of the figures are reacting with emotion to whatever has just happened in the game. Some seem upset. An angry older man in a ball cap points and snarls, a disgusted man holds his nose and makes a thumb-down gesture, and a man with his tongue stuck out and his thumbs poked to his ears also waggles his fingers. A woman leans away from the events below, eyes averted in apparent despair, one hand clasped across her face. Other figures seem jubilant. Two men – one of whom is shouting – raise their arms in victory salutes. An ecstatic woman applauds. A small boy sitting on a man's shoulders waves his cap and cheers joyfully as the man smiles broadly and makes a thumb-up sign. Two final figures, whose attitudes are not evident, are a heavy-set man with a drink-cup in one hand, eating a very large hot dog with the other, and a man behind him surveying events below with binoculars.

It is unclear if the figures are playful caricature or disdainful burlesque. But to the extent they are passionately involved in the events before them, they are not an especially authentic image of the crowds that flock to SkyDome baseball games, who tend generally to consist of well-mannered sightseers rather than participants in the spectacle. To be sure, Jays fans are *good* fans who regularly pack the house to capacity and give their team enthusiastic, if often muted, support. True, they are generally not *baseball* fans; hardly anyone keeps score. A good index of their outlook occurred in a 1994 game with Baltimore's Orioles. The Jays entered the final inning three runs in arrears, and a large segment of the crowd, assuming matters were settled, trooped *en masse* from the stadium to avoid postgame pedestrian traffic rather than remain for an at-bat by Cal Ripken, in the twelfth year of his remarkable pursuit of

Lou Gehrig's consecutive-games record, and a possible appearance from the bullpen by baseball's all-time saves leader, Lee Smith – two small but irreplaceable moments of baseball history. But habits of this kind are beyond complaint; baseball games are democratic occasions at which people are free to come and go as they choose.

The Jays fans whom the sculptures come closest to representing are not much in evidence anymore. They used to sit in the bleachers at Exhibition Stadium, a truncated football yard where the team played its early seasons. The old grandstand directly behind left field at the Ex was a good place to watch a ball game, especially on sweltering summer days when its canopy offered shelter from the sun while folks in the unshaded, top-dollar seats along the baselines baked like chicken on a spit. With a coupon from a supermarket, a bleacher ticket could be had for a couple of bucks. The crowd reflected the price structure – at day games, there were often a lot of youngsters and 'senior citizens' – and it was frequently a fairly boisterous group that cheered and jeered liberally. SkyDome, though, does not have any bleachers. There are some semi-cheap seats high in the rafters a very long way from the field, but where bleachers should be – a distinct section of seating that fans identify as *bleachers* – are the windows of some very expensive hotel rooms and a gigantic television screen whose main purpose seems to be displaying commercials for partner corporations of the SkyDome consortium.

The issue here is not that the bulk of SkyDome's better baseball seats are reserved as business-held season tickets or are cushioned 'club' chairs on a carpeted mezzanine off-limits for the hoi polloi – segregation enforced by the facility's polite and ubiquitous blue-blazered security forces. These are digestible facts that, together with the building's two tiers of corporate skyboxes and two restaurants overlooking the field, describe arrangements apparently required to sustain the budget of a modern major-league sport franchise. The trouble, rather, is the absence of much decent seating affordable for the clientele who were once among the Jays' most avid customers.

Certainly, from an urban-planning viewpoint, a hotel adjacent to SkyDome is a good idea. People living in a district, using its streets at various hours, stimulate commercial activity and discourage crime; a large hotel helps provide a residential base that, albeit transient, puts life into the area when the stadium is not in use. But having a hotel on site does not necessarily entail placing it directly within the stadium – an idea credited by SkyDome literature to the company's first president. The television screen, meanwhile, with its constant barrage of advertisements, is for the most part an irritating distraction from trying to watch baseball at SkyDome. Apart from reruns of the odd spectacular play, it transmits no information that could not be more effectively carried by a proper baseball scoreboard – something else SkyDome does not have.

Critics of SkyDome might account for the presence of the hotel rooms and television screen by pointing out that the building is first and foremost a money-machine – not an inaccurate observation. (One pundit has even acidly observed that, from the southerly distance, the building seems to resemble a mammoth cash register.) While the cost of attending a ball game at SkyDome is consistent with prices at other newly built major-league stadiums, it is abundantly clear that the building's main function is to separate the rubes from their shekels. But that is not really the point. It is unlikely that revenue generated by the segment of hotel space overlooking centre field, about forty-odd of the seventy rooms with stadium views, significantly surpasses income that might be produced by four or five thousand bleacher seats (and any shortfall might have been recouped by a modest redesign that relocated some of the rooms). And while the television screen does earn revenue for the stadium, a smaller screen placed above and behind bleachers and used creatively would do pretty much as well; so long as their message is conspicuous, advertisers are buying the building's captive audience, not the inordinate size of the display medium.

The inescapable conclusion is that, while boisterous behaviour may be suitable for SkyDome statuary, the building's management sought to minimize the number and critical mass of rowdy fans who actually entered the facility by the simple expedient of eliminating bleachers. The absence of a scoreboard is the crucial clue here: it is not that SkyDome is a money-machine so much as that it is a money-machine conceived and built by people who do not really like baseball parks – whose vision was of a large, multipurpose broadcasting studio with docile crowds, where everything from weather to hot dogs happens predictably; critics objecting to the absence of bleachers and a scoreboard would no doubt be dismissed as woolly headed purists who do not understand how the modern stadium business works.

There is much to admire about SkyDome and its construction. It is downtown, for one thing, where a baseball stadium ought to be. People arrive on foot from car parks or transit stops several blocks away, crowding the area before and after games amid outdoor cafés, street musicians, hot-dog carts, ticket scalpers, and souvenir vendors, giving the neighbourhood a festival air that would be impossible at a suburban stadium amid acres of parking lot. Partisans of a suburban location predicted dire traffic chaos if Toronto's dome were located downtown, a forecast that badly misunderstood how cities work; SkyDome's 50,000-strong crowds are small beer beside the dense flow of commuters who daily and uneventfully come and go from the core.

Architect Ron Robbie and engineer Michael Allen, who designed the building's roof, parsimoniously solved the technical dilemma of a durable, easily retractable dome. A less overwhelming structure might be preferred, or one less insulated from its surroundings; SkyDome utterly ignores its placement within close views of a Great Lake and the downtown skyline. But in its bloated, homely, and ingrown way, the building solves the 'problem' of selling sufficient tickets to support a baseball franchise that plays an April to October schedule in an Ontario climate. (Is this really a problem? Boston, Cleveland, and Detroit have, after all, with similar weather, supported major-league baseball for decades. For most of those decades, though, baseball's payroll structure was a system of legalized peonage, and in the years since that system collapsed, the game's owners have seemed unable to master the simple art of budgeting. Given this context and the importance to baseball revenue of television – a medium that wants a strict predictability unviolated by weather delays and rainouts – Toronto bought into the view that a stadium with an occasional roof is required.)

Besides Robbie and Allen, respect is also due the workers who built the huge structure, bolting the dome's frame together perched on narrow girders hung eighty metres in the air and clambering like mice over the top of the roof to install its outer shell, often in the middle of winter. (It is sometimes useful to recall that it is not self-esteeming men in suits who build SkyDomes.) The workers and their foremen can be credited with what may be the most notable statistic about a monolith whose literature is full of dazzling, multi-digit numbers: the naught counting the deaths that occurred during its construction.

So neither the officials who chose the building's site, the designers who conceived it, nor the contractors and labourers who built it can be faulted for their work.

The men in suits, though, are another matter. Among others, they include the Ontario politicians who negotiated the 1986 deal with SkyDome's partner-corporations, companies like Labatt's, McDonald's, and Coca-Cola, that exposed the province's taxpayers to the lion's share of debt arising from cost overruns and insulated the corporations' operating profits from this debt (profit earned, for example, selling beer, burgers, and soft drinks at ball games). The overruns eventually amounted to more than $300 million, of which the province was forced to swallow about $250 million, a figure that does not count the $60 million originally contributed by the public sector to the project. It is instructive to compare this debt-figure with the $220 million the Toronto Harbour Commission recently estimated is needed to clean decades of industrial pollution from the city's extensive eastern portlands to allow commercial and residential development there, and to contrast the economic and public benefits for the city of the latter sort of investment with those provided by a covered stadium. In three small words, we got took.

The men in suits also include the corporate brahmins who supervised SkyDome's construction and proved remarkably unable to complete the project remotely within budget and on schedule. They then accumulated a massive debt at the public's expense in a frantic effort to meet their own deadline (which they did amid effuse self-congratulation; the occasion was a Jays game with Milwaukee's Brewers in June 1989, scheduled long in advance). Whether their work projections were badly inaccurate or their management simply grossly inept, their maladroitness was among the main factors in the building's escalating cost. For this, they have been rewarded with handsome profits accruing to exclusive long-term contracts to provide goods and services to SkyDome.

One can imagine a different scenario – for one thing, competent management that was prepared to commit its long-term interests to the project in place of short-term profit-taking. One can imagine a single-purpose baseball park built without the expense of, say, mobile field-level seating that can be realigned for football games, a hydraulic pitcher's mound that can be made flat for monster-truck rallies, artificial turf that needs to be capable of quick removal for non-sport events, the hardware and technology required to adapt the building for rock concerts and Wrestlemania shows, the world's largest television screen, and a hotel built into the superstructure. All we really wanted was a ballpark. Instead, we got a very large concrete thing akin to the six-in-one camping tools advertised on late-night television that perform none of their functions especially well.

When one begins thinking of making a *ballpark*, a very different set of criteria comes into play than when one thinks of 'The World's Greatest

Entertainment Centre' (as SkyDome styles itself). Entrepreneurs and government officials in Baltimore, Cleveland, and Dallas–Fort Worth have lately made the citizens of their cities the beneficiaries of such criteria – and made SkyDome a dinosaur almost before its paint was dry. Still, Toronto's fans didn't require a Disneyesque artefact of nostalgic mythology in the manner of Baltimore's Camden Yards – just a good ballpark; and for this, there was a possible model a decade ago when SkyDome was still only an idea, Royals Stadium in Kansas City.

The insight of Rob Robbie and Michael Allen was that the best solution to the problem of a retractable dome was a circular building. While Royals Stadium, completed in 1973, is an expressway facility placed in suburban isolation, it is also among the simplest and most elegant ballparks in the majors and, as it happens, is quite nearly a circular structure. It is bittersweet pleasure to examine pictures of Royals Stadium and imagine what Robbie and Allen might have created had this been the problem they were asked to solve. (For one thing, Royals Stadium is solely and simply a baseball yard rather than a multi-purpose complex; football is played on an adjacent gridiron that shares the same parking lots.)

But if the late 1980s yielded SkyDome, they also yielded another building for baseball fans in the Toronto area. There *is* a ballpark nearby, not as close as downtown but still only a couple of hours away in Buffalo, a city that was forced to count its pennies and cut its stadium dreams to the bone and that, in 1988, built a small exemplar of a baseball park, Pilot Field. It may irk Toronto, a city of hubris with an edifice complex, to discover that the good burghers on Lake Erie did it better; but they did, for $42 million. Today we bear SkyDome because we are fans; for big-league ball, it is the only game in town. For a ballpark, though, we go to Buffalo.

———————— ◆ ————————

Under the pseudonym 'Ralph Connor,' Presbyterian minister Charles William Gordon (1860–1937) drew on his experience as a missionary in the Canadian West at the turn of the century to fashion stories that displayed Christian principles at work in the world. His main subject was frontier life – life beyond the structures and controls of 'civilization.' In these stories, the struggle to rescue souls from anarchy and loneliness and create a stable, caring community is embodied in a key figure like a teacher or minister. The battle between good and evil – the battle for self-mastery – frequently centres on a game or contest demanding skill, courage, and virtue. In The sky pilot: A tale of the foothills *(1899) a young minister ('sky pilot'), at first unable to gain the respect of his unruly flock of ranch hands, gets 'his second wind' when called on to pitch a baseball game for them.*

His Second Wind

RALPH CONNOR

THE FIRST WEEKS WERE NOT PLEASANT FOR THE PILOT. HE HAD BEEN BEATEN, and the sense of failure damped his fine enthusiasm, which was one of his chief charms. The Noble Seven despised, ignored, or laughed at him, according to their mood and disposition. Bruce patronized him; and, worst of all, the Muirs pitied him. This last it was that brought him low, and I was glad of it. I find it hard to put up with a man that enjoys pity.

It was Hi Kendal that restored him, though Hi had no thought of doing so good a deed. It was in this way: A baseball match was on with The Porcupines from near the Fort. To Hi's disgust and the team's dismay Bill failed to appear. It was Hi's delight to stand up for Bill's pitching, and their battery was the glory of the Home team.

'Try The Pilot, Hi,' said some one, chaffing him.

Hi looked glumly across at The Pilot standing some distance away; then called out, holding up the ball:

'Can you play the game?'

For answer Moore held up his hands for a catch. Hi tossed him the ball easily. The ball came back so quickly that Hi was hardly ready, and the jar seemed to amaze him exceedingly.

'I'll take him,' he said, doubtfully, and the game began. Hi fitted on his mask, a new importation and his peculiar pride, and waited.

'How do you like them?' asked The Pilot.

'Hot!' said Hi. 'I hain't got no gloves to burn.'

The Pilot turned his back, swung off one foot on to the other and discharged his ball.

'Strike!' called the umpire.

'You bet!' said Hi, with emphasis, but his face was a picture of amazement and dawning delight.

Again The Pilot went through the manoeuvre in his box and again the umpire called:

'Strike!'

Hi stopped the ball without holding it and set himself for the third. Once more that disconcerting swing and the whip-like action of the arm, and for the third time the umpire called:

'Strike! Striker out!'

'That's the hole,' yelled Hi.

The Porcupines were amazed. Hi looked at the ball in his hand, then at the slight figure of The Pilot.

'I say! where do you get it?'

'What?' asked Moore innocently.

'The gait!'

'The what?'

'The *gait*! the speed, you know!'

'Oh! I used to play in Princeton a little.'

'Did, eh? What the blank blank did you quit for?'

He evidently regarded the exchange of the profession of baseball for the study of theology as a serious error in judgment, and in this opinion every inning of the game confirmed him. At the bat The Pilot did not shine, but he made up for light hitting by his base-running. He was fleet as a deer, and he knew the game thoroughly. He was keen, eager, intense in play, and before the innings were half over he was recognized as the best all-round man on the field. In the pitcher's box he puzzled the Porcupines till they grew desperate and hit wildly and blindly, amid the jeers of the spectators. The bewilderment of the Porcupines was equaled only by the enthusiasm of Hi and his nine, and when the game was over the score stood 37 to 7 in favor of the Home team. They carried The Pilot off the field.

From that day Moore was another man. He had won the unqualified respect of Hi Kendal and most of the others, for he could beat them at their own game and still be modest about it. Once more his enthusiasm came back and his brightness and his courage. The Duke was not present to witness his triumph, and besides, he rather despised the game. Bruce was there, however, but took no part in the general acclaim; indeed, he seemed rather disgusted with Moore's sudden leap into favor. Certainly his hostility to The Pilot and to all that he stood for was none the less open and bitter.

The hostility was more than usually marked at the service held on the Sunday following. It was, perhaps, thrown into stronger relief by the open and delighted approval of Hi, who was prepared to back up anything The Pilot would venture to say. Bill, who had not witnessed The Pilot's performance in the pitcher's box, but had only Hi's enthusiastic report to go upon, still preserved his judicial air. It is fair to say, however, that there was no mean-spirited jealousy in Bill's heart even though Hi had frankly assured him that The Pilot was 'a demon,' and could 'give him points.' Bill had great confidence in Hi's opinion upon baseball, but he was not prepared to surrender his right of private judgment in matters theological, so he waited for the sermon before committing himself to any enthusiastic approval. This service was an undoubted success. The singing was hearty, and insensibly the men fell into a reverent attitude during prayer. The theme, too, was one that gave little room for skepticism. It was the story of Zaccheus, and story-telling was Moore's strong point. The thing was well done. Vivid por-traitures of the outcast, shrewd, converted publican and the supercilious, self-complacent, critical Pharisee were drawn with a few deft touches. A single sentence transferred them to the Foothills and arrayed them in cowboy garb. Bill was none too sure of himself, but Hi, with delightful winks, was indicating Bruce as the Pharisee, to the latter's scornful disgust. The preacher must have noticed, for with a very clever turn the Pharisee was shown to be the kind of man who likes to fit faults upon others. Then Bill, digging his elbows into Hi's ribs, said in an audible whisper:

'Say, pardner, how does it fit now?'

'You git out!' answered Hi, indignantly, but his confidence in his interpretation of the application was shaken. When Moore came to de-scribe the Master and His place in that ancient group, we in the Stopping Place parlor fell under the spell of his eyes and voice, and our hearts were moved within us. That great Personality was made very real and very winning. Hi was quite subdued by the story and the picture. Bill was perplexed; it was all new to him; but Bruce was mainly irritated. To him it was all old and filled with memories he hated to face. At any rate he was unusually savage that evening, drank heavily and went home late, raging and cursing at things in general and The Pilot in particular – for Moore, in a timid sort of way, had tried to quiet him and help him to his horse.

'Ornery sort o' beast now, ain't he?' said Hi, with the idea of com-forting The Pilot, who stood sadly looking after Bruce disappearing in the gloom.

'No! no!' he answered, quickly, 'not a beast, but a brother.'

'Brother! Not much, if I know my relations!' answered Hi, disgustedly.

'The Master thinks a good deal of him,' was the earnest reply.

'Git out!' said Hi, 'you don't mean it! Why,' he added, decidedly,
'he's more stuck on himself than that mean old cuss you was tellin'
about this afternoon, and without half the reason.'

But Moore only said, kindly, 'Don't be hard on him, Hi,' and turned
away, leaving Hi and Bill gravely discussing the question, with the aid
of several drinks of whisky. They were still discussing when, an hour
later, they, too, disappeared into the darkness that swallowed up the
trail to Ashley Ranch. That was the first of many such services. The
preaching was always of the simplest kind, abstract questions being
avoided and the concrete in those wonderful Bible tales, dressed in
modern and in western garb, set forth. Bill and Hi were more than ever
his friends and champions, and the latter was heard exultantly to exclaim
to Bruce:

'He ain't much to look at as a parson, but he's a-ketchin' his second
wind, and 'fore long you won't see him for dust.'

--------◆--------

What fan hasn't regretted the act of an impetuous mother who threw out their entire
collection of baseball cards, only to see them accrue in value faster than real estate in
Tokyo. Dave Crichton and Randy Echlin are two of the lucky ones; they held on to their
treasures, but now must rely on bank deposit boxes for safe-keeping. The O-Pee-Chee
confectionary company in London, Ontario, no longer produces a Canadian version of
the famous Topps bubble-gum card, and for that matter Topps no longer puts gum in
its cards, but for collectors that just makes the obsolete past so much more valuable.

I'll Give You Ten Harry Spilmans for a Larry Walker

DAVID CRICHTON AND RANDY ECHLIN

ACCESSIBLE TO ALL, THE BASEBALL CARD HAS BECOME THE MOST WIDELY
collected piece of sports art in the world. The collector card has
been around, in one form or another, for over a century. Covering a wide selection of subject-matter from The Wild West to Planet of

the Apes, cards have become an institutional part of popular culture. They have been turned into playground games (the first exposure to gambling for many), used for replica engines (pegged on bicycle forks), and dispatched to shoe boxes in the attic or basement to await the ultimate fate – to be thrown out by Mom.

Always the most popular, baseball cards became a big business phenomenon in the 1980s, spawning a billion-dollar industry. Stores for card collectors sprang up everywhere to meet the demand. Card-producing companies proliferated and battled to obtain official licences from Major League Baseball. They then scurried around signing agreements to produce cards for virtually any subject, regardless of the limited appeal. Perhaps this lunacy was epitomized with the card series on 'Bass Fishermen' (with apologies to bass-fishing enthusiasts).

The cause of this immense growth was the misguided belief that collecting cards was a blue-chip investment. While it is true that some people were able to capitalize on the trade in cards, few collectors actually profited, and the business has now settled back to a more sane, realistic level.

One positive consequence is that all this industry activity has proved to be a bonanza for the baseball fan who is looking to collect for the more traditional reasons. The increased variety has provided more options, with prices to fit most budgets. In addition, the design and quality of production has improved with the intense competition. Sub-sets, contained within the traditional series and pertaining to specific subject-matter, such as 'Power Hitters' or 'Future Stars,' have contributed to the overall enjoyment of collecting.

With premium sets, regular sets, update sets, insert sets, and rookie sets, it is difficult and expensive to keep up with the variety of cards issued each year. The answer is to specialize in one or two subjects: Teams, Super Stars, Rookies, Pitchers ... whatever gives you enjoyment. For those of us in Canada, an obvious theme is cards pertaining to 'North of the Border.'

Just collect the ones that have 'eh' on them

When considering a Canadian collection, it is necessary to identify the various sub-themes. They are: (1) Canadian teams (major and minor league), (2) Canadian players, and (3) Canadian-produced sets. Let's discuss each of these individually.

Canadian major-league teams

It is still possible to collect team sets of Canada's two major-league teams at a reasonable cost. They are relatively recent arrivals on the scene, with the Montreal Expos commencing in 1969 and the Toronto Blue Jays in 1977. For the first twelve years of the Expos and the first five of the Blue Jays, there were only two major sets produced – Topps (from the United States) and O-Pee-Chee (Canadian). With the arrival of Fleer and Donruss in 1981, both U.S. releases, the annual number increased to four. Add to this Score in 1988 and Upper Deck in 1989; the non-traditional Sports Flicks, a short-lived, special-effects card distributed from 1986–89 (and revived again in 1994); and the Donruss/Leaf, a Canadian version of the U.S. Donruss issue for 1985. To these must be added the additional cards appearing in Update sets issued by the major card companies. A comprehensive collection should also include the various 'Fireman's' sets (done by fire fighters!) and other specialty issues, typified by the Zellers Expo set.

Canadian minor-league teams

T.C.M.A., the originator of card sets of minor-league teams, produced sets of the Vancouver, Calgary, and Edmonton franchises as early as 1979. More recently, Pro Cards, a division of Fleer, has brought out sets for Class A teams, such as the St. Catharines Blue Jays and Welland Pirates, and AA-level teams, such as the now relocated London Tigers.

Perhaps one of the most unique and scarce sets relating to the minor leagues in Canada is the 1990 Eastern League All-Star Team that toured the U.S.S.R. That's right, the Soviet Union. While not specifically a 'Canadian' team, it did include London players, as well as General Manager Bob Gilson, and this Canadian content, as well as the unusual nature of the set, makes it a collector's must.

Canadian players

There have been more Canadians in the major leagues over the history of baseball than any country other than the United States – approaching 200 and still counting. In addition, there have been numerous Canadian minor-league players and coaches, some of whom appear on minor-league cards.

The first Canadian to play in the National League, Bill Phillips, a first baseman from Saint John, New Brunswick, appeared on two tobacco cards in the late 1800s. Goodwin & Company of New York, makers of Old Judge and Gypsy Queen cigarette brands, is generally considered one of the first issuers of baseball cards. The cigarette cards of the early 1900s featured such Canadians as 'Mooney' Gibson, 'Pop' Smith, 'Foxy' Irwin, 'Tip' O'Neill, and Russ Ford. The early candy issues from such companies as Cracker Jack, National Chickle Company, and American Caramel Company contained cards of Jimmy Archer and Jack Graney.

The first bubble-gum cards were introduced by Goudey Gum Company of Boston in 1933. This first set numbered 240 and included Canadian Frank O'Rourke. In 1939, Gum, Inc., which later became Bowman Gum, issued its Play Ball-America set, including George Selkirk and Goody Rosen amongst its numbers. The 1948 Bowman set is considered the first of the modern era. Included in subsequent sets through to 1955 were cards of Phil Marchildon and Dick Fowler.

The year 1951 heralded the arrival of Topps Chewing Gum Company of Brooklyn. The next year, Topps issued its historic set of larger and more colourful cards that set the standard for years to come. This collection includes Canadian players such as Sherry Robertson, Dick Fowler, John Rutherford, and Bob Hooper.

Today, Canadian players are seen on such exotic card sets as Topps Stadium Club, Collector's Choice, Fleer Flair, Pinnacle Museum, Studio, and Elite. In the 1990s, there will be hundreds of new high-tech cards, with such Canadian players as Larry Walker, Steve Wilson, Denis Boucher, Nigel Wilson, and Paul Quantrill.

The best way to start collecting cards of Canadian players is to research them in the *Baseball Encyclopedia*. Once a list has been compiled, the cards available can be located in *The Sport American Baseball Card Alphabetical Checklist* by Dr. James Beckett.

Canadian-produced sets

Canadian baseball cards, while not nearly as numerous as those produced in the United States, have played a significant role in the annals of the hobby. As early as 1912, a 90-card set was produced by Imperial Tobacco for its Black Cat and Sweet Caporal brands. Most of Canada's older card sets were made by confectionary companies, including Neilson's (1921), Willard's Chocolates (1923), and Parkhurst (1952). In addition, Canadian affiliates of American companies produced distinctly different sets in 1933, 1934, 1936 (Goudey's Canadian subsidiary, World Wide Gum), and 1962 (Canadian Post Cereal). Because of their more limited distribution, these cards are much sought after.

Topps' London, Ontario, licensee O-Pee-Chee produced cards very similar in appearance to their American cousins from 1965 to 1976, having previously made a 'Batter Up' set in 1937. In 1977, the year the Blue Jays were born, a special set was produced featuring the Jays and Expos. From 1979 onwards, the distinctive O-Pee-Chee logo has appeared on the front of most issues; many players' cards have been updated with team changes from those appearing in the Topps sets.

In 1991 and 1992, O-Pee-Chee produced its Premier set. While smaller, it is a higher-quality card set. In 1993 and 1994, following the World Series championships won by Toronto, special World Series Insert Sets were created. (Sadly, as of 1995, O-Pee-Chee has announced it will no longer produce baseball cards.) Other recent Canadian card issuers include Zellers, Hygrade, Hostess, Ault, Panini, Ben's, McDonald's, and Petro Canada.

Whether you decide to collect Canadian major-league or minor-league sets, Canadian-born players, or the distinctive Canadian-produced sets, a useful guide to what is available is found in *The Charlton Canadian Baseball Card Guide*.

One thing is for certain these days. Unlike their forefathers of the 1950s and 1960s, collectors today rarely expose their cards to bicycle forks, school-yard brick walls, or even shoe boxes. Today's hobbyists jealously protect their cards in albums and plastic sleeves. It's very unlikely that Mom will have an opportunity to relegate the 1990 issues to the trash.

Happy collecting ...

———————— ◆ ————————

With the significant exception of the gold medal won by the national youth team at the World Youth Championships in 1991, Canada's international baseball success has been limited. As often as not, the triumphs are small moral victories, like that of the Canadian team at the 1967 Pan American games in Winnipeg. It was discovered that four members of the Canadian team were ex-professionals reinstated to amateur status for the tournament. It was a crime most other competing countries were guilty of, but only Canada got caught. The miscreants were sent home, and Canada staggered from one loss to another before beating the Cubans in the final game. (The loss forced Cuba to play a gold-medal playoff, which they lost to the United States.) Canadian baseball talent was much in evidence at the 1984 and 1988 Olympics – many Canadian players from those squads have gone on to major-league careers. But as Jim Davidson shows in this account, glory can be snatched away in an instant in baseball.

One Pitch Away from Glory

JAMES DAVIDSON

THE TELEPHONE RINGS A COUPLE OF TIMES BEFORE MARGARET WOODEN picks it up. I'm on the other end, calling the second of three Woodens in the Windsor phone book to see if it's the home of the man who threw the most dramatic pitch any Canadian has ever thrown in the short history of Olympic baseball.

'Um, I'm not sure if this is the right number, but I was wondering if this is where I could find Mark Wooden who used to play for Canada's national baseball team,' I stammer into the receiver.

The trace of a wry laugh can be heard in Margaret's voice. 'You've got the right one all right,' she says. 'He's the one who gave up the home run to Nicaragua.'

Well, gee, thanks mom for telling everybody. You know you're branded for life when your own mother refers to you as 'the one who gave up the home run.' And what a homer it was. Bottom of the 12th inning. Canada up 3–2, with a Nicaraguan runner on second. Two outs. Two strikes on the batter. Here comes the pitch. Boom. 4–3 Nicaragua. Game over.

Shades of Joe Carter and Mitch Williams at the '93 World Series you say. Worst thing you're expecting is a base hit that ties the game, and then, lights out. At least Mitch could say he gave up his homer to one of baseball's best players. Wooden's conquerer was a pint-sized Nicaraguan infielder nobody had ever heard of before. The shame.

But let's not get carried away. After all, baseball was only a demonstration sport back in 1984 at Dodger Stadium in Los Angeles. And that pitch wasn't the only reason Canada didn't advance to the final round and get a shot at an American college all-star team loaded with the likes of Mark McGwire, Barry Larkin, and Will Clark. And furthermore, it's not as if anyone in Canada was paying much attention to baseball anyway when other Canuck athletes were snatching real medals left and right thanks in part to the Soviet-bloc boycott.

Come to think of it, not many people have ever paid much attention to Canada's national baseball team since it first appeared at the 1967 Pan-American Games in Winnipeg. And those who do know a bit about our national ball team tell more stories about the ones that got away than the prizes caught. Stories of promising clubs that upset powerful Cuban, American, and Japanese teams, but then somehow got tripped up by one of the world's pipsqueaks just when it seemed they might be about to win something. Yes, a lot of our teams have had potential, and none more than the 1984 Olympic team. 'We had good pitching, good hitting and good defence,' says Bill MacKenzie, who was technical director for Baseball Canada at the time. 'Most years we always had at least one piece missing, but not this time. We thought we had a good shot at a medal.'

Or at least a demonstration medal anyway. Baseball didn't become a full Olympic sport until 1992, nearly a century after Baron de Coubertin revived the Games in 1896. America's national pastime, with its long tradition of crotch pulling and tobacco-juice hawking, had always struck the aristocratic old codgers of the International Olympic Committee as a tad déclassé. But the codgers relented during the run-up to the 1984 Games in the face of a strong U.S. lobbying effort, and the sport was on its way to a permanent place on the Olympic menu. Canada again made it to the 1988 demonstration event in Seoul (and again failed to advance to the medal round), and then didn't qualify for baseball's official debut at the 1992 Barcelona Games.

From Canada's point of view, 1984 was a good year for baseball to climb aboard the Olympic bandwagon. After a long period of disorganization following the 1967 start-up, Canada's national ball team started making headway in international baseball during the early eighties. Much of the credit went to MacKenzie, a former Detroit Tiger and Montreal Expo farmhand who took the technical director's job in 1978. Under his guidance, the Canadians moved from the bottom reaches of the world's top dozen to fifth, a spot they held onto most of the time from 1981 to 1983. The improvement sprang from better management and better players, as MacKenzie found a nucleus of talented athletes, primarily by scouting U.S. college teams for Canadian content.

Still, Canada's inclusion in the eight-team Los Angeles Games tournament was more a matter of luck than skill. The Canadians had lost in Olympic qualifying play the year before, but then received a last-minute invitation in early June of 1984 when Cuba joined the Soviet walk-out. The whole thing was rushed, but MacKenzie had no trouble finding volunteers willing to forgo summer jobs and barbecue nights. For a field manager, he chose Eric MacKenzie, a former catcher who'd made a brief major-league stop in Kansas City in 1955. The two men weren't related and were in fact polar opposites in personality. Bill was excitable and talkative, while Eric had a Cito Gaston–like aura of calm.

After a brief training camp in Windsor, the MacKenzies and their coaching staff picked a 20-man roster that many think was the best team Canada has ever fielded. Nine of the players later signed professional contracts, and three of them, pitchers Mike Gardiner and Steve Wilson and outfielder Kevin Reimer, went on to big-league careers. Reimer, then 20, was the most obvious prospect. He had wrists the size of cantaloupes, and at an exhibition game that summer at Tiger Stadium, he hit an upper-deck home run that left jaws hanging open. Then just a couple of weeks before the L.A. Games, he led Canada to first place at a warm-up tournament in Haarlem, the Netherlands.

But Reimer's streak ended a few hours after Canada defeated Holland 17–4 in the championship game. Along with the rest of the team, he took post-game celebrations to Klaus' Party Haus, a rather bizarre establishment that was a combination bowling alley and watering hole. After a few hours of revelry, Reimer set out on the two-mile walk back to the team's hotel. Halfway home, he realized he'd left his Team Canada jacket back at Klaus' Haus and figured someone must have pinched it for a souvenir. His funk grew as the walk progressed and by the time he reached the hotel he was riled enough to punch the door of his room.

If it had been your standard North American hotel door, no problem, but the Dutch make their doors to last. His hand puffed up on the spot, and at breakfast the next morning, team-mate Jim Eliopoulos remembers, there was a look on Reimer's face that was equal parts sheepish and scared. 'He figured he'd just cashed in his future. He thought he'd be going back to B.C. to drive a pastry truck for the rest of this life.'

So with Reimer out, the Canadians went to the Olympics lacking their clean-up hitter. And to make things more difficult, they were in the stronger of the two four-team pools, along with the skilful Japanese, the defending world champions from South Korea, and Nicaragua, which was by far the weakest of the three opponents (the United States, Taiwan, the Dominican Republic, and Italy made up the other pool). They'd only have three games in the opening round-robin, and to make it through to the medal round, they'd have to win twice. The strategy was clear. Beat the Nicaraguans and then steal one from either Korea or Japan.

They'd also have to beat a case of nerves. The program said it was just a demonstration sport, but it didn't feel like one. It was, as Canadian first baseman Larry Downes put it, two sporting fantasies rolled into one. 'Playing in the Olympics was great, but playing in Dodger Stadium made it that much better. There we were standing on that crushed brick they have on the field and taking drinks out of the same water fountain you'd see Tommy Lasorda drinking out of on TV. It was an absolute high.'

Considering that it might take Downes and company a few innings to return to planet Earth, it seemed fortunate that the Canadians had drawn Nicaragua for the opener. And they seemed doubly blessed to have a veteran like Rod Heisler pitching. Heisler, a left-hander, had been with the team seven years, longer than any of his mates. He didn't throw anything fancy, but he had a sneaky-quick fastball and plenty of guts. If anyone was bothered about playing in front of 40,000 people instead of the usual 400 or so, it wasn't Heisler.

As the visiting side, the Canadians took the field at 4 P.M. on a typically sticky, uncomfortable early August afternoon in L.A. Heisler wasn't in top form, but he was pitching well enough. The same could be said of Nicaragua's starter, Julio Moya. Both teams were getting their share of hits, but not many runs. Through seven innings, it was tied 2–2. The score held through the eighth and ninth, and Heisler and Moya both stayed in the game as it went to extra innings.

But while Heisler chugged on through a scoreless 10th, Eric MacKenzie decided to start the bullpen. Ten innings on a hot day is a lot of work for anyone, even a tough Saskatchewan boy like Heisler. It was now Wooden time. If you had assembled the 20 Canadian players for a team picture, it wouldn't have been difficult to spot the bullpen closer. Mark Wooden had that classic stopper look – chunky, round-faced, broad-shouldered – and the classic stopper personality. A strong, silent type, he let his fastball do the chattering. Wooden could get by on his hummer alone, but he was dynamite when his slider was working too. And on this day it was. After warming him up, back-up catcher Eliopoulos got a call from the dugout. It was pitching coach Dick Groch. 'How's Woody throwing?' Groch asked. 'Great,' Elioupolos said. 'His slider is really snapping.'

In the bottom of the 11th, Wooden entered and put the side down 1-2-3. Then, in the top of the 12th, Canada took its final crack at the rubber-armed Moya. With a man at second, shortstop Arnoldo Munoz let a ground ball slip under his glove, and the go-ahead run scored.

'Don't, don't, don't let the lead guy on,' Wooden thought to himself as returned to face the bottom of the Nicaraguan order in the last of the 12th. But his control was on a par with most 20-year-old power pitchers, and he drilled the first batter in the ribs. The next man up bunted the runner into scoring position, and things looked dicey. But then a quick strikeout placed Wooden, and Canada, one out away from victory.

Up to the plate strode Munoz, the ninth hitter in the Nicaraguan order. After the error in the top of the 12th, he now had a chance to pass the goat horns along to Wooden. But Munoz looked overmatched and fell behind 1-2 in the count. Then came another zinger on the inside corner. Munoz looked at the umpire. Wooden prepared to leap into the air. The ump called it a ball.

Munoz wasn't taking any more chances, and fouled off the next two pitches. Wooden looked in for the sign from catcher Rob Thomson, who in turn got his cue from Groch in the dugout. Slider. It wasn't what Wooden wanted to see. The fastball was his out pitch. But Groch, who scouted opponents thoroughly, thought Munoz would be waiting on the hard stuff.

Wooden paused to think it over. If he shook Thomson off and Munoz got a base hit, he'd look pretty foolish. And Groch knew what he was doing. So slider it was.

'I'll never forget that pitch,' Wooden says. 'I went into my stretch and I turned to the outfield and said to myself, "What am I going to do to celebrate when I strike this guy out?" Then as soon as I let go of the ball my exact words were "Oh, shit!" Then my next words were, "Go foul."'

It didn't go foul. The slider hung belt high and Munoz lined it into the left-field bullpen. Like that, the game was over. Wooden didn't move. 'I just stood there. The thought that he might hit a home run never even entered into my mind. I couldn't believe it.' None of his team-mates could, either. They'd just lost the one game they needed to win for a realistic shot at the medal round. Now they'd have to beat both South Korea and Japan. 'Oh, shit,' indeed.

As it turned out, the Canadian team couldn't have drawn a more frustrating opponent for game two than the Koreans. They use fundamentals as a weapon, boring you into submission. The batters rarely fail to move the runner along. The pitchers rarely walk anybody. The fielders rarely make errors. Of course, getting behind early is the last thing you'd want to do against Team Sominex. But that's precisely what happened. Starter Barry Kuzminski lasted all of an inning and a third. The Koreans scratched four singles and drew three walks and bingo, it was 3–0.

Canada got a run back in the fourth, but after that, nothing. To start the next inning, Korea brought in their own fire-balling stopper, Hak-Kil Yoon, and he set the last 15 batters down in order. After losing to Nicaragua in a flash, now the Canadians were losing in a very different, but equally disturbing, way. As batter after batter slumped back to the dugout, the hopes of Olympic glory died an achingly slow death. The final score was 3–1. Gloom descended. By Downes's count, there was a full 15 minutes of silence in the dressing room following the game. 'It was so hard to take,' he recalls. 'That team could have really done something and we all knew it. But now we were eliminated.'

Game three against Japan was, technically, a nothing game. Canada was out of the medal round and the Japanese were in after winning their first two. But neither team treated the match as a meaningless one. For Canada, there could be no better Olympic keepsake than a win, while the Japanese strove to maintain a perfect record. Other countries might have rested their starters, but not Japan. The Japanese always played full out. Whether they were 10 runs up or 10 down, they'd still bunt and steal bases. 'They weren't taking it easy at all,' Bill MacKenzie maintains. 'That's just not in their make-up.'

For their starter, Japan chose Atsunori Ito, who two days earlier had pitched seven shutout innings against Nicaragua. Canada countered with Mike Gardiner, a freckle-faced lad from southwestern Ontario who looked more like a paperboy than an Olympian. At age 18, he was pitching at the Olympics in front of a Sunday afternoon crowd of 48,656 at Dodger Stadium. Gardiner had naturally light skin, but team-mates remember him looking positively ashen as game time approached.

They needn't have worried about the kid. He did just fine, keeping the Japanese off balance and off the base paths with an artful mix of curves, fastballs, and change-ups. Meanwhile, the Canadian hitters rediscovered their collective stroke, taking a 5–1 lead through the fourth and then holding off a late rally to win 6–4. Gardiner lasted seven innings and gave up three runs. The save went to Wooden, who this time pitched scoreless ball for an inning and a third.

Now it was all over, and the feeling was bittersweet. On the one hand, there was a sense that something important had been proved. The Canadians had always believed they were an excellent team, and now they'd demonstrated it to nearly 50,000 people at one of baseball's greatest shrines. But beating the Japanese also made that opening-game loss to Nicaragua all the more painful. And as Japan went on to defeat Taiwan 2–1 in the semi-final and then upset the United States 6–3 in the gold-medal game, the players were left to forever wonder what might have happened if not for the 12th-inning hanging slider. They were, after all, good enough to beat the eventual champion. Could they have gone all the way if they'd made it to the medal round?

More than a decade later, Mark Wooden still gets asked about the pitch a couple of times a year. He pitched several outstanding games for Canadian teams and pitched four years in the Seattle Mariners' organization before tearing ligaments in his elbow, but the only thing anyone remembers is the hanging slider. Like it or not, he is Canada's Mitch Williams, the guy who gave up the home run.

Thanks to the wonders of modern technology, Wooden owns a videotape of the game, so he can replay that moment any time he wants to. But, as you might guess, it is the least-worn item in his tape collection. A year or so after the fact, his brother wanted a look-see, so Mark popped it in the VCR and closed his eyes. He couldn't watch. Then he tried again a couple of years back. He thought he was ready, but afterwards he wished he'd just left it on the shelf. 'When I saw myself throwing that pitch I got the exact same feeling I had right when it happened,' he says. 'I just couldn't believe it. I still can't believe it.'

———————— ◆ ————————

Every town has one. Edmonton's Mr. Baseball is the late John Ducey, who never let his residence in what was then a relatively isolated Alberta outpost keep him from shagging fly balls in 1920 off the likes of future Brooklyn Dodgers star Babe Herman, or from organizing semi-pro leagues in the fifties that gave a chance to college kids like future Blue Jays General Manager Pat Gillick. Ducy died in 1984 and the Triple A Edmonton Trappers renamed their ballpark in his honour. How appropriate for a place that is reputed to be the inspiration for W.P. Kinsella's masterful Shoeless Joe. *This 1981 letter from John Ducey was sent to Bill Humber in response to his queries about the early days of baseball in western Canada.*

Edmonton's Mr. Baseball

JOHN DUCEY

I N 1921 I WAS A BATBOY FOR VISITING CLUBS COMING INTO EDMONTON, IN THE Western Canadian Professional Baseball League. I was born in Buffalo, N.Y., August 31/08. My parents brought me to Edmonton in 1910, and I went through grammar school and high school here. Edmonton's baseball park was then known as Diamond Park. The 1921 league comprised Winnipeg, Regina, Moose Jaw, Saskatoon, Calgary and Edmonton ... a Class B circuit.

When Babe Herman was named to play 1st base for the Edmonton Eskimos, at the conclusion of the California spring training camp at Crockett, California, he was 18 years of age. A teammate, the late Heinie Manush, also made the club; Heinie was then 20 years of age. As you know, both men went on to great careers in the big leagues. These two boys were the most prominent players on the 1921 Eskimos Baseball Club.

I remember too the previous season, 1920, same league, as a young fan haunting the old Diamond Park, around the clubhouse; in those early years, us kids would shag balls for the teams (home and visitors) during batting practice ... long since abandoned. Many good players made it to the big leagues from the WCL in those two years: Tony Kaufmann, pitcher, Winnipeg Maroons; Oscar Melillo, 2nd baseman, Winnipeg Maroons; Walter (Cuckoo) Christenson, Calgary Bronks, outfielder; and 1st baseman Nelson (Chicken) Hawks, were prominent names.

A dear friend of mine, for some 60 years, John E. (Beans) Reardon, was the league's most illustrious umpire; he served two years in the WCL (1920–21). 1920 was Beans' 1st year in professional organized baseball. He graduated to the Pacific Coast League for the 1923 season, and was recommended to the National League by the legendary Hank O'Day. Beans served the National League for 24 years, and had five World Series assignments. We've kept in close touch by letter all these years, and my last visit with John was while I was attending the 1974 World Series, as a guest of Mr. Peter O'Malley, in Los Angeles and Oakland. John Reardon should have followed Umpire Billy Evans into the Baseball Hall of Fame at Cooperstown. To the shame of the Committee of Veterans, he has been passed by, to date, in the umpires' category.

For myself, I played City Senior Amateur baseball in Edmonton from 1925 through 1930, as a 1st baseman. I began umpiring in 1931 (through 1945) in Edmonton, and through Alberta and Western Canada, and umpired professional baseball in 1934 in the old Northern Class D league. I umpired semi-pro baseball in California and in Massachusetts, in 1939 and 1942–43.

I went to Springfield, Mass., in the fall of 1941 to work for Eddie Shore in the administrative side of professional hockey, in the front office of the Springfield Indians hockey club of the American Hockey League, and also worked with Eddie Shore at Buffalo in the winter of 1944–45, with the Buffalo Bisons ... a valuable experience in sports administration. After the hockey season in Buffalo, I returned to Edmonton, spring of 1945, umpired that summer, and in 1946 took over the administration of baseball in Edmonton, through 1959.

Currently I serve as Secretary for our Edmonton Oldtimers Baseball Association (labour of love), and have done so since its inception, back in May of 1964. We currently have 166 members. We have lost 79 members through death since 1964. A great group of fellows ... we hold an annual dinner each June and had our 15th reunion dinner on June 26th, 1981.

One more item: Our city of Edmonton did have an Edmonton-born boy reach major-league status as a player, with the Chicago Cubs in the early 1930s, namely Vincent (Vince) Barton, who was born in Edmonton, February 1st, 1908. His parents migrated from the U.S.A. to Edmonton. Vince left Edmonton when he was about 13 years of age with his parents, and they settled in Toronto. He developed his outfielding skills on the sandlots of Toronto, and made it to the Chicago Cubs in 1931 and 1932. He later played in the International League with various clubs, for some years. We have endeavored to trace Vince for the past several years, with no success as yet. [Barton died in Toronto, September 13, 1973, according to *The Baseball Encyclopedia*.]

The only Alberta-born and raised ball player who reached the major-league level is outfielder Glen Gorbous, who was born August 7th, 1930, at Drumheller, about 80 miles east of Calgary. Glen's dad had to sign for him with the Brooklyn Dodgers organization back in 1947, Glen being under age. He had played 3rd base for the Calgary Purity 99

Baseball Club in the Alberta Big Four Inter-City Semi-Pro Baseball League in the summer of 1947. He was signed by then Dodger scout Howie Haak, who is today the Pittsburgh Pirates' super special-assignment scout. Howie conducted the first Brooklyn Dodgers baseball school in Western Canada in 1947, at Renfrew Park, Edmonton. Glen Gorbous' career was brief: 1955 Cincinnati Reds, 1955–57 Phillies. He had all the natural talent, speed, left-handed hitter, and a major-league-plus throwing arm. The Dodgers converted him into an outfielder when they signed him in '47, because of his great arm and running speed. But Glen was more interested in hockey and lost his dedication for major-league baseball. He still holds the record in all of baseball (major, minor, semi-pro, amateur), for the longest throwing distance by an outfielder – 419 ft. (aerial) – established when he was with Omaha of the American Association back in 1957.

◆

With 'Fergie' Jenkins there are the facts and then the rest of the story: 284 major-league pitching wins – only two non-American-born players have more. Better than 3000 strikeouts (3192) against fewer than 1000 walks (997) – no one can match that achievement. Seven 20-plus winning seasons. Memberships in Canada's Sports and Baseball Halls of Fame, recipient of the Order of Canada, and the ultimate – residence in the National Baseball Hall of Fame and Museum in Cooperstown, New York, with its just over 200 members and lone Canadian. And there are the other 'facts': tragic deaths among his closest family, a drug bust at Toronto's airport when he would not implicate team-mates. He returned to the majors in 1995 with the Chicago Cubs as their pitching coach and all Canadians with a trace of compassion wished him the best. This Toronto Star *column by Milt Dunnell from March 15, 1966, finds Jenkins before his first full season in the majors – with the Cubs. The Phillies traded him to Chicago on April 21.*

One Man's Family Is His Fan Club

MILT DUNNELL

C LEARWATER, FLA. – FERGUSON JENKINS HAS ALL THE USUAL REASONS FOR wanting to be a big league pitcher – money, recognition, the good life of the big time and the security of a baseball pension. But the most powerful incentives are back in his hometown, Chatham,

Ontario. Fergie's father – he is Ferguson, too, as were his own father and his grandfather – has clippings and trophies to prove he was quite a ball player with a semi-pro club at Hershey, Pennsylvania.

At that time Jackie Robinson and the late Branch Rickey had not been along to break down the barriers against Negro players in organized baseball. So Fergie's father never had the satisfaction of knowing for sure whether he could have made it as a big leaguer. His own hopes and ambitions are wrapped up in his son, who is getting the opportunity.

So the name of Ferguson Jenkins in a Philadelphia boxscore actually would represent the dreams of two men. Then there's Fergie's mother, who began losing her eyesight when he, her only child, was born. She listens to the stories which her husband and Fergie's wife read from *The Sporting News* and the Philadelphia papers. Then she sits down and types letters of encouragement to her son. She's a touch typist.

When Fergie was a kid in the minor baseball setup at Chatham, his father used to take him to Detroit so he could watch the Tigers and enjoy the big league atmosphere. Pops may even have pictured himself out there in a Detroit uniform.

'The thing that impressed me was the way the pitchers made the ball move around,' Fergie recalls. 'I knew that was something I would have to learn, too, if I intended to be a big league pitcher.'

Because he's tall (6 feet, 5 inches now) and skinny, the manual which the coaches use in kids' ball seemed to dictate that Ferguson Jenkins, Jr., should be a first baseman. That's what he was until one day in a playoff game when arm trouble knocked out the team's star pitcher.

Jenkins assured the coach he could pitch a bit. He did even better than he said: he threw a two-hitter. Ever since then, it has been a steady, although sometimes frustrating climb towards the Phillies, who stage their spring tortures here at Clearwater.

Why would a boy whose baseball idols all were Tigers wind up as a modest bonus baby of the Phillies? Well, it's a matter of emphasis, as Fergie tells it.

'I attended one of two Detroit tryout schools,' he explains. 'As far as I know, though, the Tigers never sent anyone to see me. I had inquiries from the Orioles, the Pirates and the White Sox. They wanted to know when I would graduate from high school and they asked for clippings.

'Tony Lucadello, the Philadelphia scout, used to come around and watch me play. He kept in touch with me and sent me instructions. If the Phils were holding a tryout school, he came and picked me up. That was the difference.'

Lucadello was on hand in June of 1962, when Jenkins came out of high school. The following day, a contract was signed and Fergie invested his bonus money in a new home for his parents.

He impressed his new employers early by winning seven and losing two for Miami in the Florida State League. His earned run average was 0.95. The Philly front office must have suspected a typographical error.

Like most young pitchers, he developed arm trouble along the way. He was with Arkansas, a triple-A club, at the time, and the Phils sent him back to his former manager, Andy Seminick, at Miami.

It turned out that young Mr. Jenkins was suffering from an occupational ailment. As soon as he became a ball player, he decided he would have to start chewing tobacco. This had caused some minor infection in his back teeth and the poison was draining down into his shoulder.

'Under Seminick, I got rid of the teeth and I gave up the tobacco,' Jenkins says. 'I also got rid of the arm trouble, and I won twelve ball games.'

He got his first shot with the Phils last September. They didn't exactly pick a soft spot for him. The Phils and the Cards were tied in the top of the ninth, with two on base, when he got the call in the bullpen.

Dick Groat was the batter. Jenkins struck him out with a letter-high fastball. He went on to pitch four scoreless innings and the Phils won. Jenkins got into six more games after that and finished with an impressive 2.25 earned run average.

Cal McLish is pitching coach of the Phils. He likes Fergie's chances. Says Cal: 'What I like about him is that he throws strikes.

'Some scouts told me they didn't like his fastball. So I went down to Dallas one night and watched him work. He threw 52 fastballs before one was hit out of the infield.

'I decided I liked it.'

———————— ◆ ————————

From the time a grasshopper plague ended his pharmaceutical career in Kansas in the 1870s to his recognition on an honour roll in Cooperstown's Baseball Hall of Fame in the 1940s, all Bob Emslie thought about was baseball. Ironically, Emslie's home town of St. Thomas, Ontario, is noted also as the place in which P.T. Barnum's great circus elephant Jumbo was killed in the nineteenth century, after clashing with a train. Emslie frequently clashed with the great New York Giants manager John McGraw, who once called the long-serving umpire Blind Bob. The circus and baseball were two places in the last century where young lads, unwilling to work in a factory, could flee, and for Bob Emslie, at least, the flight was rewarded. The following account was discovered at the Elgin County Museum in St. Thomas, Ontario, among the various baseball effects of Emslie's career.

All I Thought About Was Baseball

BOB EMSLIE

IT WAS IN GUELPH THAT I GOT MY FIRST BASEBALL LESSON. AS A KID I WENT to all the ballgames there. The Maple Leafs of Guelph had a great reputation in Canada, also in the United States. They were Champions of Canada. I am quite sure it is the oldest baseball town in Canada. They had a good smart club there in the 1860s.

After moving to London, I still had my mind on baseball and my parents had their own troubles keeping me at school in the summertime. All I thought about was baseball.

Finally the climax came in the summer of 1874, when my father took me from school and sent me to learn the drug business with my brother, who had a store in Waterville, Kansas. I resided out there for two years. The grasshopper plague of 1875 put my brother out of business in the fall of 1876, and nothing else was left for me to do but return to London, my home. The two years I was in Kansas did not break me from playing baseball. In 1875, we had a club in the town I lived in, and we played in Atchison, Kansas, and St. Joe, Missouri. I played the position of left field with the Waterville Club until I left in 1876.

After returning to London, I started to learn the jewellery business, but I never finished my trade, owing to too much thought about baseball. In the spring of 1878, I pitched my first baseball game on a Good Friday, against the Tecumseh Club of London, a professional club that included such well-known players as Goldsmith and Power, Juice Latham, first base, Mike Denneen, second base, Bucky Ledwith, short-stop, Harry Spence, third base, and Joe Hornung, left field ... all noted professionals at that time. The club I pitched for was all young boys from London, all amateurs. They beat us in ten innings, 3–2. The winning run was scored on an error of our second baseman, with two men gone.

I pitched around London until the 30th of June 1879, when I decided to go out into the world for myself. I landed in a small town, Harriston, Ontario. I had heard that they had a ball club there, and I was conceited enough to think that I could help them. The following year we won the Championship of Canada. I remained in Harriston until August 1881, when I left there and joined the Toronto Club, a semi-pro team. They quit in the middle of September, and I came back home to London. I played one game with the London Club against St. Thomas. After that game, I made arrangements to remain and play with St. Thomas.

The following year, 1882, we had a semi-pro team in St. Thomas. On the 24th of May that year, we left St. Thomas to play three exhibition games with Syracuse, Rochester and Auburn. All that we had with us when we left was the shirt and collar we wore and our uniforms done up in newspapers. The manager in charge of our club kept us out on the road until the 30th of June.

On the trip we played twenty-six games, won eighteen and lost eight. On this trip, we played two games against Jim Mutrie's National League club; also two games against the Philadelphia Nationals. We lost all four by a very small margin. We played two games in Camden, N.J., against the Inter-State Team. We won both games. We played Harrisburg, Pottsville, Pottstown, Redding, Binghamton, Elizabethtown, Troy, Albany, Poughkeepsie, Wilmington, Chester and other cities. They all found us hard to beat, and just think, I was the only pitcher.

This was a lucky trip for me. After our second game in Camden, I signed an agreement to join their team, after the St. Thomas Club had finished their trip. As I said before, we got back to St. Thomas on the 30th of June, and I played my last game with them on Dominion Day, the 1st of July, against Detroit and the big four on their club at that time, Geo. (Stump) Weidman in the box. They beat us 5–3.

I arrived in Camden at 11 a.m. on July the 7th, 1882. I played left field that day for them, getting three hits. The next day I pitched against the Baltimore Club, who were in the American Association. We beat them 3–0.

I had good success for the remainder of the season, and signed for the following season, 1883. We had only two pitchers, a fellow named Sam Kimber and myself. We had a good club, too good for the league we were in. It was a foregone conclusion that we could win, and people got so they would not come out to see us. The consequence was the famous 'Merrits of Camden' having lost only five games up to August 15th, when they disbanded. The club was all signed up by Brooklyn, with the exception of Frank Gardiner, a fielder, Rooney Sweeney, catcher, and myself, the three of us signing with Baltimore.

I remained with Baltimore until 1885. A pitcher named Hardy

Henderson and myself did most of the pitching. In those days we only had a couple of pitchers on a club. My most successful year was in 1884; after that I had a bad arm which handicapped me. I was playing in New Orleans. Some promoters picked two teams to play there in the winter of 1884 and 1885: one from the National League, the other from the American Association. While playing in one of those games, I hurt my arm, back of the shoulder. I felt it go at the time. I tried everything, but it never got right. It kept getting worse all the time. From an over-hand pitcher, I tried under-hand, as it did not hurt me so much with that delivery, but I was not successful with it, and Baltimore let me go in July 1885.

I joined the Athletics of Philadelphia immediately, only staying there one month. From there I went to Syracuse, where I finished the season of 1885. The Syracuse Club won the International Championship that year. I was fairly successful there. In 1886, I signed up with Toronto, where I remained all season, only with fair success. My arm was getting weaker all the time.

In 1887, I signed up with Savannah, Ga., thinking that the hot south-ern weather might bring my arm around, but that club was short-lived, disbanding on June 1st. My arm was still bad while in Savannah, and Charlie Morton, the manager, tried to make an outfielder out of me, as I was a pretty fair hitter. Whether I would have been a success out there or not I do not know, as I never played any more ball after leaving Savannah. I came back to St. Thomas and layed around a week or two.

On the 1st day of July, Dominion Day, Toronto and Hamilton were playing a double-header, and I thought I would run down to see those two games. There was always bad blood between these teams, and I thought it would be interesting to watch. I went out to the morning game, and when it was time to start, no umpire appeared.

Some of the players knew that I was in the stand and they called for me and wished me to umpire the game. After much deliberation, I con-sented to tackle it. Both sides were satisfied. They asked me if I would work the afternoon game, if the regular umpire was not there. I said, 'Yes.' He did not show up, so I worked it. When the afternoon game was finished, both managers came to me and wanted me to go on as a regular umpire. They said they would get me the job. That night, at ten o'clock, I had a job umpiring.

I got along fine. Our good friend Charlie White, who is living to-day, was my boss – none other than the Charlie White who was president of the International League in those days. I remained with the International

League from 1887 to 1889. Mr. White gave me permission to go to the American Association in 1890 after I had signed up with the International League. Mr. Zack Phelps was president and Mr. Harry Pulliam was secretary of the American Association. I was offered more money in this association and Mr. White kindly let me go there ...

In 1891, I went to the Western League. N.E. Young, president of the National League at that time, also had charge of the umpires in the Western League. It was about the 15th of August, 1891, that I received a wire from Mr. Young, saying: 'When Milwaukee jumps to the American Association, you jump to Cincinnati, in the National League.' Milwaukee 'jumped' and I left for Cincinnati. It was on the 19th of August 1891 that I umpired my first game, and I remained there until I was retired in 1923.

In 1925–6–7 I umpired the Spring games for the Brooklyn Club in Florida. That was the finish of my umpiring career. I took sick in March 1928. Up to this time, I never knew what it was to be sick, but since that time, I have not been so good.

———————— ◆ ————————

Nowhere in the world is spring more eagerly awaited than in the Far North. Three months of total darkness make winter absolute there – but so too is summer, when round-the-clock light takes hold until early August. Spring in the North is more a state of mind than a season – at least by conventional southern standards. The snow on the ground and the temperature reading might indicate otherwise to an untrained eye, but if it's warm enough to get in a few innings, it's spring.

Caribou Hooves and the Midnight Sun

SCOTT FESCHUK

I T IS APRIL AND ON THIS SCHOOL PLAYGROUND, AS ON COUNTLESS OTHERS, children are getting in their first swings of spring. The chatter is as familiar as the sound of ball meeting glove. Pitchers have rubber arms or rubber noses or both, batters are urged to *sa-whing*, fielders encouraged to look alive and get in front of it and turn two. Matters holding even the faintest whiff of scholastic merit are dodged like a sizzling foul ball. Among those waiting to bat, the talk is of the Toronto Blue Jays, their prospects for the new major-league season, which has just begun, and the question of whether Frank Thomas or Ken Griffey Jr. or Barry Bonds should be proclaimed the game's best player.

The conversation stops with the crack of the bat. 'Alomar belts it deep to centre,' the young hitter shouts as he sprints from home. The outfielder looks, turns, begins to run, runs faster, and seems to at least have a chance of nabbing the ball until he stumbles, losing his footing and his momentum and ultimately his temper. After chasing down the ball and returning it to the infield, he marches back toward his position, stopping at the spot where he almost fell. He kicks something in disgust.

'Hoof,' he yells to his team-mates. 'I tripped on a stupid hoof.'

Keeping an eye peeled for stray animal parts – in this case, a discarded hoof from a slain caribou – is just one of the unique challenges of playing baseball in the Far North, in this case Pond Inlet, one of Canada's most remote communities. Lacking the lush outfield grass and well-groomed infields that are part of the sport's romance, and given only a brief summer season during which the game can be played and enjoyed as intended, baseball is nonetheless thriving among the Inuit communities of the Eastern Arctic and indeed in settlements across the Northwest Territories. An indication of its popularity: on this day, the dozen or so elementary-school kids are playing in minus 10–degree weather, on a field covered with snow and ice, with a persistent wind that is making routine pop-ups anything but routine. If this were a major-league city, the players wouldn't even have left for the park on such a day. Days like this are exactly why spring training is not held in Buffalo.

But spring is more a state of mind than a season in Pond Inlet, a hamlet of 1150 – all but a few dozen of whom are Inuit – near the northern tip of Baffin Island, about 700 kilometres north of the Arctic Circle. The thermometer flirts with the zero mark but refuses to make a commitment. In most homes, the radio remains tuned to the CBC, which updates weather in English and Inuktitut as frequently as big-city stations report on rush-hour congestion. At least 1500 kilometres from the closest tree, the only leaves in evidence are those on the Toronto hockey jerseys worn by many residents. While Canadians in the south roll out the patio furniture and gas up the lawnmower, while big leaguers break camp in Florida and Arizona and move north to start another season, there's still plenty of snow on the ground in Pond Inlet, and blizzards remain a concern.

But there too is baseball.

For many, breaking out the bats and gloves has become part of the process of ending the emotional hibernation and physical lethargy that accompany three months of total darkness. Hockey is played pretty much year-round in Pond Inlet and other communities, but it is played in the local arena, and the last place most people want to be when the sun finally returns is inside the arena. In April, the middle of the night brings only a strange, creamy blue, as if the sky can't be bothered to choose between day and night and simply blends the two. In a few weeks the sun will no longer slip below the horizon at all; in fact it won't set again until August – offering more than 4000 consecutive hours of possible playing time, inning after inning of baseball, the timelessness of the game meshing with the timelessness of the sky. There's no need for artificial lights for baseball in the North. Games start in the morning, after dinner, after midnight, whenever; the only way to determine it's a night game is with a watch.

The game itself, of course, remains fundamentally the same in the Arctic, but many of the images and sounds are not. For instance, as a group of teenagers play ball near the steep hill on which much of Pond Inlet is built, a bunch of younger kids are tobogganing nearby, their craft usually slowing to a halt in right-centre field, at which time the game is stopped briefly. A constant howl can be heard from the dog teams that are kept chained nearby on the ice that covers the inlet and will until July. Outfielders must take care to avoid the numerous boulders and animal parts – legs, hooves, antlers, and many unrecognizable chunks – that litter the makeshift playing field. Caribou are a staple of the Inuit diet, and the past winter brought with it a remarkably good hunt; a large herd of caribou passed close to the community (too close for the animals' own good). In this particular game, the head of a caribou serves as third base, making it as much the 'shot corner' as the 'hot corner.' On closer inspection, it becomes apparent that the brain is missing from the skull; some Inuit hunters enjoy eating this delicacy with crackers.

As the game proceeds, as a hard-hit foul bounces off a snowmobile at a nearby house and the frozen ball leaves its calling card on the arm of the daydreaming second baseman, it is impossible to go too long without looking at this area's unique landmark – a massive iceberg, easily the height of Fenway Park's Green Monster, stuck just a few hundred metres from shore. It became lodged there when the inlet froze over in November and provides an odd backdrop to a game synonymous with summer.

Across the North, baseball brings with it special quirks and challenges that might spoil the sport for purists but seem to enhance its appeal to those who reside there. Grass is almost unheard of. The dirt on most fields is mashed-potato thick and difficult to manoeuvre in. The uneven and often rocky infield causes such wild and unpredictable bounces that some parents force their children to wear mouthguards or helmets.

In Iqaluit, the region's major centre located near the southern tip of Baffin Island, it is difficult for players to hear one another on the main ball field, what with passenger jets landing nearby and the hum of generators from the neighbouring industrial area. Outfield collisions are all too common. In Yellowknife at summer's peak, mosquitoes can be so plentiful and so nasty that their victims end up in the hospital. The toughest position on a baseball team is not in the field but in the third-base coach's box, where an inadvertent swipe or scratch or slap could send the team's corpulent catcher on a suicide run to second. For those sitting in the stands, the fielders often appear to be engaging in a bizarre form of calisthenics as they dance and swing in an effort to shoo away the insects. In Rankin Inlet, a hamlet of 1800 on the western coast of Hudson Bay, wind is as much a part of the game as heckling the umpire. To locals, there are only two types of wind: if you're still standing, it's a breeze; otherwise, it's fair to call it a gust. A sudden breeze can turn the scrawniest of hitters into the Babe on steroids; a sustained gust can send a pitcher's ERA ballooning well past his shoe size.

The magnitude of the change in life-style the Inuit of the Eastern Arctic have undergone over the past three decades is difficult to overstate and has much to do with baseball's rise. 'It's hard to pass on our traditions when you're fighting against cartoons and baseball games on TV,' says Josh Idlout, who manages Pond Inlet's only hotel. 'Television is a very powerful opponent.' Mr. Idlout's father, for instance, grew up on the land and hunted for survival, while Mr. Idlout had a very different upbringing in a northern settlement. This created a sizeable generation gap between them. That gap from their parents has grown to Grand Canyon proportions for the current generation of teenagers and those in their early twenties, who have been raised with an array of southern influences beamed to their isolated hamlets by satellite and cable television and shipped in daily by aircraft.

Indeed, with the infusion of television and consumer products from the south, Inuit youngsters tend to model themselves after their contemporaries in major Canadian and U.S. cities rather than their parents, and largely have embraced the culture of the south at the expense of their own. On the school playground, young teens pretend to be the muscle-bound mouthpieces of so-called professional wrestling, hurling insults and elbows at each other. On the community radio, a young woman pleads to borrow a Nintendo video-game controller – her unit broke, she explains, during a furious bid to shatter her brother's high score in Tetris, a popular game. Inside the school, students recap the best lines from the previous evening's sitcoms and recite naughty bits from comedians such as Andrew Dice Clay and Eddie Murphy.

It is largely because of television that baseball has become so popular in the North. Hockey has been available forever on the CBC, and it retains its role as a primary focus of life during winter, but cable and satellite dishes began to arrive in northern settlements at about the same time the Toronto Blue Jays started to play big-league ball with any sort of competence. The Jays are now as ubiquitous on TV as *Cheers* reruns and are as much a part of northern life as they are of southern culture. A generation of Inuit children grew up with Dave Stieb. They have learned the intricacies of baseball from television, learned whom to admire and whom to mock, learned how to arrange their groin area while stepping out of the batter's box and how to kick plenty of dirt when arguing with the umpire. Indeed, not all the lessons would bring a smile to the face of purists. During one game in Pond Inlet, a young teen took a soft pitch in the arm but flopped to the ground as though plunked by Randy Johnson. He got up, brushed the snow from his jersey, and rushed at the pitcher. Others have picked up taunts made popular by Hollywood. It is perhaps a tad surprising to hear the phrase 'Pitcher's got a big butt,' a line from the film *Rookie of the Year*, coming from a tiny Inuk leading off from first base.

Baseball is popular in the North for different reasons than those that explain its success elsewhere on the continent. There is not much interest in the history of the sport in the Arctic, not much talk of past greats or landmark moments. The beauty and purity of baseball is pretty much lost in its translation to the tundra, and the much-ballyhooed symmetry of the game vanishes awfully fast when most games are casual and feature anywhere from four to fourteen fielders. Baseball thrives instead because it represents a celebration of the present. The door to the Arctic summer opens for only a short while, and many enjoy running through it with a glove on one hand and a bat in the other.

---◆---

Until 1949, Newfoundland had only limited contact with mainland Canada. As a British colony, the island enjoyed cricket as its main game at the turn of the century. St. John's historian Paul O'Neill, however, notes that around 1912, 'a sportsman of the time observed that in the old days, when there was one mail a month, it was possible to play cricket, but with daily mail service in St. John's, businessmen could no longer afford to take time off.' Baseball gradually made its way around Newfoundland, a journey consummated in the fall of 1993 when Rob Butler, the son of a man from Butlerville, a Conception Bay community of 200 families, was a member of the Toronto Blue Jays' World Series–winning team.

1913: Newfoundland Baseball Takes Hold

RUSSELL FIELD

ENERAL FELIX DIAZ GAINING THE MASTERY IN MEXICO CITY,' SCREAMED the headline. Beyond the Mexican Revolution, mention was also made of a memorial service to be held at Massey Hall in Toronto for the Scott party that had died in an effort to reach the South Pole. Dr. Wright of Toronto, you see, was a member of the expedition. The newspaper was the St. John's, Newfoundland, *Daily News* and the date was Thursday, February 13, 1913. Elsewhere on the front page, much smaller and in the bottom corner, was an advertisement that announced: 'A General Meeting of the Baseball Clubs will be held this Thursday evening at 8 o'clock, at the office of the Imperial Tobacco Company. At this meeting plans will be made towards putting Baseball on an organized basis and establishing a four-team league.'

The earliest recorded baseball game in Newfoundland took place between local men at the Parade Grounds in St. John's on May 29, 1901. Three years later the sport had gained enough in popularity that it was included in the athletic events at the annual Mount Cashel Garden Party on Saturday, July 23, 1904. Mount Cashel was a St. John's boys' orphanage (whose name now connotes scandal and shame rather than philanthropy) that has since been demolished.

Despite these early beginnings, baseball has only recently come to be associated with Newfoundland (which did not become a part of Canada until 1949) through an odd coincidence. Former Blue Jays reserve out-fielder Rob Butler, though Toronto-born, has his roots in a small New-foundland community outside of Bay Roberts called Butlerville. His return to the island to visit family after the 1993 World Series attracted national media coverage. Butler remains 'a bit of a local hero,' according to Ken Dowe of the provincial baseball association.

Rob Butler's 'fame,' however, has little to do with the history and development of baseball in the province. No Newfoundlander has ever played major-league baseball. Both *Total Baseball* and *The Baseball Encyclopedia* list Jim McKeever, who played briefly in 1884 with Boston of the Union Association, as being from St. John's. McKeever was actually born in Saint John, New Brunswick. In reality, baseball did not become established in Newfoundland until well after McKeever's death in 1897. Already a popular sport in Canada and the United States, the game was played by employees of the colony's foreign-owned businesses. Companies like Imperial Tobacco, the Reid-Nfld Company, and the banks had Canadian- and American-born managers who played baseball informally. But the game did not become organized until that winter of 1913 when the St. John's Amateur Baseball League was formed.

At the meeting on February 13, R.G. Reid (of Reid-Nfld) and J.O. Hawvermale (of Imperial Tobacco) were named president and vice-president of the league. Initially, four squads entered the league: one each of Reid-Nfld, Imperial Tobacco, and bank employees, and a fourth of 'city sports.' But at the end of February, employees of Imperial Tobacco and the city's five banks (Bank of Montreal, Bank of Nova Scotia, Canadian Bank of Commerce, Royal Bank of Canada, and the Government Savings Bank of Newfoundland) announced their intention to compete as one team under the name 'Wanderers.' Employees of Reid-Nfld, a railway company that constructed the trans-insular line across New-foundland at the turn of the century, would be known as the 'Red Lions.' The 'Shamrocks' were composed of 'some West End "fans" and boys from "Merrie England."' A fourth team was added when the Benevolent Irish Society (B.I.S.) decided to enter a nine in the league.

Interest in baseball continued to build throughout the spring of 1913. Practice grounds were obtained for the league teams. Bell Island, Grand Falls, and Bay Roberts expressed interest in joining St. John's in competing in an inter-town series. And, for only ten cents at Dicks & Company of St. John's, the 'Biggest, Brightest, and Best Book and Stationery Store in the City,' local fans could obtain their copy of Spalding's *1913 Baseball Guide*. The appearance of this well-known publication was not the only American baseball influence in this isolated British colony. Bats, balls, and mitts for the league clubs had to be imported from Canada and the States, where the game was already well established.

The Wanderers and Red Lions were the league's more experienced clubs. Made up of Imperial Tobacco, bank, and railway employees who had been transferred to Newfoundland, they had learned the game in their Canadian and American homes. Typical of the early Newfoundland baseball enthusiasts was Timothy Hartnett, player-manager of the Wanderers. Born in 1890 in Brooklyn, New York, Hartnett had come to St. John's in May 1912 as an assistant manager with Imperial Tobacco.

The inexperienced native Newfoundlanders also looked beyond their island for assistance in learning this new game. At the end of May 1913, a group of McGill University engineering students, who were on their way to Bell Island to gain some practical mining experience, defeated a team representing St. John's 22–19 in front of a large group of both curious and interested onlookers.

Before league play began, the b.i.s. Athletic Association announced that their nine, most of whom had never played organized baseball before, were making great strides 'assisted and coached by some members of the society who have played the game abroad.' The s.s. *Stephano*, a passenger ship under Captain Clarke regularly stopped in St. John's en route from New York and Halifax. The b.i.s. baseball team twice played exhibition matches against squads formed from the *Stephano*'s Canadian and American passengers. The July 11th game lasted only one inning before heavy rains forced its cancellation, with the visitors ahead 6–1. Their next match, on July 24th, was called because of darkness with the *Stephano* nine ahead 17–3.

Clearly, the b.i.s. team had a long way to go if it hoped to be competitive. Despite its initial inadequacies as a baseball squad the b.i.s. was (and still is) an interesting group, unique to Newfoundland. The oldest charitable and social organization in Newfoundland, and possibly North America, the Benevolent Irish Society was formed in 1806. Members were Irish or descendants of Irish people, but the society was non-sectarian and its benefactors were selected without regard to religion or country of origin. Besides donations to the elderly and needy, the b.i.s. operated schools and orphanages. As a social group, the society put together dances and theatre productions, as well as fielding a baseball club.

With the addition of the b.i.s. nine, the St. John's Amateur Baseball League had four teams that would play a 12-game schedule (each side meeting the other three teams twice). Games would be played at Stancombe Field on Wednesday afternoons, a commercial half-holiday in St. John's. The eventual league champions would be awarded the Allen Cup. Offered by G.G. Allen of Imperial Tobacco, it was a silver trophy, gold-lined, with an ebony base and suitably inscribed. Each member of the championship team would receive a watch fob from H.E. Spalding Bros., the well-known New York sporting-goods manufacturer. In addition, local tailor Mark Chaplin offered a silk waistcoat to the player who hit the league's first home run.

The league's two most experienced clubs, the Wanderers and Red Lions, opened the schedule on June 11. St. John's Mayor Ellis threw out the ceremonial first pitch before 400 spectators, the threatening weather reducing the crowd to a gathering smaller than expected. The Wanderers, behind the hitting of Tim Hartnett, captured the colony's first organized league game 13–8.

The report of the game in the *Daily News* the next day described the action in terms familiar to the colonists: 'Winning the toss, the Wanderers took the "outs," or as cricketers would say sent the other side in first.' The newspaper, however, was quick to praise this new pastime: 'One point in its favour is that there are no delays, and there is excitement from start to finish.'

For the following Wednesday's contest between the B.I.S. and Shamrock clubs, both newcomers to the game, a scoreboard and players' benches were in place. Attendance for this game between local players swelled to 900 – the location of some fans interfered with play – as the B.I.S. was victorious. A fence, separating fans and the diamond, was installed for the next game at Stancombe Field. At that contest, the league by-laws along with simplified rules of the game were available to fans at five cents a copy. St. John's was a city excited about, but still learning, baseball.

For subsequent games, benches were constructed around the diamond – the Stancombe Field version of a grandstand. Spectators were charged a small admission fee to these seats to help defray league expenses. The benches were crowded with 500 fans on July 2, when the Shamrocks, showing remarkable improvement, lost a close 5–2 decision to the Red Lions. Any optimism on their part was short-lived, as the Wanderers pounded the local boys 41–7 the following week, behind the pitching of the versatile Tim Hartnett. Players, however, came under criticism after this game for smoking on the field during play. Despite this reproach, for the next league game Imperial Tobacco offered 100 Kismet cigarettes to every player who homered and 50 for every two-base hit. No one collected the 100 Kismets, but many Red Lions players left Stancombe Field that day with 50 cigarettes.

The league's two premier clubs, the Wanderers and Red Lions, met on July 23 for the first time since opening day. The Red Lions, led by their star first baseman Arthur Hiltz, book a 6–2 lead into the seventh (and final) inning. Then the Wanderers, aided by two Red Lions throwing errors on potential double-play ground balls, scored 14 runs (eight of them unearned) for a 16–6 victory. Tim Hartnett was again the star for the Wanderers, going 5-for-5 at the plate. After this game, league competition was suspended for a month so that the inter-town series could be played.

Baseball contests between Newfoundland communities had begun a year earlier, in 1912, when a team from Bell Island visited St. John's. In exhibition matches during the spring of 1913, Bell Island continually bested their city counterparts. Their team, composed of employees of the mining operations on the island, entered the inter-town series confident of victory. Grand Falls was a pulp-and-paper town. The Canadian and American managers of the local paper mills were experienced ballplayers, and Grand Falls also expected to field a competitive team. Bay Roberts, home to the Commercial Cable and Direct Cable companies, many of whose employees had played baseball before, was unable to organize a team for 1913, but looked forward to doing so in the future.

The first game of the inter-town series took place on August 2. The St. John's squad was composed entirely of Red Lions and Wanderers players. J.O. Hawvermale, vice-president of the St. John's Amateur League, was the team's manager and Arthur Hiltz of the Red Lions its captain. St. John's defeated the home-town Bell Islanders 37–26, in front of several prominent St. John's citizens who had made the short journey to the 'iron isle.' The rest of the series' games were scheduled to coincide with the visit of the Grand Falls club to St. John's the following week for the annual regatta. On their way, the 'paper men' stopped at Bell Island to play the local team. Grand Falls, with two McGill graduates in their line-up, emerged victorious 9–7 when the home team failed to score after loading the bases with one out in the ninth inning.

After this game, Grand Falls headed to St. John's, where they met the city nine the following day at St. George's Field. The Grand Falls hurler Burg, whose curve ball had baffled Bell Island, mysteriously came down with a cold (perhaps during the victory celebration) and was unable to pitch against St. John's. His replacement could do little right and the home-town side hammered the visitors 44–6 in seven innings.

The remainder of the series' games were to be played between the three teams during the following week in St. John's, but rain forced the cancellation of every game. On August 12, with the paper mills' summer shut-down over, the Grand Falls team was forced to return home. It was decided that Bell Island and St. John's would travel to Grand Falls on September 4th to conclude the series and award the R.G. Reid Cup.

With the delay in the inter-town series, the league hastily resumed play in order to finish the schedule while the weather remained favourable. Play held true to form, with the exception of the first game after the league's hiatus. The Shamrocks defeated the Red Lions, many of whose regular players were out of town, by one run in a five-inning game. The highlight of the contest was the league's first home run, struck by the Shamrock's first baseman Harzent. He was awarded the Chaplin vest, as well as a shirt, collar, tie, and socks offered by the K. and A. store and 500 Gem cigarettes. Surprisingly, two more round-trippers were clouted later that day.

League play finished on September 10, with the Shamrocks defeating the b.i.s. team to clinch third place. First place, as well as the G.G. Allen Cup and Spalding watch fobs, went to the Wanderers, who completed an undefeated six-game schedule. The inter-town series had wrapped up the previous week. Bell Island was unable to travel to Grand Falls and forfeited its two games. The home side and St. John's played two games to determine the colony's dominant baseball team. After splitting the contests, St. John's was declared the winner of the series and was awarded the R.G. Reid Cup. It was left to the *Daily News* to recall baseball's first season in Newfoundland: 'The whole series was a decided success, and we must thank those of our American cousins who were instrumental in introducing the game ... very little was known about the game here except by those who had either played it at college or who had been residents for some time in Canada or the States. Our people, however, with their proverbial intuition caught on quickly and now we have as enthusiastic a bunch of fans as can be found anywhere.'

St. John's league play and the inter-town series survived the Great War, which claimed many of the colony's best men. The local players continued to improve, as witnessed by the b.i.s. league championship in 1917. Newfoundland baseball underwent a resurgence in the 1920s. Men like Tim Hartnett and J.O. Hawvermale, who had championed the game in the early days, were replaced by the likes of John B. Orr and Paddy Grace.

The game's popularity declined during the Second World War, when Shamrock Field, the primary diamond in St. John's, was used as a military camp. Baseball returned in 1947 when St. Pat's Field in St. John's was opened. That year the city's amateur baseball association was founded. Today it operates six-team junior and senior leagues, involving over 1000 players aged ten and older. Inter-city competition also returned, in 1948, when Corner Brook defeated Grand Falls and St. John's to capture the inaugural McCormack Trophy. Baseball in Newfoundland has retained its local character through two wars and entrance into the Dominion of Canada. There is no pretension to anything grander. In keeping with the spirit of 1913, baseball in the province remains focused on healthy competition and enjoyment of the game.

———— ◆ ————

Baseball in Atlantic Canada has swerved throughout its history from periods of commercial success to ones of sharp decline, when its entrepreneurs could no longer afford the cost of imported professionals. In those times of retreat the local game has returned to its sandlot origins in places like the one captured here by David Folster, and has rebuilt its base ... eventually succumbing to the lure of the sleek pay-for-play all-star from out of province, and the cycle begins again. But there can be few more enthusiastic fans than those of New Brunswick. Historian Brian Flood has described a game of the last century in which, 'on game day, thousands left their work to attend the contest. The Saint John streetcar company had to put on a number of extra cars to accommodate the ball crowds ... housewives, doctors, clerks, lumbermen, merchants, and fishermen could be seen sitting in the grandstand or standing along the sidelines.'

The Old Home Team

DAVID FOLSTER

I T IS, I GUESS, A PERSONAL RITE OF SPRING, THIS PANG OF NOSTALGIA I FEEL every year. It comes on subtly, oftentimes prompted only by a few newspaper lines under a Florida dateline; other times, drawn out of memory by a warm sun and the sight of the first pickup game of the year.

My nostalgia is for baseball teams; in fact, what were – when I saw them – the greatest baseball teams that ever played.

They were the teams that played in my hometown of Grand Falls, New Brunswick when I was growing up, and while the intervening years have wised me to the knowledge that they really weren't the greatest teams ever, they still suffer no close rivals in terms of lingering fondness. To be sure, major league ballparks have offered more polished fare; but a major league team is impersonal and remote, and the individual fan, no matter how enraptured, has not an iota of control over its destiny. He's simply a spectator in the truest sense.

Not so with a hometown team, at least not a small town home team. In the small town the lowly fan has status. He's more than a face in the crowd. He's a part-time manager, adviser, ballpark builder, concessionaire, batting practice pitcher, ticket-taker, almost whatever he chooses. In short, he participates.

This was how it was in our town. It all began just after the war. After the grey years the boys were home again, and with time to burn, they'd formed a baseball team. They called it the Cataracts, the Grand Falls Cataracts, but nobody noticed or cared about either the redundancy in name or its possible ambiguity. Having a team was all that mattered and the citizens embraced it warmly.

The Cataracts played their games at 'Vetrans'' Field, more properly known as Veterans' Field, but the only persons who used the middle syllable were some quasi-intellectuals who came to the games from somewhere downriver. It wasn't a particularly decorous ballpark, at least not at first. Oh, the infield was tolerable enough and it did have a pitcher's mound, but in the outfield a combination of long grass and hidden gopher holes made the pursuit of a flyball a steeplechase, and a bushy growth of clover back of third base permitted several low-average hitters the only triples and home runs of their lives.

The truly distinguishing feature, however, was in right-field and right-centre. There, a town roadway composed of gravel hardened to a concrete texture cut smack across, accompanied thirty feet above by electric and telephone lines. Since this circumstance turned up endless possibilities, not the least being electrocution of an outfielder, it obviously demanded a player brave of spirit and keen of eye, and I enjoyed considerable pride that it was my uncle who was regularly selected for the task, never once thinking that a chauvinistic coach might have considered him the most expendable of his nine.

In due course, as interest in the team grew and the crowds got larger, the ballpark was refurbished. Bleachers were built and snowfence stretched round the edge of the outfield. The poles and wires were re-routed to the perimeter of right-field but the roadway had to stay. It was an essential route, the shortest to the town dump.

But aware that, by removing the wires, they'd purged most of the uniqueness from our ballpark, the team enthusiasts now sought other devices to restore a distinguishing mark to it. For one, on the steep hill that rose back of right-field they carved out two tiers for automobiles and suddenly we had a natural drive-in ballpark. For another, they installed a public address system, which by itself wasn't unique but by its use was, because the announcer rarely stopped talking. From the moment he instructed the team onto the field to begin the game ('Any-time you're ready, you can take it away, Cataracts') until he gave the final score, he provided a continual commentary. For example, in addi-tion to telling who was coming to bat he also felt moved to advise his audience what the player was doing even as the play unfolded before their eyes, and further, upon occasion to interject his own brand of humour, such as:

'Adrian Berube sure got down to second base in a hurry on that play. I'd like to see him run that fast carrying the refrigerator he sold me on his back.'

It went over big. It gave our baseball a special flavour.

The Cataracts played against teams from the neighbouring commu-nities in the Saint John Valley and northern Maine, and since the skills of their members approximated those of our players, the games were always close. Aesthetically, probably they wouldn't have pleased purists – pot bellies begun in the pubs of London and nurtured in the cafés of France and rathskellers of Germany did permit some under-the-glove base hits, for example, but the other teams usually had the same problems and so the final decision was reached only after a titanic and crowd-pleasing struggle.

Occasionally the entertainment was provided by opposition slightly more distinguished in the baseball world. One year the bearded House of David team paid a visit and, using their own arc lights, played us a night game. Another year, it was the New England Hoboes, and still another, Birdie Tebbetts' Major League All-Stars.

With visitors like this, it was inevitable that in time we would become more sophisticated in our baseball appreciation. Suddenly we were no longer satisfied with a team that won half its games against the towns and villages in the environs of our valley. Victory on the field is a drug in the bleachers and now we lusted for greater triumphs. We noted that the daily newspapers that came into our area, the Fredericton *Daily Gleaner* and the Saint John *Telegraph Journal*, paid considerable sports page attention to places like Marysville and St. Stephen and Devon and Woodstock, and, being prideful citizens, we wanted a little of that attention for our own team. We decided the only way to get it was to play these braggarts from the south.

So now our baseball development entered a remarkable phase. For once encountering these teams from the farther reaches of the province we found that they were indeed staffed by skilled performers, and, for the Cataracts, victory became a sometime thing.

The solution was obvious. Either we stopped playing these teams or got better ballplayers for ours. Smitten pride wouldn't permit the first course, so soon we were scouring the countryside for mercenaries to put under our colours.

At first we drafted the best from the immediate area, talent like the remarkable Tinker, a gaunt, gnarled pitcher in his late thirties who lumber-jacked from Monday to Saturday, threw nine innings of humming fastballs for us on Sundays, and went back to felling trees on Mondays; and St. Pierre, whose stubby legs, looking like rotors when he ran, gave him the range of a setter in centre-field. Unfortunately, these athletes and others like them were destined for short careers with the Cataracts because soon our opponents fell to the same tricks and then we entered a ferocious spiral, upward for better ballplayers and outward to where they were found. Shortly we reached the very tip of the province – a contingent of five or six was brought in from Saint John for the summer, promised a weekly salary and free bed and board, and instructed that the important things in life were church, country, and the Grand Falls Cataracts, not necessarily in that order.

This band lasted a year, perhaps two. Then we were into the flesh market again, this time south of the border to the United States.

I remember clearly the début of the first American 'imports' upon our grassy stage, even their names. There were two of them, a pitcher named Hugh Riley and a catcher named Joe Lanza, and when the team held its first workout we grouped around the newcomers as though they were captives from the Planet Krypton and now we wanted to see them bend steel and stop bullets with their chests and throw a baseball that left a vapour trail. Sweating profusely, as much from nerves as from work, the two strove hard to impress favourably – and succeeded.

And in the subsequent season Riley and Lanza did indeed turn out to be competent if not superhuman ballplayers, with their presence in the line-up producing bigger crowds and bigger gates. As a result, within a year or two the last of the familiar faces disappeared from our line-up, and when our garrulous announcer said 'Take it away, Cataracts,' the players trotting onto the field were all college boys whose real home-towns were at least 500 miles down U.S. 1.

And now of course talent of this magnitude required a finer showcase. So the town threw cost and caution to the wind and created a temple for the gods. The ballpark was spruced up again, fences built (a community project in which nearly every member of the baseball-mad citizenry drove at least one nail in the wooden perimeter), lights for night baseball added, and a league formed, the Northern New Brunswick–Maine League, a good fast circuit measuring up eventually to Class D standards, with the other members, Houlton and Presque Isle in Maine, Edmundston, and for one year, Fredericton, in New Brunswick, employing talent derived from the same New England sources as our team.

Perhaps now you're visualizing Grand Falls as a bustling little city of 15,000 or 20,000, with a nice healthy industry whose board chairman was so stuck on baseball that each spring he was moved to underwrite the entire operation with one cheque.

Could it be otherwise to support a team of fourteen or fifteen players and a coach, with weekly salaries of sixty and seventy dollars and free bed and board?

Indeed it was.

Grand Falls then had a population of less than 3,000 and the lumbering and potato processing industries it harboured directed their altruism toward treats at the annual Rotary Club Christmas tree rather than college educations for some strangers from New England. No, our teams were buoyed by a combination of packed bleachers and, incongruous though it was, the demon drink. You see, in then-dry New Brunswick the only place a man could legally imbibe outside his own home was in a private licensed club. And what more practical and noble reason could there be for such a home-away-from-home than a 'sporting club' whose profits would keep the hometown team in bats, balls, and ballplayers? It was the total solution. Not only did it adequately subsidize our baseball but it was also a marvellous antidote for the drinking conscience. A fellow could chase almost any guilt with the thought that each shot he downed contributed toward a better double-play combination for the old home team.

So now we reached a new zenith – excellent ballplayers, a fast league, night baseball, and crowds which strained the ballpark to its seams.

From June to September the entire town bounded in a continuous transport of baseball mania.

Smack in the middle of all this excitement were the youngsters of the town. The ballplayers were our idols, seriously challenging even the likes of Hopalong Cassidy, Tim Holt, Gene Autry, Roy Rogers, The Durango Kid, and big league ballplayers for a place on our altar of worship. How many afternoons did we pass sitting in the bleachers doing nothing more than watching the team work out? How many hours did we spend trying to imitate a peculiar distinctive gesture of this ballplayer or that?

As you might imagine, the presence of the ballplayers also attracted interest from the other sex. In the healthy country air of northern New Brunswick, you do not unleash a contingent of fifteen well-muscled young men in a tiny community without attracting tremendous female interest, especially young American men from such exotic places as Springfield and Hartford and Providence. Therefore shortly after the season began each summer a half-dozen or so of the town's comeliest girls could be found at each game, a row of seats behind the Cataracts' dugout, there to root, root, root for the old home team and more particularly for the new boyfriend.

During these years our principal rival on the diamond was our upriver New Brunswick neighbour, Edmundston. Representing the largest community in what its residents like to call the Republic of Madawaska, the Edmunston team, called the Republicans of course, provided the opposition in the greatest baseball struggles I have ever seen. The games were always close, always fraught with drama, always tumultuous. It was the greatest of rivalries. To Cataract fans the Edmundston Republicans were the embodiment of evil and were treated accordingly.

Naturally the main target of our abuse was the most skilled Republican, a shadowy mirthless muscleman named Johnny Catello. With single strokes of his bat Johnny Catello despatched the joy from Grand Falls hearts on more evenings that I still care to remember. He found the right-field dimensions of our ballpark ideally suited to his capabilities and seemed able to drop home runs amongst the tiered automobiles almost at will. We hated him.

The league stayed at its crest three or four years. Then, barely discernible at first, its popularity began to ebb. Attendance dropped a little one year, then a little more the next. Slowly but inexorably the decline continued and moved to the point where the profits of the sporting club could no longer keep the ink black and we all knew it was only a matter of time. Finally one year in the mid-fifties it was all over. Our silent spring had arrived.

There is no difficulty in ascertaining the reasons. The novelty had worn off; and television was sweeping the land, its purple glow luring people like insects to light. What is more difficult to figure is the fact that none of us seemed saddened by the passing. Baseball-mad though we'd been, we were now able to accept the demise with dry eyes.

But now I do miss it, fervently. Several years and several miles removed from Grand Falls, I'd like nothing better than to go to 'Vetrans'' Field again, wedge myself into the jammed bleachers, and give Johnny Catello and the Edmundston Republicans the biggest razzing I could manage. I recognize it wouldn't be quite the same, of course. Maybe you can repeat history and bygone days in general terms but not in their details and certainly not in their psychological effects. Still, I'd like to do it anyway. Therefore, let it be known that, as far as I'm concerned, anytime you're ready again, 'you can take it away, Cataracts!'

◆

Sunday baseball seems innocent enough to us today, but as Robert Fontaine remembered in his autobiography The Happy Time *(1945), attending a ball game around the turn of the century could have a theological dimension. Puritan Ontario was close-minded on the issue of Sunday sport, but Quebec, which followed the liberal practices of the European continent, saw nothing wrong with the pursuit. When Toronto mayor Alan Lamport finally supported a partial repeal of the Sunday baseball ban in his city in the early fifties, he was vilified and voted out of office.*

God Hit a Home Run

ROBERT FONTAINE

LONG AGO WHEN I WAS VERY YOUNG MY MOTHER AND FATHER AND I moved to Canada, to the lovely city of Ottawa.

We settled down in one half of a double house, next door to my several unusual uncles, my grandfather, and my aunt Felice, all of whom spoke, as we did ourselves, a strange language. It was a mixture of corrupt French, literally translated idioms, and, in time, the salt of French-Canadian patois.

There are but few memories of the first years in Ottawa. They are only bright fragments, like the little pieces of colored glass in the small hallway window at the stair landing.

The time, however, that God hit a home run is very clear.

My father played the violin and conducted an orchestra for a two-a-day vaudeville theater, so he had little time for diversion. In what spare moments he had, he turned to baseball. In spite of his sensitive, debonair temperament, he loved the game. It refreshed him, perhaps, because it was so far from his métier.

I remember well how many times he begged my mother to go with him to the twilight games at Strathcona Park. There was just time for him to see a game between the end of the matinée and the beginning of the evening performance.

My mother seemed always too busy.

'I must get the dinner, you know,' she would say, with the faint, calm, resigned, Presbyterian air she often assumed.

'Dinner!' my father would exclaim. 'We will stuff our pockets with apples and cheese.'

'What about the Boy?' my mother would ask.

My father would look at me.

'The Boy is already too fat. Regard him!'

'It is only,' my mother would smile, 'because he has his cheeks full of shortbreads.'

If it was not dinner she had to cook, it was socks she had to darn or blouses she had to make for me, or the kitchen floor she felt the need of shining.

All this made my father quite sad, even though, at each invitation, my mother promised to accompany him 'some other time.' Still, he never abandoned the hope that he would, in time, have the warm joy of explaining the principles of the intricate game to her. I suppose he knew that she was proud of his artistic talents and he wanted her to be pleased with his athletic knowledge, too.

One warm Sunday in the summer, when I was five or six (who can remember precisely those early times of coming-to-life when every week is as a year?), my mind was occupied with the American funny papers and the eccentric doings of one Happy Hooligan, he of the ragged, patched coat and the small tin can on the side of his head.

My father came into the room where my mother was dusting the china on the mantel and shining the golden letters on the sign that proclaimed: *Jesus Christ Is the Unseen Guest in This House.*

There was, by the way, nothing else to do in Ottawa on a Sunday in those days but to dust religious signs and plates on the mantel or to read the papers. All stores were closed. All theaters were closed. There was prohibition, too, as I recall, so there was not even a bar where one could sit and dream. True, one could go across the Inter-Provincial Bridge to Hull, in Quebec province, and return with a secret bottle of wine, but it could not be served in public.

No, Sunday was the Sad Day in Ottawa.

But to return to my father. He spoke to my mother with some hesitation: 'The Boy and I ... we ... we go to a game of baseball.'

My mother turned from the plates and regarded my father coldly.

'On Sunday?' she inquired.

My father ran his finger the length of his nose, a gesture which always indicated an attempt at restraint. Then he removed the band from his cigar as nonchalantly as possible.

'But naturally,' he replied. 'Do I have some other time to go?'

'You can go, as usual, to the twilight games.'

My father bit off the end of his cigar.

'Bah!' he exclaimed. 'Baseball for seven innings only is like dinner without cognac at the end. It is like kissing the woman you love good night by blowing it from your fingers. No. Baseball in the shadows, when the stars are appearing, is not in the true spirit of the game. One must have the bright sun and the green grass.'

My mother looked at my eager, shining face and then looked back at my father.

'What is wrong,' she said, smiling faintly, 'with kissing a woman you love good night by blowing it from your fingers?'

My father put his arm around her and laughed.

'The same thing that is wrong,' he said, 'with making from sour cherries an apple pie.'

'You can't make an apple pie from sour cherries.'

'*Eh bien,* you can't kiss a woman good night this way ... you can only kiss your fingers.'

He touched his lips to the back of my mother's neck.

I coughed impatiently at this dallying. My mind was fastened firmly on baseball.

'Papa,' I said anxiously, 'we go now? Yes?'

'You come with us,' my father said to my mother. 'Eh? We will stuff our pockets with apples and cheese and make a picnic. Red wine, too, perhaps.'

'And an onion,' I said, loving onions.

'Some other time,' my mother said hastily. 'Certainly not on Sunday.'

'Ah!' my father cried. 'Always some other time. Do you promise some time soon?'

'Yes,' my mother replied without much conviction. I suppose the thought of sitting on a hard bench for hours, watching that of which she knew nothing, frightened her. I felt, though, that in time my father's plaintive eagerness would win her over.

'Why,' she questioned, as if to soften the blow, 'do you not ask Uncle Louis or Uncle Felix?'

'Uncle Louis will be full and will chase butterflies across the diamond. Uncle Felix will wish to measure the speed at which the baseball arrives at the catcher. Besides, they are gone up the Gatineau to bring back the Boy's grandfather.'

'Grandpa is coming?' I asked happily.

'Yes. He will stay next door as usual and sleep here.'

I laughed. 'Why is it that Grandpa stays next door and sleeps here?'

My father shrugged.

'When you are old you sleep where you wish.'

My mother was at the window, fixing the small jars of ivy that stood there.

'It looks like a thunderstorm coming,' she said. 'Grandpa and the uncles will get wet. You and the Boy, too, should not go out in a thunderstorm.'

Our entire family was frightened to death of thunderstorms. At the first deep roll in the Laurentian Hills or up the Gatineau we huddled together in one room until the sun broke through, or the stars.

My father spoke bravely, though, on this occasion: 'It will probably follow the river.'

He did not mention the fact that there were three or four rivers it might follow, all of which came, in the end, almost to our back yard.

'Look!' my mother exclaimed, as a white flash lit the horizon's dark clouds.

'Bah!' my father said nervously. 'Heat lightning.'

'To me,' my mother countered solemnly, 'it looks like chain lightning.'

'Chain lightning ... heat lightning ... it is miles away, *n'est-ce pas*? It is not hear, is it?'

'*Maman*,' I begged, 'let us go please, before the storm begins.'

'*Voilà*, a smart boy!' my father said proudly, patting me on the head.

My mother sighed and adjusted the tiebacks of the curtains.

'Very well,' she said sadly, 'but you know what Louis says – he pays too dear a price for the honey who licks it off thorns!'

'Honey ... thorns,' my father repeated, rolling his eyes unhappily. 'It is baseball of which we speak now.'

'All right,' my mother said. 'All right. Only, just be careful. Don't stand under trees or near cows.'

'No,' my father agreed, 'no cows and no trees.'

He kissed my mother gently on the lips, and I naturally understood there would be no further discussion. I put on my best straw sailor, a white hat with the brim curled up and with a black elastic under the chin to keep the bonnet from the fury of any possible gales.

My mother regarded me with sadness, tucking in the string of my blouse. It was as if I were soon to be guillotined.

'It just doesn't seem right,' she said slowly, 'on Sunday.'

My father lit his cigar impatiently.

'We must be going,' he announced hastily. 'The game will commence before we arrive.'

My father took me by the hand. My mother put her arms around me and hugged and kissed me. It was as if I was going away forever to become a monk.

'Be careful,' she said.

'Yes, *Maman*,' I said dutifully.

'And pull up your stockings,' she added.

On the trolley car going up Rideau Street I was happy. The wind blew through the open, summer seats and the sun was not too warm.

It is true I should have been in Sunday school at my mother's Presbyterian church, learning about the Red Sea turning back. Instead, I was on my way to the very brink of hell. For Hull, where my father whispered confidentially we were going, was well known to be a place of sinful living, and the sulphur that drifted daily from the match factories was enough to convince me of the truth of the report.

'Papa,' I asked, 'is it true Hull is wicked?'

'Not in the part where they play baseball,' my father assured me.

A faint flash of lightning startled me a little.

'Papa. I have fear Uncle Louis and Uncle Felix and Grandpa will be struck by lightning.'

My father smiled.

'Louis and Felix are too fast for the lightning.'

'And Grandpa?' I plucked nervously at the tight elastic under my warm chin.

'Grandpa is too close a friend of the Lord to suffer from such things.'

I felt better after this. I reasoned that if the Lord was a friend of Grandpa, then Grandpa would no doubt see that nothing happened to Papa and me.

We changed cars presently and were soon crossing the bridge into Hull and the province of Quebec.

I looked down the dirty, roaring falls that ran the factories.

'No sulphur,' I observed.

'Not on Sunday,' my father said.

This pleased me a great deal. On the one hand, Grandpa and the Lord were good friends. On the other, the Devil did not work on Sunday. I was in a splendid strategic position to deal with Evil.

We descended from the trolley on the main street of Hull.

'We can walk from here,' my father informed me. 'At the theater, they say it is not far out on this street.'

Soon we found ourselves in the midst of hundreds of jabbering French-Canadians, all speaking so quickly and with such laughter and mockery that I could not follow them. The patois, too, was beyond my young understanding. What is more, every other building on the main street of Hull was one of swinging doors from which came the strong smell of ale, making my head dizzy.

'What do they say, Papa? What do they all say so fast?'

My father laughed.

'They say that Hull will beat Ottawa like a hot knife enters the butter! The pitcher of Hull will fan every batter of Ottawa. The batters of Hull will strike the ball every time into the Lachine Rapids, which is many, many miles away. In the end, they say, everybody will become full as a barrel of ale except the people from Ottawa. They will return home crying and drink lime juice and go to bed ashamed.'

I clapped my hands happily at this foolishness which sounded like a fairy tale – the white balls flying by the hundreds, like birds, up the Lachine Rapids.

A man reeled by from a bar as I was pondering the flight of the baseballs. He began to shout loudly. 'Hooray for Ottawa! Hull is full of pea soups. Down with Hull and the pea soups!'

The crowd picked him up and tossed him on high from group to group, laughing all the while, until, at last, he admitted Hull was the fairest city in all Canada and pea soup the most delicious dish.

I laughed joyfully. 'It will be a good game, no?' I asked happily.

'*Mais oui*,' my father chuckled. 'With the Hull and the Ottawa it is like with David and Goliath.'

It had become quite cloudy and dark when we made our way through the grounds to the ancient wooden stand. In the gray distance the lightning continued to dance.

My father patted my head gently. 'Heat lightning,' he said uneasily.

'I know,' I said. In spite of the fact that I knew Grandpa was a friend of the Lord and that the Devil had taken the day off, I nevertheless felt a little nervous. After all, I *had* skipped Sunday school for the first time. And we *were* so far from home!

My attention turned from the storm for a time as the Hull team began field practice amid great roars of approval that drowned out the rumbling thunder. The crowd began to chatter happily and proudly like many birds screaming in our back yard.

'All the world,' I said, 'speaks French here.'

'*Mais oui*,' my father agreed. 'In Hull all the world is French. In Ottawa it is mostly English. That is why there is so much desire to fight with each other.'

'And we,' I asked curiously, 'what do we speak, you and me?'

'Ha!' my father exclaimed, patting my knee, 'that is a problem for the French Academy!'

Since I did not know what the French Academy was, I placed my small chin in my hands and watched the Ottawa team as it came out on the field.

Groans and jeers now filled the air. Bottles, legs of chairs, programs, and bad fruit were thrown on the field like confetti at a wedding.

Two umpires and several groundkeepers cleared away the debris. One of the umpires announced through a megaphone:

'*Mesdames et messieurs*, we are the hosts. They are the guests. They are from Ottawa, but that is not a sin. We cannot always help where we live. It is requested not to throw bottles while the game proceeds as this is not the fair way we shall win. I am born in Hull and also my wife and four children and I am proud of it. But I do my honest duty to make a fair game. God save the King! *Play ball!*'

The game went on evenly and colorlessly for five or six innings. The darkness of the afternoon turned a sulphur yellow and the air became filled with tension.

The rumble of thunder grew louder.

In the seventh inning the Ottawa pitcher singled and stood proudly on first base. The bat boy ran out with a sweater. This is, of course, the custom in the big leagues, so that the pitcher will not expose his arm to possible chills.

To Hull, however, it was a fine opportunity to start something.

'Sissy!' someone shouted.

'Si ... sssssyyyyyyyy!' The crowd made one long sound as if the wind were moaning. Most of them probably did not know what the word meant, but it had a pleasant sound of derision.

The pitcher, O'Ryan, stepped far off first base in an attempt to taunt the Hull pitcher to throw, which he did.

O'Ryan darted back safely, stood arrogantly on the white bag, and carefully thumbed his nose.

The crowd jeered.

O'Ryan removed his cap and bowed from the waist in sarcasm.

Once more bottles, legs of chairs, programs, and overripe fruit came down on the field like hailstones.

Again the umpire picked up his megaphone and spoke.

'*Mes amis,*' he begged, 'they are the guests ... we are the hosts.'

A tomato glanced off the side of his head; a cushion landed in his face. He shrugged his shoulders, brushed himself off, and ordered wearily: 'Play ball!'

The next pitch was hit and it was accompanied by a violent peal of thunder which almost coincided with the crack of the bat.

O'Ryan started for second base and was forced to slide when the Hull second baseman attempted to force him out. The second baseman, with his spiked shoes, jumped on O'Ryan's hand.

The Ottawa pitcher was safe by many seconds, but the crowd shouted insistently: '*Out! Out!*' with such anger that the umpire hesitated but a moment and then waved the astonished and stunned Irishman off the field.

Two thousand French-Canadian noses were instantly thumbed.

O'Ryan stood up dazedly and regarded his maimed hand. He brushed the dust from his uniform and strode quietly to the Ottawa bench. There he picked up several bats, swung them together for a while, and selected his favorite.

He pulled down his cap firmly, walked calmly to second base, and, with only a slight motion, brought the bat down solidly on the head of the Hull second baseman.

This was the signal for a riot. Spectators, umpire, players, peanut vendors – all swarmed across the field in one great pitched battle. In the increasing darkness from the oncoming storm they were as a great swarm of hornets, moving around the diamond.

My father and I, alone, remained seated. We did not speak for a long time.

I began to wish I had gone to Sunday school to have the Red Sea divided, or that I had stayed home with *Maman* and Happy Hooligan. I was coming to believe that Grandpa was not so good a friend of the Lord as he pretended and that if the Devil did not work on Sunday he had assistants who *did*.

My father spoke, at length, with the hollow sound of sin: 'Poor *Maman* would be angry if she knew, eh?'

'*Mais oui,*' I mumbled, fearfully watching the lightning tear the sky.

Papa tried to be calm and to talk lightly.

'Ah, well,' he remarked, 'it is not always so simple, eh, to tell the heat lightning from the chain lightning?'

'*Mais non,*' I muttered.

'Also, in this case, one can see the storm did not follow the river.'

'It followed *us,*' I replied nervously, almost to myself.

'Well, we are safe here, no? We are, thank the good Lord, not in the melee. Here we are safe. When the fight is ended we will go home. Meanwhile we are safe. *N'est-ce pas?*'

'And the storm, Papa?' I queried, pulling my sailor hat down over my head as far as it would go.

'The storm,' my father announced, as thunder sounded so loudly it shook the flimsy stand, 'is mostly wind. It will blow itself away in no time.'

I sighed. I will pray, I told myself. I will ask to be forgiven for going to the city of the Devil on Sunday. I will pray the good Lord forgive me, in the name of my grandfather, for forgetting to attend the opening of the Red Sea, also.

I had but managed to mutter: 'Dear Lord ... ' when the sky, like the Red Sea, divided in two and there was hurled at us a great fiery ball, as if someone in heaven had knocked it our way.

Before I could get my breath, the dry, wooden stand was in flames.

'Dear Lord,' I began again, breathlessly and hastily, 'we are not so bad as all this ... we only ... ' But my father had me by the hand and was dragging me swiftly onto the field.

By this time, the rioters had stopped banging heads and were wistfully watching their beloved stand disappear with the flames.

By the time we arrived home the storm was over and even the rain had stopped. We had been at a restaurant to eat and rest and had recovered a little when we faced *Maman*.

In fact *I* did not feel bad at all. I reasoned that the Lord had not been after my destruction but after the rioters who profaned his Sabbath with fighting. For if the Lord had been after me, He could, in His infinite wisdom, have made the ball come even closer.

'I told you we would have a thunderstorm,' my mother said angrily.

'To me,' my father replied meekly, 'it looked like heat lightning.'

'You know I don't like the Boy out in thunderstorms!'

'Ah, well, he is safe now. Eh, *bibi*? And Louis and Felix and Papa?'

'They are here.'

'Good.'

'A baseball game on Sunday is just not right,' my mother went on, refusing to be deflected from the subject. 'Look how pale and sick-looking you both are!'

My father coughed uneasily.

'Let us call down Grandpa and have some wine and shortbreads. Let us forget the rest. No?' He kissed my mother. She turned to me, relented a bit, and smiled.

'Was it a good game?'

I clapped my hands together excitedly. 'It was wonderful, *Maman*! Everything happened!'

'Wine and shortbreads,' Papa interrupted nervously.

'What do you mean, everything happened?' my mother asked, glancing sidelong at Papa.

'I must go up and see my poor father,' said Papa. 'It is now many months ... '

'One moment,' my mother cautioned. She turned and motioned for me to sit on her knee. My father sank wearily into a chair.

'Well?' my mother urged.

It was too wonderful and exciting to keep!

'*Maman*,' I exclaimed, 'God hit a home run!'

My father groaned. My mother's eyes widened.

'He what?' she asked, pale.

The words came rushing out: 'He hit a home run and He struck the grandstand with His powerful lighting and then the grandstand burned to very small pieces, all of a sudden and this was because everybody was fighting on the Sabbath and ... '

My mother let me down slowly from her knee.

'Is this true?' she said to my father.

My father shrugged and waved his delicate hand helplessly.

'A small fire. The stand in Hull is made of ... '

My mother jumped to her feet.

'*Where*?'

My father lowered his eyes.

'Hull,' he admitted slowly. 'After all, they do not permit baseball on Sunday in Ottawa. If they permit you to breathe it is something. All the world knows that.'

'Hull!' my mother whispered, as if it were a dreadful name. 'Hull! No wonder! To take the Boy from Sunday school to Hull! And on Sunday! Hull!'

'*Maman*,' I said, tears coming into my eyes, 'I will speak to the Lord ...'

'Go,' said my mother, and she sounded like a voice from the heavens, 'and wash your dirty face.'

'*Ma chère*,' my father said, trying to be pleasant, 'does one always know where a storm will travel?'

'You,' my mother ordered, 'go wipe your shoes. Look at the mud you have tracked in!'

As Papa and I went our respective ways, heads bowed, we heard her whisper once more: 'Hull!'

I knew then that she would never go to a baseball game with Papa. The memory of the Lord's home run which so barely missed us would remain, I thought, forever in her mind. She would know one of the places the Lord was going to strike and she would know now that His aim was very good, if not perfect.

———— ◆ ————

Adam Ford's amazing account of a ball game in Beachville, Ontario, on June 4, 1838, is one of the earliest and most detailed on record. It describes a game that bears many similarities to the Americanized forms of English rounders then developing in the New

England states before the game's eventual codification in its present form in New York in the 1840s. Just as amazing, however, and perhaps more so, is the story of Ford himself. Born on a farm in Zorra Township of Oxford County, Ontario, in 1831, Dr. Ford wrote about the game in an account that appeared in the May 5, 1886, edition of The Sporting Life of Philadelphia ('A Game of Long-ago Which Closely Resembled Our Present National Game'). He was by then living in Denver, Colorado, where he had quietly migrated to avoid charges of having poisoned a prominent temperance leader in his office in St. Marys, Ontario. Canada Post commemorated the 150th anniversary of the Beachville game with a stamp in 1988.

A Game of Long-ago (1838)

ADAM FORD

THE 4TH OF JUNE, 1838 WAS A HOLIDAY IN CANADA, FOR THE REBELLION of 1837 had been closed by the victory of the government over the rebels, and the birthday of His Majesty George the Fourth was set apart for general rejoicing. The chief event at the village of Beachville in the County of Oxford, was a baseball match between the Beachville Club and the Zorras, a club hailing from the township of Zorra and North Oxford.

The game was played in a nice smooth pasture field just back of Enoch Burdick's shops; I well remember a company of Scotch volunteers from Zorra halting as they passed the grounds to take a look at the game. I remember seeing Geo. Burdick, Reuben Martin, Adam Karn, Wm. Hutchinson, I. Van Alstine, and, I think, Peter Karn and some others. I remember also that there were in the Zorras 'Old Ned' Dolson, Nathaniel McNames, Abel and John Williams, Harry and Daniel Karn, and, I think, Wm. Ford and William Dodge. Were it not for taking up too much of your valuable space I could give you the names of many others who were there and incidents to confirm the accuracy of the day and the game. The ball was made of double and twisted woolen yarn, a little smaller than the regulation ball of today and covered with good honest calf skin, sewed with waxed ends by Edward McNames, a shoemaker.

The infield was a square, the base lines of which were twenty-four yards long, on which were placed five bags, thus [see figure, p. 115].

The distance from the thrower to the catcher was eighteen yards; the catcher standing three yards behind the home bye. From the home bye, or 'knocker's' stone, to the first bye was six yards. The club (we had bats in cricket but we never used bats in playing base ball) was generally made of the best cedar, blocked out with an ax and finished on a shaving horse with a drawing knife. A Wagon spoke, or any nice straight stick would do.

We fair and unfair balls. A fair ball was one thrown to the knocker at any height between the bend of his knee and the top of his head, near enough to him to be fairly within reach. All others were unfair. The strategic points for the thrower to aim at was to get near his elbow or between his club and his ear. When a man struck at a ball it was a strike, and if a man struck at the ball three times and missed it he was out if the ball was caught every time either on the fly or on the first bound. If he struck at the ball and it was not so caught by the catcher that strike did not count. If a struck ball went anywhere within lines drawn straight back between home and the fourth bye, and between home and the first bye extended into the field the striker had to run. If it went outside of that he could not, and every man on the byes must stay where he was until the ball was in the thrower's hands. Instead of calling foul the call was 'no hit.'

There was no rule to compel a man to strike at the ball except the rule of honor, but a man would be despised and guyed unmercifully if he would not hit at a [...] fair ball [...] he was out if the ball was caught either before it struck the ground or on the first bound. Every struck ball that went within the lines mentioned above was a fair hit, every one outside of them no hit, and what you now call a foul tip was called a tick. A tick and a catch will always fetch was the rule given strikers out on foul tips. The same rule applies to forced runs that we have now. The bases were the lines between the byes and a base runner was out if hit by the ball when he was off of his bye. Three men out and the side out. And both sides out constituted a complete inning. The number of innings to be played was always a matter of agreement, but it was generally 6 to 9 innings, 7 being most frequently played and when no number was agreed upon seven was supposed to be the number. The old plan which Silas Williams and Ned Dolson (these were greyheaded men then) said was the only right way to play ball, for it was the way they used to play when they were boys, was to play away until one side made 18, or 21, and the team getting that number first won the game. A tally, of course, was a run. The tallies were always kept by cutting notches on the edge of a stick when the base runners came in. There was no set number of men to be played on each side, but the sides must

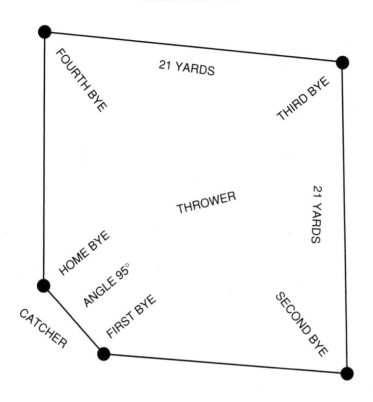

Ford's baseball field (1838)

be equal. The number of men on each side was a matter of agreement when the match was made. I have frequently seen games played with seven men on each side, and I never saw more than 12. They all fetched.

The object in having the first bye so near the home was to get runners on the base lines, so as to have the fun of putting them out or enjoying the mistakes of the fielders when some fleet footed fellow would dodge the ball and come in home. When I got older, I played myself, for the game never died out. I well remember when some fellows down at ʊr near New York got up the game of base ball that had a 'pitcher' and '[...]'s' etc., and was played with a ball hard as a stick. India rubber had come into use, and they put so much into the balls to make them lively that when the ball was tossed to you like a girl playing 'one-old-cat' you could knock it so far that the fielders would be chasing it yet, like dogs hunting sheep, after you had gone clear around and scored your tally. Neil McTaggert, Henry Cruttenden, Gordon Cook, Henry Taylor, James Piper, Almon Burch, Wm. Harrington and others told me of it when I came home from university. We, with 'alot of good fellows more' went out and played it one day. The next day we felt as if we had been on an overland trip to the moon. I could give you pages of incidentals but space forbids. One word as to the prowess in those early days. I heard Silas Williams tell Jonathan Thornton that old Ned Dolson could catch the ball right away from the front of the club if you didn't keep him back so far that he couldn't reach it. I have played from that day to this and I don't intend to quit as long as there is another boy on the ground.

Yours, Dr. Ford

——————— ◆ ———————

American born, Adam Gopnik spent his youth and university years in Montreal, and grew up a fan of the god-like Canadiens and the very human early Expos. Though he has since returned to the States, he retains an abiding affection for each team. His training as an art historian has given him a unique perspective on the grand old game.

Quattrocento Baseball

ADAM GOPNIK

I AM BY VOCATION A STUDENT OF FIFTEENTH-CENTURY ITALIAN ART AND A FAN of the Montreal Expos. It is a mixture of callings that provides more indulgent smiles than raised eyebrows, as though my penchant for wearing my Expos cap, peak backward, to seminars at the Institute of Fine Arts were a kind of sophisticated joke, a put-on – as though I were simply one more pop ironist 'thoroughly bemused by the myths of popular culture,' as Hilton Kramer puts it, 'but differentiated from the mass audience by virtue of [a] consciousness of [his] own taste.' This kind of well-meaning misunderstanding has led me to brood a great deal on the relationship of the one passion to the other, and, more generally, on which I suppose I have to call the aesthetics of sport, and of baseball in particular. I have tried to imagine a pasture on the slopes of Parnassus where Bill Lee plays pepper with Giorgione, and Fra Filippo Lippi calls off Warren Cromartie.

To be sure, it has been submitted by a few nearsighted observers that I admire the Expos precisely because they are *not* like Carpaccio or Sassetta, because they 'provide an outlet' for my need to be attached to something that is neither Catholic nor half a millennium away. It has occurred to others – for example, to my wife, whom I met in a Verrocchio seminar – that I am attracted to the Expos because participation in their cult provides a very close modern equivalent of the kind of communal involvement with spectacle which was so crucial a part of the original experience of fifteenth-century Italian art. My passion for the Expos, she argues, is at heart a way of re-creating an essential piece of the Quattrocento aesthetic – fellowship achieved through a formal object – which the passage of time has replaced with one or another kind of detached and devitalized 'appreciation.' It is a nice theory, and may go a long way toward explaining my early equal passion for the Montreal Canadiens, but I don't think it has much to say about the Expos. In 1981, the Expos won their division and participated in the Championship Series for the first time, and surely, if my wife's theory is correct, this should have been sheer epiphany for me; I should have felt as the people of Siena felt when they marched through the streets with Duccio's 'Maestà.' Yet, while I found that series by turns elating and heartbreaking, I was struck most by how *different*, how disagreeably different, it was from my everyday, high-summer experience of watching the Expos play. By the sixth inning of the final match, my 'involvement' with the destiny of the Expos had become so intense that I no longer took any pleasure in the game. I wanted only a climax, a *result* – my triumph or my doom. It was, in short, sport deprived of anything like a detached aesthetic experience – or anything like the pleasurably removed delight I take in a Carpaccio or a Giorgione – and I sensed, suddenly, that it is precisely the kinship of my normal experience of baseball with my normal experience of Italian painting that has held me, and this suggested, in turn, that there must be some substratum of pure aesthetic experience, divorced from symbolism or civic feeling, that can account for the curious twinning of my obsessions.

There's no shortage of literature on the supposed aesthetic appeal of various sports; most of it involves assimilating the activities of one or another sport to the practice of one or another of the performing arts.

This is the kind of comparison that is accomplished with a few pious references to the athleticism of Villella or the balletic grace of Lynn Swann, say, or with a few lyrical descriptions of acrobatic catches. There's nothing wrong with one kind of creative endeavor imitating the forms and strategies of another – every student of fifteenth-century Italian painting knows that it discovered itself only when it began to aspire to the condition of poetry – but I think it's obvious that playing baseball has nothing to do with dancing. Most of the actions central to the game and expressive of its essence – waiting out a fly ball, making sure of a grounder – are only minimally 'dramatic' or fluid of movement. It is possible to achieve real distinction as a baseball player while attaining grace perhaps only in the most religious sense: one thinks of the earth-bound Woody Fryman, and of Rusty Staub, who hit like a god but ran like a mortal. In football, of course, the spectacular catch is much more to the point. It is also really quite rare, and football fans do indeed seem like fans of the older performing arts in their willingness to put up with hours of deadening boredom and repetition in exchange for one or two epiphanic moments (although even in this they seem to me more like lovers of the opera than like lovers of the dance). That is why the N.F.L. is so well served by its highlight films: 'N.F.L. Week in Review' can include in a half hour everything that was heart-stopping in the previous week's games without altering their essential meaning. The response of organized baseball, the syndicated program called 'This Week in Base-ball,' is inevitably dull and unrealized; the only equivalents the producers can find for the self-contained moments of football lie in the weekly montage of mistakes and curiosities – flubbed catches, rhubarbs with umpires – that can be wrenched from their context without losing whatever meaning it is they have. That is the kind of 'highlight' that Joe Garagiola now takes onto the 'Tonight Show,' too, to everyone's apparent delight, and it suggests the depressing thought that television is now aggressively trying to reduce baseball to the aesthetic of pro football.

'In its special mode of handling its given material, each art may be observed to pass into the condition of some other art,' writes Pater in the most famous passage on aesthetic transferal. Baseball, I believe, aspires to the condition of painting. The blank, affectless description of any particular moment in the game has in common with great painting a certain puzzling first-glance banality. A child sits on the lap of a woman who sits on a rock. A very old man is seen against a neutral background in dim light. A fuzzy black square rests on a fuzzy maroon rectangle against a blood-red background. Now baseball: A man stands, stares, rocks, and throws a ball – almost too quickly to be seen – at a second man. The second actor, frozen in place, lunges at the near-invisible object with a club. Two other men, one dressed in formal clothes, squat and watch them. We see this action repeated, unchanged, again and again. Surely this sounds more like what goes on in a performance space in SoHo on an off night, or like a passage from one of the lesser works of Robert Wilson, than like a public spectacle that could become the national obsession of a restless and impatient people. Baseball can't be grasped by a formalist aesthetic; the appeal of the game can't be understood by an analysis of its moments. As in painting, the expressive effect, the spell, of baseball depends on our understanding of context, of the way what is being made now collects its meaning from what has gone before and what may come next. E.H. Gombrich has championed this view of how the meanings of pictures must be understood – not as a series of acts but as a series of choices within a context, an organized medium. The weight of Giotto becomes apparent only against the weightlessness of Duccio; the humidity of Giorgione becomes apparent only against the clarity of Mantegna. And just as Masaccio comes to alter irrevocably our understanding of Giotto, so each inning alters irrevocably the meaning of every inning that has preceded it: Henry Aaron's first at-bat in 1974, as he approaches Babe Ruth's record, suddenly lends an entirely new meaning, an unlooked-for centrality, to some nearly forgotten Aaron home run back in 1959. The significance of every action in the game depends entirely on its place within a history, on our recognition of it as one possibility, one choice, within a series of alternatives. The batter swings freely, the way the painter paints, but the swing itself is bound about by the ghosts of every other swing.

Just as painting, then, seems able to be better grasped by a historical than by a purely critical imagination, so baseball's most inspired observers are essentially historians, and do their best work at a distance. Baseball inspires reminiscence not because of the sentiment of its devotees but, rather, because the meaning of its forms – of a crucial lapse, a fabled stat – can only be clarified by time. Statistics, like the best kind of art history, are not basically an attendant or peripheral activity. They are the means by which the act become articulate. And in baseball, as in painting, the presence of history – of the weight of tradition – is both bequest and burden. Each game, each season must recapitulate all the cycles of the larger history, from nascent opportunity to exhaustion. Spring is the time of Giotto, where there is an April freshness and the rebirth of miraculous possibility. July is the Quattrocento, where history begins to give shape to that possibility, to set problems without precluding any outcome. August is baroque: the weight of history, of the season's corrosive and insistent patterns, demands an inflation of effects and complicated new forms – shuffled rotations, patched line-ups, gimmicky plays. September is wholly modern: the presence of tradition becomes oppressive and begins to generate anxiety; we turn self-conscious, pray that nerve and daring, the bravura gesture, alone may see us through.

October, my memory and my father remind me, was once both climax and renewal. The World Series celebrated our escape from history, and held out the promise of another spring, as though we could applaud Frank Stella and then begin all over again with the Arena Chapel. Now we escape from the context of the season only to enter the horrible context of prime-time entertainment, as if, just as in much contemporary art, there were nothing left for us at the end but an extended mockery of the same values that our calling once upheld. There was a time, just a few years ago, when the World Series was dominated by the Dodgers and the Yankees. No accident, it seems to me, for these two teams have precisely the kind of smug, sneering hardiness that I associate with much postmodern art and architecture. The Dodgers seem like a Robert Venturi version of a Monticello house: a familiar vernacular form like team spirit, which was once touching in its innocence and good cheer, is transformed by the Dodgers into an effect to be cultivated and exploited. The tastes of the fan, of the gallery-goer, are jeered at and gratified at the same time. The Yankees, too, seem to me to operate by taking an archetypal bit of folklore – the interfering owner meets the prima-donna player – and turning it into something rigged and artificial, mechanical in its self-consciousness. (Think of how natural and funny this trope seemed just a few years ago in Oakland!) Steinbrenner's exploitation of the Yankees' tradition is exactly like Michael Graves' exploitation of classical architectural form: not an imaginative extension but a cynical appropriation. October these days seems to share the central, miserable feature of postmodernism – the displacement of the vernacular into a mode of irony.

Am I so bitter about October because of the continuing failures – once last-minute, now apparently sealed by the third week of the season – of my Expos over the past few years? Perhaps – although the Expos, with their prolific, uncynical energy, did seem to promise precisely the kind of natural, eager, unforced voice that art and baseball alike demand at the moment. Of course, a few turncoat Expos fans have now placed their aesthetic bets on the increasingly successful Toronto Blue Jays. I don't know; the Blue Jays seem to me suspiciously skilled at embodying the virtues of their city: dogged adherence to a goal and the subordination of the individual to a team ethic. I feel about the Torontonians' methodical approach to the pennant more or less the way that the Sienese painters' guild must have felt about the Florentine discovery of linear perspective – that this is precisely the kind of depressing gimmick you would expect from a town like that. The difference between the Expos' André Dawson, who many people came to think was the best player in baseball simply because he *looked* like the best player in baseball (he never really was), and, say, the Blue Jays' Jesse Barfield, is precisely the difference between a Sassetta saint and a Masaccio saint. Their guys are probably a lot closer to the real thing, but ours look more holy.

If I can find any consolation in recent Octobers, it is this: While meaning in baseball depends on context, perhaps only part of that context is provided by public history, by the official chronicle of box scores and All-Star ballots. For each game belongs to a private chronicle, too. Perhaps there is somewhere a fan who sees the Yankees or the Dodgers not in the context of the history of the game but in the context of his own history, whose real unhappiness ennobles their squabbling, and whose rituals (the cap worn just so, the radio placed just so), unknown to them, guarantee their victories. If he exists, then there is hope for rebirth in April after all.

◆

As a prelude to the first World Series game played in Canada in October 1992, Sports Illustrated *magazine provided Canadian writer Alison Gordon with the opportunity to give traditionally under-informed Americans 'a few polite (naturally) pointers' about their neighbours to the north. (Ms Gordon, who covered the Blue Jays for the* Toronto Star *from 1979 to 1983 and has written several baseball mysteries, is the granddaughter of Charles W. Gordon, whose pen name was Ralph Connor – see 'His Second Wind' in this collection.) Under '*B *is for BUNTING' she observes that bunting is 'a very Canadian thing to do,' whereas the home run is American. Well, Bobby Cox and the Atlanta Braves* were *forewarned: a successful sacrifice bunt by slugger Dave Winfield set up the winning run for the Jays in Game 3, while a failed bunt for a hit by Otis*

Nixon in Game 6 ended the Series in favour of Canada's team. We'd like to say, 'Excuse us,' but we won't.

Canada from Eh to Zed

ALISON GORDON

A is for AMERICANS, which all the Blue Jays are, all the ones who aren't from Puerto Rico, Jamaica or the Dominican Republic. There are those who would make a big deal out of this, but we haven't noticed anybody counting how many Atlanta Braves were born in Georgia or, for that matter, have aboriginal blood in their veins.

B is for BUNTING. In the United States, it's red, white and blue. In Canada, it's our favourite offensive weapon. Just ask Jimy Williams (he who learned how to spell his name from Dan Quayle.)

Williams, the Atlanta third base coach is, of course, a former Blue Jay manager. In the winter before taking over as the Jays' skipper, he was trotted around the annual banquet tour to rally the fans. At a dinner in Ottawa, Williams was asked, not for the first time, if he planned to use the bunt more than his predecessor had. 'What is it with you Canadians?' he asked, clearly exasperated. 'You all think the bunt is God Almighty.'

Well, why not? Bunting is a very Canadian thing to do: obedient, modest, self-effacing, efficient, polite. As a baseball tactic, it practically screams out, 'Excuse me.' The home run is American; the bunt is Canadian, and when the bunter is done, he trots politely to the dugout, embarrassed by the applause.

C is for CUSTOMS, which you have to clear before you can come here to watch the World Series. You must have some identification – a passport if possible – but there are no skill-testing questions.

You have to leave your weapons at home if you want to come north. Our gun-control laws are stricter than yours, so handguns are not welcome. This week border guards are probably confiscating tomahawks, too.

D is for DOMINICAN REPUBLIC, the other nation with a significant rooting interest in this Series. Dominican fans figured to be rooting wholeheartedly for the Blue Jays, what with pitching sensation Juan

Guzman being a national hero in the Dominican Republic now, and Manuel Lee and Alfredo Griffin being not far behind. But then, of course, Francisco Cabrera, another Dominican, did his ninth-inning number for the Braves against the Pirates, becoming an instant celebrity and creating some confused loyalties down on the island.

E is for EXCUSE ME, which is what a Canadian says when you step on his foot. Apology is the Canadian way, part of our national inferiority complex.

F is for Jane FONDA, last Friday's 'Sunshine Girl' in the tabloid *Toronto Sun*. On its front page the paper ran a full-colour picture of Mrs. Ted Turner wearing a Blue Jay sweater, holding up her fingers in a victory sign. The *Sun*, known mainly for its pinup photos, right-wing views and bite-sized articles, explained in fine print that the photo had been taken a few years ago, when Ms. Fonda was not yet a baseball wife. Which didn't stop Torontonians from posting it on every fridge door in the city.

F is also for the folks at FITNESS ONTARIO, who lead the exercises that make up the seventh-inning stretch at SkyDome, a quaint custom of which we are sure Ms. Fonda will approve.

G is for Cito GASTON, who has so far brought three division championships and one pennant to Toronto in four seasons as the Blue Jays' manager. And every night on the phone-in shows, someone says he should be fired. Go figure. The players love him because he leaves them alone and lets them do their jobs. The know-all fans hate him because they can't see his wheels turning. That he is also one of only two black managers in baseball is something Canadian fans stopped noticing a long time ago.

H is for HANLAN'S POINT, in Toronto, where Babe Ruth hit his first professional home run. You could look it up. H, therefore, is also for baseball HISTORY, which I bet you didn't think we had.

I is for IGLOOS. There are very few of them in downtown Toronto. Ditto dogsleds, beavers, grizzly bears and moose. How can you tell an American tourist? He's the one who brings skis along for a holiday in July.

J is for Peter JENNINGS. Did you know he's Canadian? So are Paul Anka, Anne Murray, Oscar Peterson, Michael Myers, Alex Trebek,

Robert MacNeil and Donald Sutherland. We may be an alien nation, but we're a bigger part of your culture than you know. Watch out.

K is for KILOMETRES, kilograms, litres and degrees Celsius. It's 100 metres from home plate to the leftfield corner at SkyDome. Like most of the civilized world, Canada is metric, so our measurements may seem a bit strange to you. Don't worry about it. We'll translate. (You may have noticed already that we spell like the British: Devon White labours in centre field.)

L is for LANGUAGES, of which we have two official ones, English and French. Atlanta rightfielder Dave Justice thinks he knows all about it. In a pre-Series interview, he described a visit to Toronto. 'I didn't go walking around much,' he said, 'because if I got lost and I encountered someone speaking French, I knew I had no chance. So I just kind of stayed in my hotel room.'

He needn't have worried. In Toronto he would have been more likely to encounter someone speaking Italian or Portuguese. But American fans should perhaps learn a few French phrases in preparation for next year's all–Canadian World Series, when the Montreal Expos will represent the National League. A strike is a *prise*, an out is a *retrait*, and a home run is a *circuit*.

M is for funny MONEY: Our two-dollar bills are pink, our five-dollar bills are blue, and our 10-dollar bills purple. We haven't got any dollar bills, just coins we call loonies. This is because they have the image of a loon on the flip side of the portrait of Queen Elizabeth, although these days a lot of us think that it's because anyone who believes the dollar has any real worth is ready for the loony bin. Over the years, Blue Jay players have been known to laugh at our money all the way to the bank.

N is for the NETWORKS. Not that we want to point any fingers. That would be rude, and Canadians are never rude, but we wish some of the television commentators in the U.S. would do their homework and get some basic facts right. Excuse me, CBS, but Toronto is on Lake Ontario, not Lake Erie. And CNN, for your information, Duane Ward and Tom Henke are not a 'lefty-righty tandem.' They both pitch from the right side. And very well, too. This kind of thing drives us bonkers.

O is for O CANADA, the Canadian national anthem, never before played at a World Series game until now. It's easier to sing than yours.

O is also for OK BLUE JAYS, the irritating song played during our seventh-inning fitness break.

P is for the PRIME MINISTER, Brian Mulroney, who is in almost as much trouble as your President, and also for the PREMIER of Ontario, Bob Rae. He's a socialist (that's allowed up here) and a real baseball fan. The son of a diplomat, he rooted for the Washington Senators when his family was posted there. He was also Richard Nixon's paper boy, and some analysts assume a connection between the size of the tips Mrs. Nixon gave him with his eventual leftward leanings.

Q is for QUEEN ELIZABETH II, who is the Canadian head of state. There has been some confusion about what will happen when the Blue Jays win the World Series. Will President Bush invite them to the White House? Why should he? They're Canada's team. We think they should be invited to Buckingham Palace. ('Will that be milk or lemon with your tea, Mr. Alomar?')

R is for the ROYAL CANADIAN MOUNTED POLICE. You'll see their scarlet tunics and flat-brimmed hats during the opening ceremonies, but don't expect to see them directing traffic in those getups. The Nelson Eddy paraphernalia is strictly for the tourists.

S is for SEA GULLS, which you won't see inside SkyDome, for which Toronto slugger Dave Winfield is grateful. When the Blue Jays played in Exhibition Stadium on the lakefront, sea gulls were natural outfield hazards. In 1983 Winfield, who was then playing for the Yankees, astonished everyone, including himself, by killing one when he tossed a warmup ball toward the bullpen. He was arrested by an overzealous member of the local constabulary and charged with cruelty to animals.

Whenever Winfield returned to Toronto, sea gulls with long memories gathered in rightfield and dive-bombed him, anxious for vengeance. This year he's mobbed only by adoring fans.

T is for TORONTO, home of the Blue Jays. You may think you've never seen it before, but you probably have, in the movies, masquerading as New York, Chicago or Boston. When it's imitating New

York, however, the moviemakers bring in prop garbage to litter the streets.

U is for UNITY. On Oct. 26 Canadians will be voting in a referendum on national unity. The measure is complex (suffice it to say you vote either Yes or No), but it's sort of like your upcoming election: Each alternative is as distasteful as the other.

Some of the tall foreheads in political office hope that the presence of the Blue Jays in the World Series will make all Canadians feel so warm and fuzzy that we will vote Yes. Others feel that this is wishful thinking and that the Yes Team must be pretty desperate to be looking to the ball diamond for salvation. Still others believe that since the referendum is nonbinding, it's nothing more than an extremely expensive opinion poll and we might as well forget it and enjoy the ball game. You can see why the World Series is a welcome distraction.

V is for Otto VELEZ, an original Blue Bay and part of the small tradition we have scraped together in 16 years in the big leagues. Longtime fans took a moment to remember him and all the others who had the misfortune to be Blue Jays at the wrong time.

W is for the WAR OF 1812. We won. You lost. Nyaah-nyaah.

X is for X-RATED interludes. There haven't been any since May 15, 1990, when an amorous couple in one of the stadium-view hotel rooms at SkyDome found an original way to pass the time during a boring game against the Mariners. After the love-birds were spotted in their window by a killjoy columnist who blew the whistle on them, all guests checking into those rooms have to sign an indemnity agreement not to make whoopee with the curtains open.

Y is for YANKEES, the hatred of whom is the one thing fans in Atlanta and Toronto have in common.

Z is for Z. We pronounce it Zed. You wanna make something of it?

———————◆———————

Zane Grey liked baseball and played it as a child with his brother Romer, who eventually played pro ball in Buffalo around the turn of the century. On one of Buffalo's trips to Guelph, Ontario, to play an exhibition game Romer was amused to hear about a visit to that town back in 1873 by the best team in America, the Boston Red Stockings. He told his brother Zane about the cavalier fashion in which the Boston pros treated the small-town rubes by inserting a lively ball into play that skipped awkwardly over the heads of the poor Guelph fielders. From such happenstance do authors draw their inspiration. Grey was no exception, taking the details of this game played a quarter of a century before his brother's visit and spinning a short story that appeared in the 1915 collection The Red Headed Outfield. *One can only assume that the fur traders Grey mentions were in town for a convention.*

The Winning Ball

ZANE GREY

ONE DAY IN JULY OUR ROCHESTER CLUB, LEADER IN THE EASTERN LEAGUE, had returned to the hotel after winning a double-header from the Syracuse club. For some occult reason there was to be a lay-off next day and then on the following another double-header. These double-headers we hated next to exhibition games. Still a lay-off for twenty-four hours, at that stage of the race, was a Godsend, and we received the news with exclamations of pleasure.

After dinner we were all sitting and smoking comfortably in front of the hotel when our manager, Merritt, came hurriedly out of the lobby. It struck me that he appeared a little flustered.

'Say, you fellars,' he said brusquely. 'Pack your suits and be ready for the bus at seven-thirty.'

For a moment there was a blank, ominous silence, while we assimilated the meaning of his terse speech.

'I've got a good thing on for tomorrow,' continued the manager. 'Sixty per cent gate receipts if we win. That Guelph team is hot stuff, though.'

'Guelph!' exclaimed some of the players suspiciously. 'Where's Guelph?'

'It's in Canada. We'll take the night express an' get there tomorrow in time for the game. An' we'll hev to hustle.'

Upon Merritt then rained a multiplicity of excuses. Gillinger was not well, and ought to have that day's rest. Snead's eyes would profit by a lay-off. Deerfoot Browning was leading the league in base running, and as his legs were all bruised and scraped by sliding, a manager who was not an idiot would have a care of such valuable runmakers for his team. Lake had 'Charley-horse.' Hathaway's arm was sore. Bane's stomach threatened gastritis. Spike Doran's finger needed a chance to heal. I was stale, and the other players, three pitchers, swore their arms should be in the hospital.

'Cut it out!' said Merritt, getting exasperated. 'You'd all lay down on me – now, wouldn't you? Well, listen to this: McDougal pitched today; he doesn't go. Blake works Friday, he doesn't go. But the rest of you puffed-up, high-salaried stiffs pack your grips quick. See? It'll cost any fresh fellar fifty for missin' the train.'

So that was how eleven of the Rochester team found themselves moodily boarding a Pullman *en route* for Buffalo and Canada. We went to bed early and arose late.

Guelph lay somewhere in the interior of Canada, and we did not expect to get there until 1 o'clock.

As it turned out, the train was late; we had to dress hurriedly in the smoking room, pack our citizen clothes in our grips and leave the train to go direct to the ball grounds without time for lunch.

It was a tired, dusty-eyed, peevish crowd of ball players that climbed into a waiting bus at the little station.

We had never heard of Guelph; we did not care anything about Rube baseball teams. Baseball was not play to us; it was the hardest kind of work, and of all things an exhibition game was an abomination.

The Guelph players, strapping lads, met us with every mark of respect and courtesy and escorted us to the field with a brass band that was loud in welcome, if not harmonious in tune.

Some 500 men and boys trotted curiously along with us, for all the world as if the bus were a circus parade cage filled with striped tigers. What a rustic, motley crowd massed about in and on that ball ground. There must have been 10,000.

The audience was strange to us. The Indians, half-breeds, French-Canadians; the huge, hulking, bearded farmers or traders, or trappers, whatever they were, were new to our baseball experience.

The players themselves, however, earned the largest share of our attention. By the time they had practiced a few moments we looked at Merritt and Merritt looked at us.

These long, powerful, big-handed lads evidently did not know the difference between lacrosse and baseball; but they were quick as cats on their feet, and they scooped up the ball in a way wonderful to see. And throw! – it made a professional's heart swell just to see them line the ball across the diamond.

'Lord! what whips these lads have!' exclaimed Merritt. 'Hope we're not up against it. If this team should beat us we wouldn't draw a handful at Toronto. We can't afford to be beaten. Jump around and cinch the game quick. If we get in a bad place, I'll sneak in the "rabbit."'

The 'rabbit' was a baseball similar in appearance to the ordinary league ball; under its horsehide cover, however, it was remarkably different.

An ingenious fan, a friend of Merritt, had removed the covers from a number of league balls and sewed them on rubber balls of his own making. They could not be distinguished from the regular article, not even by an experienced professional – until they were hit. Then! The fact that after every bounce one of these rubber balls bounded swifter and higher had given it the name of the 'rabbit.'

Many a game had the 'rabbit' won for us at critical stages. Of course it was against the rules of the league, and of course every player in the league knew about it; still, when it was judiciously and cleverly brought into a close game, the 'rabbit' would be in play, and very probably over the fence, before the opposing captain could learn of it, let alone appeal to the umpire.

'Fellars, look at that guy who's goin' to pitch,' suddenly spoke up one of the team.

Many as were the country players whom we seasoned and traveled professionals had run across, this twirler outclassed them for remarkable appearance. Moreover, what put an entirely different tinge to our momentary humor was the discovery that he was as wild as a March hare and could throw a ball so fast that it resembled a pea shot from a boy's air gun.

Deerfoot led our batting list, and after the first pitched ball, which he did not see, and the second, which ticked his shirt as it shot past, he turned to us with an expression that made us groan inwardly.

When Deerfoot looked that way it meant the pitcher was dangerous. Deerfoot made no effort to swing at the next ball, and was promptly called out on strikes.

I was second at bat, and went up with some reluctance. I happened to be leading the league in both long distance and safe hitting, and I doted on speed. But having stopped many mean in-shoots with various parts of my anatomy, I was rather squeamish about facing backwoods yaps who had no control.

When I had watched a couple of his pitches, which the umpire called strikes, I gave him credit for as much speed as Rusie. These balls were as straight as a string, singularly without curve, jump, or variation of any kind. I lined the next one so hard at the shortstop that it cracked like a pistol as it struck his hands and whirled him half off his feet. Still he hung to the ball and gave opportunity for the first crash of applause.

'Boys, he's a trifle wild,' I said to my teammates, 'but he has the most beautiful ball to hit you ever saw. I don't believe he uses a curve, and when we once time that speed we'll kill it.'

Next inning, after old man Hathaway had baffled the Canadians with his wide, tantalizing curves, my predictions began to be verified. Snead rapped one high and far to deep right field. To our infinite surprise, however, the right fielder ran with fleetness that made our own Deerfoot seem slow, and he got under the ball and caught it.

Doran sent a sizzling grasscutter down toward left. The lanky third baseman darted over, dived down, and, coming up with the ball, exhibited the power of a throwing arm that made us all green with envy.

Then, when the catcher chased a foul fly somewhere back in the crowd and caught it, we began to take notice.

'Lucky stabs!' said Merritt cheerfully. 'They can't keep that up. We'll drive him to the woods next time.'

But they did keep it up; moreover, they became more brilliant as the game progressed. What with Hathaway's heady pitching we soon disposed of them when at the bat; our turns, however, owing to the wonderful fielding of these backwoodsmen, were also fruitless.

Merritt, with his mind ever on the slice of gate money coming if we won, began to fidget and fume and find fault.

'You're a swell lot of champions, now, ain't you?' he observed between innings.

All baseball players like to bat, and nothing pleases them so much as base hits; on the other hand, nothing is quite so painful as to send out hard liners only to see them caught. And it seemed as if every man on our team connected with that lanky twirler's fast high ball and hit with the force that made the bat spring only to have one of these rubes get his big hands upon it.

Considering that we were in no angelic frame of mind before the game started, and in view of Merritt's persistently increasing ill humor, this failure of ours to hit a ball safely gradually worked us into a kind of frenzy. From indifference we passed to determination, and from that to sheer passionate purpose.

Luck appeared to be turning in the sixth inning. With one out, Lake hit a beauty to right. Doran beat an infield grounder and reached first. Hathaway struck out.

With Browning up and me next, the situation looked rather precarious for the Canadians.

'Say, Deerfoot,' whispered Merritt, 'dump one down the third-base line. He's playin' deep. It's a pipe. Then the bases will be full an' Reddy'll clean up.'

In a stage like that Browning was a man absolutely to depend upon. He placed a slow bunt in the grass toward third and sprinted for first. The third baseman fielded the ball, but, being confused, did not know where to throw it.

'Stick it in your basket,' yelled Merritt, in a delight that showed how hard he was pulling for the gate money, and his beaming smile as he turned to me was inspiring. 'Now, Reddy, it's up to you! I'm not worrying about what's happened so far. I know, with you at bat in a pinch, it's all off!'

Merritt's compliment was pleasing, but it did not augment my purpose, for that already had reached the highest mark. Love of hitting, if no other thing, gave me the thrilling fire to arise to the opportunity. Selecting my light bat, I went up and faced the rustic twirler and softly said things to him.

He delivered the ball, and I could have yelled aloud, so fast, so straight, so true it sped toward me. Then I hit it harder than I had ever hit a ball in my life. The bat sprung, as if it were whalebone. And the ball took a bullet course between center and left. So beautiful a hit was it that I watched as I ran.

Out of the tail of my eye I saw the center fielder running. When I rounded first base I got a good look at this fielder, and though I had seen the greatest outfielders the game ever produced, I never saw one that covered ground so swiftly as he.

On the ball soared, and began to drop; on the fielder sped, and began to disappear over a little hill back of his position. Then he reached up with a long arm and marvelously caught the ball in one hand. He went out of sight as I touched second base, and the heterogeneous crowd knew about a great play to make more noise than a herd of charging buffalo.

In the next half inning our opponents, by clean drives, scored two runs and we in our turn again went out ignominiously. When the first of the eighth came we were desperate and clamored for the 'rabbit.'

'I've sneaked it in,' said Merritt, with a low voice. 'Got it to the umpire on the last passed ball. See, the pitcher's got it now. Boys, it's all off but the fireworks! Now, break loose!'

A peculiarity about the 'rabbit' was the fact that though it felt as light as the regulation league ball it could not be thrown with the same speed and to curve it was an impossibility.

Bane hit the first delivery from our hoosier stumbling block. The ball struck the ground and began to bound toward short. With every bound it went swifter, longer and higher, and it bounced clear over the shortstop's head. Lake chopped one in front of the plate, and it rebounded from the ground straight up so high that both runners were safe before it came down.

Doran hit to the pitcher. The ball caromed his leg, scooted fiendishly at the second baseman, and tried to run up all over him like a tame squirrel. Bases full!

Hathaway got a safe fly over the infield and two runs tallied. The pitcher, in spite of the help of the umpire, could not locate the plate for Balknap, and gave him a base on balls. Bases full again!

Deerfoot slammed a hot liner straight at the second baseman, which, striking squarely in his hands, recoiled as sharply as if it had struck a wall. Doran scored, and still the bases were filled.

The laboring pitcher began to get rattled; he could not find his usual speed; he knew it, but evidently could not account for it.

When I came to bat, indications were not wanting that the Canadian team would soon be up in the air. The long pitcher delivered the 'rabbit,' and got it low down by my knees, which was an unfortunate thing for him. I swung on that one, and trotted round the bases behind the runners while the center and left fielders chased the ball.

Gillinger weighed nearly two hundred pounds, and he got all his weight under the 'rabbit.' It went so high that we could scarcely see it. All the infielders rushed in, and after staggering around, with heads bent back, one of them, the shortstop, managed to get under it. The 'rabbit' bounded forty feet out of his hands!

When Snead's grounder nearly tore the third baseman's leg off; when Bane's hit proved as elusive as a flitting shadow; when Lake's liner knocked the pitcher flat, and Doran's fly leaped high out of the center fielder's glove – then those earnest, simple, country ballplayers realized something was wrong. But they imagined it was in themselves, and after a short spell of rattles, they steadied up and tried harder than ever. The motions they went through trying to stop that jumping jackrabbit of a ball were ludicrous in the extreme.

Finally, through a foul, a short fly, and a scratch hit to first, they retired the side and we went into the field with the score 14 to 2 in our favor.

But Merritt had not found it possible to get the 'rabbit' out of play!

We spent a fatefully anxious few moments squabbling with the umpire and captain over the 'rabbit.' At the idea of letting those herculean railsplitters have a chance to hit the rubber ball we felt our blood run cold.

'But this ball has a rip in it,' blustered Gillinger. He lied atrociously. A microscope could not have discovered as much as a scratch in that smooth leather.

'Sure it has,' supplemented Merritt, in the suave tones of a stage villain. 'We're used to playin' with good balls.'

'Why did you ring this one in on us?' asked the captain. 'We never threw out this ball. We want a chance to hit it.'

That was just the one thing we did not want them to have. But fate played against us.

'Get up on your toes, now an' dust,' said Merritt. 'Take your medicine, you lazy sit-in-front-of-the-hotel stiffs! Think of pay day!'

Not improbably we all entertained the identical thought that old man Hathaway was the last pitcher under the sun calculated to be effective with the 'rabbit.' He never relied on speed; in fact, Merritt often scornfully accused him of being unable to break a pane of glass; he used principally what we called floaters and a change of pace. Both styles were absolutely impractical with the 'rabbit.'

'It's comin' to us, all right, all right!' yelled Deerfoot to me, across the intervening grass. I was of the opinion that it did not take any genius to make Deerfoot's ominous prophecy.

Old man Hathaway gazed at Merritt on the bench as if he wished the manager could hear what he was calling him and then at his fellow-players as if both to warn and beseech them. Then he pitched the 'rabbit.'

Crack!

The big lumbering Canadian rapped the ball at Crab Bane. I did not see it, because it went so fast, but I gathered from Crab's actions that it must have been hit in his direction. At any rate, one of his legs flopped out sidewise as if it had been suddenly jerked, and he fell in a heap. The ball, a veritable 'rabbit' in its wild jumps, headed on for Deerfoot, who contrived to stop it with his knees.

The next batter resembled the first one, and the hit likewise, only it leaped wickedly at Doran and went through his hands as if they had been paper. The third man batted up a very high fly to Gillinger. He clutched at it with his huge shovel hands, but he could not hold it. The way he pounced upon the ball, dug it out of the grass, and hurled it at Hathaway, showed his anger.

Obviously Hathaway had to stop the throw, for he could not get out of the road, and he spoke to his captain in what I knew were no complimentary terms.

Thus began retribution. Those husky lads continued to hammer the 'rabbit' at the infielders, and as it bounced harder at every bounce so they batted harder at every bat.

Another singular feature about the 'rabbit' was the seeming impossibility for professionals to hold it. Their familiarity with it, their understanding of its vagaries and inconsistencies, their mortal dread made fielding it a much more difficult thing than for their opponents.

By way of variety, the lambasting Canadians commenced to lambast a few over the hills and far away, which chased Deerfoot and me until our tongues lolled out.

Every time a run crossed the plate the motley crowd howled, roared, danced and threw up their hats. The members of the batting team pranced up and down the side lines, giving a splendid imitation of cannibals celebrating the occasion of a feast.

Once Snead stooped down to trap the 'rabbit,' and it slipped through his legs, for which his comrades jeered him unmercifully. Then a brawny batter sent up a tremendously high fly between short and third.

'You take it!' yelled Gillinger to Bane.

'You take it!' replied the Crab, and actually walked backward. That ball went a mile high. The sky was hazy, gray, the most perplexing in which to judge a fly ball. An ordinary fly gave trouble enough in the gauging.

Gillinger wandered around under the ball for what seemed an age. It dropped as swiftly as a rocket shoots upward. Gillinger went forward in a circle, then sidestepped, and threw up his broad hands. He misjudged the ball, and it hit him fairly on the head and bounced almost to where Doran stood at second.

Our big captain wilted. Time was called. But Gillinger, when he came to, refused to leave the game and went back to third with a lump on his head as large as a goose egg.

Every one of his teammates was sorry, yet every one howled in glee. To be hit on the head was the unpardonable sin for a professional.

Old man Hathaway gradually lost what little speed he had, and with it his nerve. Every time he pitched the 'rabbit' he dodged. That was about the funniest and strangest thing ever seen on a ball field. Yet it had an element of tragedy.

Hathaway's expert contortions saved his head and body on divers occasions, but presently a low bounder glanced off the grass and manifested an affinity for his leg.

We all knew from the crack and the way the pitcher went down that the 'rabbit' had put him out of the game. The umpire called time, and Merritt came running on the diamond.

'Hard luck, old man,' said the manager. 'That'll make a green and yellow spot all right. Boys, we're still two runs to the good. There's one out, an' we can win yet. Deerfoot, you're as badly crippled as Hathaway. The bench for yours. Hooker will go to center, an' I'll pitch.'

Merritt's idea did not strike us as a bad one. He could pitch, and he always kept his arm in prime condition. We welcomed him into the fray for two reasons – because he might win the game, and because he might be overtaken by the baseball Nemesis.

While Merritt was putting on Hathaway's baseball shoes, some of us endeavoured to get the 'rabbit' away from the umpire, but he was too wise.

Merritt received the innocent-looking ball with a look of mingled disgust and fear, and he summarily ordered us to our positions.

Not far had we gone, however, when we were electrified by the umpire's sharp words:

'Naw! Naw, you don't. I saw you change the ball I gave you fer one in your pocket! Naw! You don't come enny of your American dodges on us! Gimmee thet ball, an' you use the other, or I'll stop the game.'

Wherewith the shrewd umpire took the ball from Merritt's hand and fished the 'rabbit' from his pocket. Our thwarted manager stuttered his wrath. 'Y-you be-be-wh-whiskered y-yap! I'll g-g-give—'

What dire threat he had in mind never materialized, for he became speechless. He glowered upon the cool little umpire, and then turned grandly toward the plate.

It may have been imagination, yet I made sure Merritt seemed to shrink and grow smaller before he pitched a ball. For one thing the plate was uphill from the pitcher's box, and then the fellow standing there loomed up like a hill and swung a bat that would have served as a wagon tongue. No wonder Merritt evinced nervousness. Presently he whirled and delivered the ball.

Bing!

A dark streak and a white puff of dust over second base showed how safe that hit was. By dint of manful body work, Hooker contrived to stop the 'rabbit' in mid-center. Another run scored. Human nature was proof against this temptation, and Merritt's players tendered him manifold congratulations and dissertations.

'Grand, you old skinflint, grand!'

'There was a two-dollar bill stickin' on thet hit. Why didn't you stop it?'

'Say, Merritt, what little brains you've got will presently be ridin' on the "rabbit."'

'You will chase up these exhibition games!'

'Take your medicine now. Ha! Ha! Ha!'

After these merciless taunts, and particularly after the next slashing hit that tied the score, Merritt looked appreciably smaller and humbler.

He threw up another ball, and actually shied as it neared the plate.

The giant who was waiting to slug it evidently thought better of his eagerness as far as that pitch was concerned, for he let it go by.

Merritt got the next ball higher. With a mighty swing, the batsman hit a terrific liner right at the pitcher.

Quick as lightning, Merritt wheeled, and the ball struck him with the sound of two boards brought heavily together with a smack.

Merritt did not fall; he melted to the ground and writhed while the runners scored with more tallies than they needed to win.

What did we care? Justice had been done us, and we were unutterably happy. Crabe Bane stood on his head; Gillinger began a war dance; old man Hathaway hobbled out to the side lines and whooped like an Indian; Snead rolled over and over in the grass. All of use broke out into typical expressions of baseball frenzy, and individual ones illustrating our particular moods.

Merritt got up and made a dive for the ball. With face positively flaming he flung it far beyond the merry crowd, over into a swamp. Then he limped for the bench. Which throw ended the most memorable game ever recorded to the credit of the 'rabbit.'

———— ◆ ————

Many have wondered why a team as talented as the 1979–81 Montreal Expos couldn't win it all. Bill Lee, who pitched for them in those years, confessed in The Wrong Stuff *that he too was baffled by their failure: 'Maybe our stadium was built on top of an Indian graveyard, and we were paying the price for desecrating it.' When the Expos released Lee early in 1982, he spent the summer playing semi-pro ball for Les Sénateurs de Longueuil of the Quebec Senior League. The experience confirmed how much he loved baseball: 'This was the game in its purest form. No agents, no commissioners. Just a bunch of guys hitting, running, throwing, and working up a healthy sweat. Playing without salary, the players in this league showed a professional brand of competitiveness.' (Lee would later ply his trade for the Moncton Mets of the New Brunswick Senior League.) Jane Gross of the* New York Times *caught this unsalaried major leaguer at play one night in Montreal.*

Bill Lee Finds Serenity in the Good Life

JANE GROSS

MONTREAL – ON A SUMMER NIGHT IN PARC PRÉFONTAINE, BILL LEE supervised his children's romp in the grass, cheered his fastball team's unsuccessful rally and mused about the unstructured pleasures of his new life.

'It was a blessing in disguise, really,' said Lee, the left-handed pitcher who was placed on waivers by Montreal Expos on May 9 after an unauthorized departure from the ballpark on the day his friend and teammate, Rodney Scott, had been released.

On Monday night, Lee was a spectator at a fastball game, but on most days recently he has played more than he did in a 12-year career with Boston Red Sox and the Expos – sometimes as many as three games a day as a first baseman or right fielder for several different fastball teams.

Last Wednesday, Lee also joined an amateur baseball team, Les Sénateurs de Longueuil, which plays in the five-team Quebec Senior League. A crowd of 1,000, more than three times the usual turnout, showed up on a raw, rainy evening to watch Lee pitch a 4–0 shutout in which he allowed two hits, struck out nine batters and got two hits himself in seven innings. He plans to play first base in future games when he is not on the mound.

'I enjoy competing at a high level,' Lee said, 'but I enjoy this more. I enjoy being able to play every day and then go have a beer with the guys and have a beer mean something. It's a good life.'

The night before Lee's release from the Expos, club president John McHale thought the 35-year-old pitcher had had one beer too many after leaving the park in protest against Scott's release and spending seven innings at the Brasserie 77, his favorite tavern. By Lee's accounts, he was not drunk but angry. The next morning, when McHale arrived at his office, he found Lee sitting on the floor eating a peanut-butter sandwich.

'The thing I disliked about baseball always was the way they treated people they released,' said Lee, who once walked out on the Red Sox for 24 hours after they sold the contract of his friend Bernie Carbo. This time, Lee was fined $5,000 and then released, but the Expos are paying his salary until the end of the 1982 season.

After his release, Lee, who has a 119-90 lifetime pitching record, got in touch with most of the National League clubs, beginning with Cincinnati Reds, who were last in the Western Division.

'I picked the bottom team to find out where I stood,' said Lee, who chose not to apply in the American League because of his dislike for the designated-hitter rule. He said most clubs didn't even call back, and he is now considering seeking a job in Japan.

'I don't know if they have the DH,' he said, 'but I'm gonna find out.'

The attention generated by Lee's release seems to have made him something of a folk hero in his adopted city, where he lives with his second wife and this summer enjoys the company of his children, 11-year-old Michael, 7-year-old Andy and 5-year-old Caitlan.

His first game in Longueuil was reported on the first page of the Montreal Gazette's sports section, and Claude Bérubé, the president of the Longueuil team, has been fielding many interview requests from out-of-town newspapers.

This week, Lee was hired by CJAD-AM, an English-language radio station, and is doing commentary on baseball in general and the Expos in particular.

'I started telling the truth a long time ago,' Lee said, 'and I had a following of people who believed in me. They won't stop believing in me because I don't play at a higher level.'

Lee's status has apparently distressed his parents more than him. His father warned his son that he would never get an offer without an agent. Lee's reply was, 'Dad, I don't believe in agents.' His mother, Lee said, is 'getting ulcers and stuff.'

His reply to her was 'Relax, relax. I'm having the best spring of my life. The weather's been dry. I have a lot of time to fish and I've got the kids up here and everything.'

Asked what he missed about his life as a professional ballplayer, Lee scratched his greying head. He mentioned the years of walking or jogging through the streets of strange towns on the way to the ballpark when he saw a 'a lot of people, a lot of car graveyards.' He mentioned 'the spontaneous stuff,' like playing winter ball in Puerto Rico with his friend Allen Ripley, who now plays for the Chicago Cubs, and 'shooting pool at 4 o'clock in the morning.'

Lee interrupted his rambling conversation to applaud a triple by a teammate and to tend to his children. He helped his daughter collect buds from a rosehip bush and directed his son to touch a pressure point at the base of his thumb to ward off a headache.

Then, surveying the floodlit field and the children playing in the fragrant grass, Lee fantasized about forming a league for older players who would 'travel around with their kids, play and have picnics.'

'All the nights,' Lee said, 'would be like this.'

——————— ◆ ———————

Great athletes, in any sport, seem to touch on a mythic dimension of the human spirit, where our embodied existence stretches to the limits of its gifts. That's one reason for our worship, despite their often vain immaturity, of sports heroes. It's also why some of us continue to dream impossible dreams: 'If only I had the time and the means ...' Hugh Hood gives us a parable about the range and limits of the human will, cast in the form of a wannabe big leaguer.

The Pitcher

HUGH HOOD

Il n'y a pas de mystère dans la création humaine. La volonté fait ce miracle. Mais du moins, il n'est pas de vraie création sans secret.

Camus, *La Création absurde*

THERE WAS ONCE A TIRED BUSINESSMAN LIKE YOU OR ME OR SHERWOOD Anderson, a bachelor verging on middle age, fat, flabby and 37, who suddenly received word one sunny showery blue and white April afternoon that an elderly relative had died in Australia, bequeathing him an immense legacy.

Hod Gantenbein, for that was his name, had read somewhere and remembered that the truly vicious man, stepping on an ant, hopes it hurts. The observation had so impressed him that he would tread on no living thing on the sidewalk; when he saw small green caterpillars struggling on the cement he lifted them tenderly and put them in the grass, where they might survive. He made an exception of the common *musca domestica*, that germ-carrier and breeder of disease, but even these he merely shooed out of his house with a rolled-up newspaper, rather than do them bodily harm.

When he heard of his aunt's death he was at first reluctant to receive his inheritance, on the grounds that the money was infected by the dear old lady's pain. Only a series of cablegrams between Hartford and Melbourne, which established that his Aunt Grace had died peacefully in her sleep, full of years and in the certitude of a glorious resurrection, had persuaded him to accept his property. As a general rule he was opposed to inheritance, holding that death is painful, and that it is the condition of testament. He would scorn, he declared, he would scorn to profit by another's agony.

In the middle of May the money arrived in America in the form of a draft on The Corn and Fleece Bank and Trust of Victoria and New South Wales in the amount of $200,000, a sum which Gantenbein calculated would just serve his burgeoning purposes, permitting him the five free years necessary for the project he had in mind, an imagining of which he had long despaired, but which he was now enabled to realize. And though he was a responsible citizen, holding a responsible post as the director and programmer of a fleet of punch-card machines in the Hartford home offices of Monolithic Life, he gave up his job at once, not like a foolish sweepstakes winner, intoxicated by good fortune and bereft of good judgment, but like one who sees looming before him his very last chance to enact his dearest fantasy.

So transparent were his motives that his employers indulged him. They refused to accept his resignation and told him instead that he might have as much leave as he liked, to get it out of his system, but they weren't going to let him quit, no sir, he was too valuable a man to lose.

'It will take five years,' he said, trying to be fair, 'I'm allowing myself five years, and if it doesn't work out, I'll come back at the end of that time. I wish you'd let me quit.'

'No!'

'I can't quit? Not at all?'

'Never! Take all the time you want.'

There was something about this insistence that inwardly bothered him; but he thought it wise not to think about it too much. What must he do, he wondered, to persuade them to release him? Apparently sudden riches were not enough; sickness wouldn't do it, for the company had paid all the expenses of employees who had been invalid for decades. Old age and death, he decided, would get a man out of Monolithic, and perhaps abandoned vice, but about the last he was not certain – they would call it sickness.

His money safely on deposit, he left town and motored to a health farm in upstate New York, 40 miles southwest of Plattsburgh. This curious establishment was the property of the ex–lightweight champion Gummy Broomstein, an almost legendary figure of the ring, who could stand on a handkerchief and let you swing at him all day without getting hit. That is, he could have done it 40 years ago; now when he tried it tired businessmen punched the hell out of him.

Gummy couldn't stop trying this trick though. He would spread the handkerchief carefully on the grass, stand on it, and say thickly: 'Try and hit me, go ahead, try and hit me,' bobbing and weaving all the time and keeping his hands at his sides. Then somebody would paste him one on the side of the head, and he would step off the handkerchief, looking down at it reproachfully.

'Caught me cold,' he would mumble, 'a sneak punch.'

Gummy was glad to welcome Hod Gantenbein, a new and wealthy client who had announced by letter his intention of staying at the farm for as long as a year, if it were necessary, and really getting into shape, *really*.

'Can a man of 37 *really* get into shape?' said Hod to Gummy, when they met at the gate.

'Fitzsimmons held the title when he was 40,' said Gummy, 'and look at Archie Moore. Look at Walcott.'

'Marciano stopped Walcott in a minute 40 seconds.'

'Yeah, but the thing is you had a man of 40 in there with the champion, I mean, that's unusual.'

'I don't want to box, though,' said Hod, reflectively.

'Why do you want to get in shape?'

'I intend to become a pitcher.' said Hod, whose imagination had been nurtured on *Lefty Locke of the Blue Stockings* and other Saalfeld publications of the early 1900s. He thought perpetually of the horsehide, the rubber, the initial and keystone sacks, the hot corner, the outer gardens, and his imaginative life seemed to have been checked somewhere about the end of the Christy Mathewson era.

'Well, Jeeze,' said Gummy, 'a pitcher uses all the wrong muscles.'

'Wrong for boxing, you mean, but I want to pitch.'

'How long have you got?'

'I intend to spend a year on this phase.'

'In a year I can get you ready to go fifteen rounds.'

'But can you get me ready to go nine innings?'

'Yes, I can do that too. But you'll be using *all* the wrong muscles.'

'Never mind,' said Hod, 'it's what I want to do.'

'Then I'll see you at 6.30 tomorrow,' said Gummy as he showed him to his room, 'and remember, from now on no alcohol and no tobacco, and a balanced diet which I'll draft when I've had a look at you.'

Tired from the variety of new sounds and sensations, Hod went to bed early, setting his alarm for six. He had been accustomed to rise at eight, and was looking forward to seeing a sunrise or two, feeling obscurely that the experience would ennoble him, make him a better man. It never did, of course, but then he was pretty good to start with.

Next morning after a breakfast of eggs, bacon, buttered toast and plenty of strong tea, Gummy led Hod to the gymnasium, where he meant to look him over.

'I warn you,' said Hod, 'I'm as far out of condition as possible. I've been sitting down for the last twenty years.' He put on the shorts and t-shirt and track shoes that Gummy handed him, and fidgeted embarrassedly while the trainer assessed him.

'Boy!' said Gummy. He walked around and around Hod. 'Boy!'

'Awful, isn't it?'

'You weigh around 195, right?'

'Dead on.'

'You'll lose 40, 50, pounds of that in the next two months. You're just carrying around a load of fat, no wonder all you guys have heart attacks. Look at you, look at that stomach!' He prodded Hod disgustedly. 'After we get you down around 150 you'll start to get some muscle tone, and then you'll gain. But it'll be muscle, not fat. You're around six feet tall, so you should weigh, with your bones, around 178. We're going to take it off your stomach and your ass and put it on your shoulders and chest, *and* we're going to build up your legs. If you're going to be a pitcher you've got to have the legs, and yours are like a girl's. If you did twenty knee bends, you'd have a case of jag legs.'

'How do we start?'

'We run. That is, you run.' He pointed. 'Eleven times around the track is a mile. Get up there and go a mile. Sprint the last two laps and I'll time you.'

When Hod had jogged nine laps, he couldn't sprint, so he walked the last two, and Gummy timed him in eleven minutes, 42 and seven-tenths seconds. His legs felt like spaghetti stalks and he collapsed gasping on a bench. He could taste every cigarette he'd ever smoked.

'The record for the mile is 3:54,' said Gummy coldly, 'you've got a long way to go.'

'What do we do now?' demanded Hod, tottering to his feet.

'We run some more. That is, you do.'

So for weeks he ran and ran and ran. He ran against a stop-watch in the gym. He did wind sprints for hours on the back lot, a hundred feet and stop, hours and hours. He did roadwork in the country with Gummy pacing him on a bicycle, uphill and down, he ran and ran and ran, and his wind and vision improved and his head cleared; he began to taste his food, he forgot about cigarettes, and his time for the mile came down. When he wasn't running he was doing pushups and situps and knee bends and chinning himself and throwing the medicine ball and playing squash and following a high protein diet and he began to notice some changes.

Like what? Well he didn't feel like himself any more. A man goes along for the first half of his life feeling the way most of us do, you and me and Sherwood, and he comes to believe that being human logically implies the constant faint headache, the slightly out of focus eyes, the shitty taste in the mouth, the sour stomach and the unending dosages of antacids, dandruff removers, deodorants, laxatives, breath sweeteners, and all this while he silently hates his body and mistreats it, this albatross around his oh so spiritual neck, for inflicting life on him, sleeps poorly, eats like a fool, and gives himself no chance.

Hod meant to give himself this latest of chances, and it made all the difference. Whereas he used to have troubling dreams, waking every morning with an erection and wounded sexual feelings, now he slept like the dead and was no longer tormented by desire and guilt, and he understood why Gummy and Charley and Whitey and most of the other old trainers bar wives from fight camps. It isn't done out of latent homosexuality, as he'd always naïvely supposed; it's simply that the question of women ceases to come up. There is a time for everything. Full genitality (that genial *summum bonum* of the 1960s) is not the sole end and purpose of human life. Insert the phrase in one of the old songs and it becomes absurd:

Sweet personality,
Full genitality,
That's Peggy O'Neill.

He got his time for the mile down around five minutes, and then into the fours. His heart stopped pounding and his lungs stopped burning when he went a fast mile. He would never do it in 3:54, and wouldn't have to; he didn't have the reflexes and the lung capacity of a great miler, but he pushed closer every day to the absolute outside limit that his particular body, legs just this length, rib cage this size, might at last achieve.

Then Gummy put him on a pattern of calisthenics to develop his muscle tone, working on each part of the body in turn, the shoulders and arms, the neck, abdomen, legs, joints, his weight began to move up again and finally hovered around 175 until it was evident that he was a natural light-heavyweight and would never weigh more than 178 as long as he stayed in shape. They began to spar a couple of rounds at a time and Hod at once discovered that he might be physically perfect, medically, and still be unable to box more than a single three-minute round at a time.

'When you can go fifteen fast rounds, shadow-box for an hour, work on the bags for another two hours, run ten miles, and finish with 50 lengths in the pool,' said Gummy, 'you can start throwing a ball because you'll be ready.'

'And when I'm learning to pitch I'll have to do all these things besides?'

'Sure. For an athlete you're an old man. I doubt we can bring your reflexes up to the point where you can play pro ball.'

'Yes we can,' said Hod stoutly, for he was very determined.

'The only edge you'll have on the kids will be condition. You'll outrun them and outwork them. But they'll have skills that you don't have.'

'I'll get the skills,' said Hod, 'I'll spend the next year on that.'

In the spring, when he had completed phase one of his design, he started combing *The Sporting News* for the names of out-of-work catchers. He compiled a list of six names, men who had been released in spring training. Then he sent them individual letters offering a year's employment at their last major-league salary and he received two replies, one from Joe Fritz, a cagey ten-year veteran of the majors whose throwing arm had finally gone, and the other from Luther Hollings, a promising rookie cut by the Gold Sox who had gone home in disgust.

Hod thought it would be better to work with an experienced major-leaguer, so he sent young Hollings a polite letter and a cheque for his trouble; but to Joe Fritz he sent an urgent wire, and a cheque for expenses and one month's salary. Three days later the veteran receiver appeared at the farm, a stumpy-legged man with a gnarled black face and fingers like bananas. Together Gummy and Hod explained the project, and Joe could scarcely believe his ears.

'You want to make a ballplayer out of this fellow? Has he ever played?'

'I played in high school,' said Hod, 'and it's unbelievable what you can do, if you work hard enough.'

'He's in terrific shape,' said Gummy proudly.

'I can see that,' said Joe, 'the way he can run. But you have to know the game. Can he throw at all?'

'My arm has never been used,' said Hod, 'literally. There ought to be a lot of spring in it.'

'We'll see,' said Joe, 'and you say you've got a year to work?'

'I plan to report to some training camp next spring.'

'And you're 38?'

'Warren Spahn is 40.'

'But he's one of the five greatest pitchers in history.'

'If he can pitch in the majors at 40,' pursued Hod inexorably, 'so can I.'

Joe Fritz was astonished at Hod's attitude and determination but didn't believe the thing could be done. 'I can maybe teach you enough to hang on in Class D for a month or two,' he decided, 'but you'll have to satisfied with that.'

'We'll see,' said Hod, and he led the old catcher to an improvised diamond on the back lot, where he began to throw. His arm felt strong and good.

'Is that the hardest you can throw?' asked Joe cynically.

'It is today,' said Hod, 'but it won't be next year. I've got to teach myself to get my body into the pitch. I weigh 178 and I ought to be able to get enough leverage to throw fast.'

'Right now you throw like José Morales,' said Joe glumly, 'still, it's your money. Tell you what, if you get so you can do anything at all, we'll play some semi-pro ball the end of the summer.' They began to work in earnest. First Joe had his pupil throw and throw without putting anything on the ball, to develop a smooth motion and get the necessary leverage. Gummy took movies of Hod, and the three men studied them after supper until bedtime. The ball began to buzz over the plate.

'Say,' said the catcher one morning after they'd been working together for two months, 'say, that ball took off, it had some hop on it.' He began to show real interest in the project for the first time. 'Right now you're sneaky fast, not real fast but faster than you look. But you'll have to be really fast, because we haven't time to give you another pitch.'

'Yes we have,' said Hod, 'I want a change of pace and a curve. Next year I'll pick up a slider, but I want the three basic pitches straight off, so I'll have a chance to stick.'

'Come on, then,' said Joe, 'hum that seed in there. Sneaky fast won't get you anywhere.' They threw and threw. They hammered together wooden frames of differing dimensions and erected these in front of the plate for Hod to throw at.

'This here is the strike zone that Minnie Minoso gives you,' said Joe, planting one of these frames in the ground, 'let's see how you'd pitch him.' In August Hod was working on control, pitching to the inch and a half of space that borders the strike zone, resolved that like his heroes Matthewson and Spahn he would never throw one down the pipe, an act he considered as immoral as stepping on a bug.

'You can control the straight pitch,' said Joe, one day late in August, 'and you've got a lot on it, the fast ball takes off. Maybe we better concentrate on that for the rest of the year.'

'I'll never make the majors with one pitch.'

'I dunno, you might fool them all for one swing around the league. You might win a few at the end of a season.' They were thinking about the same thing: spring him on the league at the end of a hot pennant race.

'Like Duren did, that one year,' said Hod.

'Yeah, or Joe Page or Wilcy Moore, you're good for one season maybe. We better throw you at somebody in semi-pro.' Using his extensive contacts, the old catcher arranged an appearance for them as a battery with a club playing out of Oneonta, N.Y. They drove over one Friday in early September, and next afternoon Hod shut out the opposition on two hits, striking out nineteen, throwing nothing but fast balls.

'Could he do that again?' asked the manager of the Oneonta team.

'Maybe once more with that club,' said Joe dourly, 'but he doesn't know how to mix them up, he needs another pitch.' From September through Christmas the two men, now equally dedicated to the grand purpose, worked ten hours a day on a change of pace thrown with the same motion as the fast ball, and when they had it perfected they began to develop a rudimentary curve. Toward the end of the second phase of the project Hod could throw three pitches with the identical sweeping three-quarters arm motion. He had a naturally smooth beautiful delivery, which is something not all pitchers have and which can't be acquired artificially.

'Lordy, Lordy,' said Joe Fritz, one afternoon in February, 'I wish we had another year to teach you a motion to first, and when to come in with the first pitch.'

'No time,' said Hod succinctly, 'I've got to get into pro ball this season. You've got to get me a job.'

Joe wrote letters to all his friends who were managing in the minors. Most of them showed no interest but at length Yancey Hooker, the old flychaser, now managing the Lancaster Groundhogs, agreed to give Hod a look-see, provided that he paid his own training camp expenses. Hod and Joe drove down to Lancaster, reported in at the front office, and then proceeded to the camp, at Hudson, Fla.

'Yancey Hooker, you crooked old buzzard,' said Joe excitedly when he spied the manager, 'I haven't seen you since we played together at Terre Haute in the Three I League, twenty years ago.'

'Yeah, never mind that,' said Hooker sourly, 'what about this boy Gantenbein, has he got anything?'

'Wait'll you see him,' said Joe.

Hod pitched batting practice the first week of the camp, during which Manager Hooker began to realize that this odd poised determined 39-year-old rookie might indeed have something. At the beginning of the second week he started Hod in an intra-squad game.

Out there on the hill, Hod was nervous as he took his warm-up pitches, wondering whether to come in there with the first pitch. His catcher called for the fast ball low on the outside corner, and Hod remembered that nobody these days ever, ever, delivers the ball high. He delivered the ball where it was called for and the batter drove a sharp liner back through the box. Instinctively Hod stuck up his glove to protect himself and the ball lodged in the pocket, stinging his palm, for the first out. He went three innings and didn't allow a hit, striking out five. In the third inning he came off the mound to his right and fielded a bunt perfectly, easily beating the runner with his throw, and after his stint was over he overheard Manager Hooker talking excitedly to the lone Lancaster reporter who was travelling with the Groundhogs.

'This fellow Gantenbein is going to help the club,' said the grizzled pilot with enthusiasm, 'he fields his position like a cat out there, just like a cat. Reminds me of Harry Brecheen.'

'Or Bobby Shantz,' said the reporter knowledgeably.

'No,' said Hooker, 'Shantz is just a little guy.'

'Where did Gantenbein pitch last year?' asked the reporter skeptically.

'Ganty?' said Hooker vaguely, 'he struck out everybody he faced in semi-pro ball last year, up in New York somewhere.' This was partly true, as we know.

'Ganty,' for the nickname was to cling, had no book on the hitters, but equally they had none on him. By the middle of July at the All Star break, six major-league scouts were following the club. Hod had won seventeen and lost one, and his ERA was the lowest in baseball, a startling 0.83. His contract belonged to the Lancaster club of course, and after spirited bidding for his services they sold him to the New York Toads organization. The Toads shipped him immediately to their Denver farm club where he won six in a row through August, giving him a record of 23 wins and no losses on the season. On the last day before he would be ineligible for a Series appearance the Toads called him up to the parent club to help out in the stretch drive; they were nursing a two-and-a-half game lead and faced a series with the second-place Detroit Bombs with their pitching in disarray. When Hod reported in the dressing-room, the Toads' famous old skipper Grumpy Hazebrouck took him into his office alone, to have a look at him.

'So you're "Ganty," my goodness,' said Grumpy, looking at the pitcher's face, deeply tanned and wrinkled from his summer in the sun, 'you mean to tell me you're a rookie? How old are you anyway?'

'39.'

'That's too old.'

'Warren Spahn is 41,' said Hod automatically, for he'd been repeating it to himself all year.

'By criminy,' said Grumpy, 'I may have to use you this weekend and I hope you can pitch as good as you talk.'

'I can,' said Hod, and the manager made a gesture of dismissal.

Little now remains to be told: of how Hod saved four games in a row in relief, brushing the hitters back and throwing them offstride with a judicious mixture of his four pitches – he'd picked up a slider during his summer in the minors; how in the waning days of the season he started and went the route for the win three times, finishing the season with a record of five and nothing and an ERA of 1.06; how in the Series he came on in the first game with the bases loaded and shut out the opposition for six innings, how in the fourth game he saved the win for plucky little Ernest Beecham, and how he started and won in eleven innings in the seventh game, covering himself with glory, and how, astonishingly, his Toad teammates voted him a full share in the Series money, and how at last, ten days after the season was over, on his fortieth birthday, he announced his retirement from baseball.

At the loss of 'Ganty' the world of sport was thunderstruck. At a hastily-assembled press conference at the Plaza, Hod stood composedly with Gummy and Joe on either side of him, while reporters from 500 dailies beseiged him with questions.

'We know all about you, Ganty,' chorused the scribes, 'how you suddenly quit your job three years ago to take up the diamond sport. Everybody in Hartford, and in the whole country, is talking about what you've done. It's a great triumph of human aspiration. But what are you going to do now?'

'Well,' said Hod slowly, 'I've got a lot of money and over two years left. I thought it would take five, and it only took half the time. I was out two and a half years in my reckoning.' He seemed annoyed at his error.

'Yes, but what will you do?'

'I don't know,' he said, 'I may do some big-game hunting.'

'And can you tell us as an inspiration to American youth what made you attempt this thing?'

'Of course,' said Hod simply, politely, and it was to be his last public word, 'I just wanted to see if it could be done.'

◆

Unlike Elvis's ghostly, unannounced appearances at 7 Elevens and shopping-mall openings, Babe Ruth's visits to Canada occurred during his lifetime. Moose Jaw, Vancouver, and the Guybourg Grounds in Montreal were just a few of the unlikely places he appeared. Most of all, however, Ruth enjoyed coming to Nova Scotia. Colin Howell sheds new light on the Bambino's attachment to Canada. To others he may have been the Sultan of Swat or the Behemoth of Blast. To Canadians he just may be the Canuck of Clout.

The Man Who Taught the Bambino

COLIN HOWELL

O N AUGUST 1, 1942, TWO YOUNG BOYS STOOD OUTSIDE THE CAPITOL Theatre in Halifax, waiting patiently for the Saturday matinée. The theatre marquee announced the day's feature film, *Wings for the Eagle*, starring Ann Sheridan and Dennis Morgan, another of Hollywood's characteristic wartime exercises in the patriotic veneration of the American way. On this Saturday, however, the movie lines were noticeably shorter than usual, for across town an even more powerful symbol of America's seeming virtue was readying himself to stride to the batter's box at Halifax's historic Wanderers Grounds. Halfway around the world, on the steamy South Pacific Island of Guadalcanal, Japanese soldiers would soon taunt American marines with the cry 'Babe Ruth is a bum,' but on this day the townspeople of Halifax harboured no such thoughts as they anxiously awaited the appearance of the greatest home-run hitter in baseball history.

For weeks rumours had swirled about Halifax with respect to the Babe's appearance. One had him appearing in a Halifax uniform against Mickey Cochrane's Great Lakes Naval Station baseball team, a collection of former big leaguers now in military service. This team, which included super-star pitcher Bob Feller, was considered by many to be the equal of the best teams in the talent-drained major leagues. In their flights of fancy Haligonians could envisage the likes of Cochrane, Johnny Lucadello, George Earnshaw, and Bob Feller parading their talents at the Wanderers Grounds. 'It's still not known whether the Babe will take part in whatever game is staged that night or whether he'll just bat a few over the fence in practice,' wrote an exuberant sports columnist for the *Halifax Herald*. 'Just imagine what a spectacle it would be to see him trudge up to the plate and oppose fire-ball Bob Feller on the mound.' Other rumours had the Babe umpiring the game, or suiting up against a college squad from Fordham University.

The fans can be forgiven their disappointment when none of these dreams materialized. They had to be satisfied instead with a somewhat rotund 'Bambino' coming to the batter's box dressed in street clothes and regular dress shoes. A slight drizzle added to the fans' discomfort as Aukie Titus, a young outfielder and occasional relief pitcher for the Navy club in the local Halifax Defence League, took the mound to serve up some batting-practice pitches to the Babe. Probably aware of an earlier trip to the province in 1936 when Ruth was forced to tell fast-baller Dingie McLeod to stop trying to strike him out and to throw one of those 'drug store pitches' down the heart of the plate, Titus avoided giving Ruth anything other than grooved fast balls. It was soon obvious, however, that the Bambino's old magic was gone. The Babe swung weakly at the first two pitches, and then lofted a fly ball to the cinder track in short right field before driving a few line drives down the first-base line. With every pitch the fans waited expectantly for him to muscle a ball out of the park. It was not to be. After popping up to the catcher, and swinging at and missing the next three pitches, Ruth decided to call it a day, hauled out a fungo bat and hit a dozen autographed baseballs to an outfield filled with souvenir hunters. When the supply was exhausted he returned to the stands to watch the game of the night, featuring an all-star Toronto Navy team and Halifax Navy.

Ruth had visited the province before on numerous occasions. There were hitting expeditions such as the one that took him to Westville in 1936, and hunting trips with friends such as Rufus Sutherland of Lockeport. His attraction to the province, however, had even deeper roots. During his childhood, Ruth had resided at Saint Mary's Industrial School in Baltimore, where, under the tutelage of the Xaverian brothers who administered the institution, he was instructed in the game of baseball. Of all those at the school, Ruth reserved his highest praise for Brother Matthias, who was instrumental in developing his knowledge of the game, and in moulding his character. At Saint Mary's Matthias had made all the boys learn to play every position on the field, and in this way Ruth developed both his batting and pitching skills. 'He used to back me into a corner of the big yard at Saint Mary's and bunt a ball to me by the hour, correcting the mistakes I made with my hands and feet,' Ruth recalled. 'When I was eight or nine I was playing with the 12-year-old team. When I was 12 I was with the 16-year-olds, and when I was 16 I played with the best of the many teams we had in school. All because of Brother Matthias.'

One day as I was wading through old newspapers collecting information on baseball in the Maritimes, a brief editorial comment from the *Halifax Herald* in 1923 caught my eye. Brother Matthias, the newspaper announced, was actually a Haligonian named Walter Comeford, a former star on Halifax baseball diamonds in the 1890s, whose family still resided on Brenton Street in the city. Sure enough, a quick check of the Halifax city directory confirmed the existence of the Comeford family, and I still remember the excitement of having discovered a long-forgotten Nova Scotian connection to the world's most illustrious ball player. But when I consulted my relatively extensive card-file on players whose names appeared in local box-scores before 1900, Comeford was not among them. At this point I had serious doubts about the claim. How then might I confirm the authenticity of the story? After contacting a number of individuals and institutions, I finally made contact with the person responsible for the records of the Xaverian brothers at Notre Dame University. The results, which proved the Comeford story inaccurate, were nonetheless amazing. Although Brother Matthias was not Comeford, he *was* a Nova Scotian after all.

In private life, Brother Matthias was Martin Leo Boutlier, a native of the coal-mining community of Lingan, Cape Breton. Born on July 11, 1872, to mining engineer Joseph Boutlier and his wife Mary Ann, Martin Boutlier entered the Xaverian brothers in May 1892, following in the footsteps of an older brother who had joined the order four or five years earlier. Now known as Brother Matthias, he was assigned to Saint Mary's Industrial School in 1894 and remained there until 1931, when he was transferred to Saint John's School in Danvers, Massachusetts. In 1941 he was assigned to the Xaverian Juniorate in Peabody, Massachusetts, remaining there until his death on October 16, 1944, just four years before Ruth's own death.

A towering man, standing 6'4" and weighing well over 200 pounds, Brother Matthias had a personal magnetism that served him well as prefect in charge of discipline at Saint Mary's. Although he had played a little baseball as a youth in Nova Scotia (Ruth remembers him hitting one-handed 350-foot fungos with a bat in one hand and a small fielding glove on the other), he was less interested in playing the game himself than in using it as a way of teaching young boys like Ruth self-discipline and good sportsmanship. Indeed, many people remember Brother Gilbert being more directly involved in the baseball program at Saint Mary's. But Ruth's memoirs make it clear that it was Brother Matthias who had the greatest influence upon him during his youth, indeed throughout his entire life. It may well be that Brother Matthias's influence was the source of Ruth's subsequent attraction to and apparent affection for Nova Scotia, demonstrated by his frequent visits to the province in, before, and during the Second World War. Unlike Brother Matthias's Nova Scotian origins, however, that supposition will probably always remain a mystery.

---◆---

Gambling and scandal have soured baseball history from the time of the Louisville Four, who threw the 1877 National League pennant, to the infamous Black Sox scandal of 1919, in which eight members of the Chicago White Sox conspired with gamblers to lose the World Series. More recently, Pete Rose was banished from baseball for using book-making services readily available to most fans. Larry 'The River' Humber, a noted prognosticator and frequent visitor to the gambling dens of Las Vegas, Nevada, eagerly bet on the Blue Jays in 1992 and 1993 when he saw the line posted by American oddsmakers. Luck intervened again in 1994, when the strike forced bookmakers to refund those who had wagered on the Jays. On the other hand, those holding Expos wagers at 15–1 were more distraught. Humber is author of Going for It *(1995), a winners' guide to sports betting.*

Vegas Gives Jays the Cold Shoulder

LARRY HUMBER

I FIGURED THE BEAST MUST HAVE A BIT OF GAMBLE IN HIM, SO HE'D BE CURIOUS to see what I had.

It was at the opening of a Royal Ontario Museum show on baseball in the spring of 1989 that I bumped into The Beast, Toronto Blue Jays president Paul Beeston.

I had just returned from Las Vegas – one of my favourite haunts – with a ticket on the Jays to win the 1989 World Series. The odds were generous, too generous for a team that had come very close to topping its division the year before. Toronto was a 13-to-1 outsider to go all the way in '89.

'What do you think of this?' I asked Beeston.

It took him only a moment to realize that I was holding a betting slip from Vegas. He was even quicker to react to the big price being offered on the Jays.

'That's a good ticket,' he said. 'I'd certainly take those odds.'

While the Jays went on to win their division that year, they met their match in the American League Championship Series. The Oakland A's did away with them in a mere five games, then swept the San Francisco Giants in what has come to be known as The Earthquake Series.

The Jays came very close to taking their division again in 1990. The next year, they were back on top again, but fell to the Minnesota Twins in the League Championship Series. Obviously, Toronto was becoming a team to be taken seriously.

Despite all those near misses, the Jays were able to command odds of as much as 8 to 1 to win the World Series in 1992. That was a heck of a price for a team that had a very real chance of winning it all. It was beginning to look as if Vegas didn't appreciate their talents.

As it turned out, 1992 *was* Toronto's year, the Jays becoming Canada's first World Champions. And, oh, how we celebrated. That should have made them favourites to repeat in 1993. What is it they say? The champion is the best until it's beaten.

Still, Vegas didn't get the message. The Jays were again quoted at 8 to 1 for 1993. Not only that, a trio of other teams was given an equal chance of winning. The Cincinnati Reds, the Chicago White Sox, and the Baltimore Orioles were also offered at 8 to 1. That wasn't the worst of it, though.

The Atlanta Braves, a team that had floundered for much of its long history in that city, were the overwhelming choice to win the '93 Series. Atlanta was at odds of a paltry 5 to 2. When former Blue Jay Fred McGriff joined the team at mid-season, Atlanta was considered such a shoo-in that many bet shops declined to take further action.

But all that did was to fire up the Jays. Come mid-October, it was Toronto's Joe Carter, not McGriff or Braves team-mate David Justice, who was to round the bases with his fist raised. Carter's blast gave the Jays their second successive World Championship, and sent Torontonians back into the streets.

It looks as if, in retrospect, Vegas was right about the 1994 season, a forgettable one for the most part. But it sure didn't appear that way when the pre-season odds were posted. Again, the Jays were undersold. One of the big Vegas Strip casinos had the audacity to open them at 10 to 1. Here they were, winners of the past two World Series, and Vegas figured they had no more than one chance in 10 of garnering further glory. Talk about a slap in the face!

One can only surmise that Americans are reluctant to bet on anything that doesn't reek of the red, white, and blue. Even though the Jays have almost no Canadian content – East York, Ontario's Rob Butler being the only local boy to play for them – there seems to be this perception in the States that they are something less than a top-flight team because they aren't based on American soil.

That's the way many Americans think, though. Let me take you back to the inaugural World League of American Football season, in 1991.

The league was made up of 10 teams, most of which were based in the States. But there was also a Canadian entry, the Montreal Machine, and three European teams, the Barcelona Dragons, the London Monarchs, and the Frankfurt Galaxy. The three European sides were even given their own division.

Even though all the teams were stocked largely with American players, and the coaching staffs had all learned their stuff in the States, the Canadian and European teams were viewed as being not up to the level of their American counterparts. That was reflected in the odds posted in Vegas bet shops. The three teams given the least chance of winning the league championship were those representing Barcelona, London, and Frankfurt.

Wouldn't you know it, the teams with the best regular-season records turned out to be the Dragons, Monarchs, and Galaxy, all of which finished 7-3 or better. The top U.S.-based team wound up a mere 5-5. A few weeks later in the first World Bowl, it was London over Barcelona by a score of 21–0. You would think Americans would have learned from that, wouldn't you.

If you want further proof as to how Americans undersell things foreign, consider how differently they responded to teams like the Dallas Cowboys and the Chicago Bulls after they won a couple of championships than they did to the Jays after their successes. It was like night and day.

After winning the Super Bowl in 1992, the Cowboys opened at a mere 4 to 1 to win it again the next year. (You'll recall the Jays were at 8 to 1 even after they had a World Series under their belts.) When the Cowboys won for the second time in 1993, oddsmakers rightly lowered their odds to 3 to 1 for a three-peat. The Jays jumped to 10 to 1. Now, that just doesn't figure.

It was much the same story with the Bulls, who won three straight National Basketball Association championships in the early nineties. After they claimed their second title, they slipped to a mere 2 to 1 to win a third. They again opened at 2 to 1 to win for a fourth time. But, when superstar guard Michael Jordan announced he wanted to play baseball, all hell broke loose. Even with Jordan, the greatest player in the game, on the sidelines, the Bulls were still quoted at about 4 to 1. The Jays should be so well thought of. It's a big world out there, America. Maybe it's time you woke up to it.

Vegas did get it right with regard to one Blue Jay in 1993. Several bet shops, intrigued by John Olerud's bid to become the first major leaguer to bat .400 in decades, came up with a proposition featuring the Jays' talented, but unassuming, first sacker.

At around the time of the 1993 All Star break, with Olerud still comfortably above .400, bet shops chalked up this little ditty on their boards: Olerud will/will not finish with an average of at least .358 for the season.

Why that figure, and not .400?

'We didn't want to make it .400, because we figured it would be all one-way action.' explained Jay Kornegay of the Imperial Palace Race and Sports Book, a popular Strip establishment. 'I think everybody would have bet he wouldn't do it, and we didn't want that.'

By making the number .358, bet shops managed to split the action. A number of gamblers wagered that he would top .358, while a like number figured even that was asking too much of this relative unknown (unknown throughout most of the States, anyway).

As to how bet shops came up with .358, it was simply a matter of doing a little digging. 'We looked into it pretty good,' Kornegay said. 'Most of the hitters who were around .400 around All Star time finished about where we put Olerud.'

Those who went with Olerud were rewarded in the end. They had to sweat for their dough, though. He dipped badly late in the season, hovered in the .350s for a while, then rallied to finish at .363.

That was pretty close to what the wise guys in Vegas had him pegged at. Now, if only they would get it right regarding the Jays.

◆

Harold Seymour's book The People's Game *(1990) was a noble attempt to capture the essence of baseball beyond its major-league professional structure. He explored a realm of micro-history and community, the ground out of which organized baseball first emerged around the time of the U.S. Civil War and which has become the feeder system for future major leaguers. Within this space we first give form in real life to passions later adopted as spectators. Most important, it is an independent realm in which the everyday life of ordinary people finds a heightened opportunity for physical perfor-*

*mance, emotional release, friendship, and civic participation. The following is a personal
story of one team in one league and, perhaps, the story of all our games and places.*

Just Another Roadside Attraction

WILLIAM HUMBER

I N THE LAST SUMMER BEFORE CARS, GIRLS, JOBS, AND PLANS FOR HIGHER
education completely take over their minds, young boys past childhood but not ready for adulthood play bantam league baseball
(for 14 and 15 year olds) in the town of Bowmanville, Ontario. Their
games are played in 'field of dreams' parks not unlike thousands of
other special places where ordinary people of all ages play baseball in
North America.

In 1993, over 300,000 children were registered in baseball leagues in
Canada and perhaps ten times as many people played slow pitch, softball, and t-ball in settings ranging from company picnics to local tournaments. We are, despite hockey's claim to national game status, a ball-
playing country.

I wanted to have one last summer, as well, coaching with my two
boys. Not because I'm feeling poorly or because they intend to abandon
the game, but in recognition that priorities change in young lives and
this opportunity may never come again. Darryl was too young by a
year for this level, but I moved him up with his brother Brad, who is in
his last year of eligibility. Next year, Brad will face 16 to 20 year olds
and so I suspect this may be it for his baseball career. Softball and slow
pitch are the grinding acknowledgement of growing older.

Our town is an odd mixture of small towns, suburbs, and rolling
countryside. It is made up of two old townships, Darlington and Clarke,
and in mid-season changed its name from the area municipality of
Newcastle to Clarington, which sounds more like a shopping plaza
than a community.

On a brutally cold late March day we sign up for the town's baseball
league – the boys as players and myself as an assistant coach. Local
merchants from Bowmanville, Orono, Courtice, and Newcastle Village
all sponsor one or more squads in the eight-team circuit. Our team,
Bowmanville Glass and Mirror, adopts the motto 'We bend but we
don't break.'

Building a contender

The infighting in the month before actual play resembles a Liberal Party nomination meeting. Insider trading on the stock market can get you thrown in prison. On selection evening, it's often the basis for creating a championship team. 'I've seen it all,' says our head coach Larry Wood, a police officer in real life. 'Someone knows a star kid from Toronto who's just moved into town, or kids who sat out a season so there's no rating for them. Little kids drafted to fill out a lineup are told not to show up for big games so the rest of the team can win a medal for them.'

Larry has a solid understanding of baseball strategy and is only put off by kids who act lazy in either their baseball thinking or play. Errors he never once chastises and when one kid tries to apologize for flying out, he's told, 'Just worry about putting the ball in play. Anything can happen out there. I don't want to see you looking at third strikes.'

His own son Rich pays the most attention to Larry's rhythmic assembly of signals at third base, often walking halfway up the third base line to make sure he's got them correct. I'm not sure that some of the others really know what's going on. Larry restrains his anger in mid-season when my son Brad drifts too far off third and is picked off. He represented the winning run and our best batters were coming to the plate. The game ended in a tie.

The regular season runs from late May to the end of August. Larry sets the batting order and positions the fielders. As the assistant I try to look 'coachly,' which involves a lot of pawing the ground, spitting, and patrolling the first base coaching box distributing the usual round of silly platitudes, 'Protect the plate,' 'Make him bring the pitch down,' 'Be ready to run on a missed third strike.' I learn again however that the most basic of baseball principles are either forgotten or not known by kids even though they've watched the game all their life. For instance, with two out and runners on first and second they should run as soon as the ball is hit. Many actually run back to the bag to tag up, while others wait to see if it's caught. A lapse in fundamentals will almost cost us a run at the championship later in the season.

The usual dugout chatter

We play our first game in a lovely little bowl of a ballpark in Orono, Ontario, with homes overlooking the third base side, great trees fringing the outfield and a creek bed running alongside right field. Our best starter Brad Williams shuts down the local team and Paul Annis hits a bases clearing triple for our first win.

There will be many moments like this during the season but what I recall best are the conversations. Sitting on the bench, I listen to kids talk about girls. One tells his teammates rather graphically about a recent trip to the beach. Another brags about all the phone numbers he collected at summer camp. Another even philosophizes on what his parents would say if he dated a girl of another religion. Midway through one game Darryl Komar, who the coach wishes would concentrate more on baseball, asks one kid if he's got a girl friend. The coach and I generally keep our thoughts and interest on the game at hand. But after a reply of no, the coach mumbles 'smart kid.' At no game of ours does a young girl actually show up to cheer for any 'boyfriend' on the team.

When the kids do talk about baseball it has more to do with style than strategy. My son, Darryl, takes to affecting a Cal Ripken batting stance, and in mid-season the socks of my oldest son, Brad, are suddenly halfway up his pants in obvious homage to the great black baseball leagues. In these matters kids aren't too different from today's major league players.

Few of these kids hold down anything resembling a part-time job, so their summer afternoons are dedicated to computer games and occasional practices at Bowmanville's Soper Creek Park, when Larry can fit them in around his shifts. I have to miss most of these but it's here that they work on the fundamentals. I do get to be head coach for a couple of games when Larry is away. One is a memorable affair in Orono on the July night before I'm to lead a group of 50 on an annual Seneca College trip to Syracuse and Cooperstown. It's a steamy night like many that dotted this glorious summer. I wear shorts. The league had a silly dress code that restricted such wear before this summer. I guess they realized that an adult in funny clothes is better than no adult at all.

After deftly shifting my pitchers about we arrived in the bottom of the sixth past the two hour curfew time. With the game tied, Orono has loaded the bases with two out and I pay a visit to Robert Dorigo on the mound. Halfway out he throws his glove in the air, and stamps off the mound with an expression that says, 'What's this idiot doing out here.' My Cito Gaston response to his David Wells blarney is blunt. 'What are you doing, trying to show me up?' I ask.

'Well you are coming to take me out, aren't you' he says.

'You don't know that do you?' I reply.

I then call Jeremy Forsey out to the mound. Jeremy is our best hitter and early in the season we discovered he could pitch as well. Tonight he worked the first three innings before I put him back in the field in case I needed an extra inning later. (A player can only pitch in four of the seven innings.) He could do a spot now but that would be the end of his night on the mound. Still if Orono scores now we won't have a scheduled seventh because of the time limit.

'Which one of you can get this guy out?'

Robert quickly says, 'I can.'

Jeremy looks dubious. I leave in Robert.

First pitch is a ball. Too late to turn back. Next pitch is a popup to short. We've ended the two hour period but the other team wants extra innings. I ask our guys and they yell 'Go for it.' In the top of the seventh we score one. Between innings our catcher Kevin Nesbitt talks quietly to me. 'Doringo doesn't have anything left,' he says.

In the bottom I call on Jeremy. He gets the first two guys.

Their third batter hits a screamer down the third base line which looks like it might go all the way through the endless outfield grass for the tying run. But our third baseman leaps and snares it. Our third baseman is Dorigo. I feel like a managerial genius.

The playoffs and the at-bat of the year

Coaching kids' baseball is a lovely way to spend a summer. But it's always better when you win. We finish the season in second place with 12 wins, three losses and a tie (I try to forget my son's faux pas at third). I'm constantly amazed at how young kids of 14 and 15 like Matt Marstrom and Ryan Phillips can create dazzling moments with their gloves, and at how quickly these moments are forgotten.

The playoffs begin during the first week of school. On Wednesday, the first place team, National Home Video, who lost only two games all season, both to us, are eliminated. Unlike our somewhat more disciplined bunch, they tend to be hot headed and prone to throw at players they don't like on other teams. They carry their swagger a little too forcefully and are consigned to the runnerup series by Greenaways Petro Canada from Courtice.

On Thursday, my 44th birthday, we are in Orono to play the team against which I had my managerial success in July. It's a tense affair. We come to bat in the bottom of sixth leading 2–1. With no outs we load the bases. Since our bench is near first base, I talk to Norm Lansing before he comes to bat.

'Try to hit it along the first base side.'

Norm, the only team member who gleefully counted the days until the start of school, wants to know why.

'Two reasons, Norm,' I explain carefully. 'Chances are the first baseman will make the play at first and let the insurance run score, and secondly it will get the runner on second down to third with, at most, one out.' Norm's a quick learner even if he has our team's most unorthodox batting stance. His legs take on a wishbone character but he manages to tap a few balls foul in my direction. I notice the first baseman is playing back. We later learn their head coach is away and his substitute forgets to play the infield in.

Now begins what we later refer to as the 'at bat of the season' and probably of Norm's life. Two crackling line drives just miss Matt Marstrom's dad on the fence behind our dugout, another crashes into a car in the parking lot, another I jump to miss. The coach later says he counted eleven foul balls, all down the right field side. Still they don't adjust their infield. By now almost everyone including their pitcher is laughing. Even Norm can hardly keep from convulsing. Finally, he plants a perfect hit just inside the line and we go up by a run.

My son Darryl follows with a similar hit after their catcher fails to hold a popup and we take a 4–1 lead into the seventh and last inning. Jeremy comes in to pitch. He gets the first batter but the second hits a ball through Brett Forsey's legs at shortstop. Brett looks like our most complete player but too often comes up early on ground balls. Now comes the play we might have mumbled about all winter. The batter bunts the ball slowly back to Jeremy. Sitting on the bench we know that the only run that can hurt us is the one in the on deck circle. But as Darryl later says, 'Things happen pretty fast out there, dad.'

At this point in the game you give up a run and especially a base to get an out. But Jeremy plays it aggressively and throws to second. The runner is easily safe. We are suddenly in real trouble. They get another runner on and we get an out. Then they hit a ball through Brad Williams' legs at third. The score is soon 4–3 with the bases loaded and two out. It's like a slowly evolving nightmare until Jeremy strikes out the final batter and we flood onto the field. We are into the championship round where two losses are required for elimination.

Life fully lived

Brad Williams can't be at Saturday's games so we need a good blowout to take some pressure off our two remaining pitchers. In the morning we play Greenaways. One of their players affects the Seattle grunge look and smokes cigarettes proferred by an adult. So much for innocence. But, when I see this same kid get in a car, I make a mental note to ask for a birth certificate if he drives it off the lot. Fortunately, a big inning gives us a relatively easy 12–4 win and a check-up isn't required.

Between games I take some of the kids on a walking trip of downtown Orono. The clydesdales and ferris wheel are in town for the annual fair. I point out the old town hall where Christopher Walken had his assassination scene in the film version of Stephen King's *Dead Zone*. The town has a few notable baseball connections. Native son Wyman Andrus played one major league game with Providence back in 1885. Near here, as well, is the little village of Kendal whose senior ball team is sponsored by the father of Red Sox pitcher Paul Quantrill.

Our afternoon game will send one team to the final and another into a Sunday afternoon playoff. We are playing another Courtice team, Shoppers Drug Mart, who after going 1-15 in the regular season have now upset two favourites. Our guys are cocky but not mean spirited. The smallest player on the team, Brett Blackett does what he has done all year – leads off with a walk and we score three runs. Good thing as we fight for our lives for a 4–3 victory, though there's little tension in the final few innings as they get few runners on base.

Sunday dawns like a day out of the *Dead Zone*. The soggy breath of fall heralds the end of a perfect summer but we need one victory to make it complete. In the afternoon after two rain delays Greenaways beat Shoppers. Our evening start is pushed back to near seven. The sky has cleared but darkness arrives by the second inning. The narrow banks of lights make catching fly balls an adventure. A slight mist drifts in and out of centre field off a nearby stream. I can almost imagine Wyman Andrus' lingering spirit stepping out from the trees.

We score once in the bottom of the first and that's the way it stays. Brad Williams leaves the mound after giving us four solid innings. Jeremy, in relief, has a few anxious moments in the fifth but it ends with us still leading 1–0. We can't get a timely base hit. In the top of the sixth we get one out and then the miracle of the summer occurs. We later refer to it as 'the catch.' Adam Van Londen plays a deep left field for this inning. Adam has a cheeky little-boy quality and was forever eating junk food during games. He's the kid some coaches would ask not to show up for the game so the rest of the team could win a medal for him. During the year the few flyballs hit in his direction fell in for base hits or bounced over his head for even more trouble. I can't blame him. I hated flyballs after seeing a kid misjudge a ball and lose several teeth in one of my own juvenile games 35 years ago.

The Greenaways batter launches a towering flyball to left. Adam stands poised, hovering in the general direction of the ball's flight. At the last second, as if in a scene from a hoaky movie, Adam awkwardly leaps and the ball somehow wedges in the back of his glove. Larry buries his head in his hands, and says 'Thank God I went to church this morning.' Again, we don't score in our half and we head to the seventh.

Larry has to make the decision of the season.

'Matty (Matt Brake, our chirpy first string catcher) says Jeremy doesn't have much left on his pitches. I think we owe Robert an inning,' Larry says.

He's right but I don't think I'd have had the nerve to switch pitchers at this point. Rob has a great fastball but can sometimes come a cropper when the other team slows down the play. Two quick outs follow but a third strike narrowly misses and the batter walks to first. Now the wheels are turning. Larry visits the mound, their coaches are conferencing with the next batter, our fielders are talking to each other. We hear their coach suggest a bunt but don't say anything for fear they'll change the strategy. On the first pitch he bunts up the third base line. I feel like I'm in an instant replay of last year's World Series. In slow motion, Rob runs for the ball, stumbles, picks it up and makes a pinpoint throw to my son Brad at first. The throw beats the runner by two steps and suddenly our kids are all over the field. Brad does a Joe Carter leap at first while others jump on a pile of teammates. I'm taking photos, the coach is shaking hands, we all promise to get together in the off-season. A trophy is presented, our guys do a victory lap, and slowly we dissolve into the night. It is an existential moment of glee in which life feels fully lived.

A season of baseball is a never to be repeated affair. Kids grow older, new teams are formed, lives change. My boys and I have had some wonderful moments together. In a few short years they'll be off to university and on to new lives. Their connection to one family will expand to include others. We'll see less of them, but that after all is the way of the world. This was probably our last chance for such a summer and we wore it well. And we'll not see many of these other kids again. Their futures will be different. In a few years they'll think of their coaches and perhaps baseball itself as something akin to fossils. In our moment of euphoria is also the realization that our perfect summer has come to an end and this team will never be together again as a unit.

It happens in a thousand diamonds in so many different towns and villages. We pass them on the highway, these summer roadside attractions. Games played full of meaning for a few spectators and players and of no consequence to anyone else – never to be recorded. We reclaim them only in our memory and I suppose in our continuing fascination with this great game. It may not be life itself, but it sure feels like it.

◆

This collection represents a modest assertion of the thesis that baseball is not the sole property of the United States, that it has long been a favourite pastime of Canadians too. So here comes one of our contributors (a philosopher, no less) implying that any talk of Canadian *baseball is but 'an admission of colonial inferiority'! Well, dear readers, clasp your shaky Canadian identity to your breast and press on, as Mark Kingwell explores how we just might have beaten them at their own game.*

Colonialism, Civility, and the National Team

MARK KINGWELL

A CULTURE'S GAMES SHOWCASE AND REVEAL WHAT IT CARES ABOUT. THEY help define the best aspects of our self-image: fairness, honest competition, good sportsmanship. But they also provide controlled outlets for those aspects of ourselves we regard with less pleasure: the violence, the competitiveness, which we try to keep between the lines, stylized and balletic. Games are an effective critique of life by being unlike it, by offering something outside the hurly-burly that stands in for and interprets those things we otherwise cannot see so clearly. They are not simply life by other means, but something separated off from life to reflect back on life critically. That, at least, is the hopeful picture.

Baseball has not historically played this kind of role in Canadian culture, where the national self-image is carried by hockey. The reasons are obvious. The summer is too short to make baseball a natural obsession; more deeply, the images of baseball fantasy, the cherished scenes from 'the heartland,' of raw recruits and ball-yards emerging naturally from the plains, are through and through American. We cannot easily tap into baseball tradition because it is so relentlessly American, so culturally specific – a specificity most evident, perhaps, in the visual propaganda of the recent photo collection *Baseball in America*, which gives iconic baseball images the aura of Soviet labour posters.

And yet increasingly, over the past decade especially, the Toronto Blue Jays have generated almost unprecedented popular support in Canada. This is doubly surprising to Torontonians, who are used to having the rest of the country regard them with ill-tempered scorn – an attitude they tend to repay in spades with urban arrogance, gentle condescension, and rudeness. The place of the Blue Jays in the national consciousness is also surprising because the first base of support for the team is distinctively urban, born of a tiresome Torontonian desire to be 'world-class.' The logical extension of this desire is the team itself, boasting in 1993 the largest payroll in major-league baseball, almost $43 million U.S. – a figure close to three times the size of the $14.85 million floated by Canada's other major-league team, the Montreal Expos, who ranked 24th among major-league clubs. The Jays' fans flocked to the high-priced SkyDome to see these foreign mercenaries compete against the best of the American League. If they did not really understand the subtleties of the game, as so many players and broadcasters complained, they at least understood its economics. Pouring hard-earned cash into the Blue Jay coffers was bound, sooner or later, to produce a winner.

The Jays provided these fans with all the excitement of romantic infatuation, and their rising success story became irresistible to people across the country. Along the way, the usual indices of fan support were rendered meaningless. Fans in Vancouver ignored the nearby Seattle Mariners – except as hosts to the travelling Jays. The Vancouver Triple A farm team, the Canadians, affiliated with the Chicago White Sox and the California Angels, created baseball fever – and more Jays fans. If it were not for the presence of the Canada-U.S. border, a Vancouver or Calgary fan's interest in the Jays would be peculiar, the vestige of some childhood obsession perhaps or of a long-ago player's heroism. Instead it is something now taken entirely for granted, as is the support of fans in Saskatoon and Medicine Hat and Flin Flon and Saint John and Halifax (though there is certainly little fan support for the Jays in Quebec).

The expansion of their fan base across English Canada demonstrates that the Blue Jays have become the closest thing possible to a genuinely *national* team – something that remains functionally impossible for any team playing within the United States. Yet, given all that dearly bought foreign talent, the Jays' World Series victories remain an ambivalent cultural achievement for Canada. That ambivalence needs to be understood.

We have to see, first, the place of Canadian self-image in a continental context. Partly as a matter of our national history, which consists in large measure of squabbles between imperial powers, and partly as a matter of economics, this self-understanding is importantly *colonial*. It used to be a commonplace in English Canada that our culture was roughly equal parts British and American. Over time the British presence has waned and the American influence – an influence chiefly of culture and money – has grown proportionately stronger. Because we depend on American markets for our country's economic health, and because our airwaves and public discourse are dominated to an alarming extent by American products, it is not an exaggeration to say that we stand in the relation of a wealthy de facto colony to the imperial power of the United States.

Colonial anxiety is carried into our games, especially those, like baseball, that bear the stamp of Americanness. One typical response is to become insistent about Canadian contributions to the game. For example, did you know that Babe Ruth hit his first professional home run on Canadian soil, at the old park on Hanlan's Point in Toronto harbour? Or consider the claims, familiar to baseball scholars, that the first game of organized baseball was played in Zorra Township, near London, Ontario, in 1838. Adam Ford, a seven-year-old spectator of the contest between the Zorra team and a side from nearby Beachville, wrote an account of the game, including a drawing of the knocker's stone (home plate) and the five byes (or bases). [*See* Ford, in this volume.] In 1988 a sesquicentennial re-creation of the game was played in the vicinity, an event coinciding with the induction of five players into the Canadian Baseball Hall of Fame.

But what does the re-creation, and the institution of a Canadian Baseball Hall of Fame itself, tell us about Canadian aspiration concerning baseball? The insertion of the national adjective – what we may think of as 'the pro-national claim' – is a distinctive colonial tic, a defining gesture of limitation. That there should even exist such a place as the *Canadian* Baseball Hall of Fame is an admission of colonial inferiority and self-doubt. It is the pro-national claim made into an institution, a frozen gesture of cultural weakness.

These gestures provide evidence of what communications theorists call 'strategic envelopment': the pervasive, all-encompassing cultural or economic victory of empire, which succeeds so well that it actually defines the terms of possible public discussion. This in turn creates 'double-binds' for the colonized, situations in which all available options are self-defeating. Under strategic envelopment, neither agreement nor disagreement from the dominant values retains any liberating possibilities. All arguments, pro and con, are phraseable only in the discourse of a public sphere defined and controlled by the dominant power.

Take a discussion of Canadian identity. To agree with American assumptions of sameness is merely to capitulate, to participate in my own oppression; but to disagree is simply to reinforce my subordinate position by using the limited language of insistence, a language of uncertainty. (The self-doubt evident in Canadian insistence on difference curiously parallels the civic anxiety about 'world-class' achievements.) The true victory of imperial domination is that condition in which the colonized not only fail to revolt, but also actively participate in, and embrace, their own subordination. This is a 'strategic' victory, one that defines and includes within itself all possible 'tactical' responses. Tactics, Sun Tzu said in *The Art of War*, can never defeat strategy; only strategy can defeat strategy. The triumph of imperialism is just this ability to define the available language of both consent and dissent. The only way out of this colonial double-bind is in some sense to *transcend* the available language: not, perhaps, by creating an entirely new language, but by using the internal dynamics of the existing language to critical effect.

Another sport provides an illustration. The challenge posed to England by colonial cricket shows that there is a deep critical possibility built into the dominance of cricket values, values that are deeply imperialistic. Cricket's Victorian soul was embodied in the dominant English player of the nineteenth century, W.G. Grace. A physician by trade, Grace was an 'amateur' of cricket, and a gentleman; yet he played the game with a fierceness and guile that often verged on the ungentlemanly. This is what Ashis Nandy has called the 'intrinsic schizophrenia of traditional cricket,' an instability that pitted the overtly valued virtues of good sportsmanship against the largely unmentionable, but nevertheless widely recognized and valued, virtues of aggression and drive to win (see *The Tao of Cricket*, 1989). The internal conflicts of traditional cricket were dynamic, delicately poised within the context of England's class system. But the game could not survive the process of exportation, for its class-based social balance and peculiar brand of hypocrisy were too delicate for overt challenge.

The challenge has come from the colonies, especially Australia, India, and the West Indies. Victorian cricket 'allowed Indians to assess their colonial rulers by western values reflected in the official philosophy of cricket,' Nandy continues, 'and to find the rulers wanting. The assessment assumed that cricket was not the whole of Englishness but was the moral underside of English life which the English at the turn of the century, even with much of the world at their feet, found difficult to live down.' And to the extent that they could not live down these values, the oppressors gave the oppressed the exact means of their own liberation.

These arguments complicate the accepted interpretation of the colonial appropriation of cricket, that victory was purchased at the cost of exploiting the rules and so flouting the culture of 'It isn't cricket.' (I'm distinguishing here, as Nandy does, between the official rules of a game and its 'unwritten' rules, or cultural norms.) The Trinidadian Marxist C.L.R. James once described how his own critical character was formed by becoming, as a young boy, a kind of perfect model of sportsmanship – an English gentleman in miniature, more perfect than the real thing. At first glance, this is colonial behaviour at its most obvious, a clear double-bind: *difference* in manners would be proof of subordination (the natives aren't even civilized), while *simulation* is proof of submission (the natives have no identity of their own). 'It was only long years after,' James notes, 'that I understood the limitation on spirit, vision and self-respect which was imposed on us by the fact that our [school]masters, our curriculum, our code of morals, *everything*, began from the basis that Britain was the source of all light and learning, and our business was to admire, wonder, imitate, learn; our criterion of success was to have succeeded in approaching that distant ideal – *to attain it was, of course, impossible*. Both masters and boys accepted it as in the very nature of things' (*Beyond a Boundary*, 1963; emphasis added). The initial triumph of imperialism is the masters' ability to interpret any and all behavioural responses in terms that reinforce, and never challenge, domination.

Yet the limitations James speaks of still contain an interesting critical possibility. What better way – indeed, what *other* way? – to challenge the masters than to illustrate their own ideals more perfectly than they themselves? What more liberating response to domination than to beat the masters at their own chosen game: not only the game of cricket itself, but also the civil norms lying beneath cricket? Not only to beat them, in other words, but to beat them by being more themselves than they are – to beat them, here, with civility.

The situation is structurally similar to the one facing the Canadian fan of baseball. The importance of the Toronto Blue Jays' World Series victories was that they challenged American dominance, demonstrating that (1) for the first time, a team from outside the United States could be the best in the game; and also (2) victory could be gained by calling out the best elements of the game's culture, not flouting them. The Blue Jays' victory was therefore both tactical and strategic. The Jays won the Series, and that tactical achievement is the necessary precondition of critique. But the critique was really vouchsafed by the *way* in which they won the Series, and especially in the way the fans responded – namely, with a kind of cheerful civility, the joyful largesse of the good winner. This second victory is a strategic *cultural* victory, one that in some fashion transcends the limitations placed on the colonized by imperial strategic envelopment.

This description of the Jays and their fans as 'good winners' may seem unsurprising, or trivial. Surely there are simply some good winners and some bad ones, a matter of contingency. But given the imperial/ colonial background of the Series victory, the fact that Toronto could assume the role of the good winner is more than usually significant. The good-winner role is one normally reserved for the masters, since only those who have nothing really to lose can be expected to lose gracefully. The slaves, typically, are good *losers*: they are resigned and cheerful in defeat, their traditional good humour a kind of defence against the harsh reality of inferiority. When they do manage to win – as in many cricketing victories – they are most often *bad* winners, ungracious and savage. The victory is purchased at the cost of undermining the game's critical possibilities. Poor losers in general, and colonized ones in particular, reduce games to simply more life, life by other means. When slavish resentment infects the game, the game is no longer all that it can be.

The gracious victory of the colonized is a powerful force. It is nothing like a direct bid for power, of course, a serious challenge to the mainstream domination of the imperial power. But it is an effective *critique* of that power. And it offers a reflection of the highest aspirations of power, aspirations that, as in the systematic hypocrisy of Victorian cricket, are at odds with the reality of the power's exercise. Colonial victories, when gracious, hold up a mirror to the masters – a mirror in which the reflection must seem, perhaps for the first time, cruelly accurate. This form of critique, which calls the masters to order in their own stated terms, is something that comes best from the margins, precisely the forums where the masters exercise their power most nakedly.

How does this critique function? The master, according to Hegel (an acute student of these matters), actually requires the slave to complete his identity as master. Thus, mutual recognition gives the slave an enormous, usually untapped, critical power. The master is as much beholden to the slave in psychological terms as the slave is beholden to the master in economic terms. The slave can, by reminding the master of the mere fact of his existence, unsettle the foundations of the master's domination, and hence of his identity. In the same way, colonized peoples stand in a critically privileged relation to their colonizers. They have an ability to *shame* the colonizers, to show them the precise shape and limits of their acts of imperial domination. This not only undermines the recognition that all masters must demand from all slaves; it also challenges the masters' very sense of themselves. Are we only masters, they will be forced to ask? Do we dominate? What about the other values we cherish? If the colonial challenge can make use of exactly these cherished values, its effectiveness is redoubled, for it emphasizes all the more the gap between self-image (how the masters see themselves) and reality (how they are seen by others).

The Blue Jays' World Series victories provided a vehicle for just this kind of challenge. They did so because three essential conditions were met. First, it was crucial that the Jays take on the role of a national team, that they be identified strongly with Canadian, and not just Torontonian, aspiration. It was likewise crucial that they play good baseball. Losing the World Series, however well, would have changed nothing. Finally, then, it was crucial that the victory be a good one, which is to say one that was gracious, cheerful, and civil. The victory had to be one, performed in the best baseball terms, that would bend those terms back on the dominant American culture of baseball in a critical fashion.

Examples of this civility abound: the Canadian reaction to the egregious error of flying our flag upside down, the good humour that greeted routine displays of American ignorance about Canada, indeed the re-markable *politeness* with which we suffered jokes about hitting home runs with hockey sticks and wearing parkas to the ballpark. It is pos-sible that this politeness is a cultural property of Canadians in particu-lar, or of colonized peoples in general – though I doubt this [but *see* Gordon, in this volume, under the letter 'E']. But whatever the precise origin and nature of this civility, joined with good baseball on the part of our loosely constituted national team, it proved a powerful combina-tion. The celebrated Canadian politeness, a politeness that looks at first blush like a form of weak submission, is in fact this kind of subversive response to imperial domination. Whether or not we believe in our responses, they treat insult in a particularly effective way. By setting a high standard of behaviour, we implicitly call attention to deficiencies of behaviour in others.

It remains to be seen whether Canadians will consistently find in the Blue Jays a way of seeing themselves, and thus finding identity in rec-ognition. It also remains to be seen what long-term effects, if any, the Blue Jays' victories will have on the American culture of baseball. The civility I referred to, the civility by reference to which the Canadian victory can assume its critical position, is something threatened both in Canada and in the culture of baseball. I suspect that the critical effects will be mostly contingent on how well Canada maintains its sovereignty in the coming decades. It is in the mainstream interests of American domination to assimilate Canada to itself. Canada must retain its differ-ences from the United States – remain on the critical margin – for the challenge represented by the Blue Jays' victories to have any lasting effects.

It would also help if the Jays once more played good ball ...

——————— ◆ ———————

W.P. Kinsella would make the starting line-up of any all-star baseball storytelling team. His quirky, sometimes dark and mystical, stories exemplify baseball's imaginative al-lure for writers down through the years. This tale, from The Dixon Cornbelt League

collection (1993), deals with a perennial sports (human, really) theme – the loss of the
powers of youth – played out in the daunting setting of a northern Alberta winter.

Eggs

W.P. KINSELLA

IT IS FEBRUARY. THE PAST MONTHS HAVE BEEN NOTHING BUT FEBRUARYS. I'M only thirty-one and my arm feels fine, but my fastball is gone. All last season I survived, if anyone could call it that, on cunning, an only partially successful screwball, and my former reputation as the best pitcher in baseball. My ERA was 5.97, I only appeared in thirty-six games, my record was 1-6. I averaged over twenty wins in each of the previous nine years, but when my long-term contract expired the Angels showed no interest in renewing.

'You've had a great career,' the management told me, not even in person. 'You're financially secure. Enjoy your retirement, get on with your life.'

'I'll work all winter developing a knuckleball, maybe try a split-finger fastball, perfect the screwball,' I told my agent. 'Get me a contract, with anybody.' What I wanted to say was 'I'm only somebody when I'm on the mound. I'm only somebody when the ball smashes into the catcher's mitt and the batter twists into a corkscrew. I need one more season before I can adjust to retirement.' But that would have sounded pathetic.

'Look, Webb,' said my agent, 'through the wonders of instant replay every team in organized baseball has footage of you being bombed every time you stepped on the mound last season, and you know your trouble started in the middle of the previous season.'

'I know, but I'm getting stronger,' I lied. There is something wrong with me. I feel weak, drained. Even though doctors can't find anything, I keep thinking cancer, leukemia.

'If we could claim you'd been injured it would be different, teams will hang in with you forever in hopes that you'll rehabilitate,' my agent went on. 'But there's no physical cause for your decline. One of the weaker teams may give you a Triple-A contract, gambling that you improve. Do you really want that? You don't need the money.'

Then last week the expansion Florida Marlins, a team desperate for any kind of pitching, came through: an invitation to spring training as a non-roster player, but still a chance to make the team, to prove I'm not through. Every has-been pitcher who can still lob a baseball will be in that camp. I will have to swing a bat, face a live pitcher for the first time since I was in the Pioneer League, eleven years ago.

I've pitched regularly all winter, run ten miles a day (I have my own indoor track), exercised, lifted weights. I've even taken batting practice, for I have always had a pitching machine in the basement of the multi-million-dollar house on the cold, isolated Alberta prairie where I spend the off-season.

But it is February outside and February in my heart. My pitching has not improved over the winter, if anything my fastball is weaker, my knuckleball too wild and too slow. I'm only thirty-one. But I'm tired. Twenty-fours hours a day I feel an ecstatic lethargy, as if I've just had sex.

The idea of swinging a bat again bothers me more than I care to admit. I wake in the night with a lurch, sticky and unrested. I am flying backward out of the batter's box, only as I fall the ball is following me, curving in on my face. I wait in terror for the sickening sound of baseball on bone. Then the ball is suddenly full of brilliant geometric designs, like the easter eggs that Maika and my mother-in-law Halya decorate at the kitchen table. I can smell the paint and the vinegar odor that always accompanies their enterprise. My wife, my mother-in-law, foreign, patterned eggs.

I glare at the fluorescent smirk of the clock on the night table. February, 3:00 A.M. I stare at the shape of my sleeping wife, Maika, wondering how she can rest in such tranquility, while beside her, troubled, I dodge chin music from a terroristic pitcher.

'Retire,' seems to be the only word in Maika's vocabulary these days. 'Koufax retired young,' she reminds me repeatedly. 'Don't be a Steve Carlton, begging to try out in Japan, a pathetic shadow of yourself. We have no financial worries, you'll be elected to the Hall of Fame the first year you're eligible.'

'Quit to do what?' I wail. 'I'm a baseball player. I don't know anything else.'

'You don't need to know anything else,' Maika points out. 'We have investments: this house, what? two, three million in the bank? Don't be like those old boxing champions, ex-champions, their brains all puffy, still fighting years after they should have retired with dignity.'

A completely reasonable argument. But wrong.

'If I retire, I won't continue to live here,' I say to Maika, not knowing I was going to say that. 'I think living here in Alberta has contributed to what's wrong with me.'

'But there's nothing wrong with you,' Maika says with a terrible logic that I don't want to hear. 'The team paid for the best specialists in the world to look at you – your arm, your back. Some athletes wear out before others. You just have to accept that.'

But I do not accept that. I cannot explain why I will not retire. I cannot explain to Maika or her mother Halya, who lives with us, though it is almost as if we live with her.

If I did attempt to explain to Maika, I would say something like, 'I know I'm as good a pitcher as I've always been. There's nothing physically wrong with me, there's nothing mentally wrong with me either. I think you and your mother are sapping my strength, conspiring to force me to retire, distancing me from, isolating me from baseball.' I also suspect they may be trying to kill me, may have put some curse on me. But I could never say that out loud. It would sound too crazy.

I can hear the fuss even a hint of my accusation would cause. I can feel Maika and Halya fluttering around me, trying to put me at ease, exchanging worried glances, letting me know as politely as possible that they think me mildly demented. What can I say? I have no proof, just an eerie feeling that they are doing something out of the ordinary. Something wicked.

I met Maika Osadchuk the first year I won twenty games in the Bigs. We were married as soon as the season was over. She was a flight attendant working the Los Angeles–Honolulu run. When I first saw her she was wearing a blue-bird-colored uniform that contrasted with her brown eyes and coppery skin; her hair was dark but with a twinge of fire to it. I thought she might be part Indian, or perhaps from Peru or Bolivia. She turned out to be more exotic, at least to a boy who had lived all his life protected by the green Allegheny Mountains. Her family had emigrated to Canada from the Ukraine when her grandmother was a girl. Her great grandfather had been a Cossack. She had a tinted photo of him mounted on a rearing black horse, wearing a sky-blue tunic and brandishing a curved, silver sword.

The first time I ever saw a decorated egg was at the tiny apartment Maika shared with another flight attendant she seldom saw.

'What is that?' I asked, pointing at the only decoration on the narrow, varnished mantel above the fake fireplace.

'You've never seen a painted egg?'

'It's egg-shaped, but is it really an egg?'

'Of course. I painted it myself. My mother taught me, and my grand-mother taught her. Painting eggs is the Ukrainian national pastime, like baseball here in the States.'

I picked it up, was astonished by its lightness. In spite of what Maika said, I had expected that it would be made of stone or crockery.

I turned the brilliant sphere in my hand, rolled its multicolored geo-metric designs down to the tips of my long fingers, transferred it to my pitching hand.

'The egg is always blown dry. You poke a tiny hole in each end and blow out the insides.'

'Like a vampire in reverse.'

'Sort of.'

'What do the designs mean?'

'They tell stories, some of them. They go way back, pre-Christian. They're a bit like cave drawings: history, myth, tall tales. Every home has to have one. "A decorated egg assures a good harvest," my grand-mother used to say, "and wards off evil." And then she'd shake her finger under my nose, "and assures you many babies."'

'It looks to me as if the harvest has been good,' I said, staring at Maika and smiling, 'and I don't see any evil to ward off. I'll pass on the babies though, at least until we get to know each other better.' I replaced the egg on the white candy dish.

After the honeymoon, Maika insisted on taking me home to Canada to meet her family. Her mother lived in a town called Vegreville, in rural Alberta, nearly three hundred miles north of the Montana border. As a rookie I had played in the Pioneer League, traveling to dusty towns in Montana and southern Alberta, so I wasn't totally unprepared for the dryness of the air, the high sky and open spaces. But I had never spent a winter anywhere really cold and decided my imagination was not large enough to imagine forty below.

'You're seeing Alberta at its best. The fall is the most beautiful time of year. Indian summer – the crops being harvested, everything golden.'

Everything was indeed golden, I had to admit, the sky a distant baby blue where hawks circled, thin and black as coat hangers. The flatness was awe-inspiring, an occasional red or green combine lumbering like a dinosaur, grain elevators visible in almost every direction, buoys on a golden ocean.

It was not an elevator that greeted us as the highway narrowed to pass through Vegreville, but a massive painted egg. It stood on end, some twenty feet tall, many feet in diameter, an intricate geometric design in a rainbow of colors.

Once, during the summer, Maika had demonstrated the art of egg painting. She had produced a box of dyes and watercolors and over a long weekend had transformed a large white egg into a kaleidoscopic wonder of color and design.

'Does it tell at story?' I asked.

'Boy meets girl, boy gets girl.'

We built our home on the outskirts of Vegreville. The town council considered printing postcards of THE WEBB WATERMAN HOUSE to send out with their thousands of postcards of the giant painted egg, but when Halya heard of the idea she persuaded the mayor that it would be as insensitive as the American news media. The plan was scrapped. But on warm Sunday afternoons cars arrive from as far away as Edmonton, some sixty miles distant, slowing on the gravel secondary road to behold the glass and aluminum marvel that is the family home of Webb Waterman, professional baseball pitcher.

Halya already owned the quarter section of land on the outskirts of Vegreville, or Wag-re-will, as she and the older settlers of Ukrainian descent pronounce it. My mother-in-law and her friends wear their accents proudly, like Germans wear leather pants.

I've never been sure how I came to build a permanent home in Alberta, a cold, dry, windy place tolerable only because Maika's roots are here. I remember on our first visit, walking the barren land as Maika and Halya discussed where the house would sit, where the access roads would be. I was very much in love. Maika's body could keep even the Alberta cold at a distance.

I had no idea how long a project our house would turn into. Halya was quick to adjust to having a wealthy son-in-law.

The house, built at the apex of my career, cost close to $2 million. It is over seven thousand square feet. Separated from the pool by Plexiglas panels is my pitcher's mound, an exact duplicate of the one in Anaheim Stadium, with a padded strike zone sixty feet, six inches away, and a portable silhouette of a six-foot-tall batter to give my practice authenticity. (I stand six foot seven and have a long, sorrowful face, brick-colored hair, and pale skin covered in penny-sized freckles.)

At first, except for the murderous climate, I wasn't too dissatisfied with my winter home. In my secure mansion on the edge of a small town where baseball was something Americans played, where the guys who played hockey and curling (a game resembling shuffleboard on ice) were local heroes, I was comfortable.

My mother-in-law, though she appeared to be no more than fifty, liked to pretend she was old, even infirm. Halya was a thin, sharp-featured woman, who must have been a rather beautiful brown-eyed blond. When I first met her she seldom left her house, a small frame building painted a searing bachelor's-button blue and stuffed to bursting with sofas, box chairs, and dark, wooden furniture.

Halya spent her days sitting at her highly polished dining-room table, usually wearing a garish kimono, her hair protected by a flowered babushka, coloring eggs and all the while talking on the telephone to her friends, usually in Ukrainian.

According to Maika, Halya would herd her friends into the living room to show off her egg collection and her pictures of me. She had a large portrait of me in uniform, our wedding picture, plus a collection of framed photographs of me – covers from *Sports Illustrated*, *The Sporting News*.

'I'm not sure I like her doing that,' I said to Maika, when she continued the practice after we moved into the new home, sometimes even when I was in the house. 'There's something *unnatural* about it. That collection of photographs is like a shrine.'

'She's just proud of you,' said Maika lightly.

Maika's father was never mentioned. There were no photos. 'He left when I was very young,' was all Maika had said.

'I can't stand it here any more,' I said to Maika for about the twentieth time this winter. I was mentally packing for spring training, though I couldn't leave for at least two weeks. I was not going to spend another winter staring out across the snow-crusted prairie in the depressing purple light of afternoon.

'We've been over this before,' said Maika, her voice pleasant and reasonable. 'Who would ever buy this house?'

'We can afford to live anywhere we want to. This tundra ... it's weakened me.'

Maika smiled at what she obviously considered my foolishness. 'The kids love it here, they have their friends. Besides, Mother could never leave Alberta.'

The wind-whipped snow was sculpted in ice-cream shapes along the edge of the runway where my twin-engined plane with the golden baseball insignia on the tail sat, cold and forlorn.

'Halya was here before we came, she can stay after we're gone. She'll just have a better house to live in,' I said. 'Maybe Florida, if I catch on with the Marlins. Florida is warm, green, a person's blood can circulate there. I think that's what's wrong with me, I'm like someone who has fallen through the ice on one of these lakes, my body has slowed to a standstill. If I stay any longer I'll suffer brain damage.'

I longed to challenge Maika's loyalty to her mother, to point out that her mother would have no part in any decision to move. If Halya chose to follow us that was fine. If she didn't, even better. But after all, who would *want* to continue to live in this bleak, cold, dry climate?

As I became more determined to leave Alberta for good, Maika, always a sweet and ardent lover, became more passionate, more artful.

All this winter, Maika and Halya have decorated eggs. There are eggs everywhere, in groups on china plates in the dining room, glowing like candies in soft baskets on the sideboards, on the TV, on the children's dressers. Even my daughters work with their mother and grandmother at the kitchen table, their brows furrowed, their stubby fingers colored by dyes.

Once I came upon Maika bent at the table; she had her lips against the end of a large, brown egg. The contents were dribbling into a glass.

'Eeech!' I said, immediately queasy.

'Omelettes for supper,' said Maika, but all I could see for hours was the sickly liquid trickling down the side of the glass.

Sometimes events puzzle me. I wake in the deepest hours of the night to find Maika gone from our bed. I continue to sleep, but fitfully. Eventually I feel the gentle vibrations of her feet as she crosses the carpeted room. As if aware of my restlessness, Maika frees the covers at the foot of the bed and burrows upwards. Her breath on my legs brings me erect. I hear her familiar cooing sounds, always associated with lovemaking, before I feel her mouth and tongue on me, slicing away the lethargy of sleep.

Eventually I pull her up to me and we make love for a long time, after which I fall into a deep, exhausted sleep.

Could this passionate lovemaking be part of Maika's strategy to keep me from moving to a warmer climate? I can imaging Maika and Halya discussing what they can do to thwart my plan. A number of times recently, they have looked conspiratorial, speaking Ukrainian.

I imagine Halya's leathery voice saying, 'A satisfied man does not want to go hunting. Feed him well and do your homework every night.'

But, I am going to do things my way. I will play one more year, more if I recover my strength. I will move my family to a warm climate. Maika can choose the location, but I will force *some* choice on her.

For the second time I wake with a lurch, hurling myself backward, away from a ball destined for my face, but this time the ball was a decorated egg streaking toward me.

Maika is not beside me. Must be nearly dawn. I am about to drift into sleep again when something touches my foot.

'What?'

'Shhh!' comes Maika's familiar whisper. Her warm hand reaches in under the blankets, caressing my leg.

I lie back, anticipating that Maika will follow her hand.

I hear a scuttling sound at the end of the bed, a scuffing on the carpet, the vibrations of someone moving across the floor toward the door. Has one of the children wandered in after a bad dream? I know I am not imagining it. I wait for the subtle change in air patterns that will tell me the door has opened and closed in silence. The breath of air comes, and with it an odor that cuts like ammonia.

I jerk wide awake.

The odor that frightens me is of things wizened, of decay, the vinegary smell of dyes, Halya.

I grab Maika's arm and pull her roughly to the top of the bed. Then I flood the huge room with light.

'What's wrong with you?' asks Maika, annoyed. 'It's the middle of the night.' She is tucking a dark breast back inside her blue satin night-gown.

'Halya's been in this room,' I shout. 'What's going on?'

'Go back to sleep,' says Maika.

I grab her wrist, stopping her from turning off the lamp.

'You've had a bad dream.'

'It wasn't a dream. She was here. I can smell her.'

Maika smiles her sexiest smile. 'Come close,' she croons. 'Let me cuddle you.'

I grab the bed clothes and sweep them from the bed. My long-naked body looks pale and vulnerable against the midnight-blue bottom sheet. I stare suspiciously at myself, at Maika, at the bed.

'Let me get the covers,' says Maika. As she leans across the bed she slips down the top of her nightgown exposing her dark-nippled breasts.

As my eyes get used to the bright light, I feel a little foolish. I am about to say so, about to apologize for being rough with her. Maika's hand is once again reaching for the light when I run my hand down between my legs, rub curiously, discover a sickly wetness, withdraw my hand.

I howl in anguish for it appears my fingers are covered with blood. I leap from the bed and bolt to the washroom, wrench a towel from the rack and stuff it between my legs. I've heard that, when first mutilated, victims feel no pain. In the operating-room brightness of the washroom, I examine my hand. My fingers are not covered with blood but colors. My fingers stink of paint and vinegar.

'Come back to bed,' comes Maika's voice from outside the door.

I yank the door open. 'Get away from me.' I stand above her, fist raised. When she sees my wildness she flees.

I ease the soft, white towel from between my legs. I examine myself carefully, studying the colors smeared on the towel. Turning on the shower full blast, I make it as hot as I dare before stepping in. I soap myself extravagantly, watching in fascinated revulsion as the water, tinged with blue, ochre, scarlet, green, runs down my legs, and swirls around to the drain.

Barefoot, I move stealthily through the dark, carpeted rooms. A yellowish light glows like a long scar at the foot of Halya's door. I think I can hear organ music, the muffled voices of my wife and mother-in-law, anxious, plotting.

As I lope through the rooms the eggs are lying in wait for me. I can almost hear their insidious clicking as they tremble to life.

'You can't do anything to me,' I call through the gray light of the living room to the row of eggs standing on the mantel, like monks in colorful robes. Going from room to room I gather what must be a hundred eggs; I have to make two trips. When I am finished the pitching machine is full, and the auxiliary basket overflows with the intricately decorated eggs.

The long February of my life is over. Come dawn I will warm up my plane and fly off to spring training, where the sun will cook my pale arms and forehead, where I will regain my strength, where my arm will snap on every pitch like a flag in a brisk breeze. I don socks and cleats, turn up the lights until they are bright as sunlight. I dig in at the plate, press the switch to activate the pitching machine, hold my bat high, and wait.

———— ◆ ————

Alexander Cartwright, the generally acknowledged father of modern baseball and member of the pioneering Knickerbocker baseball club in New York City in the mid-1840s, was a restless man. In 1849, in the spirit of Mark Twain, he 'lit out for the coast,' meeting in August with his brother Alfred and a former ball-playing team-mate Frank Turk in San Francisco. The friends shared baseball talk and tossed a ball for a few days before Alex left for Hawaii. On the way he discovered an aversion to sea travel, and never left the island. The ex-Knickerbockers introduced west-coast residents to baseball years before its arrival in much of the American West and Midwest. When gold was discovered on the Fraser River in British Columbia in 1858, San Franciscans were among the first arrivals and with them came baseball. It was, perhaps, one of Alexander Cartwright's least-anticipated legacies.

The Amity of Victoria, 1866–1905

GEOFF LaCASSE

ALTHOUGH BASEBALL HAS BEEN PLAYED IN BRITISH COLUMBIA FOR MORE than 130 years, very little of its history has survived to be re-counted today. Historians have almost exclusively concentrated on political or economic topics at the expense of baseball. A few articles have been written on the period after 1945. Fewer still have looked at the early professional period, beginning in 1905. Almost nothing has appeared on the nineteenth-century game, before the era of turnstiles, salaries, or imports.

The Amity Base Ball Club of Victoria, for example, was the dominant provincial team before the turn of the century. Yet we know almost nothing of the club's history, except for snippets in far-flung publications, most of which prove on closer examination to be false, half-truths, or exaggerations. We are told the Amity was the first formal team (half-true), employed the first semi-professional player (unprovable), won the first BC championship (true), had its home field in the Oak Bay Park in the 1890s (true) and featured Hal Chase – one of the great first basemen of all time – on its roster (in 1903, in fact), and so on.

A close examination of contemporary newspapers suggests that the real story, in fact, was stranger than the fiction. The Amity can trace their history back into the 1860s, first as the Olympics, later as the

Victorias, and for four decades outlasted the competition despite changes to the game, competition from other sports, and economic upheaval.

The early years (1866–1871)

In 1858, gold was discovered along the lower Fraser River. During the ensuing rush (through 1865), the first recorded baseball game occurred in New Westminster, on the Queen's birthday, 24 May 1862, and a second game a year later, in March 1863, in Victoria, then capital of Vancouver Island. Baseball failed to catch on in New Westminster, but Victoria quickly became a hotbed for competition. Between 1863 and 1866, a casual season of March–April and September–November evolved for (or by) miners wintering over in Victoria when conditions made it impossible to work claims.

In mid-September 1866, according to the *British Colonist & Chronicle* (13 September 1866), 'At a meeting of Base Ball players ... a club was formed under the name of the Olympic. Mr Gillon was elected President; and Mr E. McQuade Secretary; Messrs T. Fowler, J. Davies, and R.H. Adams, jr., were elected Directors. The club is limited to thirty members – and the names of twenty four are already booked. The playing rules of the National Base Ball Association of New York were adopted.' The Olympics were probably the first formal club in British Columbia. With no other competition, the first games were played amongst its own members, and against the local cricket team (the Olympics lost 29–17!). In November, the Olympics won their first inter-city game, easily defeating the newly formed City Base Ball Club. The City club did not survive 1866, and in 1867 competition reverted to inter-squad games ('Pretty Boys' vs. 'Ugly Beautys'), with a single game against the cricketers (another embarrassing loss), and possibly one against the Anglo-American Base Ball Club (formed in early 1867). Games were played at Beacon Hill Park, a popular site for sports from the late 1840s.

With such limited local competition, and no other BC teams until 1871, the Olympics were forced to look south, to the United States, for games. In 1868, they played BC's first international game, defeating a visiting team from the USS *Pensacola*. In 1869, the Olympics played the Rainiers of Olympia, Washington, in a home-and-home series (May 24 at home, July 4 away). Although the Olympics lost both games, the 1869 series foreshadowed what would become a popular annual event against American teams in the 1870s.

The Olympics pursued an erratic course over their first half-decade. Years of great activity were offset by years when the local newspapers reported few or no games. The reason is not hard to find. Baseball, as Victoria's leading newspaper, the *British Colonist*, noted in March 1863, was an American game. Its development in Victoria probably depended on the town's American population. For example, when the numbers of American immigrants declined (1864, 1867, 1870) with the end of the gold rush or during an economic downturn, so declined Victoria baseball. When their numbers increased (1866, 1869, 1872, and much later in 1898), baseball and the Olympics were much more visible. Two Americans, in particular, were critical to the Olympics' growth.

John C. Keenan had come to BC from Sacramento in the early 1860s to seek his fortune during the gold rush. When this did not pan out, he settled in Victoria as proprietor of a notorious gambling hall, the Fashion Hotel. From it, he dispensed baseball knowledge, probably picked up from his days as a member of the Sacramento Base Ball Club in 1860. The *Colonist* noted, on March 25, 1863, that play 'improved during the game, owing to the instruction afforded to the less skillful by Mr J.C. Keenan.' The *Colonist* later recorded a Fashion club active for a brief time in 1863. For the next four years, before he returned to Sacramento in 1867, Keenan was an energetic organizer and player. Though he was not a director with the Olympics in 1866 (British residents McQuade and Davies were the prominent members), an article published twenty years later called Keenan the father of Victoria baseball (*Victoria Daily Times*, 21 September 1888). It is also possible that Keenan may have brought baseball to Victoria, the game almost assuredly having been imported from California.

Revival (1872–1877)

Baseball's revival in Victoria in 1872 rested on the shoulders of another American. Mr Fisher was a member of the San Francisco Cricket Club, which travelled to Victoria in June 1872 to complete a cricket series begun three years earlier in San Francisco. Fisher was, amongst other things, a 'crack' baseball player, possibly a member of the San Francisco Eagles (ironically, Keenan had played for the same club in 1867). While in Victoria, Fisher worked with the Olympic club 'every evening between 7 and 8:15 o'clock, at Beacon Hill' (*British Colonist*, 21 June 1872). The results were dramatic. Intra-city competition returned, and home-

and-home series with American clubs were re-established after a three-year absence (the Olympics lost both games in July and September 1872 to Olympia, Washington).

Amity are dominant (1878–1888)

Unfortunately, at a critical juncture, from 1875 to 1878, the Olympics disappeared from the historical record. In 1875, they apparently changed their name to the Victoria Base Ball Club. In 1878, in another metamorphosis not fully understood, the club emerged as the Amity, a word said to mean 'friendly' in the South Sea Islands (*Daily Colonist*, magazine section, 16 April 1911).

The Amity of 1878 differed considerably from their predecessors. Where the Olympics and possibly the Victorias were independent teams, the Amity were all-stars, comprising the best local players regardless of club affiliation, formed to contest all important provincial and international games. This was never stated outright, but an examination of 1870s team rosters, plus indisputable evidence from the 1880s, is clear enough indication. The all-star format was not a new concept. In 1869, the USS *Pensacola* (in a return engagement) had played a team composed of the best players from the Olympics and Dominions. The impetus for change in 1878 was probably two-fold: a strong city league was prospering in Victoria by the mid-1870s; and increased competition elsewhere in BC and south of the border put more emphasis on quality play.

Whatever the reasons, by the early 1880s the Amity had consolidated its position as a pre-eminent club in the Pacific Northwest. It completely dominated teams from Nanaimo and New Westminster (baseball had returned there in 1871), and played very nearly on a par with its American counterparts from Seattle and Portland. In 1885, the Amity defeated Portland 16–12 to win its first Pacific Northwest championship.

The Amity's improvement came from a new generation of players – including Nipsy Gowen, George Borthwick, Tom Baker, and Joseph Kuna – who had developed their skills in Victoria. Gowen, for example, who began his career in the early 1870s, was an original Amity player and did not retire until after 1890. Borthwick was perhaps Victoria's greatest player in the 1880s, a catcher when this was the most demanding position. He was also possibly the first semi-professional player in BC, although the allegations of his receiving a salary of $2000 per year cannot be substantiated.

A series of letters between Gowen and a baseball supporter in July

1885 suggests the Amity operated on the largesse of players and 'cranks.' Gowen gratefully received $17.50 to help defray costs for the trip to Portland. An enclosed stadium and admission charges did not appear in Victoria until July 1889.

In September 1888, the Amity won BC's first (unofficial) championship at a tournament played in Kamloops, defeating teams from Vancouver, New Westminster, and finally Donald (an interior site) in the final, 10–6.

Amity in decline (1889–1905)

The Amity would not win consecutive BC championships, losing the 1889 championship in September to the host team, Kamloops. It was the Amity's fourth loss to Kamloops that year, the first two coming in a Kamloops tour in early July (14–1 and 12–3), the third in the round-robin portion of the tournament (5–4) a day earlier. In the final, with Kamloops leading 6–2 in the eighth inning, the Amity with the bases loaded and two out, the Kamloops pitcher March threw the ball away, and all runs scored. Kamloops protested the runs should not have scored, the umpire upheld the protest, the Amity walked off the field, and Kamloops was declared the victor, 9–0.

> The Kamloops came down like a wolf on the fold,
> Their coaching was cheeky, their batting was bold,
> They lit on Victoria with a terrible swoop,
> And plunged the Amities deep in the soup.
> (Vancouver *Daily World*, 11 July 1889)

The magnitude of the Amity losses to Kamloops was a clear signal of the changing of the guard. The older teams – Amity, New Westminster – were being swept aside by a newer, more dynamic generation led by teams from Kamloops, Donald, and Vancouver. The latter were the product of the building of the BC section of the Canadian Pacific Railway, beginning in 1881. Its construction attracted workers from the United States and eastern Canada, many of them accomplished ball players. With the line's completion in 1886, a new brand of baseball appeared in BC, with immigrant workers bringing a new philosophy towards the rules, professional leagues, betting, and salaries. Donald was probably the prototypical new club, founded as a semi-pro team in 1886. Kamloops followed suite in 1889, enticing seven members of a Minneapolis team to Kamloops to play. The Amity effort, an imported battery from Portland (Parratt and Turnbull), proved no match against Kamloops.

The Amity were also hurt by an economic depression in 1891, the retirement of key players Gowen and Borthwick (who moved to Kamloops in 1891), the popularity of new sports such as lacrosse, rugby, and soccer, and public disgust over the increasing violence and gambling associated with the game.

If the Amity were no longer dominant, the next fifteen years did bring some highlights. They were inaugural members (together with New Westminster, Nanaimo, and Vancouver) of the BC Amateur Base Ball League in 1890. Although the league was never very stable, foundering four times between 1893 and 1903, several outstanding players appeared on the Amity roster. Bill Lange (later of Chicago Nationals fame, 1893–99) may have caught for the Amity during 1890, although this has not yet been confirmed. The Amity were finalists to Nanaimo in the 1895 provincial championship and won the 1900 title. In 1903, the Amity played a very young and extremely talented Hal Chase at first base and catcher, alongside local hero Bernie Schwengers, later one of Canada's greatest tennis players.

It would not be enough. The first professional team appeared in Victoria in 1896. Vancouver, not Victoria, benefited from the 1898 Klondike gold rush and the resulting flood of people, and dominated the BC Amateur Base Ball League from 1901. In 1905, teams from Vancouver and Victoria helped found the Class B Northwestern League. With this final blow, the Amity quietly folded.

———————— ◆ ————————

'Your parishioners' golden calf is baseball.' This warning to a parish priest in Roger Lemelin's The Plouffe Family *(1948) reflects the sport's long fermentation among French Canadians at a time when other symbols of Anglo culture were emphatically repudiated. The game took hold among French-speaking Québécois in the last century as an ironic result of that culture's most traumatic crisis. Between 1850 and 1900 as many as half a million francophones abandoned Quebec in search of work in the lumber mills and shoe-making factories of New England. For a time their language and customs survived, but the American melting pot soon threatened even this birthright. Alarmed expatriates sent their young back to Quebec to be educated in the church-based*

colleges of the day. While learning to be priests, dentists, and businessmen these young people gave their largely French-speaking communities the game the Americans had taught them – baseball.

Three Cheers for Monsieur Folbèche

ROGER LEMELIN

THE FOLLOWING DAY, FRIDAY, THE PLOUFFES WERE OVERTAKEN BY DISASTER. Ovide had disappeared.

At ten o'clock that morning, according to Cécile, he had suddenly left the factory, exasperated by the gibes of his fellow workers who had heard, from Rita Toulouse, all about the antics during the evening of *Pagliacci*.

It was now seven o'clock in the evening and desolation reigned in the Plouffe kitchen where all were prostrate with silent dejection. The table was set, but as yet no one had eaten. A clamour reached them from the playground, for in a few minutes the game with the *Canadiens* was due to begin. Napolean was pacing nervously up and down the kitchen, and every time he passed Guillaume he gave him a dig with his elbow, which meant:

—Come on there, they're waiting for us!

But Guillaume, sitting at the table with his head between his hands, seemed crushed by grief and remorse. Cécile began to complain again:

—I was so ashamed today. Heavens above! Everybody was laughing at Ovide, calling him a sissy and singing 'Laugh then, Pagliacci!'

Mother Josephine suddenly burst into tears, her head turned towards Napoleon.

—I knew we'd be punished some day, because of that there Protestant. Poor child. He's such a good soul. It's easy to see that God wants him to be a priest. And now something tells me my Vide had gone and drowned himself.

—Now! Now! Théophile scolded.

—Don't say that, Mama! shouted Guillaume, who seemed to have lost his composure.

He went to the window, his nose glued to the pane, and stared at the playground, in bewilderment. A light breeze was blowing. The sun, on its way down, bathed everybody and everything with its slanting rays of transparent light, making the bricks of the houses glow, giving to the playground an unsubstantial look, an exciting beauty to the women, and to the men the appearance of big children. Merry groups of brightly dressed people kept emerging from the streets, and settled along the edges of the diamond where players in red or yellow sweaters were strolling about. Bats twirled, balls were struck and caught, and disputes which ended in bets rang out here and there among the impatient onlookers.

—S'pose we had it announced over the radio, Napoleon said; then we could go and play our game.

At his post, Guillaume stiffened up suddenly and looked as though he wanted to break the window with his head. Was that really Rita Toulouse arriving beside Stan Labrie? She was laughing and pointing to the house with a piece of paper in her hand. The letter! Ovide's letter, which was allowing Rita to speak to Stan Labrie at last. Guillaume fell back a step and clenched his fists.

—Damn that girl! Just wait!

With Napoleon at his heels, he tore down the steps and ran to the diamond. The colourful scene and the noisy crowd were transformed into an indistinct and shifting mass before his misty eyes. Everywhere he looked, he saw the family parlour, and in it a very narrow coffin: Ovide's. Guillaume was blaming himself for this death. He paid no attention to the shouts that greeted his arrival on the diamond. His threatening glance searched for Rita Toulouse. But the pastor Tom Brown, with Denis Boucher and the boys on his team, were already crowding around him.

—Quick, Guillaume, warm up a bit; you're late, said the pastor, handing him a ball and a mitt.

He pushed them aside and tried to force his way through the fans. He saw Rita Toulouse sitting on the enemy's bench, laughing loudly, and pointing him out to Stan Labrie who was beside her.

—What's the matter with you? asked Denis, seizing his arm.

—Let go of me! It's that Rita Toulouse. Look at her! She's making fun of me to Stan Labrie. Let me go and push her face in!

—Hold on! You wouldn't do that!

Denis was straining to hold him back. He was non-plussed. His forehead was damp with sweat. His future as a reporter depended on the success of this baseball game. The priest hadn't arrived; the crowd was impatient; and here was Guillaume threatening to beat up Rita Toulouse. He didn't understand Rita's change of front, nor what had happened at the Plouffes', and he hadn't time to think about it. All he could see at the moment was a fit of jealousy which he must appease at any price. Guillaume was carrying on like a madman.

—Listen, he said, are you crazy, attacking a woman? Act like a man!

—Let me go, I tell you!

Tom Brown, the club supporters, and a distracted Napoleon surrounded them.

—See here, said Denis, breathing hard. Don't get upset. Stan Labrie's no competition. He's a queer. He can't have any children, or love a woman. Don't give him another thought! Rita's barking up the wrong tree!

—Well! exclaimed Guillaume, calming down and looking in a puzzled way at Denis.

The latter, relieved, slackened his grip. Guillaume still looked angry as he stood there motionless, thinking. Suddenly he said:

—If that's the way it is, I'll go and tell her mother. She's going to find out what kind of a girl she's got. Be back in a minute.

There was no time to stop him. He was already off, running madly. The pastor raised his arms in dismay, and Denis swore. The players were grumbling and the crowd, with cat-calls and applause, was clamouring for the match to begin. In anguish, Denis looked in the direction of the rectory. Had the priest changed his mind? Had he feared ridicule at the last minute? All at once the youth gave a joyful cry. A group in cassocks was crossing the field. Denis ran to the mound, lifted his arms, and called for silence.

—Ladies and gentlemen! he exclaimed. We have a great surprise for you. Monsieur le curé Folbèche has agreed to pitch the first ball of this game. Here he comes, right now. Three cheers for Monsieur Folbèche.

The parishioners, at first dumb with surprise, began to shout their approval. Monsieur Folbèche was accompanied by his three curates, the school principal, and three church-wardens, brought by him as a measure of prudence, so that if there were any humiliation to suffer, it would be shared among eight. Hearing the cheers directed at him, Monsieur le curé, eyes staring and heart pounding, walked along more quickly. His escorts were mopping their brows and, between breaths, discovering a new Monsieur Folbèche. The group filed past the first lines of onlookers scattered about the field.

—Thanks for coming! The crowd is waiting impatiently for you, Monsieur Folbèche, Denis exclaimed, as he joined him.

—All right, all right! I'm here, he said gaily.

Monsieur Folbèche's eyes shone with unusual friendliness. He walked as though his soles were made of chamois. The old priest, habitually so reserved, distributed more bows than a cardinal on a mission to a foreign diocese. He crossed the diamond, elated by the shouts and applause which greeted him. The group was now surrounded. Denis warded off undesirables.

—This is the Reverend Tom Brown. I told you how much he admired your magnificent garden and your beautiful parsonage.

The pastor, who wore a white cap and was in his shirt sleeves and without a collar, his neck protected by a handkerchief, wiped the sweat off his forehead. For an hour, he had not spared himself in giving professional advice and knocking grounders and high-flies to the players.

He shook hands vigorously with Monsieur Folbèche, who reciprocated uneasily.

—Glad to know you, Monsieur le curé. I admire you. At your age, playing baseball to please your parishioners!

Monsieur Folbèche attempted a timid smile. He was relieved of a great weight. Because of numerous sermons in which he had recounted imaginary and always victorious arguments in English with Protestants, he had feared that the Reverend Tom Brown, when he met him, would begin to argue the superiority of his religion in the language of Shakespeare.

The pastor moved towards the big bench reserved for guests of honour, to the right of the home plate.

—Come and sit here, gentlemen! Just a moment. Let's turn the seat a little to the left so that you won't have the sun in your eyes.

The two already seated stood up: the pastor's fiancée, a tall girl whose eyes were hidden behind dark glasses, and Napoleon, who was watching the horizon anxiously to see if his brother were coming. Denis Boucher went back to the mound again and announced:

—The game will be opened by Monsieur le curé Folbèche, pitcher; the Reverend Tom Brown of Cincinnati, batter; and the Reverend Brother Principal, catcher. Play ball!

Monsieur Folbèche went slowly to the mound. He had been given a new ball which he now examined, turning it round and round in his fingers. Mechanically, he asked the price of it and, to cover his embarrassment, made an impish face at the Principal who was pounding the mitt with his large fist, doubtless because he was delighted at the chance of returning a ball on equal terms; for Monsieur Folbèche usually looked down upon him from the height of his priesthood, and now and then allowed himself to make ironical remarks. As the pastor grasped his bat and walked over to the plate, Denis Boucher appealed to him once more:

—For goodness' sake, do as I asked you. My future depends on it.

The pastor smiled, struck the plate with the bat, and turned towards the priest who, in his agitation, had put the ball in his pocket. The curious crowd was reduced to silence by the importance of the event. Monsieur Folbèche, who had never even consented to play cards, was opening a baseball game! Was a new era beginning? He raised his arms:

—My children. I am not used to playing. So, you must excuse my awkwardness. Laugh if you like; it's a holiday. I came because I'm very fond of you and I want our parish club to begin this game under happy auspices. I should like also to thank the Reverend Tom Brown, who returns to the United States tomorrow, for the fine sporting spirit he has shown. I also wish to welcome the *Canadiens* who, in spite of their superiority, were kind enough to meet our club in an exhibition match.

The umpire gave the signal. Monsieur Folbèche squeezed the ball with all his strength and stared at the batter. The missile rose feebly, about as high as a man's head, and moved out past the plate. Tom Brown sprang, made a great swing, and missed. At first the crowd gave an astonished murmur which quickly swelled and burst into frenzied shouts.

—Strike him out, Monsieur le curé! Strike him out! You can do it!

The three men left the diamond, Monsieur le curé rubbing his hands with satisfaction and bowing to his wardens with a great flourish of his hat. But from all sides, although it was not the custom, there was a demand for them to return to the diamond until a definite result had been obtained; either the pastor should withdraw after three balls, or make a hit. Monsieur Folbèche was the first to accept, eagerly seizing the ball as someone brought it to him.

They cheered, and Monsieur Folbèche, as happy as a child, threw a high ball which the pastor, having taken a too vigorous swing, missed again. This time, even the *Canadiens* applauded. The crowd was jumping, whistling, and thrilling with a new pride: that of being Catholic baseball fans. Delighted, Denis smiled and made gestures of encouragement and congratulation to the priest who, overwhelmed by success, stood with his legs spread apart and his arms dangling. Father Folbèche was regaining his children's affection by joining in their sports. He was jubilant. His face alight with the spirit of the game, he wished these moments might last forever. As for the pastor, who had agreed to play the role of loser out of friendship for Denis, he felt rising up within him, before this crowd who seemed to be taking the priest's success seriously, the religious self-respect that slumbers in the heart of every Protestant minister. His unhappiness ripened into a decision when he saw the tense attitude of his fiancée, to whom he had not explained his generous deception. He grasped his bat resolutely: the comedy was over. Monsieur Folbèche, who was looking off into the distance, seeming to listen to the heartbeats of the breathless crowd, turned around briskly and threw a perfect ball which smacked into the Principal's mitt while the pastor, taken by surprise, turned completely around, carried away by his tardy swing.

There was a long shout. Hats were thrown into the air. A band of men left the crowd and rushed at the bewildered priest. They hoisted him on their shoulders, singing:

—He has won his epaulettes, maluron, malurette!

Tears of happiness appeared in Monsieur Folbèche's eyes as he cast a triumphant glance over his enraptured flock. The victory of truth shone forth: Protestantism had been struck out by Catholicism. Denis Boucher forced his way through.

—Bravo! Bravo, Monsieur le curé! What did I tell you?

Monsieur Folbèche was deposited on the ground. Feverish and breathless, he took Denis by the arm and answered:

—You can come to the office presently. Your letter is ready.

Dumb with joy, Denis did not even say thank-you. The priest looked furtively towards the pastor and whispered to a paralysed Denis:

—We can beat these Americans without even practising! That's the first time I've played. Not bad, eh? And my cassock was a nuisance. Oh! if I only had the time!

The pastor, annoyed and silent, looked at his wrist-watch. Where was Guillaume? Napoleon burst into a joyous shout:

—There he is, coming now. Viourge! Just in time!

Guillaume was led quickly to the mound. He had regained his composure and was smiling defiantly. Ovide was avenged.

The match began.

———————— ◆ ————————

The genius of baseball was its designation of fair territory within a 90-degree arc of the field, permitting spectators to first stand and then sit alongside the diamond, unlike cricket whose 360-degree sweep condemned the crowd to a distant view. William Cammeyer of New York first charged fans, or kranks as they were then known, to watch games in 1862 and hence was born the ballpark, which continues to evolve both magnificent and quirky interpretations of the ideal form. One such field, Tecumseh Park in London, Ontario, has been a baseball site since 1877, when the London Tecumsehs, refusing to buckle to the admonishment of several tavern-keepers promoting a ballpark site near their establishments, instead built a park in the suburb of Kensington. Today that ballpark, known as Labatt Park, is an easy walk from the downtown and gives the same delightful view of the old Court House and the Thames River.

Canadian Baseball Paradise Gardens

ARTHUR LIERMAN

S MALL-TOWN BALLPARKS ARE FASCINATING, ECCENTRIC PLACES OF DISCOVERY that I love to visit – to investigate or simply to enjoy. Even though I prefer to sit along first base, I usually end up wandering around to various vantage points throughout the park in search of the most enlightening views. Gazing over the lush green playing field, with its peculiar angles and dimensions, and the configuration of the quirky grandstand, bleachers, and concession booth, I realize once again how landscape and architecture can create a simple setting that reinforces the glorious role of a ballpark, which I believe is to focus and complete a true baseball experience. I often pause and contemplate the thought that such places are 'baseball paradise gardens.'

Of all sports fields, the baseball diamond is the only field of play where varying configurations, orientations, and especially dimensions have continued to prevail as welcome elements that embody the character of the game. The recent success of the old-style 'ballpark' (not to be called a 'stadium' any more) design movement in major-league baseball and the competition between cities with their retro-ballpark proposals to attract minor-league teams highlight both the importance of detailed design and the meaning such public buildings provide for baseball and the community. Apart from reinterpreting the unique qualities of the old parks, however, this ballpark renaissance has responded to the desires of baseball teams and fans alike to create an identifiable and intimate place to celebrate the game, the team, the fans, and the community.

Each genuine ballpark has its own signature elements, whether planned or not, that make for a unique identity. However, beyond the more obvious short porch in right or tall wall in left, some of the true pleasures of ballparks include the subtle features that create a sense of anticipation – of arriving at a special place, set off from its surroundings, for an important community event. Their often rusty and weathered architecture returns one to the simpler days of the past. The gravel driveways, grassed parking lots, wooden bleachers, and tree-lined backdrops help to define their idiosyncratic appeal. In Canada, although ballparks may not be as prominent as hockey arenas or community centres, they too are true cultural public forums with a striking yet delightful sense of place and meaning that bring people together, focus them, and unify them.

On many memorable afternoons and evenings, I have visited two such places in southwestern Ontario with the picturesque qualities that typify the beauty and romance of ballparks. Having grown up in London, Ontario, I have of course frequented that city's baseball treasure, Labatt Park – most often as a spectator, but just recently as a player. However, before my awakening to ballpark lore and my acquired reverence for Labatt Park, I attended many games at Emslie Field in nearby St. Thomas to cheer on my brother, who played for the St. Thomas Elgins of the Intercounty Major Baseball League.

Emslie Field is comfortably integrated within the natural landscape setting of Pinafore Park, a scenic ninety-acre recreational grounds. The quaint ball field is named after Robert Emslie, an outstanding pitcher for the St. Thomas Atlantics professional baseball team during the late 1800s, who would later go on to play and umpire in the major leagues [see Emslie, in this volume].

Complete with rolling meadows, towering trees, and lush flower gardens, Pinafore Park's pastoral context arouses curiosity and antici-pation for those heading to the ballpark. As you wind your way along the entrance drive, you are greeted by the vibrant colours and sweet fragrances of the gardens. Sounds of music from summertime concerts at the park's bandshell echo soothingly throughout the park. One's journey through this place of rustic charm is further enhanced by the century-old pavilions that welcome picnicking families and social gatherings. The park reinforces and enhances the celebration of baseball's seasonal relationships and rituals.

Amidst this kaleidoscope of tranquil images, you are greeted by a whimsical wooden fence that unveils the confines of Emslie Field, tucked into a corner of the park. The weathered aesthetic and textural warmth of this articulated fence brings to mind images of 'knothole gangs' stealing glimpses of baseball games. Past the entrance gate, a gravel laneway leads to grassed parking areas behind the grandstand and along the third-base side. The crackling sound of gravel under the tires and the comforting feeling of the soft green parking areas are carnival-like and refreshing. Harsh asphalt parking lots are not welcome here.

The ball field is situated in a low-lying area that is bordered along the left-field foul line by a grassed terrace. Many people park along the terrace, pull out lawn chairs, and spread out blankets to take advantage of the views and comforts of this natural bleacher. Low-rise apartment buildings that peer into the park along the right-field side provide an urban, balancing contrast to the heavily forested hitting background beyond the outfield fence. An aging, typical, covered steel-and-concrete grandstand anchors the ballpark behind home plate, while small portable bleachers, randomly located past the dugouts along the foul lines, complete the seating configuration.

I have often wondered about the origin of the 'dugout' – that dark, grotto-like hide-out where the players banter and fraternize, but most importantly where they seek refuge and protection from both ridicule and bad weather. Emslie Field attempts to provide big-league dugout appeal, with sunken chambers of reasonable enclosure that are entered by two narrow sets of stairs. I have always considered a ballpark to be complete only if it included, at the very least, some form of enclosure to define the players' 'den.'

From a spectator's point of view, Emslie Field offers many of the characteristic and enchanting features expected of a true ballpark. However, from a player's perspective, such as my brother's, the field is not without its shortcomings, I am told. Lacking funding for continual maintenance and proper staffing, and with its unfortunate use for high-school football games in the fall, the dry and scarred playing field almost never offers a true hop. Pitching-mound idiosyncrasies have been a continuing uncertainty. In fact, one year, after the Elgins' final game of a dreadful campaign, it was discovered that the pitching rubber was sixty-*one* feet six inches from home plate. How's that for a lack of uniformity in playing-field dimensions?

During many of the Elgins' Sunday night games at Emslie Field the same group of older folks would sit up in the grandstand cheering on their team and heckling the umpires, if not the visitors. Some of the women would be knitting; a few men would be enjoying a cigar while watching the game. Between innings, melodies from the bandshell carry into the ballpark, inviting one's mind to wander beyond baseball and the characters in the stands. Every community that still treasures small-town baseball has a similar core of true fans who enjoy the summer ritual of taking time for a lazy night at the ballpark.

London is no exception. Situated in the heart of the city and positioned within a crooked piece of property, Labatt Park is a fine example of the traditional urban ballparks of the early 1900s. The park has an incredibly rich baseball history dating back to the 1870s and is believed to be the oldest baseball grounds in continuous use in North America. It was originally laid out on a six-acre site in the suburb of Kensington and was called Tecumseh Park. The park received its new name after the hometown Labatt brewing family purchased it – and later turned it over to the city along with a $10,000 donation to help rebuild it after the Thames River flood of 1937.

Since that time, gradual improvements and additions to the park, including new grandstands, dugouts, a floodlight system, dressing rooms, and a concession area, continued. It was not, however, until the arrival of the Double A affiliate of the Detroit Tigers in 1989 that Labatt Park would achieve its present professional standards. The grounds were improved and many renovations were undertaken: adding box seats and bleacher stands, installing a new press box, scoreboard, lighting, and concessions, and building new dressing rooms and public washrooms. The ballpark has seating for 5400, consisting of a covered grandstand behind home plate and two open stands along each foul line that are all connected by a concourse aisle.

Labatt Park's greatest strength, however, is the splendour of its location, nestled at the forks of the Thames River near the western edge of downtown London. The bordering land uses vary in a fanciful manner that provides engaging background settings for the ballpark. Behind home plate and along the left-field line nestle the peaked roof-lines and intimate backyards of the neighbouring houses. Beyond the outfield, towering cottonwood trees located along the river sway above the park, punctuating the skyline. The view from home plate is captivating, as if it were composed. The field's patterned lawn reaches out to a billowing hedge of lush cedars, which together create an ordered foreground for the rising skyline of downtown London off in the distance. The spectacular vistas of Labatt Park's surroundings are signature features that associate the park and the team with the city. Although these features are unplanned in Labatt Park's case, design manoeuvres for the new wave of ballparks, whether big or small, are purposely orienting their fields to face and provide views of the city skyline.

Ballpark design is successful if it provides a common thread of meaning in its details. Along Labatt Park's longest and most publicly visible boundary, once again, a peculiar wooden fence serves to announce the individual character of the park. Its extra height, impenetrable thickness, and undulating capping are characteristics that arouse one's curiosity. Attention and interest would not be stimulated had a generic fence design been chosen.

I remember going to London Majors' games at Labatt Park with my dad when I was a little boy, though I am sure I was more interested in the french fries and popcorn than the baseball game. We always parked the car in the same place, down the road two blocks and to the left from the park. I still park there now because I enjoy the experience of strolling along the intimate tree-lined streets and seeing people relaxing on their front porches. As you draw near the park you catch glimpses of the grandstand between the houses and begin to recognize the sounds of the ballpark as the announcer calls out the starting line-ups. Like the approach to the great city ballparks such as Ebbets Field, Fenway Park, and Wrigley Field, the arrival at Labatt Park furnishes a transitional baseball awakening that is an important part of the total experience of going to a ball game.

Parking inside Labatt Park's confines is a vivid experience as well. A winding route, which takes you underneath the covered wooden grandstand behind home plate, leads to a grassed parking area along the left-field side. Steel beams supporting the grandstand frame the narrow lane as a dark passage animated by the lurking silhouettes of people arriving for the game, the pounding sounds of footsteps above, and the hollow echoes of voices and cheerful music. One's view of the field is teasingly restricted, with only passing glimpses offered through the cracks of the wooden stands and over the steps rising to the concourse aisle.

The playing field is a manicured masterpiece well worth the wait. In 1989, Labatt Park won the Beam Clay Professional Baseball Park of the Year award, given annually to the top natural baseball grounds in North America. Peculiar to the field is its 'tortoise-shell' design, which assists drainage. The raised infield forms a steep lip running along the outer infield grass line from foul line to foul line. I have often wondered how the sudden grade change affects the game. My brother, who is now with the London Majors of the Intercounty League, remarks that there is not much of a home advantage because the visiting teams enjoy playing there so much.

Apart from its eccentric grandeur and perfect 'fit' with Labatt Park's other elements, the covered grandstand offers comfort and pleasure that is vital to audience enjoyment. Good ballparks can offer more alternatives than just the selection between box seats, bench seats, and bleachers. Covered stands provide shelter and protection from the weather and are especially appreciated during sudden showers or those dreadful constant drizzles. What better place to wait out a rain delay and talk baseball than in a covered grandstand?

And what about those darn aluminum seats? Well, the less said the better. During the renovations to Labatt Park aluminum box seats, bench seats, and benches were installed in all the prime seating areas at the expense of wooden benches. Wooden bleachers were located far down the base lines, but fortunately the wooden benches in the top rows of the covered grandstand were retained.

Still, views from your aluminum seat visually connect you with activities happening outside the ballpark perimeter. Just beyond the sweeping cedar hedge is a raised riverwalk used by many for promenading, jogging, and bicycling. A distinct break in the hedge in left-centre field provides a window for passersby to catch a glimpse of the park. Similarly, those in the ballpark are able to escape baseball momentarily and experience the silent periodic movement along the riverwalk. With visual access to the ballpark maintained, the public is given a teasing perception of the park – a hint of what is going on without the place's entire experience being given away.

A description of Labatt Park would not be complete without mentioning the London Majors' clubhouse, the peculiar building located behind and between the covered grandstand and the left-field stands. This unimposing structure has been a part of Labatt Park since the 1940s. Inside, the entrance room's walls and ceilings are decorated with photographs and artefacts celebrating the Majors. Shabby couches and weathered wooden panelling produce the overwhelming scent of a musty cottage or, perhaps more accurately, a miniature men's lodge. Past a drawn curtain to the right is the heart of the team's den, the cramped dressing room with its two showers and the manager's office.

Since the departure of the AA Tigers in 1993, the Majors have been offered access to the Tigers' expansive and professional quarters, but they have declined, feeling quite content with their old clubhouse.

On Canada Day, July 1, 1994, Labatt Park received historical designation as a heritage site. The deserving proclamation was followed that afternoon by a Majors' game for which I would step in to do the announcing. Although admittedly nervous, I managed to do quite well, except for the few times when I forgot to turn off the microphone and was caught mumbling to the score-keeper.

I have now finally come full circle with Labatt Park: I joined the thirty-and-over men's baseball league and have officially played on the sacred grass.

The old small-town ballparks standing today are fortunate to have survived the wrecking ball and to have evolved over several years through a peculiar growth process of eccentric renovations that we now cherish. If we begin to understand the nuances and the inherent qualities of good ballparks, perhaps more of them will be protected and sensitively improved. By understanding the importance of the experiences of arrival and departure, of the visual connections between the ballpark and its surroundings, and of elements like the undersides of grandstands and the sounds of gravel driveways, I believe we can help to preserve and enhance the beauty and romance of the ballpark. Sound design ideas can be applied to all levels of ballpark design, even for a little-league diamond or a slo-pitch complex. However, one must realize that not everything can be planned when designing a baseball paradise garden. After all, the perfection of a ballpark lies in its imperfection.

◆

Canadians like to think of themselves as different from Americans when it comes to race relations. The country largely lacks the stark heritage of slavery. Perhaps that's why Branch Rickey chose Montreal as the setting for the integration of organized baseball in the modern era when he signed Jackie Robinson in 1946. As David McDonald makes clear, however, Canadians had quickly adopted many of the unsavoury features of the American apartheid system that settled in following the Civil War. One of the saddest was the unwritten ban on gifted black ball players from playing for established teams by the 1890s. As late as the 1920s Ontario amateur baseball authorities were seeking direction from Judge Landis, the commissioner of baseball, on the advisability of allow-ing a black youth to play in their tournaments – a question completely out of the jurisdiction and moral purview of Landis.

Jim Crow Comes North

DAVID MCDONALD

O N THE EVE OF JACKIE ROBINSON'S DEBUT WITH THE MONTREAL ROYALS IN 1946, an editorial in the Chicago *Defender* remarked: 'It is ironi-cal that America, supposedly the cradle of democracy, is forced to send the first two Negroes in baseball to Canada in order for them to be accepted.'

More ironical than the *Defender* realized. For Robinson and his team-mate, pitcher Johnny Wright, were not the first African-Americans in baseball. Far from it. At least 75 blacks had played organized ball before the turn of the century, including two in the major leagues. What is more, some 60 years before Montreal welcomed Robinson, Canada had played a shameful role in their exclusion from the game's mainstream.

In the spring of 1887, baseball's racial attitudes were amorphous – not exactly fluid, not yet hardened. No blacks had appeared in the major leagues since 1884, when the sons of an Ohio physician, Moses Fleetwood Walker and his brother Welday, had played for the American Association Toledo Blue Stockings. But there were tantalizing indications that several clubs, including the New York Giants and the Philadelphia Athletics, might be willing to follow the defunct Toledo club's lead, should the ambivalent winds of public – and, more important, baseball – opinion declare themselves favourable.

As in 1946, baseball's 'third league,' the International League, would be integration's proving grounds in 1887. American cities with sizeable black populations, like Newark, Buffalo, and Rochester, would be in-volved in the experiment. But equally crucial to its outcome would be the attitudes of such comparatively racially homogeneous cities as Toronto and Hamilton. By season's end some kind of critical mass would be reached, and the prospects for integrated baseball would sink like a stone.

Five clubs in the ten-team International League recruited black play-ers in 1887. Altogether, at least nine would play in the league that summer, including ex–major leaguer Fleet Walker and dominating left-hander George Stovey in Syracuse, slugger Frank Grant, back for his second season in Buffalo, and veteran all-rounder Bud Fowler in Binghamton.

'How far will this mania for engaging colored players go?' The U.S. publication *Sporting Life* demanded. 'At the present rate of progress the International League may ere many moons change its title to "Colored League."'

If signing 'colored' players had indeed become a mania, it was one that showed no evidence of spreading north of the border. Professional baseball had been played in Canada for more than a decade, but black players had been unable to establish any kind of beachhead in this country.

Binghamton's Bud Fowler, widely regarded as the first black professional, was no stranger to Canadian racial attitudes. In 1878, Fowler had joined the Lynn (Massachusetts) Live Oaks of the major-league-calibre International Association. One of the first clubs he faced was the defending champion London Tecumsehs, managed by Dick Southam. Southam complained of Fowler's presence on the field and refused to allow his team to finish the game. The Oaks' response? Release Fowler.

Fowler's second run-in with Canadian racism came in July 1881, when Guelph brewing magnate George Sleeman recruited him to pitch for his Maple Leafs in the Canadian Association. As the Boston *Herald* reported, 'When he reached Guelph and the members of the club found he was a colored youth, they snobbishly refused to play with him.'

When the rival Petrolia Imperials indicated they might be more open-minded, Fowler signed with them, only to have his new team-mates commit 19 errors behind him in his first start. For the umpteenth time in his career, Fowler was forced to pack his bag and ply his trade elsewhere. 'The poor fellow's skin is against him,' said *Sporting Life* in 1885. 'If he had a white face [he] would be playing with the best of them.'

Tellingly, the only African-American to be accepted by a Canadian team in those years was a 'very small and very fat colored boy' named Willie Hume. The Toronto club had virtually press-ganged the unfortunate Hume as their mascot during a road trip to Syracuse in May 1886. Beyond initial reports in the Toronto papers, Hume was never referred to by name. He became, like some organ-grinder's monkey, an amusing cipher, simply 'the fat Mascot in his gaudy new suit' or 'the Torontos' colored cupid.'

Press treatment of visiting African-American players was scarcely more dignified. In the Toronto *Globe*, the brilliant Frank Grant of Buffalo was the 'colored mascot' or the 'maroon' second baseman, Bob Higgins of Syracuse was 'the sable pitcher.' But nowhere in the International League was there a paper more obsessed with race than the Hamilton *Spectator*, published by former London baseball star Bill Southam, brother of Bud Fowler's nemesis Dick Southam.

'That sunburned second baseman of the Buffs is an amusing person,' the *Spectator* said of Grant. 'He is as limber as a jumping-jack, and has lots of fun with himself.'

But if Grant was 'sunburned,' then George Stovey of Syracuse wasn't sunburned enough: 'Stovey is not very black. He is everlastingly smoking cigars when he is off duty, and looks as if he had just succeeded in coloring himself a trifle.'

When Newark visited Hamilton on June 8, 1887, the *Spectator*, perhaps intoxicated by its previous racial witticisms, pulled out all the stops. 'Walker, the coon catcher of the Newarks, is laid off with a sore knee,' it said. 'It is insinuated by envious compeers that in early life he practiced on hen roosts until he got the art of foul-catching down fine.' And, in a separate item: 'Yesterday the Newarks only played half of their coon battery, and the Hams were shut out with one run. There is good ground for suspicion that it is a case in which two blacks would have made a white-wash. Anyhow, it is generally admitted that the colored pop. have a monopoly on the calsimine [sic] business.'

This time the calcimine hit the fan. On June 10, the *Spectator* ran an apology to Hamilton's black community for the 'two items referring to Newark's colored battery.' Southam blamed the slurs on a freelance contributor and a careless editor.

There is a story that 'the coon catcher of the Newarks' took personal exception to the *Spectator* piece and sought out its publisher. Fleet Walker, who had attended Oberlin College and the University of Michigan law school, and was one of the few ballplayers of his day to have studied Latin, Greek, French, German, natural philosophy, and logic, had by this point in this career abandoned polite discourse in such matters and taken to packing a pistol. To what extent his armed persuasion was responsible for eliciting Southam's apology is not known.

But a week after l'affaire Walker, the unrepentant Hamilton rag was back in fine form. First it reprinted an item from another newspaper that termed the whole Walker incident 'a harmless little joke,' then suggested (in response to an appearance by Binghamton's Bill Renfroe) that Hamilton 'rub burnt cork on one of [its own] pitchers – just to be in fashion.'

But if black players had it tough in the press, they had it immeasurably tougher at the ballpark. On May 25 right-hander Bob Higgins made his first start for the Syracuse Stars in a game at Toronto and his fielders casually committed 16 errors behind him in a 23–8 loss. In June, several of Higgins's team-mates refused to sit for a photo with him. When the Syracuse ringleader, Mississippi-born 'Dug' Crothers, was suspended by his club, a sympathetic Hamilton *Spectator* provided him with a platform to explain why 'I would rather have my heart cut out [than] consent to have my picture taken in that group.' And when Crothers was dropped by Syracuse, he quickly found employment in Hamilton.

Even league officials were not above wearing their prejudices on their sleeves. In May 1887, umpire Billy Hoover boasted that on a close play he always ruled against 'a team employing a colored player.' The Binghamton *Daily Leader* suggested Hoover 'should be driven out of the league at the toe of a boot.' The Toronto *World*, however, called him 'the best of them all.'

By the end of June, reports from Syracuse said that four International League clubs, including Toronto and Hamilton, had begun a campaign to institute a complete ban on blacks in the league. Chants of 'Kill the nigger' were beginning to be heard at Toronto ball games.

On July 14, the International League met in Buffalo and one of the items on the agenda was the problem of 'the colored element' – by now about as rare as ytterbium. This 'element' consisted entirely of Grant in Buffalo, Stovey and Walker in Newark, and Higgins in Syracuse, the rest of the black players, including the .350-hitting Fowler, having been released. The league's directors vote 6–4 'to approve no more contracts with colored men,' with Toronto and Hamilton essentially swinging the vote.

While the U.S. press was virtually unanimous in its condemnation of the International League's colour line, Canadian newspapers treated the issue with a dispassionate matter-of-factness. The Newark *Journal* editorialized that 'if Stovey, Walker, Grant or any other colored man is refused a position ... on account of his complexion he can make things very warm for the league. It has been decided that every man in this country is entitled to a living if he can earn one.' To which the Toronto *World* replied with offhand logic: 'You can't compel a club to engage you as a ball-player whether you are black or white.'

Of the nine African-American players who began the tumultuous 1887 season, only four were around on closing day. Despite establishing an International League standard of 34 wins, Stovey was released, ostensibly as a cost-cutting measure. However, Grant (.353), Walker (.263), and Higgins (20-7) were reserved for 1888. The Toronto *World* called the retention of this 'colored element ... hard to understand.' The Newark *Register* shot back: 'Read the emancipation proclamation, Canadian brethren, and become enlightened.' The *World* responded smugly – and falsely – that the Canadian clubs had had nothing to do with the institution of the colour bar.

The revamped International Association of 1888 featured three all-white Canadian clubs – Toronto, Hamilton, and newcomer London – among its eight teams. And it didn't take long for Toronto manager Charlie Cushman to toss out the first racial bomb of the season. On May 23, with Syracuse playing at Toronto, a Stars player complained about the overflow crowd seated on the edge of the playing field. Cushman acknowledged the beef by turfing not only the spectators, but also the injured Fleet Walker, who had been seated in his civvies on the Stars' bench. Outside the stadium the irate Walker talked about putting a bullet in Cushman. He was apprehended by a police detective, who found a gun in his pocket. Walker spent the night at No. 4 police station.

Three weeks later the Buffalo *Courier* reported that Walker's erstwhile target, Cushman, was 'engineering a scheme to have colored players ousted from the International Association.' The *Courier* surmised that 'Cushman's scheme will hardly go. There are only three colored men in the Association ... and they behave themselves. '

By season's end, only Walker and Grant remained, Higgins having gone home to Memphis rather than endure further abuse. In November, the Association's directors met in Syracuse. Hamilton and London agitated – unsuccessfully – for the immediate expulsion of the remaining black players. A compromise was reached: again the clubs agreed not to sign any more blacks, and should either Grant or Walker be released, no other team would be allowed to pick them up. The fate of black players in organized baseball having been decided, the delegates, including Thomas S. Hobbs of London and Alderman James Dixon of Hamilton, adjourned to a banquet given by the Syracuse club.

The reiteration of the International Association colour bar had repercussions far beyond the league itself. It meant that the major leagues were now effectively closed to blacks. Without having to formally enact a messy racial policy of their own, the majors could now simply shrug and point to a dearth of black talent at the highest minor-league level. Hobbs, Dixon, et al. had done their dirty work for them.

In 1889, amid reports that their players would strike if he returned, Buffalo made little effort to re-sign Grant. However, Fleet Walker did put in one final, lonely season with Syracuse. The first African-American player in the major leagues would also be the last in the International League until Canadians, in an unwitting act of expiation, embraced Jackie Robinson more than half a century later.

——————— ◆ ———————

As in so many other areas of life, the best work of sport is often accomplished by unsung heroes – people who work diligently and generously at something they believe in, and along the way affect the lives of countless others. Carmen Bush was such a quiet hero for over four decades in Toronto amateur baseball. Known for his strength of character and firm convictions, Carmen loved working with young people. Most of all, he conveyed his love for baseball and his respect for the patient discipline needed to play the game well – a useful approach to any area of life. His huge contribution to the game was recognized in his induction into the Canadian Baseball Hall of Fame in 1985. Tom McKillop, now a Roman Catholic pastor, was one of Carmen's 'boys.' His unusual story touches on two very different eras in Toronto baseball.

A Boy's Dream Comes True ... 50 Years Later

TOM MCKILLOP

BACK IN 1938 AT MACGREGOR PLAYGROUND IN WEST-END TORONTO, I WAS appointed a coach of the under–85 pounders for softball. David Speyers, the playground supervisor, had given me, at the age of 10, the daunting task of being a coach. I tried to copy and do and say all the right things. Then, at age 12, David saw something in me and invited me to try out for hardball with the Columbus Boys Club on Bellwoods Avenue.

The coach was Carmen Bush, an inspirational young man who gave me my first chance to play shortstop at Bellwoods Park against such great teams as the Trinity K Club and Gerrard K Club. I was the 'cake-eater' (WASP), playing with the Pollacks, the Wops, the Blacks, and the Ikes, as we called each other at that time. Every day in the summer I rode my bicycle to the park so I could sit around and talk baseball, learn how to do the double play and how to hit. We talked and talked baseball, dreaming of someday going to a baseball camp run by the Dodgers or the Cardinals.

Among my favourite moments were the times when Carm would sit in his office and we'd all gather around and listen to the Master's stories. He was Bush, the voice with the message, and we hung on his every word because we wanted to be known and recognized by him. (He was also 'the dictator': he didn't just have opinions about things, he had *convictions*.) I remember sitting there on an old radiator, just relishing it all, with my ears and heart wide open.

One year I had hurt my arm and had to sit on the bench, game after game, and wait for my chances. It was really hard as a young teenager sitting out, but my elbow pained me when I tried to throw the ball. We were now at Christie Pits, and how I pined to play. I worried and wondered if Carm really wanted me around. One hot summer afternoon, I rode my bike down to the Club and asked Carmen if I could talk to him. He invited me to go to one of the back rooms near the pool table. 'What's wrong, Tommy?' he asked. I tried to explain my dilemma. I stuttered a little and then broke down in tears. 'I want to stay, Carmen, and I want to play.' Carm listened to me and explained how he knew my arm was hurting and he didn't want me to hurt it more. 'Just rest it,' he said, 'and we'll get you in there.' That's all I needed to hear. I went out filled with hope.

The years went by in high school. Carm had taught me the essentials of the game and not to worry about things like my batting average. 'Just do your best, Tommy, your hits will come.' I began to travel with my friends to different baseball camps and was overawed by the uniforms of the big teams, like the Dodgers and Cardinals, worn by the coaches and the scouts. Back in Toronto we continued to live at the park and to dream secret dreams.

Finally, around 1948, I began to play at Viaduct Park in East Toronto (at the southwest corner of Broadview and Danforth). We played some great teams from Oakville and Oshawa. We worked out Sunday mornings, and just lived for the game and the friendship. Rusty Wallace, Loring Doolittle, Frankie Davis, the McMurrays, Frank McLaughlin, Bus Sadler, Joe Irvine and a host of others are still vivid in my mind. We were a bunch of characters, but completely absorbed in ball – the strategies, the game, and the talking after the game.

We followed the Toronto Maple Leafs in the International League and just about lived in the right-field stands of Maple Leaf Stadium at Lake Shore and Bathurst, hoping for a foul ball. After the games we would have paper and pencil, hungering for an autograph. Every ball player dressed in suit, shirt, and tie seemed awesome as he walked through the gate. Just to have him sign an autograph was beyond the beyond, let alone sign the ball you caught.

On Sunday evenings we would walk along the boardwalk at Sunnyside Beach with hundreds of others. (With the Palais Royale and the Bathing Pavilion, Sunnyside was one of the big social 'scenes' in those days.) Our little group would include a friend of one of the guys who had played a lot of ball and done some coaching. We would talk baseball with our mentor, talk incessantly about how to hit a curve, and recall certain plays over and over again. Baseball wasn't just everything. It was the only thing.

About 1949, the Phillies came to town for a baseball school with Cy Morgan, who was signing up young prospects. I was now over six feet tall, and slow of foot, thinking this was it for me. My secret dream had always been to be a pro ball player. But my heroes – Joe DiMaggio, Red Schoendienst, Joe Gordon, and Bobby Feller – were so far beyond my level. One of the big leaguers who was coaching hit me grounders in all directions. I was relaxed and picked up everything. He even apologized for driving the ball so hard! I recall the 60-yard sprints we had to do as the final test to be chosen by Cy Morgan. Even though I was slow, I warmed up and prepared myself for the word 'Go.' I was off and could hardly believe it when I won the sprint.

Cy Morgan called me down to the Royal York Hotel to sign a contract with the Phillies for their Class C team in Schenectady. I couldn't believe it! Would there be a bonus for signing? Maybe I'd make $150 a month. I signed and was ecstatic!

That year I played senior ball. Every game was not just a challenge but another moment closer to spring training. I remember striking out to Oakville's Al Yarnell with the bases loaded. While I tried to figure out his pattern, he just zoomed three pitches straight down the middle. We were finished for the year.

That year I was in my final year of university. I was afraid of being hurt in hockey so I cut back on my time with the Varsity Blues. There was no one locally to help me stay in baseball shape. Lloyd Percival had his own sports school, but I couldn't find out where it was.

As the year went on and my studies got more intense, I found myself tossing and turning at night, restless. I couldn't wait to go. I talked to

Carmen. He said, 'Stay for your studies.' I talked to the registrar. He said, 'Stay for the exams.' I was going crazy! My mother wrapped up a sock and tossed it to me during the winter nights in the front room as I hit it against the wall. 'I can't study. I have to go!' I told my Mother and Dad. This was my only chance.

So I flew to Atlanta, Georgia, and took the bus to a little God-forsaken place called Americus. Even Cy Morgan didn't know I was coming. After all the players had introduced themselves to Cy and one another, I quietly announced myself. Cy, startled to see me, smiled.

I was alone and lonely, the only Canadian in camp. When the exercises and games began, I was nervous. I wanted to be close to a few people, but felt the pressure to compete and produce. Finally, after a few weeks, I was asked to go to South Carolina. I left, saying goodbye to a few potential pros, and stayed another week in the new camp. Then, at last, the final word came, and it was over.

I came back through Buffalo. Humiliated that I had to go back to the local ball field and explain myself, I decided to say simply, 'I wasn't good enough.' I had lost my glove, the spikes were too tight, but in the end I was not good enough.

Incredibly, I rewrote my final exams, four in a day and a third, and got through. I took a test and decided to become a teacher. Then I threw myself into helping young people, continuing to play and coach. One of the players kept suggesting that I become a priest. I thought that he was out of his mind. Then, after teaching six years, I decided to study to be a priest. But I still played ball, till I was 36 ...

Twenty-eight years later, in the fall of 1992, after having worked with young people for 18 years as a priest and having been a pastor for 8 years, I read about the Blue Jays' Fantasy Camp. I was 64 and thought, 'Maybe ... no, that's crazy ... well, why not?' I went to Dunedin, Florida, with 23 others from Canada. There I met Bob Bailor, Garth Iorg, John Mayberry, and Willie Upshaw, and found myself living out a fantasy and an old dream.

We dressed in Blue Jay uniforms, threw a baseball gingerly, gathered in centre field and listened to the coaches, and had some hitting practice. That week we played nine games amongst ourselves and ended up at Grant Field playing against the old Blue Jays. I remember walking out to second base, my old position, absolutely thrilled. In the game, I singled to left field. At the end of the game, I gave my forty-five-year-old glove to Garth Iorg, who collected old gloves. He gave me his new one.

At the final banquet, they gave me the Iron Man Award. To me, this was the ultimate holiday of my life. I've returned three times now to Dunedin and the Fantasy Camp and made a host of new friends. It feels like this has always been my atmosphere, where I am real and feel at home.

Each year the 'campers' are given a baseball card with their picture and 'stats' on it. On my last one I wrote, 'Reflection on life deepens. Action on reflection broadens. Friendship makes it meaningful.'

A video has come out recently, entitled 'When It Was a Game.' It shows the game of baseball as it was played in the majors from the 1930s to the mid-fifties. I lived through that time, but I never thought that much later in life (in my sixties!) I'd be able to return to my life as a boy and experience the thrill of playing ball again.

———————— ◆ ————————

The essay 'Baseball Is Culture' (also delivered as a talk on CBC Radio's 'Wednesday Night' in September 1952) shocked its readers, for here was a 'low' subject being treated with 'high seriousness.' Marshall McLuhan, in fact, brought to bear on popular culture the techniques of analysis usually reserved for the fine arts – literature, poetry, painting, music. In so doing, he was updating the long-neglected practice of reading the everyday world as a book and subjecting it to critical awareness to reveal the ground of current experience and sensibility. The shock of this essay lay partly in his showing that baseball has serious cultural implications, and largely in expanding the idea of culture to include both the archetypes (guarded by academics and curators) and all the clichés. Suddenly, the snobs and sophisticates found themselves in bed with Casey Stengel, Yogi Berra, and Dizzy Dean – an abrasive alliance. For McLuhan, personally, early October was a special time of year, when he and his family followed each game of 'the World Serious.'

Baseball Is Culture

MARSHALL MCLUHAN

YES, I'M GOING TO SUGGEST NOT ONLY THAT BASEBALL IS CULTURE BUT that comics are culture, and detective stories are culture, and that pictorial advertising is culture. Of course, this puts us all somewhat in the position of the character in the French play who was thunderstruck when he learned that he had not just been talking, but talking *prose* all his life.

An English friend of mine once told me of watching some Spanish peasants making wine and treading out the grapes in a sort of choral group. He said to the wine-makers, 'It's just like the Ballet Russe!' They were delighted at this suggestion and proceeded to show him a variety of dance steps employed in other parts of the country for the same process of pressing the grapes. This episode caused him to reflect that had he told a group of English workmen that they were like the Ballet Russe they would have been insulted as though their moral lives had been called in question.

To a much greater degree than the English, Canadians and Americans separate their daily occupations and amusements from what they are pleased to call culture or the higher things. But a European or a Chinese coming to this continent would never think of distinguishing between our daily lives and our occasional pursuit of these higher things.

In the same way Canadians can see easily enough that cricket is cultural activity but they might not agree that baseball is cultural activity. We would admit that the ritual of the fox-hunt is bound up with English culture and social functioning but we are not prepared to look at hockey in the same light.

As another example, the ritual of the morning and evening paper is not thought of as part of the life of culture perhaps because we enjoy such things and because we have come to think of culture as that class of unpleasant activities in which we *ought* to engage more often. Because we enjoy the radio and the movies they are not culture, but dull lectures and stuffy books are cultural. Jack Benny and Raymond Chandler just can't be culture because they are fun.

What this adds up to is to say that we have put culture in the department of moral effort. Whereas all those affairs which fascinate and delight us, whether the daily job, the profession we belong to, or the recreations we turn to, these things which make up our real lives we have somehow come to regard as non-cultural.

Imagine for a moment, however, an outsider coming to study the culture of the American continent today. Could he not learn a great deal more from the artistic forms of our newspapers and magazines, our sports and our songs, than from our historians and sociologists? But even this comparison isn't quite fair.

Because when one of our sociologists or anthropologists leaves home to study the lives and culture of some alien and remote society he takes great pains to study the gestures and artistic qualities of the language, as well as the cooking and crafts and the social rituals of child-rearing and adult behaviour. Because, today we know that culture consists of the way in which people communicate and co-operate. Culture is a network of communication. And, surprising as this may sound at first, North American culture differs from older European culture in being more intellectual, more abstract and technical than traditional cultures that have been more exclusively linked to the soil and agriculture.

Now that may explain why on this continent we don't recognize our own culture for the richly diversified thing that it is. We still think of culture in terms that belong to other times and conditions.

In Plato's discussion of love, in the dialogue of the *Symposium*, love is presented as the universal desire for human benefit and as including commerce, gymnastics, and philosophy. Merchants, athletes, and philosophers, though not called lovers, are still seekers after happiness and the good. Yet the simple statement that baseball is culture is likely to create panic in the hearts of sports lovers.

Sports lovers as a group would not thank anybody who told them that their eager spin through the daily sports page was a cultural activity of great value and significance to society. Such a notion would probably lead them to give up the page. Still less would they be pleased to learn that, seated in the stands at the ball park, they are assisting at a highly complex ritual which was linked to the mental drama of abstract finance, engineering, and the life of the fine arts as well.

But if ball fans would turn pale to learn that they are addicted to culture, it is just as easy to imagine the dismay of the professional culture vulture when he discovers that the vulgar and plebeian sports world is as much a part of the total social process as the ethereal and refined artistic experiences of the symphony lover. The so-called vulgar arts and recreations are not a popular substitute for the high arts. And the high arts of painting, music, and poetry are not an alternative to baseball, comics, and detective fiction. They are all closely interwoven in the single network of communication which makes any society whatever a living unity. In fact, that is the clue which I shall offer as the solution to the conundrum of 'why is baseball culture?'

Baseball is a useful illustration because just now everybody is beginning to get conscious of the World Series tension at this season. The World Series definitely winds up the summer and provides a natural transition to autumn and football. Even in time of war the World Series loses none of its glamour. In fact, it acquired greater appeal during the second war as providing a bridge between army and civilian experience and as a vivid means of communication with the usual rhythms of peacetime.

On the other hand, it would be foolish to overlook the obviously aggressive character of big-time spectator sports. There can be no doubt that these contests serve both to express the energetic passions of a powerful culture and also help to educate the entire society to follow the way of energy and power. Nobody can fail to have noticed the great prestige of the national sports heroes and their power over the imagination of the very young. How many kiddies have gagged manfully over an extra dish of something that is advertised to be the breakfast of champions! The child in our world is typically paralyzed with admiration for the gladiators of sport with their big biceps and their muscular coordination. If there is a cultural message in sport the junior members of our society have not failed to get the message. And it should be the business of thoughtful members of society to decode the message in adult terms.

Considered as part of our own communication network or culture, baseball represents a carefully-staged drama. Like any other drama it follows a strict set of rules which are part of the game of creating a specific kind of participation. Nine players, nine innings, alternate offensive and defensive. If a player in the dugout should catch a fly ball it would be like the prompt man reaching out of the wings to slug a stage villain.

The role of the umpire in a ball game is an important part of this drama. He must be dramatic and decisive in his gestures. He must *earn* the dislike of both teams, and the audience, too, if possible, while remaining utterly fair and dispassionate. His indifference is that of Fate while coaches and players encircle and threaten him in recurrent pantomimes of alarm, rage, and frustration.

To hasten on to the main point, let us ask: 'Of what is baseball a dramatization, if it is a drama?' And the answer is easily found in the passion of the ball fan for statistics of runs, hits, and errors, of batting averages, bases stolen, and runs batted in during a player's life-time. Baseball is a dramatic, spectator version of one aspect of the hidden life of the so-called business world. It is a means of ritual or popular communication in a public place and collective way with the central, but abstract and specialized financial and industrial drama. The statistics of sport rightly belong beside the financial page of the newspaper. The one is the mirror of the other. And the vivid headlines over bull and bear operations are very much like those which go with the Cubs, the Giants and the Tigers.

Imagine a sports contest without spectators! It would be like playing to an empty theatre. The collective presence of a large crowd at a ball game is not just figures in the box office. It adds meaning to the game as the game generates unity and dynamism in the crowd. A great crowd at a game today generates a kind of massive power which lifts individuals out of their puny ineffectual status as individuals and unites them with the central social energies. We live in a world charged with mechanical power. But the sense and reality of that power remain abstract until they are dramatized before a great audience.

Likewise, the mechanical precision of our world is expressed in the high degree of skill and co-ordination demanded of players. Plays are plotted in advance with the care and skill of great sales and advertising campaigns.

But no one game can exhaust all the hidden drama in a great society. And football expresses more directly the ruthless power and teamwork of an industrial society. And it is typically a college game for homecoming college crowds who are for the most part not yet in the arena of business. And whereas baseball is perhaps for the poor man, football is a game preferred by those closest to wealth and privilege in our world. The two games represent divergent dramatizations.

Baseball, then, is culture because it provides major channels for the flow of shared experience in a great social network of communication. We know that the first Olympic Games were rituals of communication between man and the gods. But all games are still rituals of social communication by drama and gesture, even though today we omit the gods.

I started out with the theme that baseball is culture. And by now it should be plain that what I mean is that culture is whatever men are doing in a particular time and place. High culture develops when some men take time to think about what they are doing. But culture is not something we ought to be doing and really prefer not to do. That is the notion of culture made familiar in Maggie and Jiggs. It is the view fostered by social pretention, and consists in strangling at the opera in a boiled shirt while dreaming of corned beef and cabbage or a poker game. This continent has a very great and diversified culture which we are taught to be ashamed of and not to think about, even though we dedicate most of our daily energy to charging its communications network with millions of messages. Both the quality of our popular culture and the degree of our enjoyment of it can be increased by taking an intelligent interest in them. The business man who is aware that his activities are part of the culture of his world will tend to take more pride and to feel more responsibility in the management of affairs that affect us all. Again, the sports lover who recognizes that he is engaged in a social ritual which is closely interwoven with the entire imaginative and intellectual life of his society, will be more receptive to other forms of expression in his world.

In short, taking an intelligent interest in everyday things at once enlarges the area of attention and reveals the meaning for us all. The more specialized and intellectual our scientific technology compels us to become, the more we must depend on the new popular arts as a means of keeping up social communication, and the more intelligent we must become about these new mass media. For these media don't just permit more and more people to participate in the old cultural rituals. They have changed the content as well as the form of our rituals. The radio voice that is heard by millions cannot be allowed to utter the words proper to a private audience. The sports hero or screen star who performs before millions cannot have the same kind of public style or private life as he or she would have had before the new media multiplied their statures until they filled the public mind.

We are not only living in a rapidly changing culture, but in a radically new kind of culture. The education and techniques for training perception, previously invented to help us to cope with small segments of population or with works of art produced by private artists, these are of little help today. Because the great collective art of modern cities is not produced by private individuals. Press, magazines, sports, and radio represent arts in which those who originate the messages are so numerous as to remain anonymous.

Our present education gives us very little help in getting to understand this new public and collective art. And that is why I have chosen to draw attention to some aspects of baseball as culture.

———————— ◆ ————————

Not quite 200 Canadians have made it to the major leagues, many on the strength of their parents' timely move to the United States when the future major leaguer was not yet ready for grade school. Phil Marchildon did it the hard way. Though raised within a francophone family in the small community of Penetanguishene, Ontario, he spoke not a word of French, which dismayed Quebec reporters many years later when he pitched in Montreal as a member of the International League Toronto Maple Leafs. He didn't even make the big leagues until the age of 26, and then, having won 17 games for the 1942 Philadelphia Athletics, joined the Canadian air force. As he neared completion of the requisite number of missions to earn a trip home and a return to the A's line-up, his plane was shot down over the North Sea. He completed the war in a prisoner-of-war camp. By 1947 Marchildon again was one of the American League's dominant pitchers, winning 19 games, but arm injuries and the trauma associated with his war experience combined to end one of baseball's most unlikely careers.

Magic Summer

PHIL MARCHILDON AND BRIAN KENDALL

I F THERE IS ANY ONE GAME I LOOK BACK ON AS THE ABSOLUTE PEAK OF MY career, the point when I was pitching my best and the future seemed brightest, it would have to be Opening Day at Yankee Stadium in 1947.

In front of 39,344 New Yorkers I threw six-hit ball as we beat the Yanks 6–1. There wasn't a moment in the game when I didn't feel I was in complete control. My fastball and curve hummed and snapped, and the Yankee hitters were baffled by a new forkball I'd developed and unveiled for the first time. Even the New York fans appreciated the game I'd pitched, giving me an enthusiastic cheer when I came to bat towards the end of the game.

It doesn't get a whole lot better. Just being at Yankee Stadium for an opener was a thrill, let alone getting the start and then such a convincing win. A Marine colour guard and the Seventh Regiment Band opened the pre-game ceremonies. Ex-president Herbert Hoover was in the crowd as well as a variety of other dignitaries, including a delegation from the United Nations Security Council.

Beating New York starter Spud Chandler was especially sweet. Chandler had won twenty games the year before, including four of the five he started against us. In his nine years with the Yanks he'd beat the A's seventeen times.

Connie Mack, who loved seeing us stick it to the thirty-nine-year-old veteran, delivered his best line of the season. 'What if he did win twenty last year?' Mack snorted. 'That man's getting old and in this business you can't go on forever.'

The forkball was something I'd experimented with on the sidelines before the war and finally gotten serious about that spring, working on it with the help of our catcher Buddy Rosar and Earle Brucker, the A's pitching coach. I still felt I needed something extra besides the curve and hard one to keep the hitters guessing after my attempts at mastering a straight change had been a disaster. The forkball seemed like the perfect solution. It's a slower pitch delivered with the fastball motion. Released between the index and middle fingers, my forker was especially tough on left-handed hitters, breaking sharply down and away as much as a foot as it crossed the plate.

Bucky Harris, whose debut as the new Yank manager had been spoiled, told reporters he'd had trouble identifying my new pitch. He just knew it was nasty.

'We still don't know for sure,' he said after the game. 'I'll tell you one thing, when this fellow is out there pitching, the A's are going to be a tough club to beat this year. He looks like one of the better pitchers in the league.'

I was full of juice and confidence. 'With a few breaks I might be able to hit that twenty-win mark,' I crowed to a swarm of reporters gathered around my locker. 'And don't be surprised if we land in the first division. This is a different team than you've seen in the past. Now we know we can win.'

The big difference in the A's was that the Old Man had dramatically improved our infield defence in the off-season by drafting veteran shortstop Eddie Joost and Ferris Fain, a young first baseman. Both had great range and were as good with the glove as anyone in the league at their positions. They gave every pitcher on the staff a huge boost in confidence. Pitching was so much easier when you could count on the guys behind you to catch the ball.

Joost was only a career .239 hitter, but he made up for it by getting to first on walks, leading the league with 114 free passes. Joost also had occasional home run power, hitting thirteen on the season. Fain was just getting started on a nine-year career that would see him win consecutive batting titles in 1951 and 1952. His on-base percentage was above .400 every one of those nine seasons, and only once did he strike out more than thirty-seven times.

Fain was one of the most hard-nosed competitors I've ever seen. One day that season he was tripped by Ed Pellagrini of the Red Sox while rounding third base. After he touched home, Fain ran back to third and hauled off and punched Pellagrini for 'dirty play.' It did a pitcher's heart good to watch Fain come fearlessly charging in toward the plate when he thought the bunt was on.

Mack also added hurlers Bill McCahan, Joe Coleman and Carl Scheib, who contributed twenty wins between them. McCahan, who had been a test pilot in the war, was especially effective that year, going 10-5.

That was all it took to transform us from the laughing-stock of baseball to a squad that hung in the first division for most of the season. We already had a solid outfield in Sam Chapman, Elmer Valo and Barney McCosky, who would finish second to Ted Williams with a .328 batting average. Pete Suder and Hank Majeski were steady if not spectacular at second and third, and our catcher, Buddy Rosar, who had played in Bill Dickey's shadow while he was with the Yankees, was one of the best backstops in the league.

Every time it looked like we were getting ready to fall back that season, we'd rally and win three or four in a row. Our pitching was outstanding right from the start. Fowler, McCahan and Russ Christopher all won ten games or more.

Mack went from predicting another last-place finish in spring training to answering 'I think we can' a couple months later when asked if his A's could stay near the top. 'But whether we do or don't,' he said, 'I'll tell you one thing: These boys won't quit.'

I was feeling a little more kindly towards the Old Man. Without too much discussion he'd agreed to raise my salary to $12,000. That didn't exactly put me in the same income bracket as Bob Feller and Hal Newhouser, or even Bobo Newsom, but I considered it a reasonably fair hike. Now with Joost and Fain backing me up, I figured I'd be making as much as the big boys in no time.

The talk of baseball that spring was Jackie Robinson of the Brooklyn Dodgers, the first black to play in the major leagues. Many people seriously argued that integration would destroy the game. The owners themselves were firmly opposed to letting blacks in. Commissioner Chandler was forced to step in and overrule them after they voted 15 to 1 against allowing blacks to play in the big leagues.

Some of Robinson's own team-mates circulated a petition to get him off the team. Brooklyn boss Branch Rickey said he'd trade anyone who refused to play alongside Robinson. When reports circulated that the St Louis Cardinals planned to strike when the Dodgers arrived in town for a series, National League president Ford Frick threatened the Cardinal players with lifetime banishment.

Having played in games against blacks as an amateur back home in Ontario, I had trouble understanding what all the fuss was about. Those players who objected to Robinson's presence were mostly Southerners who had grown up with segregation. I heard a couple of team-mates say they wanted no part of playing with 'niggers.' But the majority of us felt everyone deserved a fair chance. Many players had just finished fighting in a war that was supposed to be about preserving democracy. Well, didn't blacks, or negroes as they were most often called in those days, deserve their rights too?

The fact that the owners fought integration right to the end is probably the biggest disgrace in the history of the game. Judy Johnson, who, they say, was one of the greatest of all the black ballplayers born too soon to play in the big leagues, once asked Connie Mack why breaking down the colour line had taken so long. This was after Johnson had become an A's scout and a good friend of the Old Man.

'I asked him one day,' Johnson remembered. 'I said, "Mr Mack, why didn't you ever take any of the coloured boys in the big leagues?" He said, "Well, Judy, if you want to know the truth, there were just too many of you to go in." As much as to say, it would take too many jobs away from the other boys.'

On July 5, Cleveland Indians owner Bill Veeck broke ranks with his fellow American League owners and introduced a twenty-three-year-old black slugger named Larry Doby. But it would be years before baseball completely opened the doors. Including Robinson and Doby, by the end of 1949 there were only seven blacks playing in the big leagues. I never had a black man for a team-mate.

There's no question that Bob Feller was the outstanding pitcher of his generation. He was the standard by which the rest of us were judged. If the war hadn't taken almost four seasons out of his career, Feller would probably have retired with around 350 wins instead of the 266 beside his name in the record books.

Since I was the top pitcher for the A's, you might have thought that over the years Feller and I would have pitched against one another a dozen or more times. Yet we always seemed to just miss each other in the rotation. It's also possible that on other occasions Mack decided to hold me back when it was my turn to pitch against Feller, preferring to sacrifice another starter in a game in which the weak-hitting A's weren't likely to offer much run support.

Feller and I exchanged shutouts during a Sunday afternoon double-header in Cleveland June 8, with me blanking the Indians on four hits for a 4–0 decision in the opener, and Bullet Bob throwing a three-hitter to whitewash us 2–0 in the second game. The split decision left us in fourth place, five games back of leading Detroit.

I could be wrong here, but I believe the only time Feller and I faced each other as starters was in my next outing, back home at Shibe on Friday, June 13. People have often told me that I had a lot of back luck in my career. So what were my chances of winning against the great Bob Feller on Friday the 13th?

It was close, though. Feller fanned twelve and just narrowly came out on top, 5–4, as we both went eight innings. The difference was the successive homers I served up to Joe Gordon and Kenny Keltner in the fifth.

What sticks in my memory about that game was the experience of going to bat against one of the hardest throwers in history. When Feller was in his prime – and he was still at his best or close to it when I batted against him in 1947 – he was said to throw about a hundred miles per hour. The ball looked like a pea coming in at you. Feller's motion was a tumble of arms and legs as he released the ball, making it almost impossible to pick up his release point. The ball was by you before you could move a muscle.

Was I scared? You can bet on it. Anyone who ever went to bat against Bob Feller was afraid for his life. We didn't wear batting helmets in those days, and getting hit in the head by one of his pitches would probably kill you. As far as I know, Feller never hit anyone intentionally. But like all successful pitchers he wanted the inside part of the plate and would brush back hitters who took liberties. The most frightening thing of all was that Feller had a tendency to be wild at times. Or maybe he just preferred to let batters believe that even he wasn't sure where the ball was going to go.

Although players may try to deny it, even to themselves, there's no question that fear is a factor when they step up to the plate. I know that some, including Mickey Mantle, have said they have recurring nightmares about getting beaned.

Later that season I saw Elmer Valo knocked cold by a fastball from Sid Hudson of the Senators. Valo toppled over like he'd been hit by a sledge-hammer. We watched as our trainer, Jim Tadley, put ice compresses on Valo's head, but he still didn't come to. Finally he was carried to the dressing room on a stretcher, where he regained consciousness and was taken to the hospital.

Valo was the third Athletic to be hit by an opposing pitcher in two weeks. Hank Majeski had suffered a concussion when he was beaned by Earl Harris of the White Sox, and Barney McCosky had taken a pitch in the elbow from Floyd Bevens of the Yankees.

Like a lot of former players, I'm convinced the game was rougher in the old days. Some pitchers lived by the rule that when someone hit a home run off them, the next two batters were going down into the dirt. Now players charge out to the mound ready to fight whenever they suspect the pitcher is trying to brush them back off the plate. Back then batters expected to be challenged.

A few managers openly encouraged their pitchers to throw at batters. Leo Durocher was famous for yelling 'Stick it in his ear!' from the dugout. Connie Mack wasn't like that. Maybe he'd seen too many beanings in his day. I never once heard of him ordering a pitcher to deliberately hit a batter.

What's really amazing to me is that only one player has died in a big-league ball game – Ray Chapman of the Indians, who took a pitch in the temple from Yankee submariner Carl Mays in 1920. It's worth mentioning that the pitch Mays threw was said to have barely missed the strike zone. As usual, Chapman was crowding the plate.

Rarely are brush backs actually intended to hit the batter. They're thrown to send a message for him to move back off the plate. The next pitch is then usually thrown on the outside corner, out where the batter can no longer reach it. Brush backs are a basic part of pitching strategy. I can't understand why modern players expect to be able to get up close and comfortable without occasionally having to go down into the dirt.

I wonder how they would have handled batting against Dizzy Dean. 'You all done? You comfortable?' he would yell at a batter who started to dig a hole in the box with his back foot. 'Well, get a shovel because that's where they're going to bury you.'

Although I didn't hesitate to pitch inside, I only deliberately threw at a player once in my entire career. It happened the next year in Cleveland when I was matched against Bob Lemon in the second game of a doubleheader. The Indians were pounding me all over the field and I couldn't understand why. My stuff wasn't that bad. After a few innings of this I knew they must be stealing our signs.

Finally I became so frustrated that when outfielder Hal Peck came to the plate I decided to knock him on his rear. Funny as it sounds, I chose Peck, who had played with the A's for a couple of seasons, because he was a friend. I figured the Indians would get the message I was on to them if I knocked Peck down.

'Why the hell are you throwing at me?' Peck yelled as he picked himself up out of the dirt after just managing to get out of the way of my brush back. 'I had nothing to do with it.' Peck's reaction confirmed my suspicions.

I don't have any proof that would stand up in court, but I later heard that Bob Feller, who had won the opener of the doubleheader, was hidden out in the scoreboard with binoculars stealing our signs, and was then somehow relaying them back to the Cleveland bench. Lemon and the Indians were tough enough to beat on any occasion. With an advantage like that I had no chance at all.

We hung right in there near the top of the standings on into July. My eighth victory of the season, an 8–4 decision in Boston July 3, put us into third place, six-and-a-half back of New York and a half-game behind Detroit. It was our fifth consecutive win over the reigning American League champs, a pretty good indication of how far we'd come as a team.

Another example of how much tougher we were was our ability to come from behind to win ball games. When we rallied for two late runs in Cleveland July 11 to nail down my ninth victory, it was our twentieth successful comeback of the season. Mack was right when he said we refused to quit.

Around this time I decided to abandon my experiment with the forkball. Not because it wasn't usually effective, but because throwing it was wrecking my arm.

I had developed a searing pain in my right forearm. Even before the pain started I noticed that I'd lost something off my fastball and my curve wasn't snapping like it used to. As usual I went to Earle Brucker for advice.

'You're using the forkball too much,' he said immediately. 'Take a week off, rest your arm, and when you get back into action, don't use the fork so often.'

Another lesson learned. The time to start fooling around with trick deliveries is when you've already lost your fastball, not before. My heater and curve were still plenty good enough to keep me on top. A few more weeks of throwing the fork and I might have damaged my arm for good.

My arm bounced back fairly quickly and by the end of July I had twelve wins. My thirteenth, a shutout over the Browns at Shibe August 3, tied me with the Yankees' Allie Reynolds for the league lead.

I was enjoying myself more than I had at any other time in my career. When I was right, I felt I could beat anybody in the world. Best of all, the team was winning. We knew we were good and likely to get a lot better. Mack started telling reporters that the club might only be a season or two away from a pennant.

One great outing seemed to follow another. In early August I put to-gether a stretch of twenty-five scoreless innings until I finally surrendered a run to the Senators in Philadelphia August 9. After that I coasted to an 8–1 win. I also hit my first and only big-league home run that afternoon.

I was basically a line-drive hitter, which explains why the round-tripper was so long in coming. In the third inning Sid Hudson hung a curve that I got all of and drove into the upper left-field stands. I felt like Babe Ruth rounding the bases. I waved at the boys in the bullpen, who laughed and waved back. We were always kidding each other about our hitting prowess and this would give me bragging rights for weeks to come.

'Ontario pitchers had their biggest day in the majors this year when Dick Fowler of Toronto, and Phil Marchildon of Penetanguishene, hurled the Philadelphia Athletics to twin triumphs over the Washington Sena-tors, 2–1 and 5–2,' read the lead of the American Press report on our game in Washington August 17. I had a perfect game going until Mickey Vernon tripled with one out in the seventh. Washington got to me for three more hits after that. The win was my fifteenth of the season.

Dick and I always got a kick out of being able to join forces the way we did against Washington. We both took a lot of pride in the fact that until we came along there had never been two Canadians in the same starting rotation. Now there were two good ones. Fowler's twelve wins were second best on our staff that year.

Less than two weeks later, on Tuesday, August 26, under the lights in Cleveland, I came even closer to being the first big-leaguer to pitch a perfect game since Charley Robertson of the White Sox turned the trick in 1922.

I can still see almost every pitch I threw that night. To this day, I get steamed when I think about how I was robbed.

I'd been staked to a one-run lead in the fifth when we finally got to Cleveland's tough right-hander Don Black, who had himself thrown a no-hitter against us July 10. Our run came on a double by Buddy Rosar, Sam Chapman's bunt and a single by Pete Suder.

I still hadn't allowed a hit or a walk into the eighth. With two out, Ken Keltner came to the plate, the twenty-fourth man to face me. You always had to pitch carefully to Keltner, who was one of the toughest outs in the league. He fouled a couple off and worked me to a full count. Then I threw a fastball that caught the outside corner of the plate. I was already a couple of steps towards our dugout when I realized that umpire Bill McKinley had called it a ball and Keltner was trotting down to first.

The next day a local newspaper said I went 'ballistic,' which is as good a description as any. I fired my glove from the pitching mound and ran in to confront McKinley. Rosar was already jaw-to-jaw with him by the time I got there. We ranted, kicked up dirt and called him every name in the book. Naturally, none of the arguments had any effect. Keltner stayed on first.

'What Bill McKinley apparently forgot last night,' wrote Cleveland reporter Ed McAuley the next day, 'was that when there's a doubt and a perfect game at stake, the pitcher should be allowed to keep the change.'

My sentiments exactly. Besides, I know that ball was a strike. 'It was right there, Phil,' Rosar told me later. 'It caught the corner. There's no doubt about it.'

The only good thing I can think to say about McKinley is that at least he had the good sense not to toss me out of the game for throwing my glove and arguing the call. Under normal circumstances that would have earned me an automatic ejection. But even though my perfect game was ruined, I still had a shot at a no-hitter. McKinley allowed me to blow off steam and keep going. Punishment was delayed a couple of days until American League president William Harridge issued both Rosar and me twenty-five-dollar fines.

I tried to collect myself on the mound. Don't mess up now, I kept thinking. Stay calm. Joe Gordon, the next batter, hit a drive to centre field that Sam Chapman hauled in after a long run. Just three more outs to go.

Probably my greatest weakness as a pitcher was my inability to rein in my emotions. I'd fume inwardly when a team-mate made a bonehead mistake behind me or I surrendered a critical walk or home run. Sitting in the dugout that day I got angrier and angrier at the injustice of McKinley's call. I kept telling myself to focus on the next three outs. But I couldn't. By the time I walked back to the mound I had just about lost control.

I got a break when pinch-hitter Larry Doby swung at a couple of bad pitches and struck out to start the inning. Up next was George Metkovich, who wasted no time in pumping a single into the outfield to end the no-hitter. I went numb with disappointment. Dale Mitchell stepped in and slapped a single to left centre. Metkovich sprinted to third.

Not only had I lost the perfect game and no-hitter, but the Indians then tied the score when right fielder Hank Edwards hit a sacrifice fly that brought home Metkovich. I got the next two batters out and we headed into extra innings.

By this point I'd replaced my anger with a determination to win the game no matter what it took. I'd be damned if I was going to come out of this without something to show for all my aggravation.

I was tiring but managed to keep getting out of jams. A runner the Indians put on third in the tenth was thrown out at home on a failed suicide squeeze. When they got another runner to second with two away in the eleventh, Bob Lemon, one of the best-hitting pitchers in the game, was called in to pinch-hit for reliever Ed Klieman. Lemon went down swinging.

Cleveland's top reliever, Al Gettel, came in to pitch the twelfth. Gettel retired the first two batters before Pete Suder singled, bringing me to the plate.

What followed was one of the most satisfying moments of my career. Here's how Ed McAuley described it the next day: 'But, ladies and gentlemen, there was only one story in last night's ball game and Marchildon, the slim and fiery Canadian who came back from a German prison camp to become the most effective pitcher in the American League, was easily its hero ...

'Where he really proved himself a fighting man was in the twelfth. Marchildon was angry – he was sick with disappointment – and many of the customers were booing. So Phil smashed a double to left centre, and, for all practical purposes, the game was over. Suder streaked home with what proved to be the winning run.'

The Indians' half of the twelfth wasn't quite as perfunctory as McAuley would have had his readers believe. Ken Keltner was trouble again, singling with one out. Joe Gordon hit a fly to make it two away. Then Pat Seerey, batting for Al Lopez, banged a loud foul off the left field wall. That scared me and I knew I had to end it right there. I reached back and threw one of my best pitches of the long night – a beautiful curve that caught Seerey looking. This time McKinley thrust his arm in the air and gave me the call.

By early September we started to fall back into the pack – but not with our customary thud. We continued to win more than we lost, ending the season just out of the first division in fifth spot with a 78-76 record. It was the first time since 1933 the A's had played better than .500 baseball.

The revitalized Yankees shook off the rust from the war and the turmoil of the previous season to take the pennant by twelve games over runner-up Detroit. What we found most encouraging was the fact that the spread between us and the Tigers was only seven games. Wedged in the second and third spots were Boston and Cleveland.

◆ ◆ ◆

To me the best thing about being from a small town is the feeling that people genuinely care about one another and are proud when someone from the community goes out into the world and makes good. The dinner given in my honour that November 13 in Penetang was even more special to me than the night organized by Mack after my return from the war. The difference was that I didn't have to question the motives of my townspeople. They had always been my biggest fans.

Arranged by the local Chamber of Commerce, the dinner brought together two hundred friends and members of my family at Laboureau Hall. Joining Irene and me at the head table were my seventy-two-year-old father, my brothers and two of my sisters, Elizabeth and Jeanne. Looking back, I'm especially thankful that my father was able to be there. Just a few months later he died of stomach cancer, the same disease that took my mother.

On behalf of the town, Mayor W.M. Thompson presented Irene and me with a sterling-silver dinner set for twelve. 'We are terrifically proud of you, Babe,' the Mayor said. 'Phil is a credit to this town and country in sport. We in Penetang and district wish him every possible success in 1948. I personally would like to see him win at least twenty-five games.'

Judging by the cheers of the crowd, that made two hundred of us.

◆

You'll find Sunlight Park in a dishevelled corner of an on-ramp to the Don Valley Parkway in Toronto. It isn't just our baseball past that gets so easily forgotten, but also the remembrance of Canada's history. Bruce Meyer has not forgotten, however, and he brings this moment in time back with the same resonance as Joe Carter's epic blast in 1993. A trip to SkyDome by way of the Don Valley will never be quite the same again.

Cannonball Crane and Sunlight Park

BRUCE MEYER

MORE THAN A CENTURY BEFORE SKYDOME THERE WAS 'SUNLIGHT PARK,' a tiny wooden stadium festooned in gingerbread trim, creaking beneath the weight and stomping feet of Toronto fans who came to cheer their hometown heroes. Who can forget Joe Carter's incredible blast to left in the late hours of October 23, 1993? That moment is etched in time; but of equal note is the long-forgotten play of Toronto's star of 1887, Ned 'Cannonball' Crane, whose exploits, when a championship was on the line, rank him with other immortals in the pantheon of the Hogtown game.

Cannonball Crane. Sunlight Park. Those are names from an age of innocence when baseball was played on real grass beneath an open sky; an age when a fan could show up at the ballpark, to the smell of baked potatoes and cigars, for a mere 25 cents – a fee about equivalent to today's ticket prices in the coin of 1887. Toronto's first field of dreams and its first summertime hero remain enigmatic shadows, caught only in fleeting memories, legend, and obscure purple newspaper prose.

No one bothered to photograph Sunlight Park. To this day, some historians insist that the place was a myth. The only representations available are found in *Goad's Atlas* of 1892, which depicts the semicircular stands and the oblong playing field, already parcelled off into building lots in expectation of the city's eastward expansion.

Officially titled 'The Toronto Baseball Grounds,' the place was also called 'The Park Across the Don,' 'The Old Broadview Stadium,' and, perhaps the most poetic name ever given to a baseball field, 'Sunlight Park.' It stood just south of the intersection of Broadview Avenue and Queen Street (then known as the Kingston Road) on a flat lot that had been levelled in the 1850s for use as a horse track. The Union Course had fallen into disuse with the rise of the Woodbine circuit, and the site reverted to its previous usage as a lumberyard – again, an appropriate purpose for what was to become a venue for baseball hitters. Unlike later ballparks where the ground was roughly diamond-shaped, this first Toronto stadium was a hitter's park with shallow left- and right-field zones. Centre field was another matter – a 'Death Valley' alley that would make the deepest diamonds of today seem small.

The name 'Sunlight Park' was applied to the venue almost after the fact. William Hesketh Lever purchased the land directly south of the park from Gooderham and Worts Distilleries (the malting company had used the southern lot as the site of a beef-rendering factory) in 1892, and there he built his Sunlight Soap Works. For fans attending games both before 1892 and after, the air must have been heavy with the aroma of more than cigars and baked potatoes. Although the company never participated in the ownership or operation of Toronto's early International League club, Lever Brothers' proximity to the park was responsible for the name that legend accords the place.

When Toronto entered the International League in 1885 (and was courted for a brief period by Albert Goodwill Spalding as a potential location for a National League team), the old Rosedale Lacrosse Grounds at Elm and Sherbourne streets proved to be too small to accommodate the large crowds who came to witness professional games. (Earlier manifestations of baseball in Toronto had been enacted on the cricket oval of King's College Circle at the University of Toronto and, perhaps apocryphally, on the Glengrove Avenue West racetrack near Yonge and Lawrence.)

To launch the start of the 1886 season, the Toronto management decided to build a ballpark for the extravagant sum of $7000. The grandstand was designed to be luxurious by the standards of the time. It seated 2250 paying customers, 550 of which paid an extra 20 cents for reserved seats that featured leather cushions and arm rests. For games such as Opening Day on May 10, 1886, or when the governor-general, Lord Landsdowne, came to visit (May 19, 1887), the overflow crowd from the stands stood in the foul zones and the outfield, ten deep in places, to watch the game. The entire park was surrounded by a 14-foot-high wooden fence (which stood on the site well into the 1920s), and the magnificent stands rose to the dizzying height of almost four stories.

The fans purchased their tickets at Nordheimer's Piano Shop on Yonge

Street, and they filed into the park through a narrow avenue of gothic-roofed workers cottages down a street named 'Baseball Place.' The 'Torontos' stumbled to a mediocre record in their first season at Sunlight Park, but for 1887 the management guaranteed the local faithful an all-out assault on the championship.

The Torontos had begun the season with high expectations. In March the club proudly announced that it had received league permission to sign a rising star pitcher/outfielder, Edward 'Ned' Crane, from Boston of the Union League, for twice the standard salary of $2800. With Crane, the Toronto club and the fledgling International League had a potential superstar – a player already a legend in his own time.

Crane had established a reputation in the Union League as a grand-stander long before players became known for their stunts and their egos, and earned the nickname 'Cannonball' for his long-distance throwing feats. According to Frank Butler in a memoir 'Ned Crane – the Greatest Long Distance Thrower,' Crane won a throwing exhibition in Worcester, Massachusetts, in 1879 when he was only 17. He had thrown the ball 351 feet. By the time he had become a professional ball player in 1884, Crane was able to make throws of over 400 feet (for the sake of comparison, deepest centre field to home plate at the SkyDome is 400 feet). Butler remembered one such attempt at 'showing off' in Cincinnatti in 1884: 'All the players, especially the younger ones, had a try at returning the ball to where Crane and myself were standing and there were many times I had to walk fifty feet or more to relay the ball to Crane ... Not once did any of the players at home-plate throw the ball anywhere near where Crane was standing.'

Two weeks later, when the Boston team was in St. Louis for a series, the owner of the St. Louis franchise, perhaps anticipating that an injury to Crane would put Boston out of the chase for first place with St. Louis, wagered Crane $25 that he could not throw the ball more than 405 feet. Crane agreed to do it for $50, but blew a ligament in his arm in the attempt. The throw fell a foot short of its mark. Boston finished third that year and Crane sat out most of the remainder of the season with a shoulder injury. According to Butler, and regardless of persistent injuries, however, Crane held the title as the game's longest arm.

Over the next few seasons, Crane established himself with Providence and Washington of the National League as a 'twirler' (a 19th-century name for pitchers) of considerable reputation on the strength of his fastball. In many ways, Crane was the morning star of the modern pitcher. The year 1887 witnessed some significant changes in the rules and structure of the game of baseball. For pitchers, the new game demanded power, accuracy, and speed. Crane was among a new breed of hurler who threw overhand with speed, force, and accuracy rather than side-arm or underhand with finesse. Batters could no longer call for a high or a low pitch and were at the mercy of the pitcher; nor could pitches be thrown underhand. Before 1893, the distance from the mound to home plate was only 45 feet, rather than the present-day 60 feet 6 inches. Crane's power game of hard fastballs must have seemed an anomaly in 1887, especially to those who caught him. This is supported by his rather high number of runs attributed to wild pitches and passed balls – an average of 2.4 per game – likely the result of his unique style and of catchers who were just learning how to backstop the power game.

Crane won his first game in a Toronto uniform on May 2, 1887, a 6–2 victory over Syracuse. In the fifth inning, however, Crane threw wild and allowed the two Syracuse runs to score. The wildness was to plague him all season – especially during June and July, when the club slumped and sank as low as fourth place. The wildness may have been caused by more than his power game. Crane's throwing exploits and his play in the outfield on days when he was not pitching may have contributed to the continuing aggravation of the old shoulder injury from 1884.

On May 15 Crane's wildness cost Toronto a game, a 6–5 loss to Buffalo. But the greatest moment of frustration for the newcomer to Toronto took place on May 19, when the home side was hammered 11–5 by Rochester in front of 4500 fans and the governor-general, Lord Landsdowne. The *Globe*, forerunner of the present-day *Globe and Mail*, reported the event and rode Crane not only for his poor performance but for his temper tantrum afterward: 'To begin with, Crane the pitcher was erratic and was only saved by Traffley, the backstop, from making many serious misplays at critical moments. He was battered hard and did not sustain the character expected from the highest paid man in the International League ... in the "comedy of errors" which was enacted by both teams on the field.'

As the summer of 1887 wore on, the troubles persisted. Crane continued his sporadic play on the mound, but his chief contribution during the bulk of the season was his hitting and his fielding. Gradually, Crane dethroned Mike Slattery, Toronto's most popular player of the previous season, as the most beloved by the Toronto fans, and led by Cannonball's long arm and steady bat, the struggling club finally began to put together the ingredients necessary for a championship season in the final weeks of August. Crane helped the Torontos to a 12-game charge towards the top of the standings during which he had no fewer than two hits per game either as a fielder or a pitcher. The gallant late-season charge paid off.

In the end, it all came down to one splendid day and one supremely heroic effort. *September 17, 1887.* League-leading Newark was in town for a three-game weekend series. This was the final weekend of the season. The Torontos were one game behind the New Jersey leaders in the International League standings. A win would force a deciding game. Two wins would give the Canadian team the championship. The day was overcast. A heavy autumn dew blanketed the field, and the grass was slick and shining as 10,000 spectators arrived to jam the outfield and the foul zones. The sun fought to burn through the clouds.

In the morning game of the scheduled doubleheader, Crane pitched Toronto to a 15–5 decision over the New Jersey team and ensured that Newark would have to take both of the remaining games in the series to seize the championship. The *Globe* reported that 'the situation did not call for his best,' and noted that Crane, Toronto's best pitcher and hitter, pitched only a mediocre contest. The clubs broke for lunch without any announcement of who would pitch the second game for Toronto. Sheppard, the second-best pitcher on the club, could have been the starter, but there is the suggestion in the reports that he may have been nursing an injury – these were the days before the Disabled List. The question was, Who would pitch the second game?

The *Globe* records what happened next: 'As soon as it was made clear that Crane was to pitch the second game, hundreds leaped to their feet and cheered frantically, a mighty whirl of enthusiasm took everybody within its embrace, and an astounding volume of sound shook the stands and swept down toward the city and out over the grounds like the march of a tornado.'

Crane was perfect through three innings. In the fourth he began to tire. He walked the lead-off man, and when a base hit started to move the runners, Crane scooped up the ball and ran it over to second for the unassisted out; but as he crossed second he appeared to stumble and severely sprained his ankle (possibly his push-off leg). Visibly in pain, Crane returned to the mound and walked a man before throwing wild on a third strike. Traffley, the catcher, tried to retrieve the ball among the packed spectators behind the plate – but all was in vain. Four runs scored. Newark was up 4–0.

Just when it appeared that he would throw the contest away and force the championship to a deciding game, Crane dug down deep and found the strike zone. He struck out the remaining Newark batters to end the inning and continued to set the order down through the next three frames, all the time sparing his weak ankle and showing signs of agony as he stood on the hill.

In the eighth, with Newark still ahead 4–1 and the bases loaded, Crane came to the plate. He hit a double to tie the match. But the tension wasn't over yet. With Crane still on the mound, the contest went to extra innings. He continued his stellar pitching, and had just thrown his twentieth inning of the day when his turn came to bat for Toronto in the eleventh. The stadium fell silent.

Crane watched two pitches come in for strikes. A third was a ball. On the next pitch he swung. His bat made perfect contact and the ball soared over the heads of the assembled throng in the outfield, rising higher and higher towards the distillery to the south end of the park. The *Globe* recorded what happened next: 'And then the mighty audience arose and cheered and stamped and whistled and smashed hats ... the frantic fans dashed onto the field and carried Crane aloft ... it was a great day for sports in Toronto.' That was Toronto's first taste of baseball victory.

To add to the mystique of the Crane legend, he returned to the park for the meaningless Sunday game, sore ankle and shoulder, and pitched the Toronto side to a 22–8 victory over a disheartened Newark squad. The news of his heroics in Toronto quickly spread through the ranks of professional baseball. By October, Crane had been signed to play for Mike 'King' Kelly's New York Giants in the National League. Crane, however, was unable to repeat his success for the Giants. His sore shoulder and the overwork he bore in leading Toronto to its championship caught up with him. Although he never repeated the glory of that September day in 1887, his play in the National League was enough to gain him a ticket on Albert G. Spalding's World Tour All-American Team following the 1888 season.

Crane pitched his way around the world, winning games in New Zealand, near the Colosseum in Rome, and in Paris before returning to the United States, where he and his team-mates were feted by Teddy Roosevelt and Mark Twain at a gala banquet in New York. Although his major-league statistics show no record of his Toronto heroics, Crane can be seen in a moment of slightly lesser glory atop the shoulders of the inscrutable Sphinx when the World Tour squad stopped in Egypt long enough to play a game at the base of the ancient Pyramids. And like the sands of the desert, so are the days of summer; by 1896 Cannonball Crane was dead and the Toronto franchise (which endured a four-year hiatus from 1890 to 1894) had crossed town to play on the site of present-day Lamport Stadium at a new venue named 'Diamond Park.' In its turn, Diamond Park was replaced by Hanlan's Point, where Babe Ruth hit his first professional home run in September 1914; and Hanlan's Point by Maple Leaf Stadium; and the old Fleet Street flats by windy Exhibition Stadium; and the seagull-infested Ex by the mind-boggling SkyDome.

Today, at the foot of Broadview Avenue, just south of where Queen Street crosses the Don River, Eastern Avenue cuts across the old infield, and the site of the delicate wooden structure of Sunlight Park lies buried beneath rows of Japanese cars in the back lot of a downtown dealership. An obscure street, signposted 'Sunlight Park Avenue' with a bent sign, traces the southern edge of the field and leads nowhere. It is the only hint that here Toronto's first professional baseball championship was won on an overcast September Saturday in 1887. And what a day it was.

Like the star of that championship in 1887, Sunlight Park has slipped from memory. There are no markers to record the site of the first championship, no plaques to commemorate that great September day more than a century ago, when a city held its breath and a high fly ball cleared the fence and sailed into history.

Nonetheless, there is something about the site of that first stadium that is still magical, beyond the buzz of the city's traffic, beneath the layers of concrete and years that have buried the old green field. It is still possible to stand there and imagine what it must have been like, what that crowd fifteen deep in places must have felt, what it was to go home a winner.

——————— ◆ ———————

Baseball is the great exception among Canadian team sports, having forgone, until recently, national organization and championships, as well as the dictates of amateur panjandrums often based in isolated head offices in Montreal or Ottawa. Moreover, it looked not to Great Britain for ideas and leadership but to an emerging entrepreneurial clutch of baseball impresarios whose model was American and whose motive was simple – money. Commerce drove the wheels of baseball and guaranteed its strong north-south orientation to the closest American baseball market. George 'Knotty' Lee played the game, managed teams, started leagues, sold baseball gloves named after himself, and generally established the model that inspired, for good or ill, future generations of owners, including Pierre Trudeau's father, Charles, in Montreal, Jack Kent Cooke in Toronto, and Peter Pocklington in Edmonton.

Knotty Lee: Canadian Baseball's Forgotten Pioneer

DAVID PIETRUSZA

ITCHER, OUTFIELDER, MANAGER, CLUB PRESIDENT, LEAGUE ORGANIZER, glove manufacturer. Canada's George 'Knotty' Lee was all of the above. But although he never filled any of these varied roles at the major-league level, Lee nonetheless performed them all with colour and verve. Knotty Lee – no doubt about it – is the unsung hero of early Canadian baseball.

While the Canadian Pacific Railroad's Joe Page gets much-deserved credit for setting up such circuits as the Ontario-Quebec-Vermont and Western Canada leagues, the now-forgotten Lee has a record of service to the game that more than outshines Page and just about any other Canadian in the first few decades of this century.

Born in Toronto on May 12, 1877, Lee did his first pitching for the amateur Toronto Athletic Club. He made his professional debut in September 1898 – on the last day of the Eastern (International) League season. It was against last-place Ottawa, a club that had relocated from Rochester in the wake of the Spanish-American League, and which disbanded at season's end.

Lee's performance was, nonetheless, a beauty. Said one local paper: 'Pitchers in the Eastern League will have to doff their caps to Lee, the T.A.C. pitcher. Yesterday he established a record for the league in allowing Ottawa one hit. He was in great shape, and Manager Irwin knew what he was doing when he allowed the amateur to twirl. Ottawa, of course, looked upon any amateur as a mark, but they were made the marks and fell before the curves of Lee like wooden men. Lots of the pitchers in the Eastern League would have had to do some kicking regarding the cool weather. Not so with Lee ... '

From 1899 to 1901 Lee toiled in the New York State League at such stops as Binghamton, Utica, Cortland, and Waverly, both pitching and playing the outfield. He was a respectable hitter, batting .278 in 1899, .250 in 1900, and .267 in 1901, but truth to tell not much of a pitcher. For those seasons his won-lost marks were just 11-16, 10-19, and 7-11. Back then he was sometimes called 'General' Lee as newspapers touted his appearances against 'Ulysses Grant' Thatcher or 'Mad Anthony' Wayne. Sports writers were clearly of a more historical bent in those days.

It was a tough league, in which umpires rarely survived an entire season. One arbiter, Charles Lanigan, admitted that he called a forfeit in favour of the Albany Senators, even though the visiting Binghamton Bingoes were right not to take the field. His reason? Physical fear of unruly fans.

From 1902 through 1906 Lee performed in the New England League. It's not known why Knotty eventually left that circuit, but we do know that on one occasion he was hit over the heart by a line drive back through the box. He was knocked out cold for 48 hours and some news accounts pronounced him as passing on to even greener diamonds. Lee recovered, but not everyone knew that. Once in Toronto he was stopped by someone who remarked that there was a ballplayer by the same name – but that fellow was dead. Knotty, not wishing to embarrass the fellow, admitted he was often mistaken for the deceased.

One of Lee's best weapons was a wet one. On his death the *Ottawa Citizen* described him as 'one of the first users of the now famed spitball.' According to his grandson Tim he was taught the delivery by an 'old, colored pitcher. His [Knotty's] father said that when he threw a spit ball it developed a sort of a twist or knot as it spun through the air. The name stuck with him the rest of his life.'

Lee's last known stop as a player was with the Oswego Starchmakers of the 1907 Class C Empire State League. After that he turned full force to organizing leagues and to managing. Time after time he would have whole circuits collapse, right out from under him, but he kept on going to his next challenge.

In 1911 he helped found the Canadian League (Class D in 1911; Class C thereafter), which originally featured the Berlin Green Sox, the London Cockneys, the Hamilton Kolts, the Brantford Red Sox, the St. Thomas Saints, and the Guelph Maple Leafs. Perhaps the best player the circuit produced was Ottawa right-hander Urban Shocker, who led the league in wins while at Ottawa in 1914–15.

From 1911 through 1913 Lee managed Hamilton, leading them to third place in their first two years and to sixth in 1913. From the beginning of his managerial career Lee displayed a hot temper. We read of Hamilton forfeiting a game to Ottawa in July 1913 as Lee – losing 6–4 with two outs in the bottom of the ninth – became embroiled in an argument with an umpire named Daly. 'The umpires ordered Lee out of the game,' said one newspaper account, 'and when the manager refused to go, Ottawa was given the game.'

In 1914 Lee moved over to lead another new franchise, the Toronto Beavers, but despite featuring the league's leading batter (J. Trout, .349) the club got only as high as third place and settled finally in fourth. As Toronto also fielded an International League team, the Beavers attracted little attention and disbanded at season's end.

So, in 1915, Lee moved on to yet another Canadian League entry, Guelph. He got them as far as second place, but the First World War collapsed the entire circuit, and once again Lee was reading the *Sporting News* want ads. With paying baseball nearly impossible in Canada he headed south and helped form the short-lived semi-pro Pennsylvania League. Soon, however, the United States was also in the war, and baseball was shutting down there as well.

With the war concluded, however, there could be no stopping Lee. In 1919 he helped found the Class B Michigan-Ontario League, which featured Canadian franchises in Brantford (the Red Sox/Brants), London (Tecumsehs/Indians), and Kitchener (Beavers/Terriers/Colts) that first year and a Port Huron–Sarnia club, the Saints, in 1922.

In 1919–20 Lee piloted Brantford to fourth- and third-place finishes. In July 1920 the club's owner dared to step into the dugout during a game and Lee roared: 'You may own the team, but I'm managing it. Get out.' Lee, of course, was promptly fired, but his players remained loyal and threatened a mutiny. In three days he returned to the job.

Brantford's owner was not Lee's only target. That same season he went at it with umpire Lou Fyfe, a former Federal League arbiter, when Fyfe challenged him to an on-field fight. 'Lee needed no second invitation,' commented the *Sporting News*. Both were fined $50 and Fyfe resigned from the League's staff.

In 1921–2 Lee served as the Toronto Maple Leafs' business manager. About this time he went into the glove manufacturing business, peddling the 'Knotty Lee Special,' which he billed as follows: 'Fields 1000% – Made in Canada.' Ironically, Lee had been a horrible glove man. Back in 1899, for example, Knotty fielded a lowly .747. In 1900 he fielded just .899.

Lee returned to the managerial ranks in 1925 with the Michigan-

Ontario League's London Indians. The club was paced by a number of league leaders: Joe Klein's .363 batting average, Walter Sundquist's 178 hits, and Will Coogan's 24 wins and 2.48 ERA. The Indians captured the second-half pennant, but the league disbanded at season's end.

In 1928 Lee returned to the States, managing the New England League's Attleboro Burros. His club won the season's first half, but, plagued by inept fielding, it skidded so badly in the second half that it finished just sixth overall and disbanded at season's end.

Things got even rougher in 1929, although with Sabbath baseball finally legalized in New England it should have been far easier economically. Lee hooked on with the woeful Haverhill Hills, but attendance was so poor that by July 20 the club became the Fitchburg Wanderers. In less than a month they wandered again, on August 20 metamorphosing into the Gloucester Hillies.

It was back to Canada in 1930, as Lee became president and field manager of the Class D Ontario League's London Tecumsehs. His club won the second-half flag and had the best record overall, but Knotty was still brawling. The season was punctuated by an on-field fistfight with Brantford manager 'Dixie' Walker after a Brantford pitcher's alleged balk. Police had to break up the altercation.

The league folded on July 22.

In 1933 Lee was back in organized baseball, managing the New England League's Worcester Chiefs. The Chiefs finished in second place overall, having won the first-half championship. But the league was on the verge of collapse. The New Bedford Whalers had finished first overall, but their players refused to participate in post-season play. Lee's Chiefs took on the third-place Lowell Lauriers in the playoffs, but after three games the series was washed out by rain. Shortly thereafter the league disbanded.

In 1934–5 jobs were scarce in the minor leagues, and Lee contented himself by managing the Peterboro Petes of the semi-pro Central Ontario Baseball League. Once again he ran afoul of the men in blue. In one 1935 contest an umpire named Corrigan tossed him. 'I ordered him out,' Corrigan explained, 'because he called me a foul name.' Reported one Kingston newspaper: 'Lee hedged around and tried to dodge the issue, but the officer of the law compelled him to make himself decidedly scarce, while the booing of the fans rang in the Peterboro mentor's ears.'

The minors were starting to pick up, and in November 1935 Lee attended the National Association convention in Dayton. There he was asked by Joe Carr, the National Association's promotion director, to help organize yet another new league. This circuit would straddle the U.S.-Canada border and be known as the Canadian-American League. Lee brought in three Canadian teams – the Perth Blue Cats, the Ottawa Senators, and the Brockville Pirates. Lee had originally planned on running a franchise in Kingston, but when that fell through he moved across the river and took over management of the Ogdensburg club, the Colts. As usual, Knotty made things happen. 'He had a personality that picked people up, that people liked,' recalled one local.

Lee, who wore number thirteen for Ogdensburg, almost didn't make it to the 1936 Opening Day, being detained for the better part of a week with four of his players at Prescott, Ontario (on the U.S. border), but a baseball-loving Ogdensburg alderman, 'Billy' Doe, advanced a $500 bond to free the quintet. Lee's bad luck continued, however, as his team lost thirteen in a row near the start of the season.

Having no working agreements, Lee did his best to scrounge for players. Sometimes that wasn't good enough. First baseman Danny Hargrove reported from his home in Boston, but couldn't play because his hands were covered with blisters from digging ditches for the Work Progress Administration. Pitcher Paul 'Daffy' Horonzy arrived and promised not to accept a cent in salary until he won his first game. He didn't, but his constant boasting ('We won't need any outfielders if my fast one is working right') irritated not only opponents but fellow teammates. So did a 9.54 ERA.

At Ogdensburg, however, Lee did discover a true diamond in the rough – outfielder Maurice 'Bomber' Van Robays. Originally, Van Robays had been signed by the Detroit Tigers system, but after ravaging bouts of influenza and pneumonia he was released, and remained out of baseball for two years. In 1937 Lee took a chance on him and was rewarded with Van Robays's Canadian-American League record 43 homers.

'In a close game in the ninth inning,' recalled Ogdensburg business manager Carrol Belgard, 'Knotty Lee would say, "Hit one out of the park, and I'll give you an extra five." [Van Robays would] hit one, and Knotty would say "Give him five, give him five."' In 1940 as a Pittsburgh rookie Van Robays would drive in 116 runs.

One of the highlights of Lee's career came in July 1939, when organized baseball celebrated the hundredth anniversary of Abner Doubleday's 'invention' of the game in Cooperstown, New York. At Cooperstown, in the only minor-league all-star game in the sport's history,

Lee coached for a team called the 'Doubledays' against a squad called the 'Cartwrights.' The game, however, failed to live up to expectations. Most minor leagues failed to send their top stars to the contest, and both rosters were filled with Knotty's fellow Can-Am managers, who were generally quite a bit younger than he.

Lee remained in Ogdensburg until financial troubles forced him out following the 1939 season. One of his problems was of his own making. Said the *Cornwall Freeholder*: 'The Ogdensburg Colts almost missed getting paid June 15. Manager Knotty Lee left his bag containing the cash in the hotel lobby. A commercial traveler with similar luggage picked up the bag and departed. Fortunately, he was overtaken at Gouvenour [N.Y.] and the bag recovered.'

In 1940 Lee transferred the Colts to Auburn, where they went 28-93 for a woeful .231 won-lost percentage. At one point the Colts dropped 16 straight, but Lee never gave up. 'He was something else,' said future Yankee star Spec Shea (then with the rival Amsterdam Rugmakers). 'He'd raise hell all the time. He was quite a guy. I remember him. He was quite an entertainer, I'll tell you. He argued like hell. He'd throw his hat up in the air. He'd throw it up anyway, and then they'd warn him, and a little later they'd warn him again. He'd have the crowd crazy!'

Once again, Lee reached towards the bottom of the barrel for help. At one point, he got a letter from a fellow who bragged he had terrific stuff. Knotty sent him bus fare, put him on the mound, and saw him hit the first three batters he faced. His control then got better – but only marginally. He walked the next seven. With great understatement, this Depression-era 'Wild Thing' later explained to the enraged Lee: 'I was a little off tonight.'

This pathetic team drew only 10,040 fans, and Lee was forced to sell out. It was his last stop in baseball as he moved his home from Toronto to Smiths Falls and went into the hotel business. During the Second World War Lee did a good business feeding soldiers hopping off troop trains for a rest. 'He had baseball pictures of all the big leaguers – Connie Mack and all – hung all over his beverage room, and it went over big,' recalled one of his former players. 'He had a good, clean place.'

When George Lee passed away in Smiths Falls in 1962, an Ottawa newspaper termed him 'a pioneer in pro baseball, a man who forgot more of diamond lore than many of us will ever know. Knotty loved this game of baseball from the time he was a boy, was part of its history as so many of his ilk were in the early days of the game, particularly in Canada.'

———————— ◆ ————————

There was a time, not that long ago, when Blue Jays fans spoke in hushed voices about the 'curse' that seemed to hang over their team. It began in the 1985 League Championship Series, when the Jays were up three games to one over the Royals, then seemed to give it all away. (OK, they were inexperienced.) Then came 1987, and possibly their best team to date. Striding to another division title, they lost Tony Fernandez and Ernie Whitt – and the heart of their batting order – less than two weeks from the end, and collapsed. (This time, you had to think, it was *a curse.) From then on, until the Jays dispelled their demons by quashing the Athletics in the 1992 ALCS, every failure bespoke the playing out of a dark destiny. Here, from those gloomy days, is one storyteller's attempt to penetrate these mysteries and, perhaps, cast off the bad spell.*

The Magick of the Druids

PAUL QUARRINGTON

FLOUR WAS WALKING HOME FROM WORK (FLOUR WAS A HIGH SCHOOL teacher, his subject History, his passion early Anglo-Saxon battles, the kind where groaty little men dressed in boars' fur and horny helmets bash each other over the head with clubs) when he passed a junkyard. That in itself wasn't unusual, Flour passed the junkyard every day, but on this day Flour decided to go in and pick through the junk. This, as everyone knows, is called *looking for good stuff*, and although most people give it up around the age of fourteen, Flour never had. Not that he was weird or anything, at the beginning Flour was a responsible, upstanding citizen. He just had a few odd quirks, like rearranging the money in his pockets under each new moon, or, more to the point, picking through garbage for good stuff. Besides, trash-sifting was almost a vocational requirement with him, because there was always the chance he would stumble upon historical artifacts. On this day, Flour was convinced that his search would prove very fruitful, because it was spring (the sun was like somebody's friendly fat uncle up there in the sky) and what's more, it was the first day of the baseball season. His beloved Toronto Blue Jays were opening in the city of (Flour checked his pocket schedule, even though he had it all but memorized) Boston for a three game series with the Red Sox.

Flour entered the junkyard. A tiny shrivelled man sat in a fold-up chair, playing with a dog, trying to yank a stick out of the beast's maw. Flour didn't think this was a good idea. It was a German Shepherd Dog, a mangy, vicious animal with blood-red eyes, a dog that had got drummed out of the police force for excessive violence and was now forced to make a living guarding junkyards. Flour had underestimated the shrivelled man, though, who was old and wiley. 'Hey, look,' said the tiny geezer to the dog, 'an intruder.'

The beast let loose its hold on the stick, turned and saw Flour.

We needn't go into what ensued, suffice it to say that when Flour left the junkyard a few minutes later he was pumped full of adrenalin, still trembling, and also, the possessor of a stuffed Blue Jay. Flour had found the bird in one of the junkyard's darkest corners. The shrivelled man had advised Flour against searching there. 'People shouldn't go over to that corner,' said the old man, still giggling about his nasty dog. 'Nobody knows what-all's there.'

But Flour had gone over, hoping to find relics from the Battle of Rood (which had raged for fourteen days and nights before the groaty men retired to the meadhalls). Instead he'd found a stuffed Blue Jay. It was enormous for a Blue Jay, and although insects had chewed on it, it was still plenty feathery and possessed of a fine sheen. Flour knew a good omen when he saw one.

'How much?' he'd asked the old, shrivelled man.

The man thought about that. His face collapsed and he toyed with the hairs on his chin. 'Seventy nine cents,' he'd said, the transaction was made.

Flour took the stuffed bird home and placed it, without thinking really, on top of his television set. Flour's wife Marie was used to this sort of thing, she didn't comment. Flour had after all brought home much stranger fare. Flour was the owner, for example, of a blackened nub which he claimed was the fingertip of Oswald the Odd, the leader of the Anglo-Saxon groats in the Battle of Rood. Be that as it might (we mustn't lose sight of the thread here), Flour placed the stuffed Blue Jay on top of the television set and after dinner settled down to watch the baseball game.

Things didn't start off too well for the Toronto Blue Jays; after two innings they were down by three runs. Flour paced in his livingroom. In the fourth inning the Blue Jays managed to get two men on base. Flour envied the calmness of his wife Marie, who sat on the sofa in an outrageously languid position. Flour scowled and, again without think-ing really, picked up the stuffed Blue Jay and set it down, moving it by a few centimetres. The Blue Jay at the plate connected with the next pitch, driving it over the Green Monster at Fenway Park.

Flour nodded, opened his mouth to say something to his wife, decided against it, looked at the stuffed bird. It seemed to him that the creature's hackles were ruffled.

The Blue Jays won by a score of 6 to 4, and Flour was a happy man when he went to bed. He had a strange dream that night in which the stuffed Blue Jay flew through the light of a new moon, a dream in which the Toronto Blue Jays won the World Series.

The next day Flour began his History class this way: '*Oswald the Odd*,' he quoted from the ancient text, '*placed much credence in the magick of the Druids. Before the Battle of Rood he ordered the killing of the Royal Falcon. The entrails were examined and auguries made. The body of the Falcon was placed on a pike which Oswald the Odd held as he rode to meet his enemy upon the bloody field.*'

The next day's baseball game was played in the afternoon. Flour found out on his way home from the High School (dropping in to the New World Hotel, having a draught beer with the people there) that the Blue Jays had lost, what's more, lost rather badly. Flour was de-spondent but, after all, it was only the second game of the season, by the time he arrived at his apartment Flour was his usual cheery self. Marie was dusting, puttering around with great energy. Flour saw that the stuffed bird had been moved, placed on top of the coffee table. Flour didn't make a scene, Flour was still a reasonable man at the beginning of the season, all Flour did was pick up the stuffed Blue Jay and place it gingerly back where it belonged, on top of the television set.

The Blue Jays won the third game, they took two out of two from the Cleveland Indians, they were now four for five with the stuffed Blue Jay perched on top of the television set.

Then came the Home Opener. Marie produced tickets that she'd got-ten from work. Marie worked in advertising and was always getting free tickets to sporting events, and she surprised Flour by saying, 'Come on, Flour, why watch it on tee-vee when we can be there?'

Flour smiled rather tersely, but he stood up and pretended to be happy. The first time they tried to leave the apartment, Marie said, 'Flour, aren't you going to turn off the television?'

'Oh,' said Flour. He disappeared into the livingroom for a second and came back with a large lump underneath his coat.

'What's that there?' asked Marie, giving him a poke.

Flour produced the stuffed bird.

Marie signed wearily.

Flour went back into the livingroom, placed the bird on top of the television (as close as possible to where it had been) and went to the baseball game with his wife. The Blue Jays lost seven to one.

Flour lectured his class about what he termed the Druidic Concept of Magick. He told them of necromancy. He game them a surprise quiz concerning Llewyn, Wizard of Gorsedd. Marjorie Plumm asked why they weren't studying the Fathers of Confederation like everyone else in Grade Ten. Flour smiled and told them that Oswald the Odd rode into battle carrying a small statue of Ethelred the Unready, hoping that the bravery of his ancestor should manifest itself upon the bloody field.

Flour went back to the junkyard that afternoon. The tiny shrivelled man and his mastiff were playing fetch with a length of lead-piping. Flour asked if he could visit the corner where he shouldn't go, the tiny geezer laughed and said 'Be my guest.' Even the dog was much friendlier that second visit, it trotted over and hunkered down and watched Flour sift through the junk.

Flour dug around in the shadowed corner for upwards of twenty minutes before he found something. It was a bust of Ted Williams. It wasn't really a bust of Ted Williams, it was a bust of Augustus Caesar, but Flour figured that with a black wig on it would look a lot like Ted Williams, hopefully enough to fool the gods of enchantment and war. Flour carted it home, set the wigged bust (he snatched the wig from an odd assortments box) on top of the television set. Marie said nothing. It wasn't that she didn't object, she was simply not speaking much to her husband those days. The Blue Jays won two games, they dropped the next and Flour wondered what he was doing wrong.

The following day, Flour read this passage to his class: '*They erected a huge circle of stone and, their bearded faces awash in moonlight, made calculations based on the intercepts of Cassiopeia's Chair and Orion's Belt.*' Marjorie Plumm, by the way, had gone AWOL, the better to learn about the Fathers of Confederation, those grim and stuffy men. Flour wasn't overly concerned about that, Flour re-read the phrase *their bearded faces awash in moonlight* and got very excited somewhere deep in his bones. He stopped shaving immediately. The Blue Jays went on a twelve game winning streak (putting them first in the American League East) at the end of which Flour was sporting a full beard. It would be some time before his whiskers reached Druidical length, but they seemed to do the job (in conjunction, of course, with the stuffed Blue Jay and the wigged bust of Augustus Caesar). Then the Blue Jays went and dropped three in a row to Seattle, the Boys from Beantown swept their series with the Yankees and usurped first place in the AL East.

Flour took what he felt were appropriate measures. Some people felt the measures were a tad extreme, but before we go into that, let's check the results:

The Blue Jays played a double header with Detroit, won the afternoon game by a run and crushed the Tigers in the twilighter, 12 to zip! They went on to win their next seven in a row, and opened a gap of two and a half games on the Red Sox.

Flour's principal, Kenneth Pritchard, was a man who was giving up cigarette smoking. That's the state in which he existed, *giving up smoking*, he chewed gum and mints and pencils and anything else he could get into his mouth. When Ken Pritchard called Flour into his office, the principal was chewing a pen and there was ink smeared all over his lips. 'Flour,' asked Pritchard, 'am I an unreasonable man?'

'No,' answered Flour. Even as they spoke the Toronto Blue Jays were flying to California. Flour was very concerned about the long-distance power of his magick.

'Not unreasonable,' agreed Pritchard. 'And I don't impose unreasonable dress codes, do I?'

Flour shrugged, guessing not. 'I guess not.'

'You could wear jeans and sneakers and a T-shirt with Madonna on it for all I care,' said Pritchard.

Flour nodded.

'But listen, Flour,' said Pritchard, finding something else to chew on, namely a paper-clip, 'this won't do.'

'This what?'

'This, uh.' Pritchard gesticulated the length of his body. 'This particular get-up.'

'You mean my robe?'

'Yes! That's it. Your robe. Won't do.'

'But–' Flour thought the flowing black robe was rather becoming, although he'd admit he looked frightening with the hood up, plunging the whole of his bearded face into shadow.

'What's more, Flour,' said Mr. Pritchard, 'I think your students have had just about enough of this Druidic Concept of Magick.'

Flour's wife Marie had had just about enough of that too. Mind you, it was particularly rough on her, mindful as she was of her housekeeping. There were seven huge rocks in her living room, two of which could be justifiably described as *boulders*, arranged into a circle.

Marie had heard on the radio that the Blue Jays had lost their first game to the California Angels. Marie hated it when the Blue Jays lost, not because she cared about the league standings, but because it meant that her husband would do something weird. He came in that night with a plant, a small tree really, which he sat in the middle of his circle of stones. 'There is much power in the leaf of wych-elm,' said Flour.

The Blue Jays lost five games in a row, the Boston franchise *won* five in a row, the gap between the two teams narrowed to a half game. During that week, Flour acquired 1) the jaw of a Sperm Whale, 2) the tailfeather of a Bald Eagle, 3) a jim-dandy rock, almost perfectly round, 4) a bit of cloth which (he was assured by the fellow who sold it to him) came from Ty Cobb's uniform and 5) a Toronto Blue Jays jersey, which he wore over his flowing black robe.

There was a game that evening, a game against the cursed Boys from Beantown themselves, and Flour pulled out all the stops. He bewitched the Boston team, he nailed red socks to the walls of his living-room and filled them with vile things, things that he'd dug out of the garden (at night and under a full moon), slugs and worms. The first Boston player up to bat smashed one out of the park, the ball flying high into the rowdy bleachers.

'Hey!' shouted Flour towards the heavens. He rushed over to the bust and snatched off the black wig. 'This isn't Ted Williams! This is Augustus Caesar!'

Marie came into the livingroom. Marie was bone-weary, but very resolute. 'Flour,' she demanded, 'Why haven't you been going to work?'

'Work?' Flour shifted the stuffed bird over a few centimetres and tried to change the subject, because he had in fact been fired from work. 'Did you ever realize that Blue Jays have sharp, pointy beaks and ugly claws?'

On the television, the Toronto third baseman committed an error, dropping the ball on a routine grounder. Flour sensed a weakening in the fabric of the universe.

Marie deposited a small valise near Flour's feet. Flour's feet, by the way, were black as night. He hadn't been wearing shoes for the past couple of weeks. 'Flour,' said Marie, 'you're history.'

'Uhp.' Flour swallowed hard. 'I realize that things haven't been too easy around here,' he said, 'but it's just until the end of the season. We can weather the storm.'

'Flour,' said Marie, 'a typhoon has ripped through our village. It razed our huts and carried off the livestock. The children are drowned and the wise men have fled to the hills.'

The Toronto Blue Jays were dropping balls all over the infield.

Flour gathered up his possessions, the important ones that is, the stuffed bird, the rocks, the ossified finger of Oswald the Odd. He wandered into the night.

Flour went to the junkyard. The tiny shrivelled man was listening to the baseball game on the radio ('Pitiful,' was how he judged the Toronto team's performance), the hound was sleeping near the rusting husk of a dead Chevrolet. 'Is it all right,' asked Flour, for he knew of nowhere else, 'if I stay here for a while?'

The tiny shrivelled man pointed to the dark corner, the one where people shouldn't go. Flour went there. He found an old broken television set, perched the stuffed Blue Jay on top. He arranged his stones in a circle, lining up the biggest of the rocks with Polaris. In the centre of the circle he placed all of the charms and talismans. Flour's bearded face was awash in moonlight.

The Blue Jays came back from a six run deficit.

From that point forward there was no looking back for the Toronto team.

When the Blue Jays won the World Series for the first time in their history, the manager was interviewed in the locker room. People poured champagne over his head as he spoke. He was asked to comment on the season.

'Well,' said the manager, 'we got lucky. What can I say? We got lucky.'

Flour is gone from us now, we don't know where.

In the shadowed corner of the junkyard (the shrivelled groat will advise against going there, he will giggle and say no one knows what-all's over in that corner) is a stuffed Blue Jay.

---◆---

One of the subtexts of the Toronto Blue Jays' world-championship season in 1992 saw Toronto's big-league squad, not Montreal's, become the first foreign team to scale baseball's Mount Everest. The cities' long-standing rivalry has never been virulent – that would be too un-Canadian. Still, as Alan Rauch notes, the concern of Montreal and Toronto (at different times) to become 'world class' metropolises displays some striking parallels.

Looking for Home

ALAN RAUCH

WHEN THE U.S. MARINE CORPS COLOUR GUARD CARRIED THE CANADIAN flag upside down before Game 2 of the 1992 World Series, it was undoubtedly a thoughtless error rather than a signal of distress. Yet it was, in its own way, distressing. Not only did it evoke the problems facing Canada, it reminded Atlantans, as the Toronto *Globe and Mail* noted, that 'Atlanta needs to practice giving visitors and competitors the respect they deserve.' (After all, Atlanta had bested Toronto for the right to hold the 1996 Summer Olympics.)

The spotlight, that week in October, was very much on Canada at what was surely a significant moment in its history. With the Toronto Blue Jays facing the Atlanta Braves in the first truly international World Series, sports and politics came together at an opportune moment. On the Monday following Game 7 of the series, Canadians were to vote in a referendum on a package of constitutional changes that centred (emotionally, at least) on the 'status' of Quebec in Canada.

It was a disturbing time for Canadians, whether English, French, or First Nation, who had been struggling for years to come to grips with what it means to be 'Canadian.' The struggle for me – an Anglophone expatriate who had spent half his life in Montreal and was now living in 'the States' (Atlanta, as it happened) – was perhaps different because I was geographically outside of Canada. Yet I remained attached to Canadian politics and baseball. As a boy in Montreal I was, together with my friends, proud to be Canadian. And though we weren't always sure why, the arrival of major-league baseball in Montreal was, for us, confirmation that our pride was justified.

The Expos were part of a plan intended to put Montreal on the North

American 'map.' Sandwiched between Expo 67 – the world's fair that gave the team its name – and the 1976 Olympics – which provided the club with a futuristic stadium – the franchise was intended to stake a claim for the city of Montreal, the province of Quebec, and Canada itself in the broad collective consciousness of 'America.' There was something very soothing in that, especially because of the strained political climate that marked Quebec and Canada in the early 1970s. As an 'Anglais,' I studiously learned terms like *'coup de circuit'* (home run) and *'voltigeur de gauche'* (left fielder), thinking, somehow, that made *me* more French and Canada more united. American viewers, I hoped, would see the Expos and witness – all at once – Canadian diversity and Canadian unity.

When the Blue Jays became a team in 1977, things seemed to change. Not only did the creation of the Jays play into a long-standing rivalry between Montreal and Toronto as cities, it seemed to re-create a cultural tension between English and French Canada. Toronto, which had grown in size and stature (owing, in part, to an influx of businesses from Montreal), seemed to acquire a major-league team simply as a matter of course. The Jays adopted a logo that prominently displayed the maple leaf, Canada's most easily recognized symbol of national identity, as if to claim status as 'Canada's Team.'

Montreal's large and costly Olympic Stadium, the 'Big Owe' as it is often called, didn't help. As a monument to architectural incompetence, it did little to enhance a team that was still fighting for respectability. It wasn't merely that the outsized stadium dwarfed everything within sight; it dwarfed the very baseball that was being played on the field. The stadium wasn't 'about' baseball at all, it was yet another bid to claim national and international attention. Although an embarrassment to Montreal, the failure in design proved a boon for the planners of Toronto's SkyDome, who saw an opportunity to demonstrate that Canadian baseball stadiums could actually work. Each time the SkyDome's formidable roof was opened, it seemed like a taunt eastward towards Montreal's leaden tarpaulin – once touted to be the last word in retractable roofs.

The challenge for pre-eminence on the Canadian scene was never explicit, but it was clear that the Jays and the Expos were working out something bigger than inter-league rivalry. In 1992, when the Blue Jays were effectively dominating the limelight, the Expos organization added Quebec's provincial symbol – the *fleur de lis* – as an *accent aigu* over the 'e' in Montreal's 'away' uniforms. Most of the baseball world seemed oblivious to this diacritical addition, but for those of us attuned to such subtle cues, the implications were clear: Les Expos de Montréal were giving notice that *they* were from Québec.

Still, as with virtually every sport, baseball is about winning games. And it would be a disservice to the fans of both Canadian ball clubs to suggest that they had anything less on their minds than the desire for a pennant and to appear in, if not win, the World Series. But it would also be misleading not to say more. After all, whatever enmity exists between English Canada and French Canada pales in comparison to the rivalry felt by most Canadians towards their very conspicuous neighbours to the south. No matter what divides Canadians internally, there is something peculiar that unites them when it comes to interacting with or, more properly, reacting to the United States. When Canadians look southward it is with a range of attitudes and emotions that include anger, envy, admiration, confusion, condescension, and who knows what else.

Thus, when the Blue Jays, after defeating the Oakland A's for the pennant, had only one American competitor left between them and the title of World Champions, Canadians had to take notice. Watching themselves through the hype of American television and print – which played up the series as a battle between the United States and Canada – the simplistic association that linked the Jays with *all* of Canada was both exciting and troubling.

Even in years past it would have been difficult for Canadians, broadly dispersed and very diverse, to suspend local allegiances in order to rally behind 'the first Canadian World Series team.' But the 1992 Fall Classic had an added wrinkle for Canadian viewers: the referendum. And so the Series was made more problematic by the fact that many Canadians who supported the Jays for Canada's sake on one day would reject the 'unity accord' endorsed by their politicians on the next.

It was, in the language of old-school American journalism, 'quite an angle.' But the new-school journalists ignored it completely. The *Atlanta Constitution* belligerently proclaimed in its 'World Series Preview': 'This is OUR game!' and then proceeded to chastise the Jays when they could find 'nary a Canadian' on the team's roster. The paper conveniently forgot that it was a hit by Francisco Cabrera, a native of the Dominican Republic, that got the Braves to the Series in the first place. (Nor had anyone remembered that the fledgling Atlanta Knights, of the International Hockey League, boasted very few Americans on its roster.) In fact, the very question skirted by the paper, about how to understand identity – whether in the arena of sports or politics – was central to understanding what was going on in Canadian minds throughout the Series.

The Blue Jays eventually won the World Series and the victory was sweetened because it gave Canadians just a little edge over their American neighbours. It provided one of those rare moments when Americans were obliged to take notice of Canada with, perhaps, some mark of respect. In a sense, the win belonged to all of Canada. Yet beneath the exhilaration of national pride was the constant anxiety about nationhood. The victory was, to be sure, as bittersweet for Québec as it was for the Expos. As for the referendum that followed, the 'victory' of the 'No' side merely confirmed the summer-long feelings of national self-doubt that the Blue Jays had, for a time, allayed with their confident march towards a World Series title.

Baseball likes to be celebrated for both its simplicity and its complexity. You throw the ball, you hit the ball – it's that simple. At the opposite extreme lie the subtleties of pitch counts, squeeze plays, and left- and right-handed match-ups. Both approaches underestimate the sport by looking at it within the confines of the ballpark. That was something I understood when I heard my grandfather reminisce about Jackie Robinson, biding his time with the Montreal Royals, a farm team far away from the spotlight of racial politics in America. What I *didn't* understand was that even then the politics of baseball were bigger than I imagined. The enduring memory of Montreal as a 'safe haven' for Jackie Robinson, whatever the truth to it, relied heavily on that almost casual antipathy that Canadians harbour towards the States. It might, we thought, have been *their* game, but it would progress because of *our* sense of fair play. Such formulations always seem small-minded in retrospect and this one was no exception. We didn't see that our attitude towards baseball was as closely linked to the need to define a Canadian sensibility as it was to the love we felt for the game.

In 1992 the World Series gave Americans the chance to look outward towards other cultures, but it also gave Canada a chance to look inward in an effort to understand itself. It has been observed, on more than one occasion, that the familiar rituals and rules of the game make it an intriguing and sometimes comforting backdrop for issues and events that are never quite as predictable. Thus the assurance, in baseball, that 'home' will always be there when you come around third is no small consolation to those trying to find it on the playing field of national identity.

Montreal has the unfair reputation of not being a baseball town. They worship their Canadiens, the line goes, but Montrealers won't really support baseball. Anyone who argues that view, however, will have to account for a certain piece of history – the period from the 1930s through the fifties, when the game flourished throughout Quebec and the Montreal Royals dominated the International League (one rung down the ladder from the majors). Here, Mordecai Richler vividly captures the flavour of Montreal in those years, 'a town rich in baseball history.'

Up from the Minors in Montreal

MORDECAI RICHLER

RONOUNCING ON MONTREAL, MY MONTREAL, CASEY STENGEL ONCE SAID, 'Well, you see they have these polar bears up there and lots of fellows trip over them trying to run the bases and they're never much good anymore except for hockey or hunting deer.'

Alas, we have no polar bears up here, but kids can usually heave snowballs at the outfielders at the opening game of the season, and should the World Series ever dare venture this far north, it is conceivable that a game could be called because of a blizzard. Something else. In April, the loudest cheers in the ball park tend to come when nothing of any consequence seems to have happened on the field, understandably baffling the players on visiting teams. These cheers spring from fans who sit huddled with transistor radios clapped to their ears and signify that something of importance has happened, albeit out of town, where either Guy Lafleur or Pierre Mondou has just scored in a Stanley Cup play-off game.

Baseball remains a popular game here, in spite of the Expos, but hockey is the way of life.

Montreal, it must be understood, is a city unlike any other in Canada. Or, come to think of it, the National League. On the average, eight feet of snow is dumped on us each winter and, whatever the weather, we can usually count on three bank robberies a day here.

This is the city of wonders that gave you Expo in 1967, the baseball Expos a couple of years later and, in 1976, the Olympic Games, its legacy, among other amazing artifacts, a stadium that can seat or intern, as some have it, 60,000 baseball fans. I speak of the monstrous Big O, where our inept Expos disport themselves in summer, their endearing idea of loading the bases being to have two of their runners on second. Hello, hello. Their notion of striking fear into the heart of the opposition being to confront them with muscle, namely one of their pinch-hitting behemoths coming off the bench: group average, .135.

Major league baseball, like the Olympics and the Big O itself, was brought to this long suffering city through the machinations of our very own Artful Dodger, Mayor Jean Drapeau.

Bringing us the Games, he assured Montrealers that it would be as difficult for the Olympics to cost us money as it would be for a man to have a baby. He estimated the total cost of all facilities at $62.2 million but, what with inflation and unfavorable winds, his calculations fell somewhat short of the mark. Counting stationery and long distance calls, the final cost was $1.2 billion. Never mind. To this day our ebullient mayor doesn't allow that the Games were run at a loss. Rather, as he has put it to the rest of us, there has been a gap between costs and revenue. And, considering the spiffy facilities we have been left with, it would be churlish of us to complain.

Ah, the Big O. The largest, coldest slab of poured concrete in Canada. In a city where we endure seven punishing months of winter and spring comes and goes in an afternoon, it is Drapeau's triumph to have provided us with a partially roofed-over $520 million stadium, where the sun never shines on the fans. Tim Burke, one of the liveliest sportswriters in town, once said to me, 'You know, there are lots of summer afternoons when I feel like taking in a ball game, but I think, hell, who wants to sit out there in the dark.'

'Shivering in the dark' might be more accurate, watching the boys lose line drives in the seams of the artificial turf.

'The outfield,' another wag remarked, 'looks just like the kind of thing my aunt used to wear.'

Furthermore, come cap day or bat night ours is the only park in the National League that fills a social office, letting the poor know where to get off, which is to say, the scruffy kids in the bleachers are beyond the pale. They don't qualify.

It's a shame, because the Expos, admittedly major league in name only, came to a town rich in baseball history and, to begin with, we were all charged with hope. In their opening game, on April 9, 1969, the Expos took the Mets 11–10 at Shea Stadium, collecting three homers and five doubles. Five days later, the 29,184 fans who turned up for the home opener were electrified by an announcement over the public address system. 'When the Expos play a doubleheader,' we were informed, 'the second game will go the full nine innings, not seven.'

Those of us old enough to remember baseball's glory here, the Montreal Royals of the old International League, nodded our heads, impressed. This was the big time. 'Montreal,' said Warren Giles, president of the National League, 'is a growing and vibrant city.' Yessirree. And we hollered and stamped our feet as our champions took to the field under the grim gaze of manager Gene Mauch, who had the look of a Marine drill sergeant.

I still have that incomparably bubbly opening day program. *Votre première équipe des ligues majeures.* Vol. 1, No. 1 *Publié par Club de Baseball Montreal Ltée.* 'The Expos believe they landed a real prize when they snatched Gary Sutherland from the Philadelphia Phillies. Big things are expected from John Bateman, the former Houston Astros' fine receiver. Bob Bailey impressed everybody with his tremendous hustle. Ty Cline is a two-way player. "In the field," said Larry Shepard, manager of the Pittsburgh Pirates, "Don Bosch can be compared with none other than Willie Mays." Larry Jaster has youth on his side. This may be the year Don Shaw comes into his own. Angel Hermoso is one of the fine young Expo prospects the scouts have hung a "can't miss" label on. On a given day, Mike Wegener, only 22, can throw with the best. Don Hahn was a standout performer during spring training. Bob Reynolds' main forte is a blistering fastball. Expansion could be "just what the doctor ordered" for Coco Laboy.'

To be fair, the original Expos included Rusty Staub, sweet Mack Jones and Bill Stoneman, a surprisingly effective player who pitched two no-hitters before his arm gave out. Manny Mota, another original draft choice, was one of the first to be sent packing by a management that was to become celebrated for its lame-headed dealings, its most spectacular blunder being a trade that sent Ken Singleton and Mike Torrez to Baltimore for a sore-armed David McNally and a totally ineffective Rich Coggins. It should also be noted that the Expos did take their home opener, defeating the Cardinals 8–7, and that tiny Parc Jarry, where they were to play, futile in their fashion, for another eight years, was a charming, intimate stadium with the potential to become another Fenway Park.

Opening day, I recognized many of the plump faces in the box seats on the first-base line. Among them were some of the nervy kids who used to skip school with me on weekday afternoons to sit in the left-field bleachers of Delormier Downs, cheering on the Royals and earning nickels fetching hot dogs for strangers. Gone were the AZA windbreakers, the bubble gum, the scuffed running shoes, the pale wintry faces. These men came bronzed to the ball park from their Florida condominiums. Now they wore foulards and navy blue blazers with brass buttons; they carried Hudson's Bay blankets in plastic cases for their bejeweled wives; and they sucked on Monte Cristos, mindful not to spill ashes on their Gucci sandals. Above all, they radiated pleasure in their own accomplishments and the occasion. And why not? This was an event and there they were, inside, looking out at last, right on the first-base line. Look at me. 'Give it some soul, Mack,' one of them shouted.

An article in that memorable opening day program noted that while the province of Quebec had never been known as a hotbed of major league talent, we had nevertheless produced a few ballplayers, among them pitchers Claude Raymond and Ron Piché, and that three more native sons, Roland Gladu, Jean-Pierre Roy and Stan Bréard had once played for another ball club here, the Montreal Royals.

O, I remember the Royals, yes indeed, and if they played in a Montreal that was not yet growing and vibrant, it was certainly a place to be cherished.

Betta Dodd, 'The Girl in Cellophane,' was stripping at the Gayety, supported by 23 Kuddling Kuties. Cantor Moishe Oysher, The Master Singer of his People, was appearing at His Majesty's. The Johnny Holmes Band, playing at Victoria Hall, featured Oscar Peterson; and a sign in the corner cigar-and-soda warned Ziggy Halprin, Yossel Hoffman and me that

LOOSE TALK COSTS LIVES!
Keep it Under
Your
STETSON

I first became aware of the Royals in 1943. Our country was already 76 years old, I was merely 12, and we were both at war.

MAY U BOAT SINKINGS EXCEED REPLACEMENTS;
KING DECORATES 625 CANADIANS ON BIRTHDAY

Many of our older brothers and cousins were serving overseas. Others on the street were delighted to discover they suffered from flat feet, or, failing that, arranged to have an eardrum punctured by a specialist in such matters.

On the home front, sacrifices were called for. On St. Urbain Street, where we served, collecting salvage, we had to give up American comic books for the duration. Good-bye, Superman, so long, Captain Marvel. Instead, we were obliged to make do with shoddy Canadian imitations printed in black and white. And such was the shortage of ballplayers that the one-armed outfielder, Pete Gray, got to play for the Three Rivers club on his way to the Browns and French Canadians, torn from the local sandlots, actually took to the field for our very own Royals: Bréard, Gladu, Roy.

Even in fabled Westmount, where the very rich were rooted, things weren't the same anymore. H.R., emporium to the privileged, enjoined Westmount to 'take another step in further aid of the Government's all out effort to defeat aggression!'

HOLT RENFREW ANNOUNCE THAT BEGINNING JUNE FIRST <u>NO DELIVERIES</u> OF MERCHANDISE WILL BE MADE ON <u>WEDNESDAYS</u>

This forethought will help H.R. to save many gallons of gasoline ... and many a tire ... for use by the government. Moreover, will it not thrill you to think that the non-delivery of your dress on Wednesday will aid in the delivery of a 'block-buster' over the Ruhr ... Naples ... Berlin ... and many other places of enemy entrenchment?

Our parents feared Hitler and his Panzers, but Ziggy, Yossel and I were in terror of Branch Rickey and his scouts.

Nineteen thirty-nine was not only the date we had gone to war, it was also the year the management of the Royals signed a contract with Mr. Rickey, making them the number one farm club of the Brooklyn Dodgers. This dealt us young players of tremendous promise, but again and again, come the Dodgers' late-summer pennant drive, the best of the bunch were harvested by the parent team. Before we had even reached the age of puberty, Ziggy, Yossel and I had learned to love with caution. If after the first death there is no other, an arguable notion, I do remember that each time one of our heroes abandoned us for Ebbets Field, it stung us badly. We hated Mr. Rickey for his voracious appetite.

'There has been no mention officially that the Dodgers will be taking Flowers,' Lloyd MacGowan wrote in the *Star* on a typical day, 'but Rickey was in Buffalo to watch the team yesterday. The Dodgers can't take Flowers without sending down a flinger, but chances are the replacement for the burly lefty will hardly be adequate.'

The International League, as we knew it in the forties, its halcyon years, was Triple A and comprised of eight teams: Montreal, Toronto, Syracuse, Jersey City, Newark, Rochester, Baltimore and Buffalo. Newark was the number one farm team of the Yankees and Jersey City filled the same office for the Giants. But organized baseball had actually come to Montreal in 1898, the Royals then fielding a team in the old Eastern League, taking the pennant in their inaugural year. In those days the Royals played in Atwater Park, which could seat 12,000, and from all accounts was a fine and intimate stadium, much like Parc Jarry. During the 21 years the Royals played there they offered Montreal, as sportswriter Marc Thibault recently wrote, *'du baseball parfois excitant, plus souvent qu'autrement, assez détestable,'* the problem being the troubled management's need to sell off their most accomplished players for ready cash. Be that as it may, in 1914, long before we were to endure major league baseball in name only here, George Herman Ruth came to Atwater Park to pitch for the Baltimore Orioles. Two years later, the team folded, a casualty of World War I, and another 11 years passed before the Royals were resuscitated.

It was 1928 when George Tweedy 'Miracle Man' Stallings bought the then-defunct Syracuse franchise and built Delormier Downs, a stadium with a 22,000 capacity, at the corner of Ontario and Delormier streets. An overflow crowd of 22,500, including Judge Kenesaw Mountain Landis, was at the opening game, which the Royals won, defeating the fearsome Reading Keystones, 7–4. Twelve months later Stallings died. In 1929, not a vintage year for the stock market, the Royals finished fourth. Two years later, Delormier Stadium, like just about everybody, was in deep trouble. There were tax arrears and a heavy bank debt to be settled. The original sponsors resigned.

In the autumn of 1931 a new company was formed by a triumvirate which included a man who had made millions in gas stations, the rambunctious, poker-playing J. Charles-Emile Trudeau, father of our present prime minister. Another associate of the newly-formed club, Frank 'Shag' Shaughnessy, cunningly introduced the play-off system in 1933, and two years later became the club's general manager. In 1935, fielding a team that included Fresco Thompson, Jimmy Ripple and Del Bissonette, the Royals won their first pennant since 1898. However, they finished poorly in '37 and '38 and, the following year, Mr. Rickey surfaced, sending in Burleigh Grimes to look after his interests.

Redemption was at hand.

Bruno Betzel came in to manage the team in 1944, the year the nefarious Branch Rickey bought the Royals outright, building it into the most profitable club in all of minor league baseball, its fans loyal but understandably resentful of the head office's appetite, praying that this summer the Dodgers wouldn't falter in the stretch, sending down for fresh bats, strong arms, just when we needed them most.

The Royals finished first in 1945, and in '46 and '48 they won both the pennant and the Little World Series. They were to win the pennant again in '51 and '52, under Clay Hopper, and the Little World Series in '53, when they were managed by Walter Alston. The Royals fielded their greatest team in 1948, the summer young Duke Snider played here, appearing in 77 games before he was snatched by Mr. Rickey. Others on that memorable team included Don Newcombe, Al Gionfriddo, Jimmy Bloodworth, Bobby Morgan and Chuck Connors. The legendary Jackie Robinson and Roy Campanella had already come and gone.

Sam Jethroe was here in 1949 and two years later Junior Gilliam was at third and George Shuba hit 20 home runs. In 1952, our star pitcher was southpaw Tommy Lasorda, the self-styled Bob Feller of the International League. Lasorda pitched his last game for the Royals on July 4, 1960, against Rochester, which seemed to be hitting him at will. Reminiscing recently, Lasorda recalled, 'I knew I was in trouble when I saw our manager's foot on the top of the dugout step. If the next guy gets on base, I'm going to be out of there. I turned my back to the hitter and looked up toward the sky. Lord, I said, this is my last game. Get me out of this jam. I make the next pitch and the guy at the plate hits the damnedest line drive you ever saw. Our third baseman, George Risley, gets the tips of his fingers on it but can't hang on. The ball bloops over his hand and our shortstop, Jerry Snyder, grabs it. He fires it to Harry Shewman at second base, who relays it to Jimmy Korada at first. Triple play.'

A year later the Royals were dissolved and in 1971 the Delormier Stadium was razed to make way for the Pierre Dupuy School.

On weekday afternoons kids were admitted free into the left-field bleachers and by the third inning the more intrepid had worked their way down as far as the first-base line. Ziggy, Yossel and I would sit out there in the sun, cracking peanuts, nudging each other if a ball struck the Miss Sweet Caporal sign, hitting the young lady you-know-where. Another diversion was a porthole in the outfield wall. If a batter hit a ball through it, he was entitled to a two-year supply of Pal Blades. Heaven.

Sunday afternoons the Royals usually played to capacity crowds, but come the Little World Series fans lined up on the roof of the adjoining Grover Knit-to-Fit Building and temporary stands were set up and roped off in center field. Consequently, as my cousin Seymour who used to sit there liked to boast, 'If I get hit on the head, it's a ground rule home run.' After the game, we would spill out of the stadium to find streetcars lined up for a half mile, waiting to take us home.

In 1945, the Royals acquired one of ours, their first Jewish player, Kermit Kitman, a William and Mary scholarship boy. Our loyalty to the team was redoubled. Kitman was a centerfielder and an opening day story in *La Presse* declared, *'Trois des meilleurs porte-couleurs du Montréal depuis l'ouverture de la saison ont été ses joueurs de champ: Gladu, Kitman et Yeager. Kitman a exécuté un catch sensationnel encore hier après-midi sur le long coup de Torres à la 8e manche. On les verra tous trois à l'oeuvre cet après-midi contre le Jersey-City lors du programme double de la "Victoire" au stade de la Rue Delormier.'*

In his very first time at bat in that opening game against the Skeeters, Kitman belted a homer, something he would not manage again until August. Alas, in the later innings he also got doubled off second. After the game, when he ventured into a barbershop at the corner of St. Catherine and St. Urbain, a man in another chair studied him intently. 'Aren't you Kermit Kitman?' he asked.

'Yeah,' he allowed, grinning, remembering his homer.

'You son-of-a-bitch, you got doubled off second, it cost me five hundred bucks.'

Lead-off hitter for the Royals, Kitman was entitled to lower berth one on all their road trips. Only 22 years old, but a college boy, he was paid somewhat better than most: $650 monthly for six months of the year. And if the Royals went all the way, winning the Little World Series, he could earn another $1,800. On the road, his hotel bill was paid and he and the other players were each allowed three bucks a day meal money.

There was yet another sea change in the summer of 1946. After scouting what were then called the Negro Leagues for more than a year, Mr. Rickey brought the first black player into organized baseball. So that spring the Royals could not train in the regular park in Daytona, which was segregated, but had to train in Kelly Field instead.

Actually, Jackie Robinson had been signed on October 23, 1945, in the offices of the Royals at Delormier Stadium, club president Hector Racine saying, 'Robinson is a good ball player and comes highly recommended by the Brooklyn Dodgers. We paid him a good bonus to sign with our club.'

The bonus was $3,500 and Robinson's salary was $600 monthly.

'One afternoon in Daytona,' Kermit Kitman told me, 'I was lead-off hitter and quickly singled. Robinson came up next, laying down a sacrifice bunt and running to first. Stanky, covering the sack, tagged him hard and jock-high. Robinson went down, taking a fist in the balls. He was mad as hell, you could see that, but Rickey had warned him, no fights. He got up, dusted himself off and said nothing. After the game, when he was resting, Stanky came over to apologize. He had been testing his temper, under orders from Rickey.'

Kitman, a good glove man, was an inadequate hitter. Brooklyn born, he never got to play there. Following the 1946 season he was offered a place on the roster of another team in the Dodger farm system, but elected to quit the game instead.

The 1946 season opened for the Royals on April 18, with a game in Jersey City. The AP dispatch for that day, printed in the Montreal *Gazette*, ran: 'The first man of his race to play in modern organized baseball smashed a three-run homer that carried 333 feet and added three singles to the Royals' winning 14–1 margin over Jersey City. Just to make it a full day's work, Robinson stole two bases, scored four times and batted in three runs. He was also charged with an error.'

Robinson led the International League in hitting that year with a .349 average. He hit three home runs, batted in 66 runs, stole 40 bases, scored 113 runs and fielded .985 at his second-base position. And, furthermore, Montreal adored him, as no other ballplayer who has been here before or since. No sooner did Robinson reach first base, on a hit or a walk, than the fans roared with joy and hope, our hearts going out to him as he danced up and down the base path, taunting the opposing pitcher with his astonishing speed.

We won the pennant that year and met the Louisville Colonels, another Dodger farm club, in the Little World Series. The series opened in Louisville, where Robinson endured a constant run of racial insults from the Colonels' dugout and was held to a mere single in two games. Montreal evened the series at home and returned to Delormier Downs for the seventh and deciding game. 'When they won it,' Dick Bacon recently wrote, recalling that game in the 200th anniversary issue of the

Gazette, 'Jackie was accorded an emotional send-off unseen before or since in this city.'

'First they serenaded him in true French Canadien spirit with "*Il a gagné ses Epaulettes*," and then clamored for his reappearance on the field.

'When he finally came out for a curtain call, the fans mobbed him. They hugged him, kissed him, cried, cheered and pulled and tore at his uniform while parading him around the infield on their shoulders.

'With tears streaming down his face, Robinson finally begged off in order to shower, dress and catch a plane to the States. But the riot of joy wasn't over yet.

'When he emerged from the clubhouse, he had to bull his way through the waiting crowd outside the stadium. The thousands of fans chased him down Ontario Street for several blocks before he was rescued by a passing motorist and driven to his hotel.

'As one southern reporter from Louisville, Kentucky, was to write afterward:

'"It's probably the first time a white mob of rioters ever chased a Negro down the streets in love rather than hate."'

That was a long time ago.

I don't know whatever became of Red Durrett. Marvin Rackley, of whom Mr. Rickey once said, 'I can see him in a World Series, running and hitting,' has also disappeared. Roland Gladu, who got to play 21 games with the old Boston Braves, failed to sign the major league skies with his ability. Robinson died in 1972 and in 1977 a plaque to his memory was installed in the chilly Big O. Jean-Pierre Roy now does the French-language broadcasts for the Expos and a graying but still impressive Duke Snider is also back, doing the color commentary for Expo games on CBC-TV, trying his best to be kind to an uninspired bunch without compromising himself.

The Expos have yet to play .500 ball or, since Mack Jones's brief sojourn here, come up with a player that the fans can warm to. But there is hope. Next year, or maybe five years from now, the Big O will be completed. The retractable roof will be set in place. And, in this city of endless winter and short hot summers, it will be possible to watch baseball played under a roof, on artificial grass, in an air-conditioned, possibly even centrally heated, concrete tomb.

Progress.

Softball, it might be said, saved baseball. Whenever the hardball game lost its devotees because of declining skill levels or spectator disinterest, softball filled the void. It did so in the 1920s and later, in the sixties. Baseball is a faster game, with a smaller ball requiring high skill at all positions. Softball, on the other hand, gets along with a few skilled players at key positions. Since the pitcher is the dominant performer, most players – even on the best teams – seldom get a hit; so there's less pressure for weaker players to deliver. What does this have to do with baseball? By the 1920s baseball was too advanced a game for interested females and so they opted for the less-skilled game of softball. By the Second World War they had refined the game into a highly skilled, entertaining attraction that regularly drew huge crowds throughout North America, leading to the establishment of the All-American Girls Baseball League, covered in Lois Browne's story in this collection. As Laura Robinson shows here, women's softball was a hot item in Toronto from the twenties to the fifties.

When I played at Sunnyside, I thought I'd died and gone to heaven

LAURA ROBINSON

Excited thousands, to set a new attendance mark, watched the yellow-and-gold Parksides girls defeat Supremes 5 to 3 last night at Sunnyside. It was heralded as a battle for the top, and it was that and something more. Oldtimers at the major girls' softball league games declared they had never seen a battle like it before – Parksides won by their unusual team play and brilliancy in the field.

Toronto newspaper, spring/summer 1927

AND SO PASSED ANOTHER NIGHT 'UNDER THE ARCS' AT THE SUNNYSIDE Ladies Softball stadium. From 1924 to 1956, thousands of top women players and literally millions of fans flocked to the shores of Lake Ontario in Toronto's west end to watch some of the most competitive ball in North America. Teams from as far away as Cleveland, Detroit, Montreal and California came to play against the likes of 'twirler' Thelma Golden (Goldie) and Norene Zeagman Kirby, the 'starry second-sacker' with a .364 batting average.

There were other baseball stars of the twenties and early thirties who were true pioneers in women's sport. Many, such as Bobbie Rosenfeld, who was a world-champion sprinter, multifaceted athlete, and sports journalist, and Gerry Mackie, a world-champion speed-skater, held the door open for generations of women athletes for decades to come. Once arthritis claimed Bobbie's sports career, she sponsored and coached a team called 'The Bobbie Rosenfelds' at Sunnyside.

Other early players included Grace and Toni Conacher (of the Teddy Oke's Parksides and Canadian track-and-field team), Dot Adams, Molly Trinnell, Verna Beswick, Leone Duffy, Nora Gordon, Flo Cutting, Ollie Hymus, Dora Watson, Flo and Bessie Kent, Virginia Pasquale, Fern Eagen, and Helen Kent. Many other women who played from the thirties on, when the league teams increased in number, are still alive and active in sports.

In 1994, at 77, Nora Young of East York is a competitive athlete in many sports. She played and coached at Sunnyside from 1930 to 1956 (with the exception of her time in the auxiliary services overseas during the war). Nora coached at Coxwell Park in the east end from 1956 to 1965. Her schedule in the thirties would keep today's pro athletes hopping.

She would arrive on her one-speed coaster bike at the CNE stadium to take part in bicycle races at the velodrome, borrowing one of the track bikes ridden by the men. (She rose to be a Canadian champion in that sport.) Once the race was over, she hopped on the bike and sprinted over to the Sunnyside diamond to make the 7:30 game, taking the position of left field for the Sunnyside Supremes, Lakesides, Tip-Tops, Peoples, Toronto Ladies, and Du-Vals, depending on the year. Her games usually ended at 10:30 at night, at which time she got back on the bike and rode to her west-end home. Given that Sunnyside's season went from the beginning of May to October, and that the players went out for three weekly games and a full day of practising, Nora Young was a busy, and fit, young woman.

There isn't space here to give profiles of the equally talented athletes who played at Sunnyside. A thumbnail sketch of the period will have to suffice. In 1918, after the First World War, Sunnyside was developed as a recreational area by the Toronto Harbour Commission. In 1924, a diamond was constructed on the east side of the Parkdale Canoe Club (now the Boulevard Club), and right from the start, except for a few charity games, when men played, it was a place where women came to play ball, and lots of fans came to cheer.

Photos from the time show cars and people lined up along King and

Dufferin streets, anxious to gain entry, or, if the stadium was filled to capacity, then jostling for a spot that allowed them to peer into it. In 1924, spectators cheered from a grassy roped-off area near the diamond, or perched on King Street, which was higher than the park. Wooden bleachers that provided three thousand seats were added for the 1925 season, when admission cost ten cents. Fans in boater straw hats crowded the stands, and later retired to Sunnyside Park for picnics and swimming.

In 1926, additional bleachers were built to give an added thousand spectators a view of what was becoming an extremely competitive league. Floodlights shone down, allowing doubleheaders to be played well into the evening. In fact, Sunnyside became the first diamond in Toronto to play 'under the arcs.' At this time, the roster included the Supremes, Cycles, Grottos, Maple Leafs, Parksides, Patricias, Parkdales, and Marlboros. In no time, the number of teams in the league increased, not to mention the level at which they played. While senior teams were considered the most competitive, intermediate teams provided an excellent feeder system, as did the many other 'girl' teams that played in the sports-mad city.

Companies large and small were more than willing to sponsor such popular and competitive teams, which by 1934 were surpassing every men's ball team in the city in gate receipts. Among the generous team patrons over the years were Toronto Fuels, Young Motors, Cunningham and Hill Plumbing Wholesalers, and even Sheridan Funeral Homes. But support went far beyond the commercial enterprises that wanted their name across the chests of the top female athletes in the city.

A Harbour Commission representative was always on the league's board of governors, as was Flo Cutting, the perennial secretary of Sunnyside, who had been an amazing ballplayer in the twenties. The season's opener, which a Toronto newspaper noted could take place in 'hockey-like weather,' attracted a who's who of Toronto society. And speaking of hockey, in 1926, just as spring rolled around, it was grandly announced in the Toronto newspapers that the Patricias 'Pats' were to be managed by hockey great Corbett 'Corb' Denneny. In 1936, Mary Pickford attended the opener, as did a record-breaking number of spectators.

All teams, intermediate and senior, were piped in to the stadium by marching bands for the opening game. The mayor, who attended with city council, and Harbour Commission officials threw out the first pitch. Championship trophies from the year before were presented, and after the game, festivities, which even in 1927 reflected opening days 'importance both as a sporting and social affair,' were held in such 'hot spots' as the Royal York Hotel downtown or the Palais Royale dancehall, located at Sunnyside. 'Following the banquet and presentations the players and a large number of guests tripped the light fantastic until the wee sma' hours of the morning.'

No detail was overlooked for the 'girl ball players.' They had their own groundskeeper, simply named 'Jock'; a nurse, known to the players as 'Brammie,' never missed a game; Bill Hayes, the gatekeeper and program seller, drew the lucky number for the evening game's door prize; and Jimmy Wiston (husband of player Betty Wiston) was the scorekeeper.

If the twenties were the building years, the thirties and forties were Sunnyside baseball's heyday. In the tradition of other Toronto-area players, the 'girls' toured North America; and women ball players flocked to Toronto to take on the legendary league, travelling for days for a tournament at Sunnyside. Sometimes, however, it was play with other Southern Ontario teams that revealed how advanced Sunnyside women's ball had become.

A 1931 Toronto newspaper clipping describes a game between the Sunnyside Maple Leafs and the Caledonia team, a native group from the Six Nations reserve near Brantford: 'The full-blooded Indian girls played clever softball, and they would hold their own with the majority of teams in Toronto.' Caledonia players Lil and Alice Green starred for their team. A July 25, 1949, clipping of an exhibition game between the Sunnyside Fuels and the Brantford Burtols states, 'Alice and Lil Green led the Brantford attack with a triple and double apiece.' In Canada Aboriginal women could excel as athletes and play at Sunnyside, thirty years before they were granted the right to vote.

In other ways, women ball players were allowed to exist in a liberated, new world, while their unathletic sisters were straight-jacketed in the confines of traditional femininity. Not only was a state-of-the-art stadium built for their games, but members of the media covered every game from May to October, and wrote regular, lengthy features about players and coaches. Players were well respected in their communities and were fêted by Toronto's élite. Employment and accommodation were arranged by sponsors if a player moved to Toronto from another community.

While the twenties-girls wore blue serge bloomers, leggings, and jerseys, there was a wide variety of team uniforms in the latter years. Margaret Nosworthy (Ryan), who played on four championship teams between 1948 and 1952, says she was never at a loss for classy threads. 'We had blue satin skirts, and jerseys with a V-neck and cuffs to wear on Sundays. But, even better were our leather team jackets and zoot-suit pants, all tailor made. Boy, we looked sharp. They gave us suitcases for travel, and on the field we wore flannel pants that reached below the knee and matching flannel tops. When I played at Sunnyside, I thought I'd died and gone to heaven.'

Women softball players could only ascend to heaven for four more years after Margaret played. By 1956, the stadium was slated for demolition. The private and élite Boulevard Club was to be built on the increasingly valuable waterfront property. The glorious days of women's ball also met the wrecker's ball.

But listen closely the next time you're on the waterfront of Toronto's west end. Can you hear the echo? Is it the band playing at the Palais Royale as the Supremes celebrate another championship season? Or is it .404er Irene Aldred cracking yet another one over the fence and bringing the capacity crowd to its feet as she shores up another win at Sunnyside?

———— ◆ ————

No sport has inspired more writing than baseball. A game filled with characters and events, it has an inherent narrative quality. Furthermore, as Marshall McLuhan convincingly argues elsewhere in this volume, baseball can be seen as a genuine form of culture. This writer would maintain, however, that baseball can even aspire to the ranks of high culture, that is has operatic potential.

Notes for a Baseball Opera

JOHN ST JAMES

THE FIRST BASEBALL STORY I EVER READ WAS PROBABLY DOUGLASS Wallop's *The Year the Yankees Lost the Pennant* (in a 1955 *Reader's Digest* condensed version). I was 12 years old and had become a baseball fan in the midst of the Yankees' incredible five-year stretch of world championships (1949–53). My enthusiasm for the game came not from my father, who was a football fan, mad for his Ticats (I was born in Hamilton), but from my maternal grandmother, whom I visited every summer in Sault Ste Marie. She was a Tigers fan (the family had lived for several years in Soo, Michigan).

Searching, perhaps, for a stability that my turbulent family did not offer, I became a Yankees fan about 1951. My mother, in keeping with her sometimes morose personality, was a Dodgers fan. In retrospect, she probably made the more realistic choice: life is more likely to frustrate and disappoint us (like the Dodgers or the Red Sox or the Expos) than to offer us triumph after triumph the way Casey Stengel's Yankees did for their fans. Still, it was glorious while it lasted. (Maybe genes count for something in these choices too; my brother became a Red Sox fan.)

Today's fans cannot comprehend how invincible the Yankees seemed in those years. Even in the occasional year when they *did* lose (like 1954), there was the feeling, the *certainty*, that they would be back. Thus, Wallop's story of a Washington Senators fan willing to make a pact with the Devil to help his team topple the mighty Bronx Bombers was not all that fanciful in a way. For Yankee-haters, anything was worth a try. To a smug 12-year-old Yankees fan, the story was quaintly amusing. I knew nothing of the Faust legend, of course, and even if I had known its details, I still wouldn't have *understood* why Joe Hardy was willing to sell his soul to 'Mr. Applegate' to lead his Senators to victory.

I drifted away from baseball in my twenties, not, as I thought then, because I had more important things to do, but rather, as I now suspect, because I couldn't deal with the Yankees' demise, their stark mortality, after 1964. Over a decade later, the Blue Jays rekindled my love of the game, but also taught me the humility that any real fan must have. When defeat, rather than triumph, is assured, year after year, a fan learns to appreciate how hard-won victory can be in sport, how delicate the fabric of a winning team, how almost inevitable it is that some unlucky twist of fate will bring a good team down. The Jays of 1987 were testimony to these ago-old certainties of sport: a trim, efficient, confident squad, rolling to victory, then stunned by two body blows (the loss in quick succession of Tony Fernandez and Ernie Whitt in the last games of the season) that sent them reeling into a fatal tailspin. As we all remember still, the end was grim.

Still, from losing most of the time, the Jays had 'advanced' to losing tragically (snatching defeat from the jaws of victory). And, whether they won it all or not in those years from 1985 on, there was lots of dramatic baseball to be savoured and a vivid cast of hometown favourites: the dynamic young outfield of Bell, Moseby, and Barfield, the steady third-base combo of Iorg and Mulliniks, Ernie, Mookie ...

Somewhere along the line, I realized that the *drama* of baseball was one of its greatest appeals for me. So, for instance, even though the 1987 season ended for the Jays with that fatal losing streak, the last two series with the Tigers were compellingly dramatic: seven games, each decided by a run. The Jays' off-years in the late eighties, 1986 and 1988, offered high drama in the post-season: the Mets' remarkable turnaround of the 1986 Series against the seemingly forever-doomed Red Sox and, in 1988, the Dodgers' surprising smothering of the mighty Athletics in five games, somehow brought about by the hobbling Kirk Gibson's astonishing two-out, two-strike homer in Game 1 off Dennis Eckersley. The next year, 1989, God saw fit to take part in the proceedings, as a devastating earthquake hit the Bay area in the middle of the Oakland–San Francisco Series. (Was Jose Canseco's monstrous fifth-deck homer at the SkyDome during the ALCS an omen of the shattering events to follow?)

In 1991 came one of the greatest World Series in recent times: a seven-game classic between the Twins and the Braves (both teams, by the way, had finished in *last* place in their divisions the year before). There were three extra-inning games (of 12, 11, and 10 innings); five of the seven games were decided by one run; in five games, the winning run scored after the seventh inning; and *four* contests were decided on the game's final swing. And then there was Jack Morris, pitching a magnificent 10-inning, 1–0 shutout in Game 7. This was exquisite stuff: endings that no one could have expected, heroes who seemed to carry an entire team on their shoulders. My love of the game was being nourished by experiences that had nothing to do with whether *my* team won or lost.

Of all sports, baseball seems to offer the widest range of dramatic possibilities. It is composed of individual moments – punctuated by each pitch – that coalesce into the story of each game. Though fully a team sport, it is played out in focused encounters and moments of action – pitcher/batter, batter/fielder – that draw each participant briefly 'stage centre.' Astonishing things ('I've never seen *that* before!') happen in baseball because the possibilities are so varied, so wide open.

As my appreciation for the drama of baseball has grown in recent years, this passion of my leisure time has somehow grown closer to another of my life's essential nourishments, music. I attended a choir school as a boy, and grew up making and absorbing music. Though I ventured in my teens and twenties into rock music (and now enjoy jazz), I've continued to find classical music endlessly interesting and exciting. And lately, thanks to an unexpected move on my wife's part from light country music to the Three Tenors (!), I've begun to explore the highly charged and dramatic world of opera. At its best, opera is complete theatre: music, narrative, and visual spectacle artfully wedded to portray (whether in melodrama, comedy, or tragedy) some compelling aspect of the human story – compelling because it touches on the story we are writing with our own lives.

Now, it would be foolish to claim that the drama of sport is of this magnitude (though for Philly fans in the '93 Series, seeing Mitch Williams on the mound did elicit the feelings of 'pity and fear' that Aristotle said are essential to great tragedy). But drama, in the sense of an unfolding spectacle of events leading to some resolution, is surely one of the things that attracts us, even addicts us, to sport. We may not always grasp, or feel in control of, the 'drama' of our own lives, but we can gain immense pleasure and release (with little risk) from the dramatic 'events' played out on a baseball diamond (or hockey rink or tennis court).

Perhaps it's just my need, in middle age, to make sense of my life's odd collection of interests, but lately baseball and opera have been converging in my imagination. If opera can be termed a complete art, baseball can justly be called a complete sport: a delicate balance of individual and team effort, enacted within a structure that allows for unlimited possibilities (not to mention, there's no clock). In a way, baseball and opera are made for each other.

Early in the 1992 season I chanced to encounter at a Jays game a man I had not seen in almost 30 years: Father Owen Lee. He had been a professor of mine at the University of Toronto, an eloquent champion of Latin poetry (Horace and Virgil). In recent years I had become reacquainted with him over the radio, as an urbane and delightful commentator and quiz participant on the Texaco Metropolitan Opera Saturday afternoon broadcasts. Though he is a classics scholar by trade, Father Lee is known to millions as an opera expert blessed with an astonishing memory (he rarely misses a question in the quizzes) and, more important, a resonant understanding of the human depths that this great art can reach and illuminate.

Though we talked a bit about opera at the game, our conversation was far from profound. Father Lee has a mirthful disposition and a sharp wit, and understands that occasionally the *downright silly* must be given pride of place in human affairs. So, while I speculated on the make-up of a batting order of all-star composers (Rossini leading off, Mozart batting third, Beethoven – well, what about Mahler? – in the clean-up slot), Father Lee noted the operatic qualities of certain current players (Kelly Gruber, blond and thickly muscled, reminded him of a young Siegfried; ex-Jay George Bell was definitely a *primo uomo*, the male counterpart of the *prima donna*). It was great fun.

Our next contact was after the 1993 season, when Father Lee sent me an intriguing baseball/opera quiz that he had written for *Opera Quarterly* magazine: 25 questions providing operatic and baseball clues to the names of past and present baseball stars ('A' to 'Z,' with 'X' excluded). Thus, at 'B' we find: '*Carmen* composer / *Lakmé* song (tolling Toronto-Chicagoan with record 3 HRs in '88 opening game).' Answer: George Bell.

I fared well on the quiz, going 19 for 25. It was delightful to throw these apparently incongruous entertainments together and have a bit of fun. To my surprise, however, in the days that followed I could not dispel the baseball/opera connection from my mind. I wondered, Are baseball and opera *really* incongruous, from two different spheres of human interest? Then I remembered Douglass Wallop's story, and realized that there was a baseball *musical* already on the books: *Damn Yankees*. If the Faust legend could remain alive in this hugely successful Broadway show (and movie) about baseball, surely a baseball *opera* was not an outlandish notion.

Now, I am neither a musician nor a skilled storyteller, and an opera requires both for its creation. So the best I can do here is to offer some ideas for a baseball opera and throw out a challenge for others to meet. In the spirit of this volume, however, I would hope that a *Canadian* musician and librettist would be the first to realize this lofty goal. For what it's worth, I'll offer (*gratis*) a possible plot-line and central group of characters to work from, pointing out that a story *somewhat* like this was used by a great nineteenth-century opera *meister* in one of his finest works.

First, the locale. As this book demonstrates, baseball has been played just about everywhere in Canada. In choosing a setting for our opera, then, one needn't be restricted to obvious (and over-exposed) places like Toronto and Montreal. An unassuming small town will do just as well. Some place in southwestern Ontario or the Prairies would make sense, but I would opt for a more dramatic setting, the Atlantic coast. Though not often associated with baseball, the sea is a mythic presence in human legend, literature, and music, and could provide a powerful, mysterious backdrop for our story (somewhat the way the cornfields of Iowa did in Kinsella's *Shoeless Joe*). My choice, then, is the town of Lunenburg, Nova Scotia.

The time is the 1920s. The men of Lunenburg work hard; their craft, of course, is shipbuilding – wooden ships. But they also appreciate the rugged pleasures of sport; since the 1870s they and their sons have played baseball. These hardy craftsmen have brought to their play the same pride and precision manifested in their ships. Over the years, their team, the Lunenburg Larks, has become famous for its pitching. In some ways, their unique skills, appreciated less and less in a world that no longer has need of sailing ships for its commerce, have been chan-nelled into the 'Lunenburg style' of pitching: precise, finely tuned, subtle – the antithesis of the brash, electric, fast-paced world that is threatening their livelihood. As Babe Ruth is reshaping the game of baseball at the major-league level, young Maritime players are drawn more and more to the new 'power game.' After all, how can a deftly executed hit and run compare with the towering splendour of a home run? Young pitch-ers, to survive, feel they have to match power with power, and are turning away from the 'old fashioned' finesse epitomized by the Lunenburg game.

It's here our story begins. Walter Knight, a skilled apprentice ship-wright, who's recently moved to Lunenburg from Halifax, is an avid ball player. A tall, strapping fellow blessed with a resilient, whiplash right arm, Wally was a sensation on the sandlots of Halifax, overpow-ering hitters with his hard stuff. Though he could have played for any team in the Halifax area, there was only one squad he wanted to join – the Lunenburg Larks. It is not just the legendary skills of the Larks' pitching staff that has drawn him down the coast, however. More than anything, young Walter wants to win the hand of Evie Goldsmith, whom he met the previous year at a Lunenburg mid-summer fair. They are deeply in love. But Wally is an outsider, and can only achieve his sweet goal of marrying Evie if he can win over her father, William, who (as it happens) is the Larks' owner. Now 'Whitey' Goldsmith had been a ball player in his youth and is not unsympathetic to the young man's quest. But he is old-fashioned and believes young Walter has to pay his dues. So he offers him a chance to play for his team – strictly as a reserve – and learn the Lunenburg style of play. *Then* he'll see ...

Wally, young and impatient, has loftier goals: he wants to crack the Larks' starting rotation. The team is solid this year and looks as though it can go all the way to the provincial finals, if not the Maritime championships. Wally knows that if he can help the Larks knock off their main South Shore League rivals, the Liverpool Larrupers, 'Whitey' Goldsmith will be proud to have him as his son-in-law. In anticipation of such a late-season opportunity, Wally has been working on a special pitch: a low fastball that looks pretty hittable coming in, but rises suddenly at the last moment, confounding the hitter. With the radiant Evie shimmering in his mind's eye, Wally calls this exploding riser his 'prize' pitch [key aria at this point].

The tradition-bound Lark pitchers are cool in their reception of Wally Knight. The crusty old manager, Hec ('Six Toes') Messer, is set in his ways and none too impressed with 'new' pitches; the old style suits him fine. (He's bitter, too, since *his* promising ball career was tragically cut short by a shipyard accident.) Reluctantly, he takes Wally onto the staff, but will only use him out of the bullpen, for mop-up work. Fortunately, Wally has an ally in the kindly pitching coach, Hank ('Socks') Shuster, who sees the young man's potential and keeps working on 'Six Toes' until the old man finally agrees to give the young Knight a chance. It's mid-August, the dog days, and the starters are wilting. Messer figures he's got nothing to lose. Wally performs well in a start against Yarmouth.

The Larks are gearing up for a crucial Labour Day–weekend series against the Liverpool Larrupers. Connie Nightingale, their ace, is set to pitch the important opening game, but, with a week to go, goes down with a sore shoulder. Young Wally is given the start, and baffles the Larruper hitters with his zinging riser. The rejuvenated staff silences their bats for the rest of the series, and ... Well, you can figure out how it ends.

I'm not sure yet how to bring the sea into this opera. Perhaps Wally could be visited by a ghostly apparition from the sea (like Joe Jackson emerging from the cornfield) who inspires him to pursue his quest of the lovely Evie. It could be his father, tragically lost at sea when Wally was a boy, or perhaps some epic baseball figure, known for his hard work and steely determination: someone like Honus Wagner, the 'Flying Dutchman.' (Come to think of it, he was still alive in the twenties; it will have to be someone else.)

Finally, there's the matter of a title. I wouldn't want to hamstring the genius who is going to put all this together, but I rather like *The Masterflingers of Lunenburg*.

———————— ◆ ————————

'A guy who's played one game in the pros is like a former State Senator,' Wilfred Sheed wrote in Diamonds Are Forever, *'a big man in most neighbourhoods, and any saloon, as long as he lives.' Mel Kerr from Souris, Manitoba, played only one major-league game, and that as a pinch runner, in 1925. Seventy years later, his 'glory' lives on in the pages of Jim Shearon's* Canada's Baseball Legends: True Stories of Canadians in the Big Leagues since 1879.

Mel Kerr – How Brief Was His Glory

JIM SHEARON

Kerr, John Melville
Born: Souris, Manitoba, May 22, 1903
5'-11^1/$_2$", 155 lbs, Batted left, threw left
Career highlights: Pinch runner, Chicago Cubs, 1925

MEL KERR WAS A GREAT AMATEUR ATHLETE OF SASKATOON. STANDING just under six feet and weighing 155 pounds, he was slim and quick. A Saskatoon newspaper report described Mel as the city tennis champion, an all-star halfback for the city's senior football team, 'a phenomenon at basketball' and the individual champion at the annual Saskatchewan track and field games.

A photograph of the four-man relay team shows Mel Kerr in company with Jimmy Skinner, later coach of the Detroit Red Wings hockey team; Vern DeGeer, who became a sports columnist with the Montreal Gazette; and Colborne McEown, future Vice-President of the University of Saskatchewan. It is an impressive foursome.

When Mel Kerr signed a major-league contract with the Chicago Cubs in January 1925, the Montreal Gazette, 2,000 miles away, announced the news. Mel was assigned by the Cubs to the Saginaw Aces of the Michigan-Ontario League, and it was there that he played his first game as a professional, May 6, 1925, in bitter cold weather.

The London Free Press reported that it had snowed in the morning, 'Hardly a thousand fans turned out and they were shivering even in overcoats.' Mel Kerr played left field and batted second. He put down a sacrifice bunt in his first appearance and doubled later in the game. Kerr had one putout in the outfield as Saginaw lost 4–1 to London.

The 1925 season had been a hard one for Chicago managers. Bill Killefer, a catcher who originally came to the Cubs from the Phillies with Grover Cleveland Alexander and helped Chicago to win the pennant in 1918, had been fired in July with the Cubs in seventh place. Rabbit Maranville, the Cubs' shortstop, replaced Killefer then was fired himself, after 53 games, when the team showed no improvement. George Gibson, a former catcher from London, Ontario, who had been a scout and coach for the Cubs was asked to finish the season while management looked for a new leader.

According to a newspaper story from Chicago on September 3, 'The new boss had just returned from a trip to the bushes in search of young ivory to bolster a sagging team.' Gibson had scouted the Michigan-Ontario League and one of the players he saw down on the farm was Mel Kerr, left fielder of the Saginaw Aces. The rookie outfielder played 136 games for the Michigan club and made 147 hits, including 31 doubles, eight triples and one home run for a batting average of .283. Kerr had 21 stolen bases and made nine errors in the outfield, most of them during the first month of the season.

The Sporting News reported, 'Outfielder Mel Kerr, the Canadian youth who was farmed out last spring, has been recalled, but he is such a kid and so lacking in experience that it probably will be necessary to give him another season in some butter and egg circuit.'

Mel had two hits in his final game at Saginaw on Sunday afternoon. Monday he took the train to Chicago. Wednesday, September 16, 1925, he made his major-league debut at Wrigley Field. The Cubs and the Boston Braves split a doubleheader. Grover Cleveland Alexander shut out Boston 3–0 in the first game; but four different pitchers couldn't contain the Braves in the second game.

As the Cubs came to bat in the bottom of the ninth, trailing 8–4, Tommy Griffith was announced to bat for the pitcher. Griffith had batted .302 for Cincinnati in 1915 and had played for Brooklyn in the 1920 World Series. He stroked a single to right field. Manager Gibson called Mel Kerr from the bench and sent the Prairie youngster to run for the pinch-hitter.

Was it a tactical decision, or an act of kindness from one Canadian to another? It was Kerr's first appearance in a major-league game and it proved to be his last. Chicago sustained a brief rally and Mel scored a run, but the Cubs lost 8 to 6. Two weeks later the season ended. Mel played professional ball for another six years until a shoulder injury ended his career, but he never played in the big leagues again. Mel Kerr's major-league career lasted barely 15 minutes.

———————— ◆ ————————

No one knows more about Saskatchewan baseball's history than lawyer David Shury, who even started a provincial baseball hall of fame in his home town of North Battleford in the mid-eighties. He has never forgotten the day in August 1963 when the legendary Satchel Paige and his squad of barnstormers suddenly appeared at a local game. Paige had always warned others not to look back; as he was fond of saying, 'Something might be gaining on you.' On this day eight years before the famous black player's eventual induction into the Baseball Hall of Fame, Paige's fortunes were at a low ebb.

The Last Barnstormer

DAVE SHURY

ONE SUNDAY AFTERNOON IN AUGUST OF 1963, KEITH ERNE AND I WERE taking tickets at the gate at Abbott Field in North Battleford. We were just about ready to pack everything up and close off sales and watch the rest of the game between the North Battleford Beavers and the visiting Unity Cardinals.

At that point I looked up and saw two old cars pulling up the hill and into the parking lot adjacent to the ball park. Out of the cars poured 11 or 12 black persons who looked like they could be ball players. As they headed over to the ball park gate I recognized the leader as Leroy 'Satchel' Paige. I recall hearing that Paige and his All-Stars had been in the province barnstorming earlier that summer but I didn't recall hearing of anything from them in the past couple of weeks and I just assumed they had left the province.

Paige and his All-Stars had fallen on hard times. He readily admitted to me that they were out of money and were supposed to be in British Columbia (I believe at Kamloops) that afternoon. However, they did not have gas to get there. The team was absolutely destitute and had not had a decent meal for several days. Keith and I invited them into the ball park and I sat with Satchel during the rest of the game. Satchel showed interest in the game and stated to me that he never watched a baseball game that he did not enjoy – and never watched a game without learning something.

This team had come into southeastern Saskatchewan several months before but had not raised very much money – and now they were broke. The North Battleford team put Satchel's team up in a local hotel and saw that they were fed. The Unity team arranged an exhibition game against them at Unity for the next evening and told Satchel they would be donating the entire proceeds to them.

On the Tuesday evening of that week, North Battleford had an exhibition game against the All-Stars and donated the proceeds to them, so that with ourselves and Unity helping out, enough money was raised to get them back to the States.

When Satchel passed away in Kansas City, Missouri on June 8, 1982 of a heart attack, one month shy of his 75th birthday, I felt as a lot of other people did: that organized baseball should hang their heads in shame.

Satchel had turned professional at age 17 but because of baseball's unwritten color bar he did not make it to the majors until age 41.

In August 1963 Satchel pitched one inning and then the rest of the game was pitched by a lanky right hander whom Satchel passed off as his son, Satchel Paige Jr., but who in actuality was Sherman Cottingham. Sherman came back and played for North Battleford for two seasons, 1964 and 1965.

It is hard to explain to the younger generation that for 60 years – up until 1947 – no blacks were allowed to play in organized baseball. In April 1887 in Newark, New Jersey, Cap Anson refused to let his Chicago White Sox take the field because the Newark club in an exhibition game had announced that a Canadian-born black was slated to pitch for Newark. This was the beginning of the unwritten color bar which lasted for the next 60 years until Jackie Robinson took the field in 1947 for the Brooklyn Dodgers. A year later, at age 41, when most players are retiring, Satchel Paige became a rookie on Bill Veeck's Cleveland Indians.

I had seen Satchel pitch once, prior to 1963, and that had been during an exhibition game against the Saskatoon Commodores in 1958 in Saskatoon. At that time he was a member of the touring Cuban All-Stars.

Satchel, of course, was well known throughout the province, having pitched here with John Donaldson in a tournament held in 1931 in southern Saskatchewan against Virden, Manitoba in the finals of a two-day tourney. In 1935 when he was a member of the Bismarck, North Dakota semi-pro ball team, a number of exhibition games were played throughout the province. Actually his name comes up fairly regularly when oldtimers talk about playing against him. I am certain he found Saskatchewan to be far more hospitable than much of the United States.

One only wonders what sort of records Satchel Paige might have set had the color bar not existed.

When I watched the Tuesday night exhibition game in Abbott Field that August 1963 evening, little did I realize that I was probably watching the last game played in Saskatchewan by a touring group of black barnstormers.

———— ◆ ————

The Class D Cape Breton Colliery League, at the lowest rung of organized baseball, was part of the elaborate feeder system of minor-league clubs through which young men hoped to progress to the big leagues. Few made it that far, but most had fond memories of their time spent pursuing a dream and of the people they met in places like Sydney Mines, Glace Bay, and New Waterford, Cape Breton. After the German invasion of Poland in 1939, umpire Chuck Whittle recalled meeting league president Judge Campbell. 'We came to the conclusion that the Colliery League would never operate again with the war upon us and American players sure to be restricted in their travel. I remember how sad it was seeing the players with tears in their eyes when they realized they wouldn't be returning. They hated to leave Cape Breton.'

Cape Breton Colliery League

SPALDING *OFFICIAL BASEBALL GUIDE*

WEATHER CONDITIONS UNPARALLELED IN THE HISTORY OF CAPE BRETON Island during the first weeks of the 1939 pennant race of the Cape Breton Colliery League, and the declaration of war in Europe during the latter part of the season, combined to make the 1939 pennant race a poor one for the four clubs from a financial viewpoint.

At the commencement of the season, a League decision was reached to step the classification up from Class D to Class C, with the result that the brand of ball played during the season was the fastest ever seen in Eastern Canada. Under the capable leadership of Judge A.D. Campbell and a capable board of governors, the League played to a conclusion, the only change in the original schedule being its curtailing by one week, in order that Canadian soldier recruits could use the ball parks for training purposes, Canada entering the war before the end of the regular schedule.

The 1940 season opens brighter, with all teams having a number of splendid players under contract, as well as reliable managers available for at least three clubs, with the fourth having several playing managers to select from. There is also a hope that the Cape Breton Colliery League, the only professional organized base ball league operating in Canada with all Canadian clubs the past three years, will get what they have not been able to secure in the past, some practical assistance from their big brothers in the United States.

United States players who were engaged by all clubs proved on the whole to be an exceptionally fine lot, and as a result of their playing, base ball has been given a great impetus among the young native players.

Sydney, with a well-balanced pitching staff, won the League schedule and the final playdowns, mostly through their superior pitching.

Waterford, after leading the League the greater part of the season, came apart in the playdowns, when their ace pitcher, 'Specs' Spiers, was unable to hurl a game in the finals for them, after he had pitched Glace Bay Miners out of the picture in the semi-finals.

The Miners from Glace Bay finished third, under the management of Roy Moore. They failed to hit their stride until well along in the season, but too late to land better than third place.

Sydney Mines had no less than four playing managers during the season, the last being the major leaguer Billy Marshall, who with a skeleton team finished the season.

A world's record was set by the Glace Bay and Sydney Mines teams, when they played four consecutive games, each ending in a tie, two of them going extra innings. On August 22 they played a 2–2 draw, on the 24th the score was 4–4, on the 26th it was also 4–4 and on the 30th 2–2. In all, the teams played 38 innings, with the runs scored being 12–12.

Outstanding pitching feat of the season was the no-hit, no-run game hurled by playing manager Al Smith of the Sydney team, on June 30th at Sydney, when he blanked Glace Bay 3–0. Smith fanned six of the thirty-two men to face him, walking five, three of them first up in the inning.

Sydney also had the two outstanding players of the 1939 season, Bernie Pearlman, who captured all pitching honors, and Abe Abramowitz, leading first baseman and all-round League hitter.

The Cape Breton Colliery League was signally honored last season when its president, Judge A.D. Campbell, was chosen by Judge Bramham, president of the National Association of Professional Base Ball Leagues, to act as chairman of the commission which supervised the 'Little World Series,' between the winners of the International League and the American Association.

The Glace Bay club, which operated the franchise in that town the past three years, will, it is planned, by succeeded be a new group of base ball enthusiasts, with some of the old executives to assist them.

– D.H. MacFarlane, Glace Bay, N.S.

STANDING OF CLUBS AT CLOSE OF SEASON

Club	Won	Lost	Tied	Pct.
Sydney	36	20	1	.643
New Waterford	31	25	1	.554
Glace Bay	26	25	5	.510
Sydney Mines	14	37	5	.275

Championship play-off – New Waterford defeated Glace Bay, two games to one; Sydney defeated New Waterford, four games to none, with one tie.

───────◆───────

Most young Canadians have developed their baseball skills in playground settings. Climate restricts the amount of time schools can devote to the game. A significant exception has been Assumption College, established in 1870 in Windsor, Ontario, by Brasilian priests as an elementary to post-secondary institution whose main purpose was to prepare young males for the priesthood. (It later evolved into the University of

*Windsor.) With Detroit and its significant baseball heritage just across the river, it's
not surprising the sport was well received at Assumption.*

Assumption College's Mighty Five

TONY TECHKO

Assumption's close proximity to Detroit made it natural to look to the United
States for sports competition, inspiration and in some cases opportunity.

Dr. Dick Moriarty, Sports Historian, University of Windsor

ON EASTER MONDAY, 1908, THE PRESIDENT OF ASSUMPTION COLLEGE, Rev. D. Cushing, gave some students permission to attend an American League game at Bennett Park, situated at the corner of Michigan and Trumbull, in Detroit. He knew that the Cleveland catcher that day would be none other than Justin Jay 'Nig' Clarke, a young man he had known well at the school as the talented receiver for the Assumption Stellas. Clarke impressed his faithful with two hits and kept the highly touted Ty Cobb and his Detroit Tiger team-mates from stealing a single base.

If the students considered that to be a good day, it was a pity that they had not been present at Ennis, Texas, on June 15, 1902, when Clarke, catching for Corsicana of the Texas League, went to bat eight times and hit eight home runs in one game. That dramatic feat in the dead-ball era established a professional baseball record which still stands.

Justin Clarke enrolled at Assumption in September of 1894, more than one hundred years ago. He was a 12-year-old kid of mixed Scottish–White Wyandotte Indian ancestry from 'Hell's Corners,' at the intersection of Texas Road and the Third Concession in Essex County, not far from the town of Amherstburg, Ontario.

By the time Clarke came to Assumption baseball was very popular at the school. Back in the spring of 1871 the game had made its debut in a somewhat different form. For one thing, the equipment used was limited to say the least. Such easily recognizable things as gloves, masks, and shin or chest protectors were not in vogue. The essentials consisted of two or three balls, a bat or two, a home plate, and a group of young men willing to compete.

The rules were different too. The ball was pitched underhand and caught by the catcher on the first bounce. Before a batter was allowed to take first base on a walk he had to watch seven bad pitches go by. Another interesting feature was the right of the batter to call for a pitch of his liking: high, low, or middle.

The earliest recorded baseball game in Detroit was played in 1857, a contest between the Early Risers and the Franklin Club. The earliest recorded organized baseball team in Windsor was the Eurekas, founded in 1878. It would appear from those dates and the introduction of baseball at Assumption in 1871 that baseball came to Windsor from the United States, possibly by way of Assumption College.

During the Depression year of 1933, Rev. Charles Armstrong, an Assumption graduate and native of Stratford, Ontario, was ordained a Roman Catholic priest and assigned to his alma mater to teach science and coach in the sports program. He heard that a young man from the Gordon McGregor Continuation School, Henry Arcado 'Hank' Biasatti, had decided not to return to school in favour of a job at a local industrial plant.

Father Armstrong visited Biasatti and his parents at their home and was able to persuade the young man to enrol at Assumption to complete grades 11 and 12 of his high-school education. Biasatti, a high-scoring cager and stylish first baseman, became one of the finest all-around athletes ever to attend the Basilian high school. He fashioned careers in basketball and baseball that led to the Toronto Huskies in 1946 and the Philadelphia Athletics in 1949, earning him the distinction of being the only Canadian to play in the major leagues of professional basketball and baseball.

In 1948, a native Torontonian, Rev. Ronald Cullen, was transferred to Assumption from Catholic Central in Detroit. He began a baseball program at the school that produced three major leaguers: Reno Bertoia, John Upham, and Joe Siddall. Baseball people have been most complimentary about the manner in which Father Cullen coached the game. The work ethic and dedication to task produced not only outstanding performers but teams that won local, provincial, and national championships.

Without benefit of a single game in the minor leagues, Reno Peter Bertoia, only 18 years of age, made his major-league debut with the Detroit Tigers in 1953 against the legendary pitcher Leroy Robert 'Satchel' Paige; he struck out. A bonus baby who signed for a reported $25,000, Bertoia played in ten major-league seasons, compiling a batting mark of .244. Perhaps his greatest moment of baseball glory came during a

May month early in his career when he led the American League in hitting, with an average of .398, while the great Ted Williams was still playing.

A gifted storyteller, Bertoia, who was inducted into the Canadian Baseball Hall of Fame in 1988, sometimes entertains people with recollections of his playing days. He remembers Ted Williams greeting him in his rookie days with the words 'Hi, Bush.' Awe-struck, he could only reply, 'Hi, Mr. Williams.' He also recalls a long Sunday afternoon in Fenway Park when the Red Sox thrashed the Tigers unmercifully. Detroit couldn't do anything right that day. Finally, late in the game, as umpire Bill McKinley called a third strike on a Tiger batter on what manager Bucky Harris thought was a missed call, Harris yelled out in total frustration: 'They shot the wrong McKinley.'

In the summer of 1959, John Leslie Upham was signed for the Philadelphia Phillies by Tony Lucadello, the same scout who signed Ferguson Jenkins. In his second season of professional baseball, Upham, playing with the Class C Bakersfield team of the California League, batted .356 and led the league's outfielders in fielding with a .976 mark. He made the all-star team and seemed destined for big things in baseball.

But the following year, with Buffalo of the International League, as the season barely got under way, Upham, while sliding, suffered a severe knee injury that required surgery. The speed that enabled him to run the sixty-yard dash in 6.5 seconds or better was gone. His meteoric rise as an outfielder was dealt a serious blow.

Eventually, John Upham turned to pitching, his mainstay as an amateur, more and more. He hurled for the Chicago Cubs in 1967 and 1968 under manager Leo Durocher. But once again an injury, this time to his pitching arm, brought an abrupt end to his nine-year professional baseball career.

As a coach, Upham has worked with many Canadian youngsters both locally and nationally. He has been involved with teams in the Canada Summer Games, the World Junior Championships, the 1988 Olympic Games in Seoul, Korea, and the 1991 Pan-American Games in Havana, Cuba.

Joseph Todd Siddall was the fifth ballplayer from Assumption to play in the major leagues. A fine defensive catcher, Siddall began his pro career in baseball after a short stay at Central Michigan University on a football scholarship.

On Monday, September 6, 1993, more than 40,000 fans were in the seats at Montreal's Olympic Stadium to experience a bit of baseball history. On the mound that day for the Montreal Expos was Denis

Boucher, a southpaw from Lachine, Quebec, and behind the plate was Joe Siddall from Windsor, Ontario. This was the fifth Canadian battery in major-league history. The first, on July 13, 1883, featured James 'Tip' O'Neill from Woodstock, Ontario, then a pitcher who started for the New York Metropolitans. His catcher was John Humphries of North Gower, Ontario.

Assumption College began as an educational institution in 1857, before Canada came into being. Jesuits, Benedictines, Basilians, and the layman Theodule Girardot all tried in vain to make the school a success. It was not until 1870 that the Basilian Order on its second try, this time under the leadership of Rev. Dennis O'Connor, set in motion an educational and sporting tradition that has continued to this day.

Assumption, with its emphasis on the motto 'Teach me goodness, discipline and knowledge,' has seen sport as a vehicle to realize some of those objectives. The 'Mighty Five' of Justin Clarke, Hank Biasatti, Reno Bertoia, John Upham, and Joe Siddall have accomplished something for Assumption that no other Canadian school has done – sending five of its graduates into the ranks of major-league baseball.

———— ◆ ————

Each baseball season is a sweeping piece of history, featuring bold heroes, tragic figures, epic struggles, and remarkable, never-seen-before events – a microcosm of human history in its grandeur and folly. Long and wearing, ultimately, for most teams, the season is often called a campaign (as in war). The Montreal Expos' first, in 1969, was a gruelling long march. As Dan Turner demonstrates, in this excerpt from The Expos Inside Out *(1983), the Expos added some quirky grace notes to the ongoing symphony of world events.*

The History of Canada and the World: April–October 1969

DAN TURNER

There's one thing people forget about that team. And that's how hard we tried.

Manny Mota, July 1982

F OR SOME PATHETIC CITIZENS, SPORTS IS EVERYTHING. AS THE PHILOSOPHER Stephen Douglas Rogers has pointed out, fan is short for 'fanatic.' Twisted as it will seem to the reader, there are those who become so engrossed in the day-to-day doings of professional athletes that they lose touch with the important events of their times. But while this phenomenon is prevalent in large American cities, it's rare in cosmopolitan Canadian centres such as Montreal and Chicoutimi. While a sports team as fascinating as the Expos will serve as an entertaining and healthy diversion for the good burghers of such communities, almost all of them will keep a finger on the pulse of those happenings that determine their fate, the fate of their children – indeed, the fate of mankind. With this civilized approach to life in mind, here is what was important to the hundreds of thousands who added the Expos to their spectrum of interests in the team's first year of being.

Main characters:
Pierre Elliott Trudeau, elected prime minister-for-life of Canada, June 25, 1968.
Charles de Gaulle, first president of the fifth Republic of France (1890–1970).
Ho Chi Minh, orig. Nguyen That Thanh, Vietnamese political leader (1890–1969).
Country Joe and the Fish, musical group, played at Woodstock.
Maury Wills, premier shortstop of the 60s, finished his career with 586 stolen bases, languished in minor leagues for several years before starring with Dodgers, chosen early in expansion draft by Expos, who may have reminded him of the minors, then sent back to the Dodgers.
Rusty Staub, owner of Rusty's Restaurant, New York.
John Lennon, singer and songwriter (1940–1980).
William Hambly Stoneman, one of 26 major-league pitchers to have thrown two complete games in which his opponents did not hit safely.
Richard Raymond 'The Monster' Radatz, 6'6", 235 lbs., appeared on the cover of both *Time* and *Life*. Between 1962 and 1965, throwing for some terrible Boston Red Sox teams, saved 100 games, winning 49 games and losing only 32. Over those four years he pitched 538 innings, giving up 396 hits and striking out 608 batters.
Elroy Face, 5'8", 155 lbs., 1969 room-mate or Richard Raymond 'The Monster' Radatz, pitched 16 National League seasons, saving 193 games, winning 104 and losing 95. In 1959 he won 18 games, lost one on a ninth-inning single by Jim Gilliam, and saved ten more.

Richard Milhous Nixon, president of the United States of America
from 1969 to 1974.

1969
April 7: 150,000 people lined Montreal streets to greet their new baseball team, many of the younger fans flashing the V peace sign as the
players paraded past.
April 8: The Expos, came, saw, and conquered in New York, winning
their opener 11–10 over the Mets.
April 14: Jarry Park was packed as the Expos stormed back to win
their home opener 8–7 over the St. Louis Cardinals.
April 17: The emergence of talent continued as Bill Stoneman no-hit
the Phillies 7–0. Don Bosch did his Willie Mays imitation in center field,
making a great sliding catch to preserve history.
April 21: Four parachutists descended toward the mound at Jarry in
between-game festivities during a double-header. Three of them missed
the park, one injuring himself by hitting a parked car. Pitcher Carl
Morton had set the tone, an errant tone for them, in the first game,
walking five batters and hitting another in four innings of work.
April 26: Morton served up a hanging curve ball to Pirate pitcher
Steve Blass, who smacked it for a three-run triple. Expo manager
Gene Mauch removed both Morton and catcher John Bateman from the
game.
April 28: Charles de Gaulle resigned as president of France after his
new constitutional proposals were turned down in a referendum. De
Gaulle's feelings were identical to most of the Expos' starting pitchers:
'Après-moi, le déluge.'
April 30: The Montreal Amateur Baseball Fan Club held a luncheon
to honour Don Hahn for having been the outstanding Expo at spring
training. General Manager Jim Fanning filled in for Hahn, whom he
had sent to the minors four days earlier.
May 8: Mauch dazzled with his footwork at Jarry, kicking a rosin bag
to deep short and punting a baseball into the dugout after being ejected
for protesting a balk call on his pitcher. Balks, he said later, are 'insig-
nificant technicalities' that shouldn't alter the course of the game.
May 14: The Expos committed five errors as the Astros clobbered
them 10–3. 'We own Abner Doubleday an apology,' said Mauch apolo-
getically.
May 15: U.S. President Richard Nixon proposed a gradual, twelve-
month withdrawal from Vietnam.

May 17: Tito Francona of the Braves hit a two-run homer to beat the Expos in the twelfth – a legacy for his son.

May 20: Elroy Face celebrated the launching of Apollo 10 to the moon by serving up three home runs in relief. All fell short of the ionosphere. But just.

The Expos had expressed interest in trading slugging first baseman Donn Clendenon to the Mets for a package that would include sophomore pitcher Nolan Ryan, but it was leaking out they were no longer interested because Ryan was said to be having arm trouble.

May 22: Montreal Mayor Jean Drapeau flew off to Europe to lobby for the 1976 Olympics.

May 24: In his first start Jerry (Hard Luck) Robertson allowed only four hits in six innings, striking out nine. The Expos lost to Cincinnati, 4–3.

Gazette sportswriter Ted Blackman acknowledged American newspaper reports that seven days earlier Mack Jones had called him to the back of the team bus, where in 'a momentary loss of cool' Maury Wills had demanded that Blackman no longer use his name in stories, then slapped him in the mouth.

May 26: Apollo 10 splashed down safely with Stafford, Cernan, and Young aboard. The first frogman in the water was Louis Boisvert, who was born in Montreal.

May 27: The Chinese government of Mao Tse-tung threatened to wipe out the Soviet Union 'resolutely, cleanly, thoroughly, and completely.'

May 28: The Expos lost their eleventh straight to the Dodgers. A description of the game's key play: '[First baseman] Bob Bailey started to charge the bunt but stopped when [pitcher] Larry Jaster fielded it. [Second baseman] Gary Sutherland stood behind first base instead of on the bag. Bailey ducked to give Jaster a clear path and the pitcher threw it in the dirt for a two-base error. Sutherland wasn't even there to make the try.' (You had to credit Bailey for ducking.)

Blackman, who had said he had forgiven Wills for slapping him, had nonetheless started describing the back-up shortstop, Bobby Wine, as 'a symphony on spikes.'

John Lennon and Yoko Ono held a public live-in in a Montreal hotel bed.

May 29: Starter Jim 'Mudcat' Grant shook off the agony of the Expos twelfth straight defeat and announced he would open a disco in Montreal and call Mudcat's. Grant explained that if he was going to dance every night it might as well be at his own club. His record was 1-6. Pitching from the Jarry Park mound, he said, was making him sore.

May 30: The Expos lost their thirteenth straight, losing 3–2 to the Padres. They had held the lead three times in the previous 117 innings. Average offence during the 13 games: 2.5 runs per game. Average defence: 6.5 runs per game.

May 31: The Expos lost their fourteenth straight, again 3–2 to their expansion rivals, the Padres, as Johnny Sipin hit his first, and second-last, major-league homer for the opponents.

June 2: Premier Bertrand proposed holding a referendum to determine Quebeckers' wishes on the status of the province in confederation.

June 4: Maury Wills, the Expos' eleventh pick in the expansion draft, announced his retirement after 'a nice visit' with General Manager Fanning, who said he had no doubt that Wills was sincere.

Mudcat Grant announced his disco would not be opened since he had just found out he had been traded to St. Louis. 'That cools the scene,' he explained. The Expos lost their seventeenth straight, 8–3 to the Giants.

June 5: 'Wegener was doing fine until he faced Murderers' Row,' observed Expo manager Mauch. The team lost its eighteenth straight when starter Mike Wegener weakened in the fourth, giving up four straight hits to Giants' catcher Jack Hiatt (.196), shortstop Hal Lanier (.228), second baseman Don Mason (.228), and pitcher Mike McCormick (.156).

June 6: Maury Wills announced he had reconsidered his retirement on advice he had received from thirty friends.

Two pitchers were released: relievers Carroll Sembera and Steve Shea. Shea's ERA was the best on the club, Sembera's was second.

The Expos, having lost nineteen straight, arrived in Vancouver to play an exhibition game against their top farm team, the Mounties. Coach Bob Oldis spoke passionately in an attempt to inspire the parent club. 'Go get 'em boys,' he said. 'This is a sudden-death game, the winner to complete the remainder of the National League schedule.' The Mounties won, 5–3, but Oldis reneged.

June 7: They lost again: twenty straight. A month of non-stop losing. Manny Mota and Coco Laboy asked a Spanish brother for a blessing. Mauch commended their attitude: 'I'm pleased they asked for a blessing and not the last rites.'

June 8: The Expos nipped the Dodgers 4–3 in Los Angeles to end their losing streak, with Elroy Face sewing up the victory in relief. Called upon in the bottom of the ninth, with the Expos leading 4–1, he gave up one run on an infield out, allowed a bloop single, and sent home another run with a balk. Slow Rusty Staub, who had homered, scampered deep to right to catch a ball a foot from the fence, ending the game. At the beginning of the streak the Expos were 12-17. They had slipped to 13-37.

June 9: Wills and Manny Mota, the Expos' first pick in the expansion draft, were traded to the Dodgers for Ron Fairly and change. Wills, who had been manipulating to get out of Montreal, responded to Fanning's informing him of the deal by saying, 'Well, I guess that's it' and walking out of Fanning's office, slamming the door in his face.

Fairly, from a long tradition of Dodger winning, was at least cheery. 'It'll be fun trying to win with the Expos,' he guessed.

George Pompidou was elected president of France in a landslide.

June 16: Donn Clendenon was traded to the Mets for pitcher Steve Renko and others. Renko would have a long journeyman's career with six teams, pitching well enough to survive. No mention was made of Ryan, whose arm was now fine.

June 17: Newcomer Kevin Collins, obtained in the Clendenon trade, impressed the pre-game crowd by smashing six pitches into the upper deck at St. Louis' Busch Stadium. Unbeknownst to anyone he had exactly matched the half-dozen home runs that would be his total major-league output.

June 19: Mudcat Grant, traded to St. Louis two weeks earlier after compiling a 1-6 record with the Expos, pitched 5⅓ innings of scoreless relief against his old club to pick up a win.

June 25: Mauch was jeered as the Expos drop both ends of a double-header to the Cardinals, 8–3 and 8–1, before a capacity crowd of 30,219, with Grant picking up another win. Mauch conducted the jeers with his hands, as though he were leading an orchestra.

Leanne Mauch, the manager's daughter, sat in the Jarry stands with Lowell Palmer, a young Cardinal pitcher who had shut out the Expos the previous day with a three-hitter. Reporters called it treason. Palmer was to have a five-year career, winning 5, losing 18, and compiling a lifetime ERA of 5.28. His problem was wildness.

July 1: Newly acquired Ron Fairly slammed his right fist into his left hand and broke a bone in the fist. Fairly was philosophical, saying he once knew a pitcher who broke his arm in four places trying to throw a curve.

Prince Charles was installed as Prince of Wales.

July 2: Dan McGinn, a little lefthander with a terrific sinker, came in in relief and retired ten members of the league-leading Chicago Cubs in order, striking out six of them. The Expos lost, 4–2.

July 3: Cub pitcher Dick Selma was forced to towel off his greasy scalp on the mound after Rusty Staub noticed the ball approaching the plate in a strange way.

Leo Durocher, the newly married Cub manager, was not in the dugout as the Expos squared off against the Cubs. The Cubs publicity office announced he was not honeymooning but was sick, and had regurgitated seven times the previous night. One Chicago newspaper called it a record for a National League manager on Canadian soil.

July 5: A heated battle of words erupted between several players, including Rusty Staub, and pitching coach Calvin (Coolidge Julius Caesar Tuskahoma) McLish. McLish refused to allow the lights to be doused on the bus back to the hotel in Philadelphia so the players could drink their beer in the dark, and he called the players 'spoiled.'

'When I played we carried our bags a mile from the railway station to the hotel. We never had buses on the runway and a porter to carry our bags. Nowadays they want everything.'

July 6: Gary Waslewski, obtained from St. Louis for Mudcat Grant, pitched a one-hitter and gave up only one walk, hitting a two-run double in his own cause and facing the minimum twenty-seven batters, to win his first major league game in more than a year.

July 15: El Salvador guerillas invaded Honduras following a series of violent soccer games between the two countries.

July 17: Willie Stargell became the first player to hit a home run into the swimming pool behind Jarry's right-field scoreboard, 450 feet from home plate.

Prime Minister Trudeau was pelted with grain in Saskatoon, as demonstrators brandished placards exhorting him to 'Hustle Grain, Not Women!'

Substitute first baseman Ty Cline went 4-for-4, scoring two runs as the Expos beat the Pirates 5–4.

July 20: Apollo 11 landed on the Sea of Tranquility. 'That's one small step for man, one giant leap forward for mankind' – Neil Armstrong.

Police said a complaint will be laid against Senator Edward M. Kennedy for leaving the scene of an accident.

The Expos swept a pair from the Mets on home runs by Jones, Bailey, Wine, and Laboy.

July 23: The National League won its seventh straight All-Star Game behind the home-run power of Willie McCovey and Johnny Bench. Rusty Staub of the Expos made it to the on-deck circle, but not to the plate.

July 26: The Expos became the first team in the league to turn one hundred double plays. Mauch was not surprised. 'It makes it a lot easier,' he said, 'when you give up that many bases on balls.'

July 29: The highly strung Adolfo Phillips, recently acquired from the Cubs, had been batting lead-off but was asking to be removed from that position. 'Everywhere the pitchers are not so good but I don't hit them,' he explained.

Mauch called starter Jerry Robertson 'a great man with a lot of courage.' The Expos had been supporting Robertson with an average of half a run a game. Despite a decent ERA of 3.95 he would finish the season at 5-16.

August 5: Claude Raymond was presented with a gold medal by an organization called Palestre Nationale for being the best French Canadian in baseball. Raymond was to fashion a 5.25 ERA with the Atlanta Braves before being released and joining the Expos. He beat out Ron Piche, the only other candidate, who was pitching at Tacoma.

August 7: Prime Minister Trudeau took 'a stunning redhead' with him on the Grouse Mountain Skyride in North Vancouver. He told reporters her name was 'Miss Patterson,' but she was later identified as Margaret Sinclair, 21.

August 9: Police were looking for suspects in the murder of pregnant movie actress Sharon Tate and four others.

August 10: The Expos had lost 13 of their last 15, leaving them with a 35-79 record, 36 games behind the league-leading Chicago Cubs. The New York Mets were in second place, 7½ games behind.

August 14: Room-mates Dick Radatz and Elroy Face, two of the premier relief pitchers in the history of baseball, went out in tandem at Jarry Park. In a relief stint against the Cincinnati Reds Radatz walked three, threw a wild pitch, and was replaced by Face, who served up a bases-loaded home run to Johnny Bench.

August 15: Elroy Face was given his unconditional release by the Expos. It was his second of the year, having been previously released by the Detroit Tigers, and it marked the end of his career.

August 18: Dick Radatz was given his unconditional release by the Expos – also his second of the year (the Tigers again) and the end of the line. His arm, he said, was as good as it ever was, even when he was on the cover of *Time*. 'It's all mental.'

The Woodstock Music and Arts Fair oozed to a muddy conclusion on farmland near Bethel, New York, having attracted 500,000 rock fans for a weekend concert.

The Expos lost 9–3 to the Dodgers. Relief pitcher Larry Jaster walked Jeff Torborg (.185) to get to pitcher Claude Osteen, whom he then walked on four pitches. Up strode tiny lead-off man Maury Wills (.222 with the Expos, .297 with the Dodgers), who then smacked the only grand-slam home run of his thirteen-year career.

August 21: The Padres rallied for a run in the tenth to beat the Expos 1–0, for Montreal's eleventh loss in extra innings. They had never scored, let alone won, in extra innings.

August 22: Expos pitchers issued 19 walks – four of them forcing in runs – in losing a double-header 7–5 and 10–2 to the Giants. Bob Bailey hit his hundredth career home run and the public address announcer appealed for the historic ball. Eight of Montreal's finest children showed up, all holding baseballs.

The Expos were 39-87, 38 games behind the Cubs.

August 23: Quebec Justice Minister Remi Paul announced an all-out war against terrorist bombings in Quebec, saying the populace would ensure 'these terrorists don't even crawl out of their caves, which reek with the stench of vermin.'

The Expos' millionth customer passed joyously through the turn-stiles.

August 24: Former Prime Minister Lester B. Pearson, a rabid baseball fan, watched his first live Expos game and said he found the team 'staggeringly exciting.' The Expos lost to the Giants, 6–4.

August 26: First baseman Bailey, who had once played third for the Pirates, amused reporters with a self-deprecating anecdote about himself and Pirate coach Harry 'The Hat' Walker.

Walker, it seemed, had once told Bailey outright that he was the worst third baseman in the league.

'No I'm not,' Bailey had fumed.

'Name a worse one,' challenged Walker.

(Long thoughtful pause) 'I guess you're right,' conceded Bailey. Laughter all around.

Bailey didn't mind being the butt of a joke but he quit telling the story in 1970, when the Expos moved him from first back to third. He played there regularly for the next five years – although not quite as well as he had at Pittsburgh, when he was in his prime.

September 1: Padres pitcher Ray Sadecki, hitting .118, was walked three times by Expos ace Bill Stoneman, once with the bases loaded. Sadecki brought his bases on balls total to six in the last two games he had faced the Expos. 'It's just one of those things,' he said modestly.

September 3: Ho Chi Minh, Vietnamese nationalist leader who led insurrections against the Japanese, French, and Americans, died in Hanoi. A spokesman at the Western White House in San Clemente, California, said President Richard Nixon would have no comment.

Bullet Bob Reynolds, a pitcher called up from Vancouver, arrived with his hair died orange. 'Imagine that,' said Mauch. 'Things like that tell me a man isn't concentrating on baseball. I need people who think baseball every waking minute.'

September 4: 'Victory is exhilarating,' Mauch told reporters. 'It's the only thing that keeps you going over a 162-game schedule.' The Expos had dropped 18 of their last 21.

September 10: The team has been stricken with spasms of fine pitching. Steve Renko won 6–1; Howie Reed lost 1–0 on a five-hitter; Jerry 'Hard Luck' Robertson won 3–2; Mike Wegener lost 2–1, giving up only two hits in 7⅓ innings; Bill Stoneman won 3–0 on a five-hitter – his fifth shutout. In another game Wegener gave up only five hits and two runs over 11 innings, striking out 15.

But then the Mets took over first place from the stumbling Cubs with a double-header win over the Expos.

September 14: The Expos whomped the foundering Cubs 8–2 to cap a four-game winning streak – the longest in club history.

September 18: Singer Tiny Tim, 40-ish, announced he would marry 17-year-old Vicki Budinger, whom he had met at John Wanamaker's department store in Philadelphia.

The Expos had fallen 44 games behind the league-leading Mets.

September 19: 17,084 fans went wild as the Expos swept the Phillies 10–6 and 3–1 in a double-header, storming back from a 6–0 deficit in the first game. Rusty Staub belted homer 28 and Ron Fairly his eleventh in an injury-shortened season. And broadcaster Russ Taylor, his fish net a Jarry Park institution, poked it out of the broadcast booth and finally caught a foul ball.

September 20: Sonny Wade's touchdown pass with 31 seconds left in the game led the Montreal Alouettes to their first CFL victory in more than a year.

Veteran Woodie Fryman, pitching for the Phillies, gave up 12 hits in

9 innings but struggled to a 6–4 win over the Expos on John Callison's three-run homer, which Jose Herrera caught over the outfield fence, then dropped.

September 23: The Expos had won eight of their last twelve games and were being mentioned in dispatches as 'the fast-closing division doormats.' Rusty Staub was hitting .298 with 28 home runs and everywhere people asked themselves, 'Will he round off his numbers?'

Manager Dick Williams was fired by the Boston Red Sox. At his home in Peabody, Massachusetts, Williams attributed his dismissal to lack of communication with his players.

September 25: Shea Stadium in New York was stripped of everything not nailed down by exultant fans as the Miracle Mets clinched the pennant.

The Expos lost 6–2 when Jim Fairey lost a ball in shallow center, leading to a six-run inning. Fairey said he had noticed the sun come out, but didn't think it would bother him.

September 26: The St. Louis Cardinals sat out their regular players and beat the Expos 12–1, with the Expos committing three errors and second baseman Kevin Collins losing a pop-up in the sun.

September 28: An elegant club-house party was held to celebrate the closing of the Expos' first season, a bevvy of four-star chefs laying a table groaning with turkey, chicken, and ribs. The event was marred by the disappearance of one of Mrs. Charles Bronfman's favourite silver forks.

Bob Gibson whitewashed the Expos 2–0 in the final game of the year at Jarry Park, with 23,754 fans sitting through a cold drizzle, many of them under blankets. No balls were lost in the sun and in an emotional 30-minute finale the players' caps were given away in a raffle. 'This is a year,' manager Mauch told his soaked audience, 'that I'll never forget.'

Terrorists bombed the Rosemount home of Mayor Jean Drapeau. No one was injured.

October 1: Pirate rookie Al Oliver hit a run-scoring single in the ninth in Pittsburgh as the Pirates beat the Expos in their second-last game of the season. The Expos committed six errors (Bateman, Jestadt, Fairey, Jones, and Sutherland with two) to better their record of five.

October 2: The Expos lost 8–2 to the Pirates, but their six-game losing streak was terminated by the ending of the season. Staub hit .302 – tenth best in the league, with 29 home runs. As a team the Expos played 52–110, tied for eleventh and last with their expansion-mates, the San Diego Padres.

The United States detonated a one-megaton thermo-nuclear device

4,000′ underground on the Aleutian island of Amchitka without setting off the earthquake some scientists had feared.

October 3: Paul-Emile Carindal Léger, looking wan, was mobbed by 250 admirers at Montreal International Airport as he returned for a three-month break from his missionary work in Africa.

The daughter of NDP Leader T.C. Douglas, wife of actor Donald Sutherland, was arrested on charges she had purchased hand grenades for the Black Panthers.

U.S. Marine Lance Corporal Normand Corbin, 21, became the fourth Montreal youth to die serving in Vietnam.

October 4: Anna-Machi Malani, a 20-year-old model, was chosen Greece's 'Miss Mini-Skirt of 1969' at the annual wine festival in Daphni.

Parts of Saskatchewan were hit by a snow storm, accompanied by 55 mph winds, that left a five-inch blanket over Prince Albert.

——————— ◆ ———————

In a country as vast and sparsely populated as Canada, the arrival of radio had a special magic all its own. And for many Canadians, radio broadcasts of sporting events such as the Stanley Cup and the World Series were high points on the calendar. The play Babe Ruth Comes to Pickle River *deals with the advent of radio in a northern Ontario gold-mining community. The year is 1932, a good while past radio's appearance in Canadian cities, but Pickle River is too far north to get any kind of decent reception. So Roy Little, an ex–gold miner with big ideas, decides to start a radio station 'right here in town.' With some difficulty the station begins to establish itself in the community, but there is resistance from some quarters, resulting in a plebiscite to determine the station's fate. As it turns out, the plebiscite is to be held on Saturday October 1st, the day of the third game of the 1932 World Series.*

Babe Ruth Comes to Pickle River

NELLES VAN LOON

Percy Elliott, the editor of the local paper, appears to have convinced Roy that his decision to start a radio station is just so much talk.

Roy: After Percy left, I sat there thinkin' for awhile 'bout what he'd said about me and Babe. I have t' admit I thought maybe he was right about me. But I knew he was wrong about Babe. Y' see what Percy was always forgettin' is that Babe changed the game. That's right. Before Babe came along, they were afraid t' swing for the fences 'cause strikin' out was like fartin'. A guy'd come back to the bench after the big strike three and everyone'd move away from him.

But Babe started out as a pitcher, y' see, and nobody really expected him t' get a hit. So he just went up there and swung as hard as he could. Heck, y' could say he practic'ly invented the home run. That's right. And if he struck out, well it was more excitin' to see Babe strike out than it was t' see most guys get a hit.

'Course I never saw him play – but I can still remember how clear I could see him that night, standin' at the plate with that big gut a his hangin' out over those skinny legs, holdin' that bat like it's a toothpick, and swingin' so hard he just about screws himself int' the ground.

'Steeeeeerike.'

He misses by a foot, but the crowd loves it and it gets me back t' thinkin' about the radio station. Y' see I'd heard that Elmer Clark down at the Paper Company was tryin' t' get rid of the radio transmitter they'd bought t' keep in touch with their wood cutters. But I'd also heard you had t' have a licence t' start a radio station and Ottawa was gettin' mighty stingy with 'em.

Anyway, Babe is still wagglin' his bat, and he looks over at me and says, 'Never mind the licence, keed. If you're gonna do it, do it. If not, forget it.'

'Steeeeeerike.'

He misses again, but the crowd is still with him, and he digs in a little deeper, and says, 'I'm not seein' the ball as good as I used to, keed. But if that guy tries t' sneak a fast ball by me, I'm gonna pound the piss out of it.'

I hear the crack 'v the bat [*sound effect*] and a huge cheer [*sound effect*], and I see the ball sailin' over the centre field fence, and I think t' myself, 'Why not, eh? Why the hell not?'

After much difficulty, Roy and Jane (his right-hand gal) get the radio station off the ground. But there is the usual resistance to change. Here, at a meeting of the community club, the local barber suggests that the fairest way to deal with the issue would be to hold a plebiscite.

Percy: Order, order. Mattera fact ... mattera fact, a plebiscite is a real good idea. Looks like the only question is when we're gonna hold it. Guess a month from now oughta be about right. So looks like we're lookin' at ... let's say the first Saturday in October.

Nap: Tell him it's a dumb idea, Roy.

Roy: There's no way we can lose, Nap.

Nap: It's a dumb idea.

Percy: All in favour?

Jane: And just like that, the motion carried. I looked over at Roy who suddenly looked like he'd seen a ghost.

Roy: Hey ... hey! Wait a minute! On October first, the World Series is gonna be on.

Scotty: Is that right, Percy?

Percy: Yes sirree, Scotty, the World Series is gonna be on. And every person in town is gonna be in fronta the newspaper office waitin' t' hear the scores. And when the last man is out, every person of votin' age is gonna step inside and vote for the good old days.

Nap: I told you it was a dumb idea!

Roy [To aud.]: Last thing I remember is Babe sayin', 'Y' forgot t' watch out for the curve ball keed.'

Here, Roy attempts to explain to Jane why their chances of winning the plebiscite are slim, at best.

I couldn't for the life 'v me see how we were gonna win the plebiscite without gettin' the Series. Well next t' Christmas and the first of July, the Series is the biggest event of the year. Percy puts out a big banner over the newspaper office which says, 'Pickle River Stadium' and he gets some 'v the women t' set up a lunch counter t' sell hot dogs and pop.

If it's a weekday game, it's mostly women and the business men who close up shop for th' afternoon. After school, the kids come runnin' over, and at four, when the miners come up, they all come over t' find out how the game went and talk baseball with Percy. If it's a weekend game, then everyone is there from noon time on. And after the game, if the weather's nice, everyone goes over t' the school yard for a weiner roast.

But it wasn't easy tryin' t' get Jane t' understand.

Jane: Surely to goodness people who've spent hard-earned money on radios aren't going to vote against us.

Roy: There's still a lota folks out there who don't have a radio yet. All they care about is baseball, and right now they get their baseball from Percy.

Jane: But it's just a game. An *American* game at that.

Roy: Hey, it's our game too. Babe Ruth hit his first professional home run in Toranna. Hanlan's Point, September 5, 1914.

Jane: That's nothing more than an accident of time and place.

Roy: Hey, my uncle was there.

Jane: So was mine, for all I know. But so what?

Roy: He saw it happen. Not in Baltimore, not in Boston, not in New York. In Toranna. Toranna, *Canada*.

Jane: Okay, if you think baseball is so important, you deal with the baseball problem, and I'll do what I think we need to do.

Roy: Only trouble is there's nothin' we can do about the baseball problem.

Jane: You're not quitting on me are you?

Roy: I'm just tryin' t' tell y' the way things are around here.

Jane: The way things are is that if you're so sure the game is that important, then do something about it.

Roy: But you just said ...

Jane: Never mind what I just said. Do you want to win the plebiscite or not?

Roy: Well, she had me there, so I got on the phone, which is tough enough when you're makin' local calls, but when you're callin' outa town, it's sorta like makin' hand signals in the fog. But one day I managed t' get some guy from CBS. We'd only talked a minute or so when he was already t' make us an affiliate station – which'd mean runnin' up a special phone line all the way from the nearest affiliate t' the Pickle River telephone office and from there into the studio. It was all lookin' pretty rosey for gettin' the Series till he said,

'Where exactly *is* Pickle River?'

I told him it was three hundred miles north 'v North Bay, and that was the end of that.

On the day of the plebiscite, all appears to be lost. But in the words (even though anachronistic in this case) of the great Yogi, 'it aint over till it's over.'

Roy: The day of the plebiscite, I went over t' the studio, but I was just goin' through the motions.

Nap: So what do we do today?

Roy: Not much. Everyone's gonna be in fronta the newspaper office anyway.

Nap: Who knows? Maybe it will rain in Chicago.

Roy: It isn't gonna rain, Nap.

Nap: How do you know?

Roy: I picked up one of the Chicago stations for a few minutes last night.

[*Sound of telephone ringing.*]

Roy: How many times do I have t' ask Millie t' stop sendin' through incomin' calls?

[*To aud.*] Turns out it's my Uncle Joe from Toranna. Seems he's got a new radio and he's all excited about pickin' up the ball game. I guess Nap got wind 'v what we we're talkin' about 'cause he starts wavin' his arms around tryin' t' get my attention.

Nap: Tell him to turn on the radio.

Roy: I didn't know what he was gettin' at so I just ignored him. But he was real excited about somethin'. So I put him on the phone.

Nap: Hello sir ... Nap. Nap Lapointe. Would you please turn on the radio and hold up the phone to it ... The weather's been very nice up here too ... Anyway, I would really appreciate it if you would just hold the phone up to the radio ...

Gee that's too bad. [*Beat.*] Well, maybe you could move the radio over to the phone.

Roy: Nap, you're gonna give the poor guy a hernia! [*To aud.*] But the kid wont get off the phone.

Then he started pointin' from the phone to the mircophone and I thought I knew what he was gettin' at. So I got on the phone, only when I go t' talk t' Uncle Joe, it's Aunt Maggie who's on the other end wonderin' when I'm gonna come and visit.

Finally I get Uncle Joe back on the line and I get him t' turn up the radio as loud as it'll go.

Nap: Can you hear it?

Roy: I hand the phone to him and let him listen for himself, but I can tell from the expression on his face it isn't gonna carry int' th' old microphone we bought from the Kinsmen.

Okay Uncle Joe. I'll call ya when I got more time t' talk.

You too. G'bye Aunt Maggie.

Nap: I guess we could try it anyway.

Roy [*To aud.*]: I can tell from the way he says it that he knows it isn't gonna work. Anyways, talk about perfect timin'. In comes Percy, who's about the last person I wanta see right then.

'Mattera fact,' he says, 'I heard Jack made you another offer.'

'So?'

'So you gonna take it?'

'No.'

'Folks are gonna miss ya.'

'Thanks for the push, pal.'

'Don't go blamin' me,' he says. 'I toldja what was gonna happen and you wanted t' play the big shot.'

'Some people still care about this place. Seems t' me you used t' be that way.'

'Never mind the bullshit, Roy. Mattera fact, you're lookin' after your own ass the same as everyone else. The only difference is, you're no damn good at it. Maybe this time you'll learn somethin' for a change.'

One thing y' might 've noticed 'bout Percy is that he likes t' get in the last word and then walk out the door before y' c'n answer him back, but this time I wasn't gonna let him pull that little caper, so I says,

'They're callin' for rain in Chicago.'

'Says who?'

'I picked up one of the Chicago stations late last night. If y' don't believe me, go and check the wire.'

'Bullshit!' he says and stomps out the door, but I can tell I got him worried.

Nap: Hey, you made that up.

Roy: Yeah. Too bad we can't make up today's ball game.

Nap: Hey, that's not a bad idea.

Roy: Whatya mean, Nap?

Nap: We'll make it up.

Roy: Make what up?

Nap: The ball game! We can get the information from the phone and we can fill in with the rest.

Roy: Now wait a minute, wait just a minute, Nap. Wh-wh-who's gonna do the t-t-talkin'?

Nap: You.

I tried to explain about my stutter, but I can hear Babe sayin', 'Forget the stutter, keed.'

But I'm thinkin' what's the point? The mine is gonna close down one day anyway.

'We're *all* gonna close down one day, keed. That's why we have t' give it our best shot while we're still here.'

'No one's gonna believe I'm at Wrigley Field.'

Nap: Oh yeah? What's this?

[*He claps two pieces of wood together.*]

Babe Ruth hittin' a double down the line.

Roy: Right then is when Jane came in, and I remembered about the willing dispension of unbelief.

And now, the moment of 'truth.'

Roy: For you folks who are just tuning in, we're in the top of the fifth inning at Wrigley Field. It's the Yankees four and the Cubs four. They say it's pretty windy ... I mean it's real windy out here. Forty mile an hour wind blowin' in' off the lake.

[*To Jane*] I can hardly hear it.

[*He drinks some water.*]

Jane: You're doing fine. Just pretend you're there.

Roy: Like I said folks, there's a forty mile an hour wind blowing in from centre field, and forty mile an hour wind or not, Babe Ruth has already hit a home run t'day.

Not bad for a thirty-eight-year-old who practicl'y got off the sick bed t' play in this series. The Babe has been takin' a lota razzin' from the Cubs because he gave them the gears about not votin' a full share t' his old buddy, Mark Koening. And you can bet the Babe would really love t' do somethin' t' make the Cubs eat crow. And know what? I'll bet he isn't finished yet. No sirree, I got a feelin' the Babe has got somethin' special up his sleeve and he's just waitin' for the right moment. So don't go away folks, or you might just be missin' somethin' real special.

Jane: Hey!

Roy: Yes siree, folks, it's a perfect day for baseball – nothin' but sun and open sky over the grass here at Wrigley Field.

[Jane reminds him about the wind.]

'Cept for the wind, of course. We got the uh ... veteran Tony Lazzeri steppin' up to the plate right now and uh ... err ...

[Roy is suddenly silent.]

Jane: Keep talking.

Roy: It's Millie.

Jane: What?

Roy: Somebody wants the line.

Jane: Give me the phone. And keep talking.

Roy: What am I s'posed t' say?

Jane: Anything! [*To Millie*] What seems to be the problem, Millie?

Roy: Well folks ... seems we had a small problem with our equipment.

Jane: Let me talk to the Toronto operator.

[While ad libbing, Roy drinks a lot of water.]

Roy: As I was sayin' it's a real fine day for b-b-baseball ... yeah a real fine day ... not a cloud in the sky ... but uhm ... it seems we got a little f-f-f-f-f-fog movin' in off the lake. Must be the wind. Yes sir, that f-f-f-fog is movin' in real quick.

Roy: Yeah, the f-fog is comin' in real heavy all of a sudden.

Uhm ... the third base umpire seems to be sayin' the g-g-game is gonna go on, and the home plate umpire seems to be pointin' at the sky. Now the first base umpire is comin' over and he's pointin' at his eyes. The home p-plate umpire is callin' over the second base umpire, but the second base umpire is talkin' with the sh-sh-sh-ortstop.

Jane [To operator]: Yes, I understand, but we have an emergency too.

Yes, we have a very sick man whose dying wish is to hear the World Series on the radio.

You ask whoever it is whether it's more important than the dying wish of a man who worked his heart out in the mines.

	That's absolutely correct. Morally, if not legally, you could be responsible for his death.
[*To Jane*] I can't do this.	
	[*To Roy*] Keep talking!
The sh-shortstop seems to be saying play on, but the second baseman is	[*To operator*] You're enjoying the ball-game too?
pointing to the sky. So now we got the	Well, it's like I always say: if you can't enjoy the World
shortstop and the second baseman and three umpires talkin' t'gether.	Series, there must be something wrong with you.
	I can't tell you how much this will mean to him.
Holy c-c-c-cow, folks, You're not gonna beleve this. Now the third baseman is getting into the act.	
	[*To Roy*] Keep talking!
	If there are any questions, you just have the phone company call us after the game.
[*Jane hands Roy the phone.*]	[*To Roy*] All systems go.

Roy: Ah, the f-fog is clearing up. Yes, the wind has just moved in again and lifted the fog. And we have a Yankee hitter comin' up to the plate. Yes, we got the Babe himself standin' at the plate.

[*Faint sound of train whistle in the distance.*]

Jane [*To herself*]: Oh no!

Roy: Like I said, the Babe has already hit a home run into this forty mile an hour wind that's comin' in off the lake.

Apparently ... I mean in fact ... someone just rolled a lemon up to the batter's box. Ruth snaps a few words at the Cub bench and takes called strike one.

The Babe smiles and holds up one finger.

Charley Root delivers the pitch ... outside, for ball one. Babe seems to be taunting Root to throw him something he can hit.

Here's the pitch ... ball two.

The crowd lets up a bit, and so does the Cub bench.

[*Louder sound of train whistle in the distance.*]

Jane [*To Roy. Stage whisper.*]: I'd better get going.

Roy: I hear that ... I mean I see Presidential candidate Franklin D. Roosevelt is here today in a train ... I mean in a box near home station ... I mean home plate ... Yes sir, there he is right over there larger than life.

Here's the pitch. Called strike two.

Ruth holds up two fingers.

A couple of Cubs move out in front of the dugout and yell at Ruth ... who waves them back to the dugout. Charlie Root says something from the mound, and the Babe shouts something back.

Root bends over to pick up the resin bag ... he's taking his time with this awesome hitter.

[*Sound of train whistle drawing near.*]

Jane [*To Roy. Stage whisper.*]: I've got to go.

Roy: Wait a minute, something remarkable has just happened. I'm not quite sure I can believe my ears ... I mean eyes. The Babe has just pointed towards the deepest part of the ball park ... He seems to be saying that's where he intends to hit the next pitch.

Jane: Don't overdo it!

[*Roy gestures to indicate that he's only saying what he's heard over the phone.*]

Roy: Babe has really got this crowd goin' folks – there is definitely somethin' in the air!

Jane: Come on Babe!

Roy: Here's the windup, here's the pitch. It's a deep drive to centre field.

[*Sound of two pieces of wood being clapped together a few moments too late.*]

It's going, going ... and ... it's still going. It's a home run.

It's a home run, it's a home run ... it's a home run ... holy jumpin' Jehosophat ... it's a home run. And what a home run. To the deepest part of the ball park, right where the Babe said it would be. The longest home run ever hit in Wrigley Field.

Baseball fans all over Pickle River, I mean, all over the world, will be talking about this *forever*.

——————— ◆ ———————

Nineteen seventy-five was one of Reggie Cleveland's best years in the majors. Starting and relieving for the Boston Red Sox, he was 13-9 with a 4.43 ERA. Most important, he went 10-3 after July 6 and won four straight games at the end to help the Sox hold off the Orioles for the Eastern Division title. He became the first Canadian to start a World Series game, the fifth of the 1975 Series, but wasn't a match for Don Gullett and the bats of the Big Red Machine, losing to Cincinnati 6–2. He appeared again in Game 7, with the Reds leading 4–3 in the ninth and the championship almost in their grasp. In between was Game 6, one of the greatest in Series history. Reggie's line for the Series, like his career 105-106 record, was unspectacular, but how many kids from Swift Current (or Moose Jaw or Windsor) get to be part of World Series history?

From Swift Current to the '75 World Series

LARRY WOOD

THE BRIGHT, SHINY, FIRE-ENGINE RED CORVETTE POSES SLEEK AND SHEIK IN the new-car showroom of the northwest Calgary dealership. 'Yep,' says the big right-hander who used to be from Swift Current, Sask., taking note of a visitor's hypnotic fix and flashing a Cheshire grin, 'you can write me a cheque and drive her away.'

Just like that! Five figures, a signature and a so-what shrug. No sweat, eh?

Well, they always said the big right-hander from Swift Current, Sask., was the easy-going, docile, country-boy sort. They said he'd spin the wheel and rarely be fazed by the results – strikeout or walk, ground ball or line drive, popup or gopher.

In fact, he admits now that, if he was blessed with a re-run of his 37 years on this earth, he'd probably revise only one or two of his moves.

'I'd watch my money a little closer,' he muses. 'And I'd never sign another five-year contract in a year like 1978.'

'I thought it was the right move at the time. I wanted to buy a little farm down in Texas. How was I to know that baseball salaries would start going through the roof a couple of years later?'

The big right-hander, who used to be from Swift Current, Sask., laughs off the memory.

'When I signed, I was well-paid. When I retired, I was under-paid. But here am I back in another fun business. Not bad. Of course, there's no better way to go than 11 years in the big leagues.'

Eleven and change, to be precise. Which definitely isn't too shabby for a genuine Canadian-bred – any genuine Canadian-bred.

For Reginald Leslie Cleveland, it was sufficient to enshrine him in the Canadian Baseball Hall of Fame the other week. He's the only Canadian-born pitcher ever to draw a World Series starting assignment. He ranks second only to Ferguson Jenkins among Canadian-born winners in The Bigs. No other Canadians have won 100 games.

'But Fergie was in another class,' says this big guy who won 105, lost 106 and posted a career ERA of 4.01.

'He was up there with Gibson, Seaver, Palmer. I played with him and I fish with him and I know him well.

'Fergie threw nothing but that sinking slider and it'd paint the corner at the knees. Me, I lived off the fastball and the hard slider.'

Definitely the kind of pitches that are more liable to get in the way of a bat. But astutely delivered, the kind that sustain the paycheques for 16 years, too.

'I guess that World Series start was life's big highlight,' Cleveland is allowing, thereby severely understating the case.

Oh, he lost the battle, the pivotal fifth of the 1975 renewal at Riverfront Stadium in Cincinnati. His Red Sox lost the war, too, at the last gasp in a seventh game they were leading 3–0 after five innings. But there are a few million guys who can't say they participated in that World Series, which ranks with history's most memorable.

Recalled Sparky Anderson, as late as four months ago:

'I don't know that there's ever been a better World Series than the one in '75.'

For the big right-hander from Swift Current, Sask., it all seemed to happen, well, just like that. And it's probably no coincidence his latest business revolves around speed machinery. Two decades back, St. Louis scout Bill Sayles discovered a speed machine of a different kind in this guy's 17-year-old right arm.

'I was just a kid who threw hard,' Reggie recalls. 'At that age, I couldn't make the ball do anything. But the heat was all that interested them. They teach you how to pitch. They don't even want to know if you can hit or field. If I'd been a third baseman or an outfielder, forget it. I'd never have had a look-see.'

So much for the obvious question – how does a kid from Swift Current, Sask., wind up in the majors and stay there for the best part of a dozen summers? Which is tantamount to asking, how do you win $10 million in the Loto?

'I wasn't even living in Swift Current at the time,' he says, just for the record. 'I left there when I was seven. My dad was in the air force up at Cold Lake.'

But the kid used to visit his grandparents in the summer, work in construction and play ball for Jackie McLeod's Swift Current Indians.

'It wasn't a bad way to spend the holidays,' he reflects with the characteristic shrug.

How good is not bad?

The year was 1965. There was a ball tournament tied into the Moose Jaw fair. A guy named Sammy Shapiro – 'Your typical carny type from Florida, four feet high by four feet wide, always talking' – happened to wander in on an Indians' game. A kid named Cleveland happened to be pitching.

Now this guy Shapiro fancied himself as a bit of a baseball authority, you understand. On account of he just happened to moonlight in his off-season, which was early spring, as an umpire at the St. Louis Cardinals' training grounds in St. Petersburg.

You can guess the rest. Shapiro watches the kid, wires the Cards about this hotshot who can throw bullets, a legit scout is dispatched to the hinterlands, he confirms the kid's velocity has major-league potential and signs him on the spot.

And so began the second 16 years, more or less, of Cleveland's life.

One of balls and strikes and another rendering of the Star Spangled Banner every day. In good towns and bad, but, mostly, with good organizations who treated a guy fairly.

There was St. Pete, then Eugene, Ore., where Reggie 'broke in' throwing to Bill Plummer, the Cannons' new manager. Then St. Pete again, Lewiston, Idaho, St. Pete again, Little Rock, Tulsa, St. Louis.

It was September of his fourth year when he finally made it to The Bigs. One game. Four innings.

The next year – 1970 – it was 16 games, 26 innings.

In 1971, he went directly from spring training to the Cards, started 99 games over three seasons, won 40, lost 37. Then it was over to Boston for four seasons, 153 games, 110 of them starts.

'I never could stick in the starting rotation at Boston. So I became a sort of jack of all pitching trades – starter, long relief, short relief, mop-up, you name it.'

By April of 1978, when he was sold to Texas, his reputation was that of a fireman. He'd actually been wooed by Milwaukee, but the Red Sox wanted to move him out of their division. The Brewers' Harry Dalton got his man, anyway, in a December trade with the Rangers.

'Three years in the Milwaukee bullpen and that was it. They released me. I suppose I could have shopped around, but I was ready to get out. So was my shoulder.

'That last year was The Strike Year. When they settled it, they wanted us back and in shape in a week to 10 days. That's when the shoulder started to do the talking.'

Does it bother him now?

'It hurts every time I think about pitching,' he quips.

'Actually, I could probably still throw harder than the average pitcher and it wouldn't hurt.

'But,' he adds, jabbing at an ample middle, 'to get myself in shape and pitch four innings? Uh-uh. The shoulder's worn out. It's a common problem with ex-pitchers.'

The big right-hander from Swift Current, Sask., wasn't exactly the body double of Mickey Lolich. But he always was prone to gaining weight.

'It was the lifestyle. A lot of fast food, a lot of beer. I'd start the season around 195. I'd be 220 by October.

'But, they didn't care if you weighed 400 as long as you were winning. Baseball coaches figure if it's not broken, don't fix it. You never hear from them unless you're going bad. In which case you hear all kinds of things.

'One year at St. Louis, I was 11-4 at the all-star break and I was up to 210 pounds. I lost seven of the next eight and, coincidentally, dropped 10 pounds, too. And Red Schoendienst kept telling me, 'you should gain some weight, boy.'

'Red was a good manager, but he had the horses. Don Zimmer was probably the best I played for. He was the kind of guy whose moves could help you win five or six extra games, and that's all a good team needs.

'George Bamberger was another good one. Those guys rarely changed anything. Everybody knew what they had to do and they went out and did it. And if you had the horses, you won.

'Deron Johnson was the other side of the coin. He'd screw up everything with constant changes.

'Managers don't win games. The players do. A good manager will win with a good team, but a bad manager will lose with a good team. They can't make good teams a whole lot better and they can't make bad teams good. But they can make good teams bad.'

How about the owners?

'Some of them are astute businessmen who like to cry poor. But when a franchise comes up for sale there's no shortage of buyers. And they haven't folded too many lately.

'At the time of '81 strike, salaries were 29 per cent of revenues. In 1930, they were 31-to-34 per cent of revenues. You can't blame the players for trying to get what they can. It's a competitive world out there.

'The way it's going, there'll eventually have to be a ceiling. But it won't happen as long as you hear of a guy like Toronto's controller saying he can make a $500,000 profit look like a $500,000 loss with the stroke of a pen' ...

Now, the big right-hander who used to be from Swift Current, Sask., is content to become a Cannons' fan. He moved his family to Calgary in November, in the wake of a four-year withdrawal from baseball in the Dallas–Fort Worth area.

'After 20 years, it was time to turn a page and come home,' he explains.

Just like that.

Drawn from a collection of 'stories of men and sports' entitled We Won't Be Needing You, Al *(1968), this piece, explains Scott Young in his introduction, 'came from the days when I covered Northern League baseball for the Winnipeg Free Press, and rode the old buses with the young players. I wrote [this] story 10 years or more after the incident [in the late 1930s] that prompted it; the release of a catcher called Jack Allendorf. When it was published in* Collier's *a U.S. Army captain at a base far out in the Pacific picked up the magazine one day after lunch and started to read and then leaped to his feet (if any upward move by Allendorf could ever be called a leap) and yelled, "Hey, you guys! Here's a story about me!" In the story he is Allen Menckendorf.'*

We Won't Be Needing You, Al

SCOTT YOUNG

ALLAN MENCKENDORF WALKED FROM THE DUGOUT WITH THE SPLAYED stride made necessary by his heavy leg guards. He was thick in the thighs and chest and shoulders, the biggest among the thirty or so young baseball players shagging flies and playing pepper ball and warming up along the side lines. Although his tanned, fleshy face looked a few years older, he was twenty-two and blond and had to shave only every other day.

Already the hot prairie sun of this day early in June – the first warm day of the Manitoba summer – had made the beginning of a black sweat mark between his shoulder blades. He stood alone near third base, his mitted left hand doubled against his thigh, and watched the stands fill with men in shirt sleeves and women in bright hot-weather dresses. Boys in white coats yelled peanuts, popcorn, ice-cold drinks. Over the long grandstand, the sky was a pure blue broken only by the slender fluttering flags.

Here came Bud, the pitcher, waving to a pretty dark girl, his wife in the stands. Now he was grinning over his shoulder at someone in the Maroons' dugout.

'Quit laughing at your own jokes, Bud,' the catcher said with a shy grin. 'Warm up good. Today you've got to give me something to remember you by.'

The pitcher stopped smiling and pounded his fist slowly into his glove. 'Too bad you've gotta work today,' he said. 'They shouldn't work you today.'

'It isn't that I won't be having a long rest,' the catcher said.

'What're you going to do?'

'Go home and look for a job.'

'Baseball?'

Menckendorf had thought this out and his answer was ready, but to him his voice sounded too earnest. 'No more than semipro. If I can't even hold a place on a Class D club, there's no use throwing good years after bad. I'll get a job and play Sunday ball.' He couldn't help what he said, then. 'I probably ought to quit altogether.'

There was a silence. Bud had been with the club two years, one less than Menckendorf, and was doing well enough that he could expect a try with a better club, maybe next year. He was only twenty and he didn't know except by instinct how to act with a man who had failed.

'Let's me and you win this one,' he said, and smiled full into Menckendorf's face and walked along the third-base line and took up a position to throw.

Menckendorf crouched and his mitt thumped with the southpaw's first pitch. The cries of the young ballplayers taking infield practice were high and urgent above the murmur of the growing crowd. Bud was throwing easily at first and Menckendorf tossed them back just as easily, the routine of the thump and the throw releasing his mind for random enjoyment of the sun and the crowd.

Thump, throw, thump, throw, thump ... Bud began to bear down. He had a single bad fault. When his curve didn't break, it came in shoulder-high and fat. Bud called it his balloon ball and laughed about it, but Menckendorf knew it worried him all the same.

'No balloon balls today,' Menckendorf called suddenly.

Bud grinned.

Players were streaming off the field into the dugout, but the pitcher and the catcher stayed with their warmup until the last possible minute and then stood at attention while the band played the anthem. The anthem ended and Menckendorf slipped into his belly pad and ran toward the plate with his mask under his arm. Infielders and outfielders ran out into position, yelling at each other.

A clear voice came from the crowd. 'Hey, Twinkletoes! Show 'em what they're losing!'

Menckendorf tipped his mask in the direction of the voice and smiled bleakly as he whipped it over his head and crouched behind the plate.

On the fifth warmup pitch he stood and threw to second, slightly off the bag. He was accurate if he took a step before the throw, but that step often gave a runner the instant that made him safe instead of out, and for two years Menckendorf had been trying to perfect a throw from his crouch, or without taking a step. He still couldn't do it well more than half the time.

The first batter for the Grays, the opposition today, stood near the batter's box, rubbing dirt on his hands. He spoke sideways to Menckendorf: 'What's the matter with Marty?'

'Split a finger yesterday.' Marty was the Maroons' first-string catcher. The other one, Anderson, was pretty good too; but for some reason Joe Bentham, the manager, had picked Menckendorf to work this last day. Al Menckendorf liked Joe. It wasn't Joe's fault that Menckendorf wasn't a better catcher, and Menckendorf knew that.

'See by the papers you're being released,' the batter said.

Menckendorf straddled the plate to get the throw-in from third and tossed it out slowly to Bud on the mound.

'Yeah,' he said, and crouched again, laying two fingers behind his glove to call for the fast one and setting the target low and just over the outside corner of the plate.

Bud came in a little higher than he should have and the batter hit it on the ground to deep second and Menckendorf was off at the crack of the bat, running like a plow horse to back up first. The second baseman took the bounce and flipped the ball to first, and the man was out. Menckendorf pulled up near the coaching line and trotted back into position, breathing a little harder than normal. The sharp twist in his chest that came with every infield ground ball receded, and he thought, as he always did, that it was too bad they used this ball diamond for football in the fall because it always pocked the infield some, and the groundsman never had it in proper shape before July. Menckendorf worried on every ground ball because he had seen a lot of bad bounces on this field.

Bud struck out the next man and got two strikes on the third batter. He had a lot of stuff today. Waiting for the pitch, Menckendorf reflected that maybe this season would be the one that would make Bud a really good pitcher. Menckendorf hoped so. He was fond of Bud and Belle, and he hoped for them, as he had once hoped for himself, that the passage of years would take them up into the good leagues. Then Belle would sit among the tens of thousands and watch Bud throw strikes to some other catcher, past the best hitters in the world.

The pitch. Swing and miss. Strike three.

Menckendorf trotted to the dugout steps and settled himself in a cool corner, not bothering to remove his equipment because he was batting seventh and he'd have lots of notice if he had to hit in this inning. For a couple of minutes, while the warmup pitches were being thrown, he watched Schull, the third baseman for the Grays, a man almost as big as Menckendorf. When his teammates threw the ball to Schull it always came soft and easy.

Schull had hit .404 last year to lead the league in batting, but when he went to a triple-A training camp this spring he fielded so badly that they put him in the outfield and he kept catching fly balls right between the eyes until finally they gave up on him. He'd spent a couple of weeks with a Class B club until the manager decided that he didn't need hitting quite that badly, and now Schull was back in Class D again, hitting .392.

The manager, Joe Bentham, dropped down beside Menckendorf in the dugout. Menckendorf was a little embarrassed. Joe had told him three days before about his release. It hadn't been too much of a surprise. This spring the ownership of the Maroon franchise had changed. The old management hadn't much money and Menckendorf probably would have played on with the Maroons for years if there hadn't been this sale.

The new owners, a group of businessmen who didn't mind spending, brought in Joe Bentham as playing manager. Just last year he'd played left infield with St. Paul. He could murder this Class D pitching. They'd spent money to get him. They were spending money elsewhere, too. Marty and Anderson, the other catchers, were both new and both good and Marty was twenty, Anderson nineteen. So when Joe had called him into the bare little office back of the dressing room on Wednesday, after practice, Menckendorf had guessed why.

'Al,' Joe had said. 'I'm sorry, but we asked waivers on you and nobody bid. After Saturday you'll be a free agent.'

Menckendorf had said nothing, twisting his big square hands together painfully.

'You know we've got to get the player roster down to seventeen men by Saturday,' Joe said.

'Yes.'

'We don't need three catchers.'

'No.'

'We won't be needing you, Al.'

'You, you won't.'

'What will will you do?'

'I don't know.'

There was a silence for a minute and then Menckendorf got up, his eyes still averted from Joe's and started to try to thank Joe for being as good as he could.

'Don't go,' Joe said. 'Sit down.'

Menckendorf sat down again.

'I don't know much about you, kid,' Joe said. 'Where are you from?'

'Minneapolis.'

'What did you do before you came here?'

Menckendorf was brief with his words but his memory was complete and now the commonplace became poignant. He ran through the teams he'd played with. 'Legion ball.' (In the state tournament he'd been his club's second-best hitter, and pro scouts signed the best hitter and the third and fourth best hitters and a kid shortstop who was a whiz but could hardly hit at all.)

'Semipro with a brewery team.' (The Sunday they had foot races before the game everybody laughed when they matched Menckendorf and a fat old pitcher from the other team. Menckendorf won by only a few feet, although he'd run as fast as he could.)

Then old Ed Bush had come along one Sunday and signed him to go to the Maroons the next year to catch for this team that he, Ed Bush, owned and managed. (God, the excitement of that evening, telling Mother and Dad and the two sisters in the living room of the high old brick house three blocks from the ball park in Minneapolis; the excitement of that night in bed, unsleeping, the roar of the great crowds in Chicago and Philadelphia and New York in his ears. In the flickering light that came through his window from the streets he could see the large glossy prints – some old, some new – of Roy Campanella and Ted Williams and Mickey Mantle and John Roseboro and Roger Maris; he'd wondered what they were like, man to man, the way men would be when they played with the same ball club. When spring came Bush told him he could make an extra twenty dollars a month driving the bus and he drove it for a month and then a pitcher wanted more money, so Bush gave the pitcher the job of driving the bus.)

'I don't know, kid,' Joe had said, and his voice was kind and sort of unhappy. 'It's up to you, but maybe this is a good thing. You're still young and you can get into some other business. All you've got to do is try as hard as you have in baseball, and you'll make a million at anything else.'

In the dugout now, Joe was on his feet, leaning his hands against the rim, yelling as Frenchy Aquirre, the center fielder, stretched a short hit into a double with a wild slide to second. In the minute or two Joe had sat beside Menckendorf no word had been spoken.

Bud slid along the bench and nudged Menckendorf, and Menckendorf grinned at him.

'Someday when we're coming back up from the other end of the league we'll drop in at your place in Minneapolis and see you, Twink,' Bud said. 'Maybe we'd better let you know in advance, and we'll come for dinner, the whole team, and it'll cost you so much you won't be able to buy that new convertible for another two weeks.'

There was another crack of the bat and Frenchy was streaking for third. Then he took off in a looping dive and slid the last three feet on his chest, stopping with his outstretched forefinger on the bag, while Schull disgustedly looked down at Frenchy's grinning, sweating face.

'You oughta be happy just catching one for a change, Schull,' bawled Bud, 'without worrying whether you tag the guy or not!'

Schull threw the ball back to the pitcher, who eyed the runners on first and third and got ready to deliver. Two on, nobody out. Menckendorf started to unfasten his belly pad.

'Come on, you bum,' Bud was saying to Gus, the cleanup man, who was fingering the bats outside the dugout. 'No use me pitching this no-hitter if you don't get me some runs.'

For no really logical reason, Menckendorf remembered the day Bud had joined the club on the road last season. Nineteen, not yet married, cocky. On the way home in the aged, chugging club bus he had poked a water pistol out of the window beside him and poured a perfect shot into the shocked face of a driver who was passing with his window down.

They'd passed the car a second or two later. It had stopped beside the road and the driver swore and shouted and wiped his face and shook his fist.

Gus, the first baseman, bawled Bud out.

'It didn't hurt him,' Bud protested.

'It might have.'

'I'll mind my business. You mind yours.'

'When I was a rookie I knew enough to let other people do the talking and play the jokes.'

'When you were a rookie, you weren't as good as I am.'

Bud was a favourite in the club now. He'd stopped playing practical jokes but he still kidded a lot. Last year the trainer had loaned him a bottle of smelling salts after he was beaned by a line smash back through the box. He'd been dizzy for a few days, needed the smelling salts, but he'd never remembered to give them back. This spring, Mac, the trainer, who was no smarter than the law demanded, had asked for his smelling salts.

'They're all gone,' Bud said slowly.

The trainer blew up. 'All gone! You can use smelling salts a thousand times and they're still good!'

'Look, Mac,' Bud said quietly. 'I used them up.'

The rest of the players in the dressing room were grinning at one another.

'You know that I work in a coal mine in Mississippi in the off season,' Bud told the trainer. (Actually, he was a cashier in a Crookston bowling alley.)

'Yeah?'

'Down there we use mule carts. We go along about a mile down, see, and I shovel this cart full of coal. Then I lead the mule along the slope and dump the coal and it's taken up to the surface.'

'Yeah?' The trainer's attention was rapt, and completely trusting.

'Well, this mule, see, kept balking. I'd throw coal from behind, drag from the front, do everything, and the mule wouldn't go.'

'So?' said the trainer, puzzled but eager. 'What's this got to do with my smelling salts?'

'So,' said Bud, 'one day I remember these smelling salts. I'd kept them in case I had dizzy spells again. I walk up to this mule and I shove the end of the bottle to the mule's nose and the mule breathes in the smelling salts.'

'Yeah,' said the trainer. 'What happened?'

'The mule went like hell. But every trip after that he'd balk and I'd have to use the smelling salts and by the time March came around this year there just wasn't even a smell left in that bottle.'

'By gosh!' said the trainer in wonderment, shaking his head as he went about packing towels and equipment.

The third Maroon up bounced one toward second, and the Grays' shortstop held Frenchy on third before he forced the runner at second, allowing the batter to reach first on a fielder's choice. Gus socked a long double to center and two runs scored. Joe was up now, batting fifth, and Menckendorf slipped out of his belly pad and unbuckled his leg guards.

Bud was out in front of the dugout now, jubilant at the lead his mates were getting for him, yelling: 'Hit this one, Joe! Hit it!'

In the few seconds before the pitcher began his windup, Menckendorf reminded himself without emphasis that this was his last day, that Joe (contrary to custom, really) had given him his walking papers in advance, that after today he wouldn't know what Bud was doing or what Gus was doing or what Joe was doing. Later today he would head home to the big house in Minneapolis (his bags were already at the bus terminal) and tell his mother and dad that he'd been released. His old room would be waiting for him and his mother would make half a ton of doughnuts because Menckendorf loved doughnuts and his mother always thought that if a man's stomach was full of food he loved, damage to other parts of his being or his ego took care of itself.

Joe slapped a single to left field and Gus scored. The next man up hit to right and the Grays yanked their pitcher. With men on first and second, Menckendorf hit a line drive over the left-field fence, a few feet foul. On the next pitch, he caught the top of a slow curve, and the ball bounced in front of him. The pitcher threw to the shortsop at second for one out and the quick throw down to first was there while Menckendorf was still two steps off the bag, throwing his heavy thighs and knees out as he ran and, even in the intense effort, hearing the groan from the crowd at the quick end to the rally.

Menckendorf kneeled, putting on his leg guards, and there was a hard lump in his throat that he couldn't swallow. Why couldn't that foul have been a few feet closer in? Fair, it would have scored three more runs. He slipped into his belly pad and trotted to the plate and took the ball from Anderson, who'd been warming up Bud. Anderson didn't speak. He was too young to know much about failure. Bud came down from the mound and Menckendorf went out to meet him.

'Tough luck, Twink,' Bud had said. 'You really powdered that one.'

'Let's mow 'em down, Bud,' Menckendorf said, and turned back to the plate.

They held the three-run lead for the next three innings, but were held hitless themselves by the Grays' second pitcher. In the fifth Bud was nursing along a two-hitter when one of his curves failed to break. It came in like a balloon and Schull, without effort, dropped it into the right-field stands for a home run.

There was some desultory clapping from the crowd for the ease with which Schull hit, and as he rounded third he waved his cap at the crowd, a crooked grin on his big, rather stupid face; but as he came down the base line Menckendorf noticed that the grin faded quickly. The only man at the plate to shake his hand was the next batter, and Menckendorf was glad that he was playing with Joe and Bud and Gus and the others; and quickly again came the thought that this was the last day.

The Grays' next man singled to left and went to third when an easy grounder off the next pitch took a bad hop over the shortstop's shoulder. The men on first and third both broke with the next pitch, and Menckendorf pretended to pitch to second but threw to the shortstop, who whipped the ball back home fast. Menckendorf kept a tight clutch on the ball and stuck his hands into the flying spikes coming at him.

'Out!' the umpire yelled with his thumb in the air.

The runner disconsolately dusted himself off and limped away.

Menckendorf tossed the ball back to Bud and sucked at the blood from the new gash on the side of his right hand. He crouched to give the signal for the pitch.

They were getting into the low end of the Gray's batting order now. Bud struck out the next man. With two out, the pressure was off a little. The runner on second danced around but Bud ignored him and threw two curves past the hitter before he missed the corner for a ball. On the next pitch the batter hit a high pop foul, and Menckendorf whipped off his mask and followed it and thanked God that it wasn't in the sun and involuntarily began to circle under it and then desperately realized he was misjudging it and heard the crowd yelling and dived full length and caught the ball for the third out.

'Make it look tough, Twinkletoes!' yelled a deep voice from the crowd. Some of the fans were laughing. Menckendorf kept his head down as he walked to the dugout and looked up only when Bud came in, bouncing on his toes. 'You should take that show on the road, Twink,' he said. 'I'm telling you, I thought for a minute you weren't going to get it.'

Bud and Menckendorf grinned at each other. There was a look almost of tenderness in the pitcher's eyes for an instant before he went on down the bench, kidding somebody else. A couple of others met

Menckendorf's eyes and grinned but the rest, especially the men new to the club this year, ignored the incident. Menckendorf stared out at the diamond and wiped the sweat and dust from his face with a towel. He rubbed his big square hands along his thighs and noticed how dirty his uniform was. It was always like that after the first couple of innings of a game, and that dive for the foul had added the final touch of grime. A good catcher would have got that foul easy, he thought. Lots of time. Marty would have had it without wasting a step. Marty's a good catcher.

'How's the finger, Marty?' he called along the dugout.

Marty, who had been quiet and self-conscious with Menckendorf ever since the news of his release, smiled a grateful smile. 'Not bad, Al. Not bad.'

The second time Menckendorf came up to bat, in the last of the fifth, he popped to the second baseman. Then he was crouched again behind the plate in the hot prairie sun, and the wet black sweat mark had seeped down his shirt to his belt, and his mitt was thumping with the warmup pitches. Bud threw one very high, and, as Menckendorf trotted back to the screen for it, conscious of the effort of moving these heavy awkward legs, he remembered the time a girl behind the screen had asked her escort, 'Why do they call him Twink?'

He remembered the male voice. 'Short for Twinkletoes.' And then the mingled laughter. They couldn't know that he'd heard, because baseball crowds don't understand the acoustics which will allow a player to ignore the huge roars and hear only the small clear voices.

Crouched there behind the plate while the umpire whisked it clean and a batter rhythmically tapped his bat first on one foot and then on the other, Menckendorf grinned wryly. Twinkletoes.

Strike, ball, foul, single to left, stolen base, fly to right, strike, strike, strike, ball, strike, ball ...

The innings went on. They were getting to Bud a little and in the seventh added another run and in the eighth tied the score. Three all, one out, men on first and second. The pitcher who'd held the Maroons scoreless since the first was coming up to bat when the Grays' manager made his decision. He sent in a pinch hitter, gambling on taking the lead now and then holding the Maroons with a new pitcher in their last two times at bat. Immediately, a pitcher began warming up in the Grays' bull pen. The pinch hitter lined one to first, Gus doubled the runner off the bag, and the side was retired.

Bud didn't have much of a grin when he came off the mound that time. He sat swearing vigorously to himself at one end of the bench as

Gus fanned, yelled when Joe rattled a double off the wall, groaned when the new pitcher, another left-hander, picked Joe off second and then got the next batter on a long fly. Menckendorf, who'd removed his leg guards, put them back on hastily and ran out to the plate.

This time his practice throw to second, from the crouch, was on the mark, and he felt good and added his deep shout to the peppery yells of the infielders. Hold them now, and then he'd be first man up in the last of the ninth and even if the Maroons couldn't score there'd be the tenth with the top of the batting order coming up. And maybe he would score. It would be his last time to bat, his last stop before the blank window of the bus and the flowing flat countryside as he rode home alone. Something to remember ...

Bud got his stuff back, as he often did when the heat was really on. Sometimes he'd strike out five and six men in a row at the end of a game after seeming to have blown up in the middle innings, and Menckendorf had a feeling this was going to be one of those times. Bud struck out the first man, and Twink roared encouragement and pounded his mitt and argued with the umpire over a close one and they got the second one by a strike-out too. The third man walked, but on the first pitch to Schull, the next batter, Twink fired to first from his crouch; and, although his throw was high, the runner had hesitated and Gus caught him off the bag for the third out.

In his mother's dining room (he always pictured himself as a boy, at home; no man, an oversize boy) maybe the team would come in some-day on the way north or south, and they would all talk baseball and old times and ask Twink what he was doing. Mother and Dad would laugh with delight at his nickname, and Bud would kid Mother and tell her that Twink used to fire water pistols at passing motorists from the bus, and that was why no other team in the league would have him. The long dining-room table would be set with coffee and platters of dough-nuts, and Marty wouldn't feel so hot, eating them, because he'd be thinking that he and Anderson really had taken Twink's job.

As he stripped off his pads in front of the dugout, to get ready to bat, Twink caught Marty's eye and grinned.

'Nice throw, Twink,' Marty called.

Menckendorf was trembling a little, swinging three bats briefly and then picking one and stepping into the batter's box with his normal left-handed stance and then stepping swiftly back out again.

A thought had just come to him. The pitcher was a left-hander and Twink hadn't hit against him before, since he'd come into the game in the eighth. In Legion ball, when Twink was playing his best baseball, he'd been a switch hitter. He'd switched some in semipro, too; batting left against right-handers and right against left-handers, getting the slight advantage of having the ball cross to him. He'd done it the first year here, until the day a sports writer wrote tersely that Menckendorf should concentrate on learning how to hit from one side before he tried hitting from both. It was the same sports writer, a little older and a little more tolerant now, who'd written an affectionate farewell column about him in this morning's paper.

Twink rubbed his hands in the dirt, switched his grip on the bat, and stepped across the plate to bat right-handed against the southpaw.

There was an instant of silence followed by Bud's yell to the pitcher, 'Yay! He'll outwit you, you dumb southpaw!'

The first pitch was a ball. Twink crowded the plate, hunched over it, his mind a blank except for a racing consciousness of excitement.

The second pitch was a ball. There was no signal from Joe about what to do.

The third pitch was a cripple and Twink leaned into it and as he dropped his bat and started to run he saw it soaring toward the scoreboard in left center, bouncing along as he rounded first. He remembered that once Gus had got a home run inside the park on the same kind of hit. He noticed with a piece of his eye that the center fielder was bending for the ball as he neared second. He knew that two poor hitters were coming up next for the Maroons. He thought as he rounded second that, if he made third, a long fly from either of them or even a deep infield grounder might bring him home with the winning run.

He forgot for the instant that he was Twinkletoes Menckendorf and not Jesse Owens. He saw Joe's up-raised palms – the signal to stay on second – when he was so far along the base line that he was lost anyway and then he was thudding laboriously down on the hunched figure of Schull. The long heave from the outfield bounced once, Schull wheeled quickly to tag him, he was sliding for the base ... He was seeing the umpire's hands flattened toward the ground to signal him safe while Schull reached down to pick up the ball he had neglected to catch before he tried to tag the runner.

And he was seeing Joe's face white for a second before he grinned a slow grin, half of amusement and half of astonishment, and turned toward his men in the dugout, shaking his head while he clapped his hands and yelled at the next man up to bat.

And he was listening to the razzing Schull was getting from Bud and the others – listening with an embarrassment that he recognized as sympathy for this other man who, despite his magnificent hitting, was in some ways an even greater dub than Twinkletoes Menckendorf.

He was thinking: A fast runner would have made third easy; a good ballplayer would have caught Joe's signal soon enough to stay at second; here I am at third and I can score the winning run.

The batter, eighth in the line-up, a shortstop who was hitting .211, nine points less than Menckendorf, slapped a fly to center field, and Twink scored the winning run. He had to slide. And even in the midst of the cloud of dust, while Bud was hauling him to his feet and Joe was thumping him on the behind, he was thinking: A good man would have been home without a slide.

Then he straightened up. Some of the fans were yelling at him through the wire. There was affection and good humor in what they said and the way they said it. Twink walked through the passage under the creaking stands into the dressing room and yelled back and forth in the showers with the others, none of them mentioning that this was good-by except Bud, who had dressed quickly to join Belle and came up to Menckendorf and said in a low voice, 'Belle and me, we'll see you at the bus, Twink.'

Half dressed for the street, he stopped and opened his senses to remember the smell of sweaty bodies and liniment, and the clatter of lockers and the beefing of the shortstop because that bad hop in the fifth had been scored as an error against him; the wet towels on the floor; Marty, silent, with his hand outstretched; brief words of good-by as players hurried outside to meet their girls; the audible counting of Mac, the trainer, as he checked in from the cleaners a bundle of road uniforms for use next week; the look of Joe as he grinned with his lips compressed and shook his head with the same amazement every time he caught Twink's eye; the wet plank floors; two naked, lean, brown kids throwing soap at each other and laughing. He slipped on his jacket and picked up his bag and looked around at it all, carefully and without hurry, because although his bus was leaving for the south in an hour and he wanted to be sure to catch it, this was all disappearing and he must remember.

◆

Jimmy Rattlesnake (1909–72) from the Hobbema Reserve in central Alberta made his name as a barnstorming professional and is today recognized by the awarding of a trophy named after him to the outstanding player on Team Canada's senior baseball team. The game was introduced into many native communities in North America through reservation schools and proved amazingly adaptable to local circumstances. Since it required only a bat and ball, costs were low. Women were among the earliest players in games like the 'old fashion,' a cross between rounders and softball, which flourished in Atlantic Canada before the Second World War. In the days when tournament ball was the thing in western Canada, when Indian people were dying of white men's diseases and close to starving on Hobbema, pitching gave Jimmy Rattlesnake a reprieve, even leading to an occasional T-bone steak. However, it couldn't save him, as told in this docufictional account, abridged from To Run With Longboat: Twelve Stories of Indian Athletes In Canada *(1988).*

The Smilin' Rattler

BRENDA ZEMAN

RATTLESNAKE, common name for any of the poisonous American snakes of the general Crotaulus and Sistrurus, characterized by the possession of a loose, horny rattle at the end of the tail.

I F A FELLA WHO KNEW BEANS ABOUT RATTLESNAKE WAS TO GO SOLELY ON this here photo of Jimmy,' says Laurel Harney in his Edmonton living room, 'he'd think, shoot, the guy looks harmless enough: legs like a damn scarecrow, no ankles to speak of, cheeks so hollow he could be mistook for a famine relief victim, and his wrists, just look at his wrists.'

I am caught staring at the fawn eyes in the photo, at their gentle beauty. I examine a wrist which is connected to a long slender hand gripping a baseball. 'The wrists are awfully delicate,' I offer.

'Delicate, you say! Couldn't be much bigger'n the wrist on that ballernina I saw dancin' on the TV last night. A bag of bones he was, but on that diamond it wasn't his bones that seemed to rattle.'

'He must have been a sight,' I say politely. But the image he's painted makes the back of my neck prickle.

'Oh Jimmy could throw,' says Harney, 'threw what we called 'a saw-dust ball.' Catchers used to feel like they was stickin' their hands in a sack fulla rattlers. I was luckier than those Indian boys over on Hobbema. Those guys didn't use catchers mitts, too poor for that, I guess. I re-member Jimmy laughing about it. But the guys that showed me their bent or broke fingers didn't laugh much. They just shrugged and said Jimmy was like his sawdust ball, you never knew what he was gonna do next. In that sense he was a real Indian.'

'What do you mean by that?'

'Well for one thing, places meant nothing to him. He'd show up anywhere. Took him out to Victoria in '43, got him a job in the shipyard and put him to work fannin' longball hitters. But workin' in the ship-yard drove him crazy, just insane with the noise from the rivet guns.

'One night my wife and I found him walkin' down the street alone in Victoria. He said, "Harney, I gotta go home. I'm too lonesome." So we took him out for a steak, and boy, could he light into a porterhouse. After he wiped his plate clean, he said, "Harney I gotta go home." I got him released from the shipyard. Kept this photo for forty years. Only real Indian I ever met.'

'I'm sure my Dad would like to meet him. He's sort of an amateur sport historian; he could maybe write Jimmy's life up somewhere.'

'Hobbema's the place Jimmy come from, place he went back to. When-ever I hear about Hobbema, I think of Jimmy. Heard there was a mur-der over there just last week. 'Course I've never set foot on the place myself.'

In the distance I see a woman stuffing cans and bottles into a black plastic bag. It doesn't make sense. Hobbema, they tell me, is rolling in petro-dollars. I pull up to the ditch on the other side of the road and lean out the window of my car. The woman looks up from the ditch and stares at me. Doesn't say anything. Now I'm really nervous. I'm new here, but I've yet to see a dark-skinned woman in a bandanna with her teeth framed in gold. Does Hobbema have gypsies? I wonder.

In a moment a man surfaces from the ditch, his right arm in a sling with a T-shirt, PUERTO VALLARTA, crossing his torso.

'I'm looking for Jimmy Rattlesnake. You haven't run into him, have you?'

'Chimie Rattlesnake?' the man says in an accent nothing like Cree.

'He was a great Indian baseball pitcher.'

'Beisbol,' beams the man, 'I luv *beisbol*! That's how I hurt my arm eight years ago, I was playin' secon' base for Sayulita down in Meh-hee-co. Son of a beetch runs into me on secon' base. Last year I hurt it again skiin' cross the country in Wetaskiwin.'

'Really?' I say. 'I've heard there's at least a couple of old men on this reserve on the permanent disability list with broken or dislocated fingers.'

'From *beisbol* or skiin'?'

'From catching Jimmy Rattlesnake's pitching.'

'Es dangerous this Chimie Rattlesnake?'

'He had a very good curve.'

'A bery good curve?'

'Good control.'

'Good control?'

'And he was a southpaw.'

'Ah,' says the man sagely, 'es dangerous for sure. Just like Fernando Valenzuela.'

I strike out, no sign of Jimmy Rattlesnake anywhere down miles of road on the reserve. In the Muskwachees Mall on the Ermineskin Band portion of the reserve I sit down with a cup of coffee to figure out my next move.

The priest is new to Ermineskin. He places the heavy book on his desk and turns the pages slowly, making his way down the lists of births and deaths. 'Here it is, Jim Dummy Rattlesnake, son of Peter Dummy Rattlesnake and Marguerite Moignon Rattlesnake. Born 1909. Died 1972.'

Phyllis Rattlesnake, a daughter of Jimmy's, is a tall woman with strong, even features and black hair to her shoulders. 'My Dad,' she says over the priest's shoulder, 'used to always sign his name 'Jimmy D. Rattlesnake,' but he'd never tell me what the "D" stood for.'

Joe Smallboy knows. Joe's got a crooked finger. Joe and his wife Dorothy Rowan Smallboy have come in from Smallboy's camp. Joe's Dad led a group from Hobbema to a more traditional way of life in the bush when alcohol was permitted on Hobbema in 1968. Dorothy's Dad went with Joe's Dad.

'My mudder was cousin to Chimie's Dad,' says Joe. 'Dat old man didn't speek, didn't hear, they oost to call 'im "Dummy." Had 'im one racehorse, dat horse some kind of half t'orobred, s'post be. He oost to run dat horse all over. Trained dat horse at old track Hobbema, oost to train 'im old Indian way, had to, hands and feet, no talkin'.'

'Joe's Dad,' Dorothy can't wait to break in, 'was a farmer and they would do their work durin' the day and in the evening they'd practise pitching. My husband here,' she smiles at Joe, 'I had to teach him to be a real Indian.'

'Ya gotta be happy wit it,' laughs Joe. 'Dat's why I got dese braids,' he says, holding a greying one up. 'I t'ink Chimie learn 'bout pitsing in schole.'

'And Joe's dad told him to keep at it,' says Dorothy, ''cause maybe he could beat the white boys at their own game.'

'We oost to call 'im "Chuckboy," dat Chim Rattler, or "Chimie Da Tall One." I oost to cats for him. He warms up, Chimie, says, Wats out! Boy it was a hard pits! After dat I tell Chimie I move first base. Boy, dat a hard place play wit Chimie too. He t'row first base, gotta be hard! I got first base glufs too, special make, you know. I move backstop, first base, centrefield. I tell Chimie I like play centrefield when I play wit him. Chimie laugh 'bout dat, Chimie like to laugh.'

Louis P. Crier is busy looking at the middle finger on his left hand. He takes hold of it, turns to me grinning and breaks into English.

'He's the one who broke this finger,' he laughs. Louis P. moves his right hand away from the crooked finger. He turns his left hand to the inside so that he is facing me directly with his middle finger stuck up like an obscenity. He is so busy examining it that he does not notice me looking at Jimmy's oldest daughter Sylvia Moocheweines, Sylvia looking at me, both of us trying to stifle our laughter. When he looks up, he catches the joke and starts to laugh with us.

'Jimmy did it when we were boys and he would pitch and I would catch. Great days. I was wearing a catcher's mitt, big mitt and the ball was comin' straight at me and I was gonna catch it. Then that ball went a different way, hit my finger right on the top. Jimmy come runnin' from the mound and he just pulled my finger like this, he put it in place.'

Louis P. is deep in thought. 'People have good habits and bad habits. Like Jimmy, he was a good sportsman; at the same time he likes his booze. But in baseball he had one bad habit I won't tell you about.'

After some time he yields to coaxing.

'After the ball crosses the plate he always pulls pants up like this.'

Louis P. tugs vigorously at the waistband of his trousers. 'Never fail. You know, that Jimmy, sometimes I come to think of him and it makes me feel real good.'

The late afternoon sun warms us as we leave Louis P.'s place. Sylvia's memory has been pleasantly jogged. 'See this road here,' she says as we hit Ermineskin, 'I remember my Dad working on this road. And you know what? After he did a little bit of work, he'd stand and look at it, then he'd pull his pants up just like Louis P. said.'

As we drive on, I hear Sylvia laugh softly as if her father were still standing by the side of the road.

'I sure wasn't smiling the day I married Jimmy,' Isabelle Morin Rattlesnake says. 'I was seventeen, he was forty. Our wedding day he was drunk falling all over. We were supposed to get up there and dance. I didn't feel like dancing. I just about back out at the last minute from that wedding.'

She didn't, though, because her family wanted her to marry him. 'Me, I had five brothers, died from t.b. Good boys, those boys. Jimmy's whole family died from t.b. I guess I'm strong, I survived. And Jimmy too. Playin' baseball and workin' away, that saved Jimmy's life.'

'None of my ten kids died, I really looked after them. From the start when I got married, I got to be a good hunter. Jimmy was a good guy when he wasn't drinkin'. He was good to us, a good worker and when the kids were sick he was really watching them at night. It's bad for me when Jimmy died, why did he have to leave us then?'

There is silence for a moment. Suddenly she blurts, 'Jimmy sure had better aim with a baseball than a gun.' And then she is laughing outright. 'One day, not too long before he died, Jimmy got so excited, I don't know why, we had lots of meat in the 'fridge that time. He seen a deer not too far from this house, over there in the trees. He come runnin' to the house. 'Where's the gun?' he said. 'It's in the closet,' I told him. So he run for the gun. Then he run out and shoot that deer not too far from ...' Isabelle whispers something.

I tell her I can't hear her.

She whispers a little louder, '... the asshole.'

She covers her mouth to stifle her laughter and in a moment we are both laughing out loud.

'We used to laugh about that, Jimmy and me,' Isabelle says, 'what a hunter he turned out to be.'

Lawrence Rattlesnake is a big man, and strong. At thirty-four, he's the same age as Jimmy was in Laurel Harney's photo. 'He used to tell,' Lawrence says, 'his main reason for playing ball was that he liked the idea of travelling around so much, just to see the country. Even now when I'm away, old men will come up to me and tell me how good he was and how easy he was to get along with. Everybody liked my Dad.'

Lawrence's chin trembles, his voice becomes even softer.

'I was twenty when my Dad passed away,' he speaks with effort. 'I was with him till he died, right to the last minute.'

Lawrence tries to steady his voice. 'He'd been drinkin' all night, and when I woke up he was downstairs. I didn't really know what he was doin'. My wife and I left to get some groceries and since we had no vehicle, we hitch-hiked to Hobbema and caught a cab back. By the time we got to the house he was on the front step vomiting. He said, 'Take me to the hospital, son, I didn't mean to drink it, it was a mistake.'

'He couldn't walk so I carried him to the highway. His heart stopped two or three times while I was carryin' him. Finally, I got to the highway and flagged a car down. We tried to hurry. Then there was no point hurryin'. His heart stopped for the last time, he was lyin' in my arms. He used to have a hiding place for his booze and he grabbed the wrong bottle. My Dad, he'd drank gasoline antifreeze.'

Lawrence is silent. Then he says, 'I'm proud of my Dad but I don't want to go down like he did. I've got a good job in Ponoka and I don't want to lose it. I'm takin' steps to stop my drinking. I want to make something out of myself like my Dad did. He had one downfall, that was it. You should tell the whole story because it's the truth.

'A person when he catches on to a dream,' says Lester Fraynn, 'he would like to fulfill that dream. And sometimes, before that person realizes it, the dream passes him by. I'm really sad the way my late Uncle Jim left us. We have a way, the Indian people, when somebody passes on, when you go to the funeral, you don't go there and start bragging up a person, you don't start blaming them for things that went wrong his life either. But we're only human and when we see people leave, especially the way he left, people ask why. And being human, as far as you live on this earth, you can't really understand anything.

'The only way I can say it is that I like to remember my late Uncle Jim as he was, as a gentle person and as an athlete. There are so many stories about him, like about him eating x-number of pancakes before a game. That number keeps getting bigger as the years go by. My Uncle Jim would like those stories: he was a humorous person. I can still see him smiling,' Lester chuckles gently, 'I can still hear him laughing even before he turns the corner and comes into my view.'

——————— ◆ ———————

Rick Monday's 9th-inning home run for the Los Angeles Dodgers in Game 5 of the 1981 National League Championship Series will forever be a defining moment in the history of the Montreal Expos. The team of the eighties, as they were dubbed, have never again come so close to a World Series appearance. Whether Monday's home run changed the prospects of major-league baseball's survival in Montreal is problematic. What is indisputable, as Dan Ziniuk surveys it, is the long and cherished heritage of baseball amongst Québécois, for whom the game is the ironic demonstration of both an independent spirit and an interest in things American.

L'équipe de Denis Boucher

DAN ZINIUK

MAJOR-LEAGUE BASEBALL WRESTLES WITH TWO INTERCONNECTED VISIONS of its future. One sees it abandoning small markets unable to compete economically, the other has it reaching into new international territories beyond the United States to embrace a more global market.

To date major-league baseball's only contact with an obvious foreign culture has been in Montreal. (Toronto's foreignness is too abstract for Americans or even Canadians to understand fully, but it is nonetheless real.) Montreal is one of the troublesome markets that major-league ownership is not compelled to save, but at the same time is a test case for the potential success of the game's globalization efforts.

No one suggests Montreal is a small-market city for hockey; many wonder why the Expos have become a small-market team. The easy response is to dismiss Montreal, the province of Quebec, and French Canadians as somehow inferior baseball fans. Let's be frank ... they got lucky in 1968. Jean Drapeau had just put on a great show at Expo 67 and the $10-million asking price for a franchise a year later made no sense for a sport experiencing declining public interest. Even Montrealers showed little interest in the process. Only two French-language media representatives from *La Presse*, and no English media, showed up at the expansion vote.

In their first five years, despite unpredictable weather and the small, makeshift diamond of Jarry Park that held barely 30,000 fans, the Expos consistently outdrew their three expansion cousins and many established teams. Expos players and coaches were astonished by the fans' support. Don Zimmer, a team coach, said of the team's 1971 season opening parade, 'I never saw anything like it. I'd been in World Series parades in Los Angeles and Brooklyn, but they were never anything like that.'

No one who knows Quebec's baseball history should have been surprised. The game had caught on first among French Canadians. The English élite was too immersed in developing a national foundation for sports like lacrosse, football, and cycling. Francophone culture, on the other hand, was in a state of crisis. Between 1850 and 1900, a half-million French Canadians left the province and went primarily to the newly emerging textile and shoe-making towns of industrial New England. They found jobs all right, but lost their children, who abandoned a Québécois background in favour of the Yankee possibilities before them.

Alarmed, French-Canadian émigrés sent their rebellious teens back to Quebec for a good high-school and seminary education and, hopefully, a successful inculcation into the values of their parents. Like the teenagers of today, these youngsters had their own ideas, and not surprisingly they brought to Quebec the hobbies and fascinations of their American upbringing. One of these was baseball. In the community of St.-Hyacinthe, whose population was 96 per cent French, the return of these natives had an immediate impact. At the 1876 St.-Jean Baptiste celebration, the high point of the day was a 'bangup baseball game.'

Through the latter part of that century and into the twentieth, French-Canadian ball players and entrepreneurs were leaders in the growth of the game in the province. They played a prominent part in the formation of 'la ligue provinciale' in the latter stages of the nineteenth century, and continued to be the driving forces in similar leagues that rose and fell up to the arrival of the Expos. French Montrealers supported the city's fabulous International League teams to such a fanatical extent that even regular weekday game tickets became unobtainable without the aid of a ticket scalper – probably the only such occurrence in minor-league baseball history. So widespread were problems of scalping and gambling at Delormier Downs that Commissioner Happy Chandler forced team management to hire additional security. The storied Montreal Royals, a team whose ownership changed hands during a Depression era high-stakes poker game, won seven International League pennants, seven IL playoff series, and three Little World Series between 1941 and 1958.

French Canadians rallied to that team despite limited access. Radio broadcasts were only in English, but French-speaking Quebecers listened anyway, and brief inning-ending reports in French concluded with the French-speaking voice turning the mike back to the anglophone host with the words 'O.K. Bill Simms.' O.K. Bill became a francophone hero on the strength of that reference. Still, even Quebec baseball contained deeply independent, nationalistic views, best described by Roland Beaupré to Jean Blouin in their oral history of provincial baseball, 'Monsieur Baseball' se raconte. Two examples will suffice. 'Edmond Larivière played under the name Ed Wingo. One day he told me, "to succeed in this sport, you need an English name."' 'I can tell you that honest Americans compared Roland Gladu to Ted Williams ... If he wasn't French Canadian, he would have played in the Majors. He never got justice. Even in Quebec, we were the *white niggers* of baseball.' Beaupré, a fiercely proud francophone, documents numerous similar slights of French-Canadian players on the baseball diamond.

If there was a defining moment in Quebec's baseball history, and indeed its evolution as a culture, it was in the days following the end of the war in Europe. In the summer of 1945 Richard Wright, the black American author of the hugely successful *Black Boy*, sought a respite from the intractable race divisions of his country and booked passage on a boat to Europe. His tour was thwarted by war conditions, however, so instead he went to Quebec and lived anonymously on the Ile D'Orléans for two months, and relished the opportunity to 'live with the earth rather than against it.'

Are there connections between Wright and the announcement in the fall of that year that Jackie Robinson would integrate organized baseball the next season by playing for the Montreal Royals? We don't know, but one suspects a convergence of observation. New York sports writers said that Branch Rickey chose Montreal for the integration of baseball because there was no discrimination in Canada. They were wrong; the discrimination was less overt, but the element of truth worked in Rickey's favour.

The Robinsons left their southern California home for the foreign environment of Montreal in early 1946, and Rachel Robinson recalls that she was offered lodging at the first place she inquired. That didn't happen in the United States. There was always obfuscation, argument, dispute, and rejection. In Montreal there was acceptance. At season's end, when the Royals won the minor-league baseball championship, the locals caught Robinson up in their wave of excitement and carried him through the city. 'It was the first time a black man ran from a crowd with love rather than hate on its mind,' said a Louisville sportswriter who witnessed the scene. This incident is generally forgotten. It should not be.

A few years later Roger Lemelin alluded to that very moment in celebrating a priest's baseball triumph in his novel *The Plouffe Family*. The baseball-ignorant padre had struck out a visiting American minister intent upon signing French Canadians to baseball contracts in the States, and his parishioners carried the priest about, singing the very words – '*Il a gagné ses épaulettes!*' – immortalized by the supporters of Robinson.

The Montreal Expos were able to build on this proud baseball heritage in their early years, but their initial success began to fade after the 1973 season, and attendance dropped for three consecutive years, coinciding with the dispersal of the original fan favourites and the struggles of the first crop of home-grown players. In 1979 the Expos became a contender and baseball fever returned to Montreal, lasting through 1983, when attendance peaked at 2,310,651. By season's end the Expos heard almost as many boos as cheers. Attendance fell by 700,000 the next year, and further in years ahead. By 1986 the team drew only 1,128,981. Things have been worrisome since.

Despite having won 79 more games than any other National League team from 1979 through 1994, there has been widespread speculation that Montrealers are at best lukewarm baseball fans. An analysis of the team's recent attendance suggests that their support is so highly conditional on success that there can be no reason for optimism about the franchise's future.

To be fair, Montrealers behave this way because of the way they interpret the signals they receive. Like everything else in Quebec, the manner in which Québécois respond to baseball is influenced by the dominating current of Quebec nationalism. In order for any commercial enterprise to be successful in the province's market-place, the seller must familiarize himself with the nationalist culture and its needs.

In the team's early years, players raved about playing in Montreal.

Many lived there year round, giving the team visibility and leaving the impression that players wanted to be Montrealers. Marriages to 'local girls' by players like Ken Singleton encouraged a psychic bonding between the team and the community. Montrealers may not have loved the Expos as much as they loved the idea of having the Expos, for the team's presence suggested that Montreal, and by extension Quebec, were major league. The players' actions confirmed that Québécois confidence was well founded and thus appealed to both civic pride and Quebec nationalism. In short, the psychic needs of the market-place were met.

Rusty Staub's career demonstrates how goodwill was created. The best player on the early Expos team's, Staub made a sincere attempt to integrate into both the French and English scene. By trying to communicate with fans in their own tongue, Staub fulfilled the nationalist need for recognition while immortalizing himself in the hearts and minds of Québécois sports fans. Management, however, never fully understood what this gesture meant to their francophone clientele. Staub was traded after the 1971 season, but the Expos had a second chance to build on this goodwill after his re-acquisition in 1979. They made a fatal mistake in not making Staub a permanent member of the organization at the time.

Likewise, the dream of seeing a native star emerge faded through the 1970s. Pitcher Claude Raymond from St.-Jean, Quebec, had joined the team during the 1969 season after a lengthy career, but there was no one to follow him after 1971.

A final blow was the arrival of free agency and rising salaries in the mid-seventies. Wealthier ball players became more picky in their choice of residence and included 'no trade to Canada' clauses in their contracts. Only the move to the new Olympic Stadium and the emergence in the late 1970s of a great team led by Gary Carter, Andre Dawson, and Steve Rodgers stemmed the tide of fan rejection.

After several years of near misses, however, spectator disillusion turned into bitterness. Players were booed, and pitcher Jeff Reardon said that the Expos' management treated players better than other teams did as compensation for the city's terrible fans. He further implied that this view was generally shared by his team-mates.

Concern about the Expos' future in Montreal began in the mid-eighties. By then, however, Québécois nationalist sentiment was such that nothing less than a bonafide star player, able to converse in French, would suffice to turn the tide. A brief glimmer of hope was provided when Canadian Larry Walker arrived on the scene. He even made an attempt to learn French. 'When I spoke to a crowd in French, they went nuts. It made me want to learn so much more, so that I could talk to them in their own language.' Unfortunately, the former hockey player from British Columbia never lost the image of foreigner. As his stardom emerged, he dropped his French classes and, eventually, moved to Florida.

While Montrealers are no doubt hypersensitive about the impressions of others, the Expo situation also demonstrates the insensitivity of the baseball industry – that is, its failure to understand the ingredients necessary for developing a good image in the mind of local customers. Montreal is a test case of the benefits and challenges of globalization. Baseball owners can tackle the distinct problems facing foreign franchises, or they can claim it is too difficult and leave the issue to individual franchises to solve.

Before the 1992 season, Expo team president Claude Brochu identified the problem as being of a psychic nature: a lack of a 'sens d'appartenance.' Brochu said, 'If we understand the Quebecer – the French side – he has to feel part of it. He has to feel he can communicate, he can talk to people.' Unfortunately, attendance in the following seasons and player Mike Lansing's malapropos comment 'We don't need to hear that crap [French], everybody here speaks English' suggest that this awareness developed too late in the game. The extent of September 1995's damaging front-page headlines and the editorials condemning Lansing will be revealed in seasons to come; in Montreal baseball has suffered from an image problem serious enough to kill the franchise since 1991. For the price they would pay to join, major-league baseball owes Mexico City, Caracas, Tokyo, or any other foreign locale the benefit of increased sensitivity.

——————— ◆ ———————

On the eve of his induction into the Baseball Hall of Fame in Cooperstown, New York, Fergie Jenkins confessed that he had only one goal as a child: 'I wanted to be Doug Harvey, the all-star defenceman of the Montreal Canadiens.' Hockey rose to prominence in the twentieth century, becoming Canada's national game and eclipsing lacrosse in the process. Lacrosse, which competed with baseball for national team honours in the last century, has almost disappeared; but not baseball, which picks up the occasional hockey drop-out, like a Terry Puhl or a Larry Walker, and sometimes sends players the other way, like Brantford's Wayne Gretzky, who was a member of Chatham's Kinsmen Peewees who won the 1973 Canadian National Beaver baseball championship in North Battleford, Saskatchewan.

Canada's Baseball-Hockey Connection

ERIC ZWEIG

I was playing ball one day, and there were men on second and third. I came to bat with our team three runs behind and, taking a mighty swing at the pill, landed it far out in deep centre. Seeing that it was a long hit, I put my head down and ran like the wind. And would you believe it, I beat both men to the plate.

FRED 'CYCLONE' TAYLOR TOLD THIS TALL TALE TO A GATHERING OF RENFREW Millionaires team-mates during that team's trip to New York City in 1910. Taylor was professional hockey's first superstar and his box-office appeal in America caused the press there to dub him 'The Ty Cobb of hockey.' The linking of these two legends may be the first example of a baseball-hockey connection.

The comparison of Taylor to Cobb was an interesting one. Both broke into their respective sports in 1905. Both were fast and flashy, tricky and aggressive, and both rose quickly to the top in their chosen field. Taylor, in the years before the darker side of the baseball legend's personality became known, enjoyed his tie to Cobb. He was a big fan. In the off-season, Taylor would occasionally make the day trip from Ottawa to Detroit – an almost 24-hour round-trip journey by train, ferry, and on foot – to watch Cobb play. It's doubtful his counterpart ever returned the favour, though another of baseball's early immortals saw Taylor in action during his days with Portage Lake and came away quite impressed: 'There was a great cheer just after the start of the game when the star of the Pittsburgh Pirates, Honus Wagner, appeared, accompanied by the Pirates' manager-outfielder, Fred Clarke. They took seats a few rows behind the Portage Lake bench. Wagner ... had travelled from his home in nearby Plattsville to see the game. He is a real hockey fan, and he seemed greatly excited by last night's proceedings. He was on his feet many times, and afterwards said that he thought the Portage Lake player, Taylor, was as fine an athlete as he has ever seen.'

Despite his love of baseball and his great athletic skill, Taylor never played professionally. Like many early hockey players, he earned his off-season wages on the lacrosse field, and – like most athletes of his era – did so while also holding down a regular job. These turn-of-the-century heroes would likely be unimpressed by our modern two-sport athletes, since many of them, such as Harry Trihey, captain of the two-time Stanley Cup champion Montreal Shamrocks, played football as well as hockey and lacrosse. Harvey Pulford of the famed Ottawa Silver Seven went several sports better, adding championships in boxing, paddling, rowing, and squash to his football-hockey-lacrosse career.

Another of these bygone, multi-sport stars was Bouse Hutton, goaltender of the Silver Seven. Hutton played the same position with the Ottawa Capitals lacrosse team and was a fullback with the Ottawa Rough Riders. He holds the distinction of being the only man ever to play on a Stanley Cup winner, a Canadian lacrosse championship team, and a Canadian football championship squad in the same year, earning the unique hat trick in 1904. 'According to old timers,' his obituary stated in October of 1962, 'he could have played professional baseball had he been able to follow up this game during his crowded sports career.'

While lacrosse and football were the off-season choices of most early hockey stars, Bouse Hutton and Cyclone Taylor were not the only players to make the baseball-hockey connection. Several other members of Taylor's Renfrew Millionaires also played baseball. While Taylor was boasting of his speedy base-running stunt in New York City in 1910, teammate Fred Whitcroft was telling of hitting .700 for Deacon White's Young Liberals team in Edmonton two summers before. Frank and Lester Patrick also played baseball, anchoring the left side of the infield for the local nine in Nelson, British Columbia, when their family lived there in 1909, and earning praise from the town press: 'Lester Patrick, short-stop, singled home the winning run yesterday as Nelson defeated the University of North Dakota, 5–3. The single was Patrick's third hit of the game, and the University of North Dakota's Bill Hennesey, who once played for the Baltimore Orioles in the National League, said that the rangy Nelson short-stop was a fine professional prospect. He said he would so advise the Orioles, if Lester was interested.'

Apparently, Lester wasn't interested, and the sports world would have to wait for its first true baseball-hockey star.

During this early era of multi-sport hockey heroes, Canada's greatest all-around athlete was still a child. Born May 24, 1901, in Toronto, Lionel Conacher would grow up to excel in lacrosse and football, boxing and wrestling. The big money in Canadian sports of the 1920s was in hockey, however, so Conacher painstakingly taught himself to play the winter game. Though he never developed into much of a skater, he was an outstanding checker and shot-blocker throughout a 12-year NHL career. Conacher was elected to the Canadian Hockey Hall of Fame in 1994.

Like Lester Patrick, Lionel Conacher had a chance to become a baseball star as well. He signed with the International League's Toronto Maple Leafs in 1926, but showed little enthusiasm for the game. 'I don't think Conacher cared much for baseball,' says a fan quoted in the Louis Cauz book *Baseball's Back in Town*. 'I believe he played in only one game, the last of the season, and he struck out on three pitches.'

There was a man on Conacher's Maple Leafs team, though, who truly excelled at both baseball and hockey. That man was Babe Dye.

Babe Dye signed his first pro baseball contract with Hamilton in the spring of 1919. That fall, he signed his first NHL contract with the Toronto St. Pats. The following year, he came into his own in both sports. Though he bounced around during the 1920 baseball season, playing in Toronto, Syracuse, Hagerstown, and Brantford, Dye was impressive enough to be offered a $25,000 contract from Connie Mack to join the Philadelphia Athletics in 1921. Dye turned him down, saying a big-league job would conflict with his hockey career. That winter in the NHL, he had led the league with 35 goals in 24 games.

From 1921 to 1926, Dye spent his winters starring for the Toronto St. Pats and his springs and summers playing baseball in the International League, first with Buffalo, then Toronto. During those years, he was reputed to have the hardest shot in hockey. Dye led the NHL in points once and goals three times; he helped the St. Pats win the Stanley Cup in 1922 (scoring nine goals in the five-game series against Vancouver, including four goals in the final game); and became the first player in league history to score 200 goals. All the while, though, he could never decide in which sport he was better. One thing was certain, he gave the credit for his two-sport success to his mother: 'My mother knew more about hockey that I ever did, and she could throw a baseball right out of the park.' His father had died while he was a baby.

Babe Dye, who grew up with Lionel Conacher in North Toronto and played against him in the NHL, teamed up with Conacher in the Maple

Leafs outfield in spring training of 1926. They played together for the first time in a 9–8 exhibition game victory on April 9th, and, as the *Toronto Star* reported: 'Conacher ... had one hit and scored the winning run ... With Dye in centre and Conacher in left, the Leafs presented quite a home-town aspect. Dye also had a run to his credit and took care of three chances in the field. It was a great day for the NHL.'

Dye and Conacher were both on the bench when the team opened the season, but Babe was in the line-up for the home opener against Reading on April 29. It was Toronto's first game at the brand new Maple Leaf Stadium and Dye had two hits, including a run-scoring single in the five-run ninth as the Leafs rallied for a 6–5 victory in ten innings. Despite Dye's dashing debut, he was soon on the outs with the Maple Leafs brass and was released in July after complaining repeatedly of 'lameness' in his back. He finished the year in Baltimore.

Sadly, the worst was yet to come for Babe Dye. Traded from Toronto to Chicago in the NHL, he broke his leg in training camp in 1927 and missed the entire season. His baseball career was over, and, while he managed to hang on in the NHL until 1931, he scored only one goal in this final two seasons. Still, he had left behind a ten-year stretch of most remarkable athletic achievement.

No one would ever truly duplicate Babe Dye's baseball-hockey career (though Montreal Canadiens great Doug Harvey came close, playing two years in the Ottawa Border Baseball League and turning down a pro offer from the Boston Braves), but the baseball-hockey connection continued to flourish. In fact, the greatest baseball player Canada ever produced considered hockey his favourite sport.

Growing up in Chatham, Ferguson Jenkins was a three-sport star: baseball, basketball, and hockey. He was considered a top hockey prospect, but gave up his favourite game when he signed with the Philadelphia Phillies, who told him they didn't want him risking injury on the ice. 'I haven't been on skates since,' Jenkins said in an interview after being traded to the Chicago Cubs. He didn't stay off the ice for good, though. In the winter following his 25-win season with the Texas Rangers in 1974, Jenkins, unbeknownst to the club, was playing hockey in an industrial league back home. During one game, a player on the opposite team kept taking shots at him. Jenkins tells the story in *A Century of Canadian Sport*: 'I dropped my glove and let him have it – bam – and broke all the knuckles in my right hand.' Luckily, the injury healed in time for the baseball season.

Ironically, while Jenkins grew up loving hockey, the greatest hockey player Canada ever produced grew up idolizing Jenkins. In fact, Wayne Gretzky claims in his autobiography that hockey wasn't even his favourite sport when he was growing up: 'I always wanted to be a professional baseball player. I always dreamed of being a Detroit Tiger because Detroit was just a few hours from Brantford. I loved Mickey Lolich. Ferguson Jenkins of the Cubs was another hero, like he was to every kid in Canada.'

Gretzky writes that when the most famous backyard rink in hockey history melted, a pitching mound went up. Later, he played for Brantford in the Inter-County League and hit .492. He was even offered a tryout with the Blue Jays. Gretzky's other boyhood idol (and another option as the greatest hockey player Canada ever produced) also had a baseball connection. Gordie Howe used to take batting practice with the Tigers and was in business for a short time with Tigers great Al Kaline.

In the years between the careers of Babe Dye and Wayne Gretzky, the length of the hockey season increased from 24 to 84 games. In Dye's day, hockey lasted from December to April. Now training camps open in September and the Stanley Cup is decided in June. There's not much room left to pursue a baseball career. But the baseball-hockey connection does still exist. Former Expo Larry Walker, who may someday surpass Fergie Jenkins as this country's greatest baseball star, played hockey in his youth. Atlanta Braves pitcher Tom Glavine also played hockey. Glavine was even drafted by the Los Angeles Kings. If he'd pursued pucks instead of pitching, he might be playing with Wayne Gretzky today!

From Taylor and Ty Cobb at the turn of the century to Gretzky and Glavine in the games of today, there has always been a link between baseball and hockey – America's summer pastime and Canada's great winter game.

A Canadian Baseball Bibliography

The following list is provided for readers interested in delving further into the many areas of Canadian baseball touched upon in this collection. It concentrates on non-fiction sources and, though by no means exhaustive, covers all the bases for those interested in Canada's rich baseball tradition.

General Baseball Information

These sources cover the entire spectrum of professional baseball, including the records of Canadian players and teams.

Filichia, Peter. *Professional Baseball Franchises*. New York: Facts on File 1993.
Johnson, Lloyd, and Miles Wolff. *The Encyclopedia of Minor League Baseball*. Durham, NC: Baseball America Inc. 1993
Ojala, Carl F., and Michael T. Gadwood. 'The Geography of Major League Baseball Player Production: 1876–1989.' *Minneapolis Review of Baseball* 10:1 (1991)
Reichler, J.L., ed. *The Baseball Encyclopedia*. New York: Macmillan, several editions
Thorn, John, and Pete Palmer. *Total Baseball: The Ultimate Encyclopedia of Baseball*. New York: Harper Perennial, several editions

General Canadian Sports Information with Baseball Bits

These books cover baseball within the entire history of sports in Canada.

Ferguson, Bob. *Who's Who in Canadian Sport*. Toronto: Summerhill Press 1985
Guay, Donald. *Introduction à l'histoire des sports au Québec*. Montreal: VLB Editeur 1987

Howell, Nancy, and Maxwell Howell. *Sports and Games in Canadian Life.*
Toronto: Macmillan 1969

Metcalfe, Alan. *Canada Learns to Play: The Emergence of Organized Sport 1807–*
1914. Toronto: McClelland and Stewart 1987

Morrow, Don, Mary Keyes, Wayne Simpson, Frank Cosentino, and Ron
Lappage. *A Concise History of Sport in Canada.* Toronto: Oxford University
Press 1989

Young, A.J. (Sandy). *Beyond Heroes: A Sport History of Nova Scotia.* Hantsport,
NS: Lancelot Press 1988

Canadian Sources with Interesting Baseball Bits

The Canadian Encyclopedia. Edmonton and Toronto: Hurtig, McClelland and
Stewart 1985–

Moffett, Samuel. *The Americanization of Canada.* Toronto: University of Toronto
Press 1972; originally published 1907

Canadian Baseball

Barney, Robert. 'In Search of a Canadian Cooperstown: The Future of the
Canadian Baseball Hall of Fame.' *Nine: A Journal of Baseball History and Social
Policy* 1:1 (Fall 1992)

– 'Diamond Rituals: Baseball in Canadian Culture.' In *Baseball History 2.*
Westport, Conn.: Meckler Books 1989

Bowering, George. 'Baseball and the Canadian Imagination.' In *Imaginary
Hand: Essays by George Bowering.* Edmonton: NeWest Press 1988 [An essay on
baseball in Canadian literature]

Bryce, William. *Bryce's Canadian Baseball Guide.* London: William Bryce 1876
[Excerpt in this volume]

Humber, William. *Diamonds of the North: A Concise History of Baseball in Canada.*
Toronto: Oxford University Press 1995

– *Let's Play Ball: Inside the Perfect Game.* Toronto: Lester & Orpen Dennys 1989

– *Cheering for the Home Team: The Story of Baseball in Canada.* Erin, Ont.: Boston
Mills Press 1983

Kendall, Brian. *Great Moments in Canadian Baseball.* Toronto: Lester Publishing
1995

Pietrusza, David. *Baseball's Canadian-American League.* Jefferson, NC: McFarland
1990 [Minor-league ball in Ottawa, Quebec, Three Rivers, Perth, and
Cornwall]

Shearon, Jim. *Canada's Baseball Legends: True Stories of Canadians in the Big Leagues since 1879*. Kanata, Ont.: Malin Head Press 1994

Turner, Dan. *Heroes, Bums and Ordinary Men: Profiles in Canadian Baseball.* Toronto: Doubleday 1988

Western Canada

Broadfoot, Barry. 'Baseball Was the Thing.' In *The Pioneer Years: Memories of Settlers Who Opened the West, 1895–1914*. Toronto: Doubleday 1976
– *Ten Lost Years 1929–39*. Toronto: Doubleday 1973 [Selection in this volume]

Manitoba

Duncan, Hal. *Baseball in Manitoba*. Souris: Sanderson Printing 1989

Mott, Morris. 'The First Pro Sports League on the Prairies: The Manitoba Baseball League of 1886.' *Canadian Journal of the History of Sport*, December 1984

Saskatchewan

Rae, Lorne. 'It Was Real Baseball.' *Saskatchewan History* 43:1 (Winter 1991)

Shury, David. *Batter Up: The Story of the Northern Saskatchewan Baseball League*. North Battleford: Turner Warwick Printers 1990
– *Play Ball Son! The Story of the Saskatchewan Baseball Association*. North Battleford: Turner Warwick Printers 1986

Shury, David, ed. *The Saskatchewan Historical Baseball Review*. North Battleford: Saskatchewan Baseball Hall of Fame. Annual journal, 1984–91

Zwack, Andy, ed. *Saskatchewan Twilite Baseball*. Booklet, 1991

Alberta

Abel, Allan. 'Living It Up in Baseball's Bushes.' In *But I Loved It Plenty Well*. Toronto: Collins 1983 [Baseball in Medicine Hat, Alberta]

Bercuson, David. 'It's a Hit.' *Report on Business Magazine*, August 1987 [The business of baseball in Calgary]

British Columbia

Adachi, Pat. *Asahi: A Legend in Baseball, a Legacy from the Japanese Canadian Baseball Team to Its Heirs*. Toronto: Coronex 1992

Anderson, James. 'Notes and Comments on Early Days and Events in British Columbia.' Archives of the Province of British Columbia
LaCasse, Geoff. 'From Amity Wolf to Vancouver Beaver.' *Dugout Magazine,* June/July 1994

Ontario

Adams, Frank. 'Some Baseball History, Both Amateur and Professional, in the City of London.' *Canadian Science Digest,* August 1938
– 'Sundry Memories of Old-Time Baseball.' *London Free Press,* 19 May 1938
Anderson, Tom. *Memories: A History of the North Dufferin Baseball League.* Self-published, 1980
Bernard, David. 'The Guelph Maple Leafs: A Cultural Indicator of Southern Ontario.' *Ontario History* 34:3 (September 1992)
Bouchier, Nancy B., and Robert K. Barney. 'A Critical Examination of a Source on Early Ontario Baseball: The Reminiscence of Adam E. Ford.' *Journal of Sport History* 15:1 (Spring 1988)
Bowes, Lisa. 'George Sleeman and the Brewing of Baseball in Guelph 1872–1886.' *Historic Guelph,* October 1988
Bronson, Les. Unpublished paper on the London Tecumsehs Baseball Club, presented to the London-Middlesex Historical Society, 15 February 1972. Copy in the University of Western Ontario Regional Collection
Heidorn, Keith. 'Diamonds in the Rough: Baseball in Canada 1860–1890.' *Early Canadian Life,* May 1979
Palmer, Bryan. 'In Street and Field and Hall.' In *A Culture in Conflict: Skilled Workers and Industrial Capitalism in Hamilton, Ontario 1860–1914.* Montreal: McGill-Queen's University Press 1979 [Baseball in Hamilton in the 1860s–1880s]
Reed, Jeffrey. *40 Years of Baseball: The Eager Beaver Baseball Association of London, Ontario.* London: EBBA 1994

Toronto and the Blue Jays

Bjarkman, Peter. *The Toronto Blue Jays.* Toronto: W.H. Smith 1990
Caulfield, Jon. *Jays! A Fan's Diary.* Toronto: McClelland and Stewart 1985
Cauz, Louis. *Baseball's Back in Town: A History of Baseball in Toronto.* Toronto: CMC 1977 [Contains a partial bibliography]
Cheek, Tom, and Howard Berger. *Road to Glory.* Toronto: Warwick Publishing 1993
DiManno, Rosie. *Glory Jays: Canada's World Series Champions.* Toronto: Sagamore 1993

Fulk, David, ed. *A Blue Jays Companion*. South Pasadena, Calif.: Keystone 1994
Gordon, Alison. *Foul Balls! Five Years in the American League*. New York: Dodd, Mead 1984
Grossman, Larry. *A Baseball Addict's Diary: The Blue Jays' 1991 Rollercoaster*. Toronto: Penguin 1992
Joyce, Gare. *The Only Ticket off the Island*. Toronto: Lester & Orpen Dennys 1990
Martinez, Buck. *The Last Out: The Toronto Blue Jays in 1986*. Toronto: Fitzhenry and Whiteside 1986
– *From Worst to First: The Toronto Blue Jays in 1985*. Toronto: Fitzhenry and Whiteside 1985
Millson, Larry. *Ballpark Figures: The Blue Jays and the Business of Baseball*. Toronto: McClelland and Stewart 1987
O'Malley, Martin and Sean. *Game Day*. Toronto: Viking 1994
van Rjndt, Philippe, and Patrick Blednick. *Fungo Blues: An Uncontrolled Look at the Toronto Blue Jays*. Toronto: McClelland and Stewart 1985

Quebec

Blouin, Jean. *Roland Beaupré, Monsieur Baseball, se raconte*. Montréal: Les Presses Libres 1980
Clifton, Merritt. *Disorganized Baseball: The Provincial League from LaRoque to Les Expos*. Richford, Vt.: Samisdat 1982
Paradis, Jean-Marc. *Histoire illustrée du baseball rural en Maurice, 1940–1990*. Trois Rivières 1990
– *100 ans de baseball à Trois-Rivières*. Trois-Rivières 1989

Montreal and the Expos

Bjarkman, Peter. 'Montreal Expos: Bizarre New Diamond Traditions North of the Border.' In P. Bjarkman, ed., *The Encyclopedia of Baseball Team Histories: National League*. New York: Carroll and Graf 1993
Post, Paul. 'Origins of the Montreal Expos.' *The Baseball Research Journal of the Society for American Baseball Research* 22 (1993)
Richler, Mordecai. 'Up from the Minors in Montreal.' In D. Okrent and H. Lewine, eds, *The Ultimate Baseball Book*. Boston: Houghton, Mifflin 1981 [Reprinted in this volume]
Snyder, Brodie. *The Year the Expos Finally Won Something*. Toronto: Checkmark 1981
– *The Year the Expos Almost Won the Pennant*. Toronto: Virgo Press 1979
Turner, Dan. *The Expos Inside Out*. Toronto: McClelland and Stewart 1983 [Excerpt in this volume]

Atlantic Canada

Howell, Colin. *Northern Sandlots: A Social History of Maritime Baseball.* Toronto: University of Toronto Press 1995
– 'Baseball, Class and Community in the Maritime Provinces, 1870–1910.' *Histoire sociale/Social History,* November 1989

New Brunswick

Ashe, Robert. *Even the Babe Came to Play: Small-Town Baseball in the Dirty 30s.* Halifax: Nimbus 1991 [The story of senior baseball in St. Stephen, NB; excerpt in this volume]
Flood, Brian. *Saint John: A Sporting Tradition.* Saint John: Neptune Publishing 1985 [Covers the entire history of baseball in the New Brunswick city]
Folster, David. 'The Old Home Team.' *The Atlantic Advocate,* July 1968 [Reprinted in this volume]

Nova Scotia

Howe, Joseph. News item in *The Novascotian,* 1 July 1841 [Mention of bat and ball at a temperance picnic in Dartmouth is the first newspaper reference in Canada to baseball-type play.]
Russell, Burton. *Looking Back: A Historical Review of Nova Scotia Senior Baseball, 1946–1972.* Kentville, NS: 1973

Newfoundland

O'Neill, Paul. *The Oldest City: The Story of St. John's, Newfoundland.* Don Mills, Ont.: Musson Book Co. 1975 [Brief survey of baseball in St. John's]

Prince Edward Island

Ballem, Charles. *Abegweit Dynasty 1899–1954: The Story of the Abegweit Amateur Athletic Association.* Summerside, PEI: Williams and Crue 1986 [PEI's premier sports organization, including its baseball involvement]
Ledwell, Bill. 'Charlottetown's Vern Handrahan.' *Charlottetown Monthly Magazine,* October/November 1984
O'Grady, Michael. 'From Covehead to the Polo Grounds: The Story of Henry Havelock Oxley, Major Leaguer.' *The Island Magazine* (Charlottetown) 37 (Spring/Summer 1995).

Canadian Baseball Biographies

Jenkins, Ferguson, and George Vass. *Like Nobody Else: The Fergie Jenkins Story.*
  Chicago: Henry Regnery Co. 1973
Marchildon, Phil, and Brian Kendall. *Ace: Canada's Pitching Sensation and
  Wartime Hero.* Toronto: Viking 1993 [Excerpt in this volume]

Canadian-related Baseball Fiction

Bell, John, ed. *The Grand Slam Book of Canadian Baseball Writing.* Lawrencetown
  Beach, NS: Pottersfield Press 1994
Craig, John. *Chappie and Me.* New York: Dodd, Mead and Co. 1979 [A black
  barnstorming team comes to the fictional town of Trentville, Ont., in the
  1930s.]
Kinsella, W.P. *Box Socials.* Toronto: HarperCollins 1992 [Fictional account of
  baseball in Canada's West]
Meyer, Bruce. *Goodbye Mr. Spalding.* Windsor: Black Moss Press 1995

Miscellaneous

Browne, Lois. *Girls of Summer: In Their Own League.* Toronto: HarperCollins
  1992 [The story of the All-American Girls Professional Baseball League and
  its Canadian focus; excerpt in this volume]
Lowry, Phil. *Green Cathedrals.* Cooperstown, NY: SABR publications 1986
  [Items on Parc Jarry and Stade Olympique]
Tygiel, Jules. *Baseball's Great Experiment: Jackie Robinson and His Legacy.* New
  York: Random House 1983 [Jackie Robinson's time in Montreal]
Zeman, Brenda. *To Run with Longboat: Twelve Stories of Indian Athletes in Canada.*
  Edmonton: GMS Ventures 1988 [Excerpt in this volume]

---- ◆ ----

The Roster

PAT ADACHI and her father IWAICHI KAWASHIRI were fans of the Asahis in
 Vancouver before the Second World War.
ROGER ANGELL is a fiction editor for the *New Yorker* magazine and one of
 America's great baseball writers.
ROBERT ASHE is an Ottawa freelance writer.
GEORGE BOWERING is a Vancouver poet and fiction writer.
BARRY BROADFOOT is the author of several oral histories on western Canada.
LOIS BROWNE is a freelance writer and broadcaster.
STEPHEN BRUNT is a Toronto *Globe and Mail* columnist and author.
WILLIAM BRYCE was a London, Ontario, publisher and bookseller.
MORLEY CALLAGHAN was a Canadian novelist and broadcaster who once
 kayoed Ernest Hemingway.
JON CAULFIELD is a sociology professor at York University, Toronto.
RALPH CONNOR was Canada's first best-selling author.
DAVID CRICHTON and RANDY ECHLIN work in respected Toronto professions
 when not collecting baseball cards.
JAMES DAVIDSON is an Ottawa-based freelance writer.
JOHN DUCEY was a baseball official and promoter in Edmonton.
MILT DUNNELL is the dean of Toronto sportswriters.
BOB EMSLIE was a Canadian-born major-league ball player and umpire.
SCOTT FESCHUK is a reporter for the *Globe and Mail* based in Edmonton.
RUSSELL FIELD is publisher of the baseball magazine *Dugout*.
DAVID FOLSTER is a freelance writer based in Fredericton, New Brunswick.
ROBERT FONTAINE's literary career was influenced by his boyhood days in
 Ottawa.
ADAM FORD was the mayor of St. Marys, Ontario, in the 1870s.
ADAM GOPNIK is a staff writer for the *New Yorker* magazine.
ALISON GORDON is the creator of the Kate Henry mystery series.

ZANE GREY was the author of western sagas and boys' baseball books.

JANE GROSS is a sports reporter for the *New York Times*.

HUGH HOOD is a Montreal writer and university professor.

COLIN HOWELL is a member of the history department at St. Mary's University, Halifax.

LARRY HUMBER is the author of *Going for It: A Guide to Sports Betting*.

WILLIAM HUMBER was coach of the 1995 pennant-winning bantam-level Bowmanville Glass and Mirror baseball team.

MARK KINGWELL is a professor of philosophy at the University of Toronto.

W.P. KINSELLA is the author of *Shoeless Joe* and other baseball-related novels and stories.

GEOFF LACASSE writes on British Columbia's baseball history.

ROGER LEMELIN is a novelist and journalist who created the Plouffe family.

ARTHUR LIERMAN is a landscape architect based in London, Ontario.

DAVID MCDONALD is a freelance writer living in Ottawa.

TOM MCKILLOP is a Roman Catholic pastor in Newmarket, Ontario.

MARSHALL MCLUHAN was a media prophet and the author of *Understanding Media*.

PHIL MARCHILDON pitched for the Philadelphia Athletics in the 1940s; BRIAN KENDALL is a Toronto-based writer.

BRUCE MEYER is a professor of English at the University of Toronto.

DAVID PIETRUSZA is the president of the Society for American Baseball Research.

PAUL QUARRINGTON is a Toronto author, musician, and angler.

ALAN RAUCH is a professor of literature, communication, and culture at Georgia Tech in Atlanta.

MORDECAI RICHLER is a Montreal author whose works include *The Apprenticeship of Duddy Kravitz*.

LAURA ROBINSON is a freelance writer in Toronto.

JOHN ST JAMES is a Toronto editor, opera aficionado, and passable right fielder.

JIM SHEARON is the author of *Canada's Baseball Legends*.

DAVE SHURY is a lawyer and the founder of Saskatchewan's Baseball Hall of Fame.

TONY TECHKO is a Windsor-based sports historian.

DAN TURNER is an author and columnist in Ottawa.

NELLES VAN LOON is a Toronto playwright and musician who throws a mean drop ball.

LARRY WOOD is deputy news editor for the Calgary *Herald*.

SCOTT YOUNG is a storyteller and former *Globe and Mail* columnist.

BRENDA ZEMAN is a Saskatoon-based freelance writer.

DAN ZINIUK is an Ottawa freelance writer.

ERIC ZWEIG is the author of *Hockey Night in the Dominion of Canada*.

◆

Acknowledgments and Permissions

The editors would like to thank, first and foremost, Bill Harnum, Senior Vice-President, Scholarly Publishing Division, of University of Toronto Press, who conceived the idea of compiling a Canadian baseball reader and (like a certain world-champion manager) let us play our game in putting it together. We appreciate as well the enthusiastic support shown by Ron Schoeffel, UTP Editor-in-Chief, throughout this project. Thanks are also due to UTP editor Darlene Zeleney for her keen eye. In addition, we thank the following individuals who have provided valuable help along the way: John Bell, M. Owen Lee, Judi McLaren, Eric McLuhan, Maty Molinaro, Daniel Okrent, and Daniel Westreich. Finally, we cherish the long-standing (and tolerant) appreciation that our wives, Cathie and Sandra, have shown for our obsession with the Game. They know that baseball has helped to keep us young.

Grateful acknowledgment is made for permission to reprint the following copyrighted works: ADACHI: From *Asahi: A Legend in Baseball*, trans. Pat Adachi from Japanese version written by her father, Iwaichi Kawashiri. © Pat Adachi • ANGELL: Reprinted by permission. © 1993 Roger Angell. Originally in *The New Yorker* • BOWERING: From *Caprice* by George Bowering. Copyright © George Bowering, 1987. Reprinted by permission of Penguin Books Canada Limited • BROADFOOT: From *Ten Lost Years 1929–1939*. Copyright © 1973 by Barry Broadfoot. Reprinted by permission of Doubleday Canada Limited • BROWNE: From *GIRLS OF SUMMER In Their Own League*. © 1992 by Lois Browne. Published in Canada by HarperCollins Publishers Ltd • CALLAGHAN: From *New World Illustrated*. Reprinted by permission of Barry Callaghan • DUNNELL: From *The Best of Milt Dunnell*. Copyright © 1993, edited by Robert Brehl. Reprinted by permission of Doubleday Canada Limited • FOLSTER: © David Folster. Reprinted by permission • GOPNIK: Reprinted by permission. © 1986

Adam Gopnik. Originally in *The New Yorker* • GORDON: Reprinted by courtesy of *Sports Illustrated* from the October 26, 1992, issue. Copyright © 1992, Time Inc. ('Canada from Eh to Zed' by Alison Gordon) All Rights Reserved • GROSS: Originally published June 30, 1982. Copyright © 1982 by The New York Times Company. Reprinted by permission • HOOD: From *Dark Glasses*. © Hugh Hood. Reprinted by permission • HUMBER: © William Humber, 1993 • KINSELLA: From *The Dixon Cornbelt League*. Copyright © 1993 by W.P. Kinsella. Published by HarperCollins Publishers Ltd • LEMELIN: From *The Plouffe Family* by Roger Lemelin. Used by permission of the Canadian Publishers, McClelland & Stewart, Toronto • McLUHAN: © Corinne McLuhan. Reprinted by permission • MARCHILDON: From *Ace: Phil Marchildon, Canada's Pitching Sensation and Wartime Hero*, with Brian Kendall. Copyright © Brian Kendall, 1993. Reprinted by permission of Penguin Books Canada Limited • QUARRINGTON: Copyright © Paul Quarrington • RICHLER: From *The Ultimate Baseball Book*, edited by Daniel Okrent & Harris Lewine. Copyright © 1979, 1981, 1984, 1988 by The Hilltown Press, Inc., and Harris Lewine • ST JAMES: © John St James, 1995 • SHEARON: From *Canada's Baseball Legends* (Kanata, Ont.: Malin Head Press). © James Shearon • SHURY: © David Shury. Reprinted by permission • TURNER: From *The Expos Inside Out*. © Dan Turner. Reprinted by permission • VAN LOON: © Nelles Van Loon. Reprinted by permission • WOOD: Originally in Calgary *Herald* (February 8, 1986). Reprinted by permission • YOUNG: From *We Won't Be Needing You, Al*. Copyright © Scott Young. Reprinted by permission.